THE FLETCHER JONES FOUNDATION
HUMANITIES IMPRINT

The Fletcher Jones Foundation has endowed this imprint to foster innovative and enduring scholarship in the humanities.

The publisher gratefully acknowledges the generous support of the Fletcher Jones Foundation Humanities Endowment Fund of the University of California Press Foundation, which was established by a major gift from the Fletcher Jones Foundation.

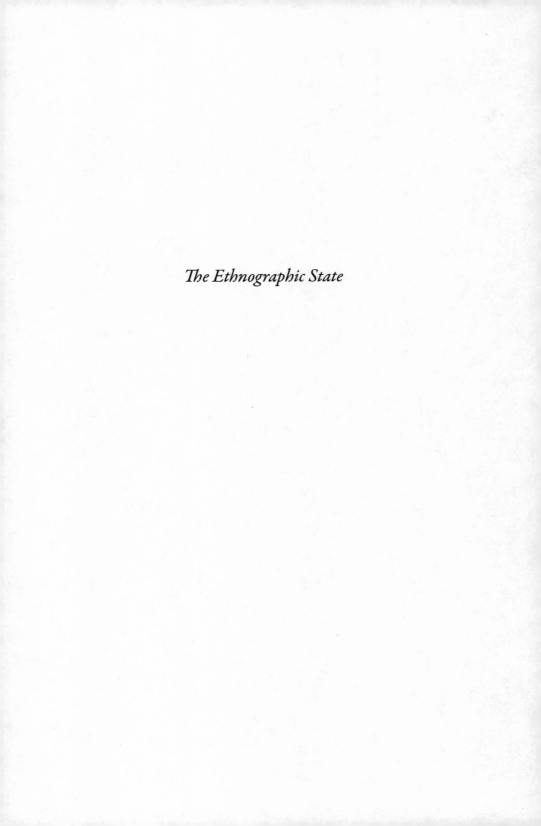

The Ethnographic State

The Ethnographic State

FRANCE AND THE INVENTION OF MOROCCAN ISLAM

Edmund Burke III

UNIVERSITY OF CALIFORNIA PRESS

University of California Press, one of the most distinguished university presses in the United States, enriches lives around the world by advancing scholarship in the humanities, social sciences, and natural sciences. Its activities are supported by the UC Press Foundation and by philanthropic contributions from individuals and institutions. For more information, visit www.ucpress.edu.

University of California Press
Oakland, California

Library of Congress Cataloging-in-Publication Data

Burke, Edmund.
   The ethnographic state : France and the invention of Moroccan Islam / Edmund Burke III.
      p. cm.
   Includes bibliographical references and index.
   ISBN 978-0-520-27381-8 (cloth, alk. paper) — ISBN 978-0-520-95799-2 (pbk., alk. paper)
   1. Islam and state—Morocco—History—20th century.   2. Islam—Morocco. 3.   Morocco—Religious life and customs.   4. French—Morocco—Intellectual life.   5. France—Colonies—Africa, North—Religion.   6. Morocco—History—1912–1956. I. Title.
BP64.M6B88   2014
964.04—dc23   2014000842

Manufactured in the United States of America

23 22 21 20 19 18 17 16 15 14
10 9 8 7 6 5 4 3 2 1

In keeping with a commitment to support environmentally responsible and sustainable printing practices, UC Press has printed this book on Natures Natural, a fiber that contains 30% post-consumer waste and meets the minimum requirements of ANSI/NISO Z39.48-1992 (R 1997) (*Permanence of Paper*).

CONTENTS

ACKNOWLEDGMENTS

When did I begin writing this book? I always envisioned that my first book *Prelude to Protectorate in Morocco* would eventually have a ghostly twin. However, I have always worked on multiple projects at the same time. Over the several decades following the publication of *Prelude to Protectorate,* while other duties distracted me, I continued to produce conference papers, articles, and chapters on what I had come to refer to as the Moroccan sociology of Islam. In the process, the present book had acquired its own spin-off, a book tentatively entitled *France and the Sociology of Islam,* which, it is hoped, will not tarry long in appearing.

The chance to have uninterrupted time to devote to this book came in 2006 when thanks to Joan Scott, then head of the School of Social Sciences of the Institute for Advanced Study, I was able to spend the fall semester in Princeton as a Visiting Fellow. In the ensuing weeks I completely rethought the project, disassembled earlier essays, discarded others, and began writing anew. A second fall semester in 2007 at the IAS enabled me to complete a first draft. My gratitude to Professor Scott is therefore beyond measure. Without her kind, unstinting support, this project might very well never have been completed.

It is a real pleasure to recognize the support of friends, family, and colleagues who sustained me in this quest. Over such a long time, there have inevitably been many. Some comrades are no longer among us, or have had the good sense to retire from the field with honor. Some will be frankly astonished that I have at last completed my odyssey among the *ethnologues.* Whether or not it was worth waiting for is not for me to say.

A number of individuals stand out for their key interventions and support in the writing of this book. David Prochaska was always available to read draft by the yard and to help me think my way out of trouble. His friendship and colleagueship have been invaluable.

A lifetime ago Larry Rosen and I spent a summer interviewing elderly Moroccan men about the early days of the protectorate. Somehow, despite interruptions, our friendship has only deepened over the years. His commitment to this project has helped see me through.

Fanny Colonna, emerita of the French National Research Center, is an esteemed friend and colleague whose life's work and continued engagement with this project have been a major inspiration to me.

Walking and talking with Paul Lubeck (then Sociology/UCSC, now SAIS/Johns Hopkins University) over the years has helped me think through the manuscript. It is his suggestion that the enthronement ceremony embodied all that the protectorate claimed to be.

More than once in the process of my completion of this book Daniel Schroeter (History/University of Minnesota) bailed me out with needed information and more. His friendship and collegiality are much appreciated.

Thanks to Ross and Jeanne Dunn for their enduring support over the years, and especially to Jeanne, who did the map.

I am grateful to the members of the Fall 2006 ad hoc Maghrebi studies reading group at the IAS (Cemil Aydin, Benjamin C. Brower, George Trumbull IV, and Max Weiss) for their colleagueship and support at a key moment in the life of this project. Special thanks to Ben Brower.

Portions of the manuscript were completed while I was in residence at the European University Institute in the fall of 2011. I am especially grateful to Professor Bartolomé Yun-Casallila, the chair of the Department of History and Civilization at the time, and to the EUI staff, who did so much to make my stay a productive and enjoyable one.

In Morocco, I have many individuals to thank. Above all is Driss Maghraoui (historian, Al-Akhawayn University), former student, colleague, and good friend, who helped me reconnect with Morocco and Moroccan scholars, including several stays at Al-Akhawayn University, and a series of lectures in Rabat in the fall of 2010. Jim Miller, executive director of the Moroccan American Commission for Educational and Cultural Exchange, arranged for Fulbright support of my travels.

I am also deeply grateful to the Moroccan scholars who critiqued an earlier version of the manuscript in 2008 at a series of roundtable discussions in Rabat organized by Driss Maghraoui and Abdelhay El Moudden. Participants included Abdelahad Sebti, Mohamed El Mansour, Ahmad Dahlane, Mustafa Qadery, and Taieb Belghazi.

Thanks to Professor Mohammed Kenbib for inviting me to present a paper at the Casablanca conference in October 2012 to promote the establishment of a Moroccan historical museum. The conference allowed me an opportunity to share my research with Moroccan historians.

Finally, thanks as well to Fatema Mernissi, who was always able to find ways to divert my attention from the Morocco That Was to the Morocco That Is; to Abdesselam Cheddadi, who was the first to point out his interest in seeing this book in print; and to Mohamed Tozy, who has understood this book from the beginning.

In Paris, François Pouillon, *vieux campagnon de route* and Directeur d'études at the Centre d'histoire sociale de l'Islam méditerranéen (Paris), provided a venue to discuss this project. Thanks to Gianni Albergoni, Claude Lefebure, Allain Mesaoudi, and Daniel Nordman for their warm greetings and pertinent remarks on this occasion. Pierre Vermeren, Professeur des Universités, Université de Paris (Panthéon/Sorbonne), provided assistance in navigating the French archives on Morocco, and moral support.

Thanks to Gregory Blue and Martin Bunton for their kind invitation to present portions of this manuscript to the Faculty Seminar of the History Department, Victoria University. Thanks to the participants for their engaged reading in the ensuing discussion.

Jonathan Wyrtzen critiqued portions of the manuscript during a stay in Morocco in the fall of 2010. Patricia Goldsworthy-Bishop was helpful in my research into the iconography of the early protectorate, a field she knows well. Charis Boutieri shared her knowledge of Moroccan historical databases. James Casey helped me locate important materials about the activities of the École d'Alger in Morocco.

Finally, thanks to Raymond and Mari-Jo Jamous, old and dear friends whose hospitality and humor sustained me throughout this project; to Stuart Schaar, a wonderful host and supportive friend; and to Kenneth Brown, editor of *Mediterraneans/Méditerrannées,* for sage comments and wry observations that sustained me. Michael Wolfe has always been available to read, discuss, and deliver trenchant observations. Muiris Macgiollabhui, able to reach the top shelf with ease in all his endeavors, was there when most needed.

Last but not least, enormous thanks go to Marian Rogers, ace copy editor, whose forbearance, acuity, and good sense of humor got this book over the final bumps in the road. Remaining errors are of course mine. Thanks as well to Cindy Fulton and Niels Hooper, my editors at UC Press. It's been a pleasure working with them both.

This book is dedicated to my wife, Carolyn, and to Poppy, Ron, and Leila with gratitude for all they have brought me.

Rabat and Santa Cruz
October 17, 2013

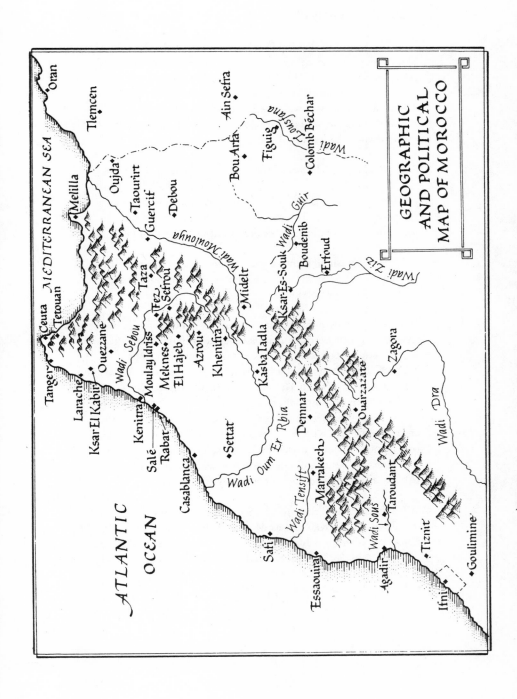

GEOGRAPHIC
AND POLITICAL
MAP OF MOROCCO

It all began with a Sufi tale.

In the reign of Mawlay Ismail (r. 1672–1727), so the story goes, Sidi Ali ben Ahmed, the marabout of Jabal Sarrar [an important religious figure of the time] was present when Moulay Rashid [the first Alawi sultan] designated his son Moulay Ismail as his successor. Also present was Moulay Abdallah, the sharif of Wazzan, who was head of the Wazzaniya, a Sufi order whose spiritual power rivaled that of the Alawis.

Sidi Ali addressed the assembled persons. To Moulay Rashid he said, "To you I give the stirrup," while to Moulay Abdallah, he said, "To you I gave the stick." That is, the Alawis should receive the temporal power, while the Wazzanis should receive the spiritual power. Unfortunately, the oral tradition stops at this point.

After Moulay Ismail came to the throne, things changed. This provides a second story of the origins of the tradition. It dates from a slightly later period.

Moulay Ismail did not appreciate the rivalry of other *sharif-s* and *zawiya-s*. He therefore commanded Moulay Tuhami (the successor of Moulay Abdallah) to appear before him at his palace in Meknes. The sultan ordered his chamberlain (*qaid al-mishwar*) and his vizir to verbally chastise Moulay Tuhami for his exaggerated claims. But no sooner had they arrived than the stomach of the saint swelled with indignation, threatening to engulf the entire room. Faced with this demonstration of his spiritual power, the chamberlain and the vizir fled to the sultan. They begged him to abandon his attacks on the sharif, who was obviously a favorite of heaven. This was not the end of the affair however.

When he learned of this miracle, Sultan Ismail went to meet the marabout. He arrived just as Moulay Tuhami was leaving his house to greet him. While Moulay Ismail was dismounting from his horse, Moulay Tuhami called on the sultan to remount, and held his stirrup for him. "It is only now," Moulay Ismail is said to have exclaimed, "that I am a real sultan."

Introduction

INVENTING MOROCCAN ISLAM

IN AN ICONIC MOMENT, Hubert Lyautey, first resident-general of the French protectorate in Morocco (1912–25), holds the stirrup for Moulay Youssef as he mounts his horse on the occasion of his accession to the throne in 1912 as the first sultan of the French protectorate. The ceremonial ritual is alleged to have originated in the precolonial period when the sharif of Wazzan, a major regionally powerful religio-political figure, held the stirrup.[1] According to the custom, the new sultan would then ride from the palace to the principal mosque and lead the Friday prayer (one of his few public ritual duties). The ritual underscored the status of the sharif of Wazzan as the premier grandee of the realm, as well as his public abasement in the presence of the sultan.

With the inauguration of the French protectorate in 1912 this ceremonial gesture was repeated. Or so we are told.[2] But the reenactment was infused with new symbolic meaning for Moroccan observers. The throne accession ceremonial encapsulated the political strategy that underlay the French protectorate. By it, the French colonial state affirmed its historical continuity and legitimacy through its deep understanding and respect for the historical specificity of Moroccan Islam. It also signaled the subordination of the French protectorate to the authority of the new sultan. Resident-General Lyautey consistently sought to present the continuity of the protectorate with the deep past of Morocco, and to suggest his great respect for Moroccan tradition. Far from being of great antiquity, however, "Moroccan Islam" has a history—one that is complexly entwined with French colonial ethnography.

Today, almost alone among Muslim countries Morocco is known for its national form of Islam, "Moroccan Islam." Yet there is little evidence that precolonial Moroccans thought of themselves as having a distinctive style of Islam. Indeed, since Islam is a universal religion, the existence of recognized national versions is not recognized. European observers before 1900 tended to agree, even as they noted the ubiquity and persistence of a variety of superstitious beliefs and practices. This is in no way to deny that the Moroccan monarchy had a long history, or that it enjoyed widespread popular support among most Moroccans. The distinction is between Moroccan Islam and Islam in Morocco. Today, Moroccan Islam stands for the unbroken history of Moroccan kingship extending from the seventh-century arrival of Islam in northwest Africa. Some authorities, on perhaps dubious grounds, have even credited its national Islam with preserving Morocco from the contamination of Islamic radicalism.[3]

WHAT IS MOROCCAN ISLAM?

Moroccan Islam has several components. First, the Moroccan monarch combined three official titles.[4] He claimed to be sultan—the Arabic title literally means "holder of power" and had no religious connotations. Many Muslim rulers employed the title *sultan,* and the Moroccan sultan was just one of them. He also claimed to be khalifa—the term is generally translated as "caliph." As caliph he was the religiously sanctioned ruler, the "Commander of the Faithful" who was endowed with supernatural powers. Finally, he was imam—in the Sunni context this term had much the same religious connotations as "caliph." *Imam* also had a more specific meaning, since it was the imam in the Sunni Muslim tradition who was charged with leading the general noon prayer on Fridays.

A second feature of Moroccan Islam is that the sultan was alleged to possess magico-religious powers. Moroccan monarchs were believed to have special powers, such as *baraka* (charisma, divine blessing), which enabled its possessor to bestow blessings on selected individuals or groups, and *sukhta,* the power to curse those who attracted his wrath.[5] Moroccan monarchs were not alone in having this power, however. Marabouts and other reputedly holy individuals were also believed to have *baraka.* They were also believed to be able to heal by the laying on of hands. Forms of sacral kingship were widespread in the preindustrial world.[6] For example, medieval French kings were believed to have the power to heal the afflicted by their royal touch.[7] Anthropologists inform us that a host of other popular beliefs (including belief in the evil eye, and magico-religious practices) were widespread not just in North Africa but throughout the Mediterranean, from Spain to the Ottoman Empire and beyond.[8]

When the European colonial offensive on Morocco began in 1900, there were lots of Muslim monarchies in the Middle East. The chief ones were the Ottoman Empire, Persia (today Iran), Afghanistan, and Yemen. (The Tunisian Bey and Egyptian Khedive were subordinate to the Ottoman sultan). Following the breakup of the Ottoman Empire only Morocco, Persia, Afghanistan, and Yemen remained. They had in common the fact that they all were isolated from the outside world by mountains and deserts and inhabited by fierce tribesmen, who migrated with their flocks and herds. Today Morocco alone remains a monarchy. The history of Moroccan Islam can do much to help us understand why this is so.

Moroccan Islam was constructed under the auspices of French colonial scholars in the early twentieth century. Its creation made possible the transformation of a fragile precolonial Moroccan monarchy into a modern state. As Morocco became French, the meanings and functions of the discourse on Moroccan Islam underwent important modifications. A measure of the success of the discourse on Moroccan Islam is that it continues to inform the post-colonial Moroccan state (see chapters 9 and 10).[9] Yet there has been little serious examination of the role played by Moroccan Islam in the modernization of Morocco.

The persistence of a tradition, in this case of Moroccan Islam, does not happen by itself. It requires a great deal of work and cunning, since it occurs against the grain of historical change. Morocco is not the only monarchy to be reinvented in modern times.[10] The British monarchy, whose pomp and circumstance can still capture the world's attention on the occasion of royal enthronements, weddings, births, and funerals, is perhaps the best-known example. British historian David Cannadine's essay "The British Monarchy and the Invention of Tradition" performs the useful task of historicizing the choices that went into staging royal events, thereby keeping the monarchy uppermost in the minds of British subjects.[11] The French monarchy too was redesigned and updated after the fall of the Bourbons in 1830, although its history is less well known. A better example for our purposes is the British Raj, whose rituals and ceremonies were invented in the nineteenth century to foster the appeal of the British Empire, with India as its beating heart. Cannadine slyly refers to this process as "ornamentalism" (he's thinking of Edward Said).[12] The retrofitting of Indian rituals of royalty and governance under British rule is the subject of Bernard S. Cohn's brilliant essay on the invention of the 1877 imperial durbar organized to proclaim Queen Victoria as empress of India.[13] At stake is the question of whether traditions and nationalisms are always there, or socially constructed. The British Raj provides many examples of British Indo-Saracenic ceremonies designed by amateur Cecil B. DeMille for the edification and entertainment of the colonized as well as the colonizers.[14]

Lyautey and his advisers were deeply impressed by the British colonial Indian example and eager to incorporate as many of its features as they could into the Moroccan sultanate as a modern monarchy. The enthronement ritual with which we began was not the only ritual that underwent a process of triage and repurposing in the refashioning of the modern Moroccan monarchy. The successive transformations of the royal parasol as an emblem of royalty in Morocco from early modern times forward have been demonstrated by Jocelyne Dakhlia in an inspiring essay.[15] With the establishment of the protectorate, former courtly rituals were examined for their suitability to a modern monarchy. Survivors included the signing of the *bay'a* and the ritual procession of the monarch to conduct the Friday prayer. The *bay'a* was a religious document in which the leading ulama and notables of the major cities of Morocco swore allegiance to the new sultan upon his accession to the throne. Having undergone periods in which it was seldom invoked, the *bay'a* was repurposed and updated under Lyautey. Today it has become, if anything, more important as a marker of the support of the elite for each new sultan. The royal processional has a similar history of intermittency. The invention of the modern Moroccan monarchy under the protectorate is an important topic. But its history has not yet been written, and it is not the subject of this book.

The French ethnography of Morocco provides a remarkable portal into the social and cultural worlds of ordinary Moroccans. To read the early volumes of *Archives marocaines* (about which much more later) is to enter a very different world from the Morocco we find in European diplomatic sources. In the pages of the early volumes of *Archives marocaines* one encounters the daily life of Moroccans, and their interactions with one another, with the government (Ar. *makhzan*), and with Europeans. The experience of reading these accounts enabled me to look past the indifference of European writings on the "Moroccan question" (as the international struggle over Morocco was called) to discover the wellsprings of popular protest and resistance in my first book, *Prelude to Protectorate in Morocco*.[16] French ethnographic writings constitute an irreplaceable source regarding the pre-protectorate social world of Morocco on the threshold of the modern world. While Arabic sources offer us access to the thoughts and actions of the Moroccan elite, they have much less to say about peasants, tribesmen, and urban popular classes.

This book examines French ethnographic and political supremacy through a bifocal lens. In so doing it seeks to clarify hitherto poorly understood aspects of the history of the inception of French rule in Morocco, and to raise a series of questions about history and theory. Finally, it draws attention to the discourse of Moroccan Islam and the persistence of the Moroccan monarchy. In addressing these questions *The Ethnographic State* underscores the importance of the historical contexts (international, financial, and political) within which key developments occurred, in shaping French research. This book focuses primarily on the period 1900–1914, when the Moroccan colonial archive was assembled. But it begins with the deeper history of French ethnography in the lands of Islam and especially colonial Algeria. It also addresses the post-1914 Lyautey era, when the template for the new academic field of Moroccan studies was laid down. Finally, in a brief conclusion it seeks to apply some of the implications of the argument to the contemporary era.

THE MOROCCAN COLONIAL ARCHIVE

I have chosen the creation of the Moroccan colonial archive as the point of entry into the complex and layered history of the invention of Moroccan Islam. The term *archive* is a conceptual tool developed by Michael Foucault to express the collective intellectual power of categories of thought.[17] The concept of a colonial archive derives from the work of Bernard S. Cohn, whose essays on British India, subsequently collected in *Colonialism and Its Forms of Knowledge,* helped stimulate research on the knowledge systems of colonial Indian history.[18] The British colonial archive of India provided the categories of the organization of its rule, as well as specific modalities by which British rule was implemented. One such was the investigative modality. Under it, the local and provincial officials of the Indian Colonial Service (known as the I.C.S.) were tasked to collect and disseminate information about Indian societies in response to official questionnaires. The results were collated and published in provincial and local gazetteers and handbooks, whose purpose was to provide reliable information to British officials charged with making policy decisions.[19] The colonial archive of India provided the symbolic capital that underwrote British colonial rule and displayed British mastery of India.

The Moroccan colonial archive signals a different intellectual genealogy at work. The nineteenth-century French sociology of Islam derived from the

Enlightenment tradition of Diderot's *Encyclopédie.* It was this tradition that animated the *Description de l'Égypte,* a study of the archaeology, geology, geography, and natural history of Egypt in twenty-three grand folio volumes. Another major series of volumes in the Enlightenment style was commissioned following the French intervention in Algeria in 1830. But soon the Algerian colonial archive was replete with racialized binaries and essentialized thinking.[20] Following the French defeat by Prussia in 1871, French policymakers were largely in agreement that French rule in Algeria had led to numerous costly blunders. Although Algerian Muslim society had been inventoried in the process, ethnography had done little to mitigate the cost or effectiveness of the conquest. Morocco provided a chance to do better, to develop policies based on a more scientifically informed knowledge of the society. The creation of the Moroccan colonial archive was thus an attempt to allay public fears through the adoption of what its proponents called "scientific imperialism." Part of a systematic French effort to gather information (*renseignements*) about Morocco, scientific imperialism was an application of the newly emerging intellectual tools of the social sciences to the governance of colonial peoples. But was it successful in escaping the discursive destiny of the Algerian colonial gospel? This remains less clear, and is a major subject of this book.

Around 1900, as the social sciences in France were in the process of assuming their modern disciplinary forms, *anthropologie* meant physical anthropology, a discipline closely tied to the measurement of skulls (craniometry) as a system of racial classification. Sociology was just emerging as a discipline under the leadership of Émile Durkheim, and focused on the study of institutions and the importance of structural "social facts," in the tradition of Comtian positivism.[21] It was concerned primarily with French society, and it eschewed the study of colonial societies and the practice of fieldwork. Ethnography was not yet a recognized discipline in France. Indeed, there was no real French equivalent to the fieldwork-based discipline of anthropology in France at this time.[22] French ethnographers *avant la lettre* collected "facts" (but not Durkheimian social facts) about Moroccan culture and society. Individuals referred to as ethnographers in this book might have little or no formal training in the subject. Some were academics—a mix of geographers, geologists, or orientalists. Others, in the absence of a discipline, were explorers (we're in the closing chapter of European explorer narratives). All shared an interest in Moroccan culture and society, and a devotion to the cause of science and *la patrie.*

The collection of facts about Morocco comprised a discursive system established by the French as the basis for their administrative policies. As in the case of India, a number of specific modalities derived from the Moroccan colonial archive. What was deemed a fact worthy of collection derived from the rules implicit in the discourse. The French claimed a superior under-standing of Moroccan Islam, by virtue of which they alone could express, organize, and make legible the diverse components of Morocco's political identity. The discourse on Moroccan Islam provided the frame within which several distinct modalities were created.

As used here, the term "Moroccan colonial archive" refers at its broadest extent to the writings in French, both published and unpublished, about Morocco and Moroccans in the period 1880–1930. It does not refer to the contents of actual French archives and libraries. A manifestation of French intellectual power about the Moroccan other, the colonial archive organized knowledge into categories based on then relevant assumptions, which over time could and did change. It provided the symbolic capital and ethnographic authority on which the discourse on Moroccan Islam was constructed, as well as the frame within which Morocco could be thought.

The Moroccan colonial archive (in the sense of an ordered and relatively complete inventory of Moroccan history, society, and culture) was an impor-tant intellectual accomplishment. French ethnographers provided an impres-sive inventory of Moroccan social groups, cities, tribal groups, and Sufi orders. At its broadest extent, this archive comprised published and unpub-lished works about Moroccan society and history. Readers interested in a more complete bibliography of Moroccan ethnography, sociology, and geog-raphy are referred to André Adam's *Bibliographie critique de sociologie, d'ethnologie et de géographie humaine du Maroc.*[23]

This book is based on a lifetime's research in French archives and private papers. It provides a unique examination of the development of the French colonial archive on Morocco and of the political struggle among French scholars for the control of research on Morocco in the period 1890–1925. It locates French experts in their multiple political and intellectual contexts, while also tracing the complex ways in which the Moroccan colonial archive was shaped by the determinants of native policy and anti-Islamic racism. In so doing, it asserts the importance of historicization. It seeks to bring the discussion of colonial representations and empire to a new level of historical engagement by inserting the Moroccan case into different political contexts: French and Moroccan domestic politics, the politics of research, economic interests, and the micropolitics of the local. Social observations, we discover, were devised experimentally, provisionally, with many gaps and artful bridges between reality as perceived, represented, and projected.

ETHNOGRAPHIC MOROCCO: HISTORY AND THEORY

As colonial history has matured over the last quarter century, it has become more adept at exploring the complex ways in which colony and metropole interpenetrated one another.[24] In common with much of the new colonial history, this book is predicated on the assumption that the metropole and the colony constituted a single field of analysis.[25] However, with the end of colonialism and the retreat of empire, our awareness of the interpenetration of the two has increased. No longer are the histories of colonizer and colonized viewed as autonomous spaces with essentialized, always divergent histories. Indeed, as I have argued elsewhere, despite a fundamental disagreement over who should hold power, nationalist and colonialist histories shared many of the same basic assumptions.[26] Now the challenge for historians is to locate colonial histories in their global, and not just colonial, contexts.

When the Morocco crisis (1900–1912) erupted, France possessed relatively little knowledge of Morocco. Indeed the Moroccan colonial archive was created in an attempt to fill this knowledge gap. French Morocco experts agreed that if France were to prevail over its international rivals, it would need more information on Moroccan society—lots of it. The ability to collect and classify facts of all sorts was central to the task of colonial administration. In colonizing Morocco, France sought to develop policies based on a scientifically informed knowledge of the society. The origins of the Moroccan colonial archive are thus to be sought in the modernist impulses of French culture and the fin de siècle historical conjunctures in which they were embedded.

Thanks to an abundant archival documentation (including correspondence, research proposals, government records of all kinds), we are able to trace the successive transformations of the Moroccan colonial archive. Between 1900 and 1912, research on Morocco was bitterly contested as different factions and research groups jockeyed for control. The polarization of research was consequential for the sedimentation of types of knowledge gathered, and changing areas of contestation. Through the history of the creation of the Moroccan colonial archive the historian can trace in detail the contexts in which particular decisions were made, and the nature of the ethnographic studies undertaken. We discover that the archive that emerged was shaped as much by the vigor of Moroccan anticolonial resistance as by the unevenness of French engagement. The Moroccan colonial archive was notable for what it contained, as well as for its gaps and silences. This fortuitous ancestry means that we can follow the interplay of knowledge and power in the development of the Moroccan colonial ethnography as we can for few other societies.

Unlike the Indian and the Algerian colonial archives, which represent the sedimentation of a century or more of studies originally undertaken for diverse purposes rather than linked to the craft of governance, the Moroccan colonial archive was produced in less than a generation and was yoked from the outset to facilitating French rule. Subsequent to the establishment of the protectorate, significant adjustments were made that only strengthened the link between ethnography and empire. Over the period under study, there were changes in the social facts that were collected, and the institutional contexts in which these facts were collected.

The French colonial archive of Morocco was remarkable for both its ethnographic richness and its depth. In the space of little more than a quarter century a systematic survey of Morocco, tribe by tribe, city by city, institution by institution, came into being. The Mission scientifique du Maroc provided the intellectual basis for the official policy of cooperation with the *makhzan* in the pre-1912 period, and subsequently the native policy of the protectorate. Resident-General Lyautey believed that France should use its knowledge of Moroccan society to nudge Moroccans onto the path of progress without provoking messy and unfortunate little wars. Things began well. But as French errant policies provoked one crisis after another, it became apparent that French understandings of Morocco were based on faulty assumptions.

Does orientalism have a history, or is it the inscription of a timeless essence? Most of the scholarly literature on colonial forms of knowledge fails to problematize the particular historical contexts (political, economic, or cultural) in which colonial representations were generated. The discourse on "Moroccan Islam" asserts the basic continuity between precolonial Morocco and the postcolonial state in which the role of the French protectorate was to introduce modernity without change. The scholarly literature asserts the specialness of Moroccan political culture, based on the central role of the Moroccan sultan (now called king). In so doing, it erases the memory of the often bitter political divisions of the pre-protectorate era. Instead, it insists on the timeless role of the Moroccan sultan, the rightly ordained commander of the faithful, a quasi-divine person endowed with vast spiritual powers. Seen from the present, the discourse on Moroccan Islam makes it possible to reimagine the sweep of

Moroccan history from precolonial to colonial to postcolonial as a continuity, instead of a radical discontinuity. In contrast, this book starts with the notion that the discourse on Moroccan Islam, far from being without a history, cannot be understood without reference to its multiple global contexts

This becomes clear if we consider the pre-Saidean critique of colonial representations. Prior to 1978 publication of *Orientalism*, the critique of colonial forms of knowledge largely proceeded through a Marxist lens. While lacking the concept of discourse, the Marxist critique of colonial representations provided a theoretical as well as moral and political explanation of the historical necessity of nationalism. But (as Said and others argued) Marxism failed to extricate itself from its Eurocentric perspective on the emergence of Western capitalism. This is because it was only partially disembedded from the thought world of post-Enlightenment European culture. Thus it remained vulnerable to the charge of being Eurocentric. Nonetheless, by justifying and moralizing the struggle of Third World nationalists and providing it with a rooting in world history the Marxist critique filled a historic role.

The 1978 publication of *Orientalism* was a bombshell. By arguing that orientalism was a discursive system, Said created a powerful conceptual tool. It trenchantly critiqued the idea that the West was the primary beneficiary of progress and that the Orient was the space of tradition, backwardness, and stasis. In summoning the Orient into existence, Orientalism (the discourse) endowed it with its characteristic negative features, seen as a series of nesting cultural binaries. As a totalizing system, *Orientalism* conceptually explained the permanence of Western dominance. It also struck a blow to Marxism, the then dominant critical trend. As viewed by Said, Marx was an orientalist (in that he shared the assumptions of European observers of the time about Europe's place in history).[27] Most important was the timing of the publication of *Orientalism*. Coming when it did, at a moment of political contestation over racism, Vietnam, and gender oppression, *Orientalism* allowed the emerging contemporary cultural critiques to cross over from race, gender, and sexual identity to the critique of empire.

However orientalism was not without weaknesses of its own.[28] We can start with the concept of discourse, which as James Clifford has argued, Said appears to have misunderstood. As developed by Foucault, discourse did not apply to individual authors, but to literature as a whole.[29] Beyond this basic misconception, within the context of Saidean theory there are other issues that have to do with its lack of purchase on historical change. Thus, according to both Foucault and Said, discursive systems lack a discernible historical origin, being in effect always already there. Further, if orientalism as theorized is a totalizing discourse of domination, then the existence of resistance and nationalism cannot be explained. It is necessary to rehearse this intellectual history to understand the intervention of this book.

This book distinguishes between the social observations of individual observers, and the discursive contexts in which their observations occurred. Such observations could be more or less pertinent, more or less able to articulate complexity, depending on the particular discursive context. Discourses themselves were not unchanging, but could be more or less permissive depending on the political conjunctures. As the Morocco crisis deepened and political passions grew more intense, the tendency to abandon complexity in favor of cultural binaries was at war with the needs of native affairs experts who required "social facts," not ideology, in order to govern. As we will see, contexts could profoundly alter colonialist imaginings—even the most consequential, such as Hubert Lyautey's imagining of Moroccan Islam.

In excavating this history I seek to provide an account of the creation of the Moroccan colonial archive (and of its most important product, Moroccan Islam) and to map its successive transformations over the years 1900–1925. In this period, the nascent social sciences in France were seeking to address the tensions of modernity in metropolitan society, while in the "colonial space" they claimed to be pursuing "scientific imperialism." The Moroccan colonial archive was thus created under the double sign of social science and high modernist imperialism.

MOROCCO IN WORLD HISTORY

By putting Moroccan history on world time and inserting it into the conjunctures that shaped its development, this book seeks to bring discussion of colonial representations and empire to a new level of historical engagement. The discourse on Moroccan Islam was developed and deployed in a specific series of international, financial, and political contexts. Against the presumption of some cultural historians that intellectual and institutional contexts mattered but little in the launching and sustaining of discourses, this book suggests a different approach. The shape of intellectual fields was determined not only by the deployment of binaries, but also by personal and political rivalries over intellectual turf, and the larger political and economic contexts in which these mundane struggles were played out. In the history related in this book, we discover that colonial representations were devised experimentally, provisionally, with many gaps and artful bridges between reality as perceived, represented, and projected. Indeed, as we'll see, contexts could profoundly alter colonialist imaginings—even the most consequential, such as Hubert Lyautey's imagining of Moroccan Islam.

Moroccan Islam was an assertion of the hegemonic power of French colonial rule that reduced the complex realities of Morocco to a few metonyms. Because it seemed self-evidently true, one could not imagine things ever having been otherwise. In an audacious rewriting of history, it recast the French protectorate as the bridge between "the Morocco that was" (precolonial Morocco) and modernity.[32] In so doing it generated the myth of the peaceful conquest of Morocco and of a beneficent monarchy under French authority. The discourse on Moroccan Islam made the violence and depredations that accompanied the imposition of French rule fade into the background, while diverting attention from the gigantic transfer of Moroccan resources to the Compagnie marocaine (later known as the Omnium Nord-africain).[33] It is above all a political fable, deliberately told to bring about a political result.

The conquest of Morocco was a world event, shaped by conjunctural developments in the global world economy, the international system of states, French and Moroccan domestic politics, and the culture of global modernity. Each played an important role in shaping the Moroccan colonial archive.

By the late 1890s, the diplomatic isolation of Morocco was coming to an end. As the scramble for Africa entered its final phase around 1900, European rivalries for colonial territory intensified. Because of its strategic position on the Strait of Gibraltar, resource endowments, and increasingly anomalous financial independence, Morocco was an attractive prize. But French ambitions were blocked by Britain, Spain, and Italy (and latterly, by Germany). In this way "the Moroccan question" helped to preserve Moroccan political and economic independence until 1912 and to block any European power from claiming the prize. These global dynamics shaped the social and political struggles within and between individual states and provide an important context for explaining how and why the Moroccan colonial archive developed as it did.

Morocco's economy was not highly developed on the eve of the Moroccan question. Its exports to the world market consisted mostly of wool, hides, and agricultural commodities. Although Morocco's mineral and agricultural resources were reputed to be great (it had been an important source of silver and copper in medieval times for western Europe), both were poorly developed. In 1900 the *makhzan* was able to exercise a degree of control over access to Morocco's land and resources.[34] Europeans were legally enjoined from owning land, though clandestine land purchases via Moroccan intermediaries (authorized by the 1880 Madrid Convention) were increasing. A sign that momentous changes were brewing was the increase in the size of the resident European population, which jumped from 1,360 in 1864 to 9,000 in 1894.[35]

After 1900, the economic clock began ticking more loudly. The state contracted major loan obligations, and the best Moroccan agricultural lands began to fall into the hands of European (mostly French) speculators. A botched tax reform in 1902 was a disaster, depriving the *makhzan* of revenue just when it was most needed. By 1904 Morocco no longer had a substantial treasury balance but owed 100 million francs and was saddled with an international debt commission.[36] These woes coincided with a series of terrible harvests, followed by outbreaks of epidemic disease. The economic dimensions of the Morocco crisis, while not as well known as its diplomatic aspects, were considerable.[37]

The convolutions of French domestic politics in the Third Republic were famously complex and contentious, and constitute another factor that affected the unfolding of the Moroccan question. French governments (sometimes two or three a year) rose and fell , while bureaucratic factions mobilized to protect economic interest groups. Between 1890 and 1914 the Dreyfus affair, the struggle between church and state, and the right of workers to organize took turns roiling the political arena and dividing families. Meanwhile, on the left and right extraparliamentary groups fought in the streets. In this context, the decision to colonize Morocco became subject to political debate. As the colonial lobby asserted the benefits of making Morocco French, it was vigorously opposed by those wishing first to liberate Alsace and Lorraine from German occupation. Moreover, the colonial group itself was sharply split over which policy might best secure Morocco for France. During the period under study French domestic politics could and did shape both the Morocco policy options of the government, as well as framing what could be thought about Morocco.

Moroccans in these years lived through a political crisis that seemed to have no end. With government stability undermined by ongoing official corruption and incompetence, its elites found themselves badly divided over what stance to take toward the threat of European imperialism. Greedy land-lords and corrupt officials tightened the social noose on the poor and power-less, who had already been undermined by recurrent famines and epidemics. *Makhzan* incompetence in the face of the looming specter of French imperi-alism further stoked fears and desperation. Threatened by populist insur-gency, many elites looked to the Ottoman Empire for models of modernity or sought private arrangements with European interests. Others, less sophis-ticated, were tempted by the prospect of jihad to oppose an imperialist takeo-ver and the growing social disorder. This led to a sharpening of social ine-qualities and a polarization of Moroccan domestic politics. By 1912, a tsunami of protest and resistance threatened to sweep all before it.

Changing French policy options and continued Moroccan resistance affected ethnographic analyses. In an effort to more fully historicize the development of the Moroccan colonial archive, the pages that follow are grounded in their historical contexts and conjunctures.

OVERVIEW

The chapters in part 1, "Ethnographic Morocco," explore the historical and discursive background out of which the French colonial archive on Morocco emerged. Chapter 1 provides a survey of the history of the French sociology of Islam, starting with the 1798 French expedition to Egypt, and its chief intel-lectual product, the *Description de l'Égypte,* a twenty-three-volume survey of Egyptian history, and concluding with the compilation of the literatures on Algeria, Tunisia, and West African Islam. The experience of Algeria was to prove crucial in a number of ways in shaping the intellectual and political context in which the ethnography of Morocco would emerge some years later.

Chapter 2 takes up the Algerian origins of Moroccan studies. It focuses on the contrasting traditions of the Arab Bureaux and the French civilian academics in elaborating Algerian ethnography. Both drew on metropolitan examples, and in the first case the tradition of the statistical enumeration of the social characteristics of particular populations governed by the French administration. The civilian academics derived their intellectual genealogy from the discipline of folklore and dialectology, both of which were undergo-ing a renewal in France at the time. Gathered at the École d'Alger under the leadership of René Basset and Edmond Doutté, the scholars of the École d'Alger felt destined to dominate research on Morocco by dint of their cultural and linguistic expertise.

Chapter 3 explores the dynamics of the struggle over control of social research on Morocco in the period 1900–1904. At the start of the Moroccan crisis in 1900 a wide-ranging political struggle over control of the ethnography of Morocco broke out. Before it was resolved it split not only the world of academics and researchers, but the French government itself, pitting rival strategies to conquer Morocco and their intellectual proponents against one another. The struggle for control over research on Morocco between the École d'Alger and the Mission scientifique du Maroc was simultaneously a struggle over how Moroccan social and political realities should be portrayed to the French and international publics. This provides the subject of chapter 4, which discusses political and discursive contexts of the Moroccan question and raises important questions about theories of colonial representations.

Chapter 5 examines the auspices under which the Moroccan colonial archive was created. We discover that most of the ethnographic research on Moroccan society was conducted as a result of the de facto collaboration of two rival groups—the Mission scientifique du Maroc (MSM) and the Comité de l'Afrique française (CAF). The MSM was based in Tangier. Its periodical, *Archives marocaines,* published remarkable studies of northern Moroccan groups and institutions. In contrast, the CAF, its main rival, sponsored study missions into the Moroccan interior, which were published in its monthly *Bulletin.* Between them, these two groups produced the majority of Moroccan ethnography before 1912.

The chapters in part 2, "Native Policy Morocco," explore the development and institutionalization of native policy research. Chapter 6 traces the institutionalization of French knowledge about Morocco under the protectorate. Drawing on the British experience in colonial India, Resident-General Lyautey and Alfred Le Chatelier sought to endow the native affairs section with a series of handbooks and gazetteers in the Indian fashion. The periodical *Archives berbères* (1913–18) and the eleven-volume series Villes et Tribus du Maroc provided facts about the Berbers of the Middle Atlas Mountains, and Moroccan coastal cities and their rural populations. Also in this period the academic research center the Institut des hautes études marocaines was established. Its quarterly periodical, *Hespéris,* became the leading academic journal of Moroccan studies.

The fraught question of French ethnography and Berber policy is the subject of chapter 7. When the protectorate was first established, France had little knowledge of the *thamazight*-speaking pastoralist Middle Atlas Berber groups. When French measures to introduce security provoked instead a series of major rebellions in the period 1912–14, a major native policy debacle erupted. Only then did the French realize that there were crucial differences between the *tashelhit*-speaking groups of southern Morocco and the *thamazight* speakers of the Middle Atlas Mountains. A policy devised for Middle Atlas Berbers, however, soon proved to have its limitations. Prematurely hailed as a success, French Berber policy became a persistent weak point of the protectorate government.

French urban ethnography and policy, the subject of chapter 8, provides another example. Even before 1900 Fez provoked great interest among Europeans, but it remained little frequented and less understood. By 1904 a comprehensive portrait of the city of Fez had been generated. But a succession of urban insurrections in 1907–8, 1911, and 1912 suggested that beneath the surface there was much that eluded French analysts. Following a major rebellion in May 1912, it was clear that something needed to be done. After the establishment of the protectorate an experiment in "guided democracy" ensued. The French authorities created an elective municipal council (Ar. *majlis al-a'yan*). But the Fez model was not extended to other Moroccan cities. Instead the French pursued municipal policies that effectively divided the native city (*medina*) from the modern one (*ville nouvelle*)—a system one critic has called "urban apartheid."[38] Chapter 8 seeks to explain why.

The chapters in part 3, "Governmental Morocco," explore how the creation of the discourse on Moroccan Islam facilitated the emergence of a modality of governmentality under the protectorate that was subsequently reinvented and deployed to justify the French conquest and to legitimize colonial rule. Chapter 9 explains how the discourse on Moroccan Islam came together over the period, incorporating many of the binaries of the Algerian colonial legacy and including the specifically Moroccan elements of sharifism and *baraka*, which together distinguished Morocco from other Maghrebi societies as an object of study. By insisting on the role of superstitious religious beliefs in sustaining the Moroccan monarchy, the founders created a Morocco that never was, one exempt from historical change.

Chapter 10 has several objectives. First, it shows how the discourse on Moroccan Islam became an instrument of governmentality, tracing the successive reinventions of the discourse on Moroccan Islam under the auspices of the protectorate, and subsequently under an independent Moroccan government. Second, it considers the reinvention of Moroccan Islam in the 1970s by Anglo-American scholars, notably Ernest Gellner and Clifford Geertz. The chapter concludes with a series of historical reflections on the Moroccan experience of applied ethnography and native policy.

PART ONE

Ethnographic Morocco

On Bled al-makhzan and Bled al-siba (1901)

The expression of *bled el-makhzan* opposed to that of *bled el-siba* is incorrect, for all of Morocco under different forms and to varying degrees undergoes the action of the *makhzan*. . . .

While a European might interpret the persistent conflict between the *makhzan* and the tribes as mere anarchy, all this is not disorder, but an order; in this apparent chaos all the living forces ended up by finding an equilibrium: the play of classes and of parties of all kinds resulted in a kind of social stasis that constitutes a durable state, as much in the tribes as in the cities.

EDMOND DOUTTÉ, "UNE MISSION D'ÉTUDES AU MAROC," RENSEIGNEMENTS COLONIAUX, 1901, 166

On Arabs and Berbers (1901)

As much in Morocco as in Algeria the ethnic division of natives into "Arabs" and "Berbers" is a vain distinction, because no criteria can be invoked on which to base this distinction. One can find Arab speakers who used to speak Berber and vice versa, just as one can find nomadic and sedentary populations among both groups.

EDMOND DOUTTÉ, "UNE MISSION D'ÉTUDES AU MAROC," RENSEIGNEMENTS COLONIAUX, 1901, 166

On Bled al-makhzan and Bled al-siba (1908)

Moroccan history is caught between two contradictory impulses: The situation of the *makhzan* vis-à-vis this national organism [the Berber organism] is about the same as that of the ancient Phoenician and Roman conquerors; like them, it is incapable of finishing its conquest and organizing it, and it has been unable to absorb for its benefit the Berber vitality, to assimilate it; all that it can do is to resist it, to contain it within its limits and to declare itself responsible for its actions vis-à-vis Europe in order to justify an authority that it is moreover incapable of exercising by its means alone.

ÉDOUARD MICHAUX-BELLAIRE, "L'ORGANISME MARO-CAIN," REVUE DU MONDE MUSULMAN 9 (1909): 43

ONE

France and the Sociology of
Islam, 1798–1890

WRITING IN THE NEW YORK REVIEW OF BOOKS in 1971 Clifford
Geertz argued that the old explanations of North African society were no
longer valid, if they ever had been.[1] When he arrived in Morocco in 1965, with
the classics of French colonial ethnography as his guide, Geertz looked immediately for the primordial groupings that he had been led to believe structured
social relations at every level. Yet on closer examination, he discovered, the concepts of tribe, saintly lineage, sufi *tariqa,* and even the extended family, tended
to dissolve before his very eyes. The French colonial literature seemed suddenly
suspect; all now was dyadic ties. What had changed of course was not just
North Africa. The observer had also changed. As a consequence of the shifting
patterns of world politics in the postwar era, as well as changes in intellectual
fashions, Morocco was suddenly of interest to British and American social scientists. With these sea changes it was perhaps to be expected that the image of
North African society in Western scholarship would be temporarily out of
focus. But so too, in a way, was the French tradition of the sociology of Islam.[2]
How and why the latter was transformed is the subject of this chapter.

IN SEARCH OF THE SOCIOLOGY OF ISLAM

The French tradition of the empirical study of Muslim societies began in 1798
with the Napoleonic expedition to Egypt and the twenty-three volumes of
the *Description de l'Égypte.*[3] A second formative moment was the work of the
first generation of French researchers in Algeria (1830–48).[4] Thereafter the
tradition emerged largely within these early parameters, its major phases cor-
responding to the shifting patterns of French colonialism. By the outbreak of

the Algerian war in 1954, it had become a mummified version of its former self, and in its evident inability to explain the outbreak of the war, or its raison d'être, collapsed of its own weight. Somehow an intellectual tradition that had begun with aspirations of bringing the fruits of the French Revolution to the lands of Islam had become instead an apologist for empire, a disseminator of racist stereotypes, and a producer of irrelevant folklore. It is no accident that the existence of this tradition dates from the beginnings of French imperialism in the Middle East in 1798 to its bloody and convulsive end in 1962 with the independence of French Algeria.

But can there be said to be a French tradition of the sociology of Islam? The very terms of such a formulation are full of traps for the unwary. Indeed, at the risk of sounding perverse, I am tempted to observe that the sociology of Islam does not exist, and that it has until recently been preeminently a French tradition. Part of the problem, part of the misconceived *problematique* of the field, is the assumption that Islam is an appropriate field for sociological inquiry.[5] The question of the relationship between the study of Muslim peoples and the discipline of orientalism, never an easy or straightforward one, is thereby posed. Then there is the fact that most of the French sociology of Islam was produced by individuals who were not sociologists at all. Rather they were colonial native affairs officers, civilian amateurs, and orientalists. Academic sociologists did not concern themselves seriously with such questions until the twentieth century. Thus we will have to consider the relationships between those whom we are calling sociologists (using the word in its broad nineteenth-century sense), and intellectual circles in metropolitan France. A third objection can be raised to the title of this chapter. It presumes that something called a *tradition* of the sociology of Islam exists. What does it mean to speak of a tradition of the sociology of Islam? Before going on to discuss in greater detail the legacy of French sociology of Islamic societies (which, as we will see, is principally a sociology of North Africa), it is necessary to consider these questions further.

To speak of a tradition of French sociology of Islam involves an intellectual exercise the implications of which we should be aware. To retrospectively construct a tradition is in some sense already to validate it, to accord it legitimacy, to assert its existence. A tradition in this sense, what Foucault calls a *discours* (or Bourdieu a *doxa*), is invested with a kind of *mana* that is highly interested.[6] In this sense, a tradition is a politically structured discourse, whose function is to dominate, control, and or orient our understanding. As we are no longer contemporaries of the period in which this discourse flourished, there is no reason for us to accept its central assumptions. Because we are not innocent consumers of its product (colonial sociology), but are forced to have reference to it insofar as we are interested in North African society, it is crucially important that we situate its practitioners against the political and intellectual background in which they flourished, and in the context of their central assumptions about that society.

Historically the study of Islamic subjects in France followed one of two paths:[7] either the discipline of orientalism, a linguistically defined field based on the critical study of texts written in oriental languages, or the less rigorous tradition of colonial studies of Muslim societies, the product of amateurs and enthusiasts, expatriate sojourners in an exotic world they sought to understand. French orientalists dominated the study of Islamic subjects in the metropole. From the time of Silvestre de Sacy (1757–1838), who can in many ways be said to have single-handedly invented the field, orientalists came to occupy positions of institutional power within the Parisian academic establishment: in the department of oriental manuscripts of the Bibliothèque nationale, the École des langues orientales, the Collège de France, and the Académie des inscriptions et belles lettres of the Institut de France. Although mastery of Islamic languages made orientalists useful in supporting French colonial adventures in North Africa, the fundamental impetus of the discipline moved in other directions. Resolutely hostile to the study of contemporary subjects and devoted to the formalist study of classical texts, orientalists looked with deep suspicion on those who studied the living languages of the Middle East. Engaged in a field that they regarded as the elaboration of "the historical science of the human spirit" (Renan), they refused to sully their intellectually noble calling with less worthy intellectual pursuits.[8] Not until the end of the nineteenth century, with the introduction of comparative linguistics and the introduction of the spoken oriental languages to the curriculum of the École des langues orientales vivantes, did the discipline undergo important changes that were eventually to lead to its renewal.[9]

What orientalism contributed to the study of Islamic societies was the concept of Islamic civilization. This had its advantages, as well as its liabilities. On the one hand, it compelled students of colonial North Africa to recognize the historical past of North African Muslims and their place in the wider world of Middle Eastern Islamic civilization. Had the concept of Islamic civilization been taken seriously, it might have inhibited the tendency to conceive of the Maghreb as an island cut off from its Mashriqi point of reference. On the other hand, civilizational studies accredited essentialist notions about the nature of Islamic history, even while it systematically devalued the study of the more recent periods of North African history. For an E. F. Gautier, the murky periods *(les siècles obscurs)* included everything after the Arab conquest of North Africa.[10] In this way civilizational thinking supported the dichotomous and racist categories of the colonial world.

Nineteenth-century French orientalists also shared with the students of Islamic societies the romantic quest for the exotic, for *dépaysment,* perhaps ultimately for the autonomous individual. Ethnographers, orientalists, painters, and writers—people like Léon Roches, Eugène Daumas, Émile Masqueray, Eugène Delacroix, Gustave Flaubert, and Charles de Foucauld— were propelled from their secure moorings in metropolitan bourgeois society into an encounter with the other, the Arab, the Oriental. One of the most striking things about this imperialism of the spirit is the watchful impersonality that characterizes the closest personal encounters, a kind of voyeurism, an emotional ethnography of the other. Even in its most intimate and personal form, that of sexual relations, one finds a strange, distanced watchfulness. The heroic couplings of Gide at Biskra, no less than Flaubert's affair with Kuchuk, or those of Isabelle Eberhardt, or indeed any number of French lieutenants of the Arab Bureaux have this quality.[11] Edward Said, who is our best guide to this encounter with the Orient, is therefore correct to insist on both its sexual nature, and its paradoxical abstraction of the other.[12] He is also right to point to the manner in which this encounter sprang from a desire for power and domination, which is the very opposite of mutuality. This romanticism was most potent in the first half of the century, but it continued to be an important current of thought and feeling until well into our present century.[13] The psychosexual dynamics of the encounter with oriental peoples are of central importance to any effort to understand the complex origins and nature of French orientalism and colonial ethnography.

Compelling as it is in certain respects, Said's analysis of orientalism is unsurprising. After all, what would one expect the colonial sociology of Islam to be, if not colonialist? Said's discussion of the *Description* is limited to a brief examination of its *Préface historique,* and fails to engage the essays in the *État moderne* that discuss contemporary Egyptian society of the period.[14] In this way, as historian David Prochaska remarks, Said "reproduces the textual, philological, and linguistic tendencies which constitute the basis of the orientalist enterprise he is so critical of otherwise!"[15] We might agree with Said that orientalism was a discursive system that created the Orient as a field of power in which France might intervene. But if our intention is to achieve a historical understanding of French colonial forms of knowledge, such a diagnosis is insufficient. French power relative to the rest of the world was neither evenly deployed nor always the same, and French forms of knowledge and understandings of colonial peoples were always changing as well in relationship to the power dynamic, but also in response to changes in France itself.[16] Overtheorized and inadequately historicized, Said's *Orientalism* provides neither a history nor a sociology of the authors of the *Description de l'Égypte*.[17]

If our goal is to develop a sociology of these sociologists, the work of Pierre Bourdieu is indispensable. He provides some useful concepts that can help us understand the ways in which to understand the evolution of orientalist knowledge (especially the fields of ethnology/sociology that are our primary concern here). If knowledge is produced in particular institutional contexts, Bourdieu suggests, it arises in specific political contexts as well. In order to better understand the ways in which the sociology of Islam developed, it is important to situate it in both its political and its scientific fields. If we perform this operation we must recognize that while the sociology of Islamic societies had an ambiguous relationship to French orientalism, it was frankly marginal to intellectual currents in France, an insignificant back eddy to the unrushing stream of French *science*. This is all the more true of its relationship to the emergent discipline of sociology. The major figures of French sociology, from Auguste Comte and Frédéric Le Play to Émile Durkheim, Marcel Mauss, and Claude Levi-Strauss were little interested in the Maghreb, or Islamic societies generally. Nor were their disciples. French ethnography of Islamic societies developed in a kind of intellectual ghetto, clearly subordinate to the metropolitan world, a little tradition against the greater French tradition. This explains why despite a vast ethnological literature, no significant contribution to general sociological theory can be found in French studies on North Africa.[18]

It is in the examination of the relationship of the sociology of Islam to the French political field that we encounter the reasons for its distinctive shape. Although it was marginal to metropolitan *science,* the sociology of North Africa was much closer to the French political arena. Often, it was dominated (to its detriment) by political questions. Thus the study of the nature of the system of landholding in rural Algeria was from the outset a highly charged political question for French settlers, and the literature on *arch* land reflects this fact.[19] The bitter struggle for the control of research on Morocco at the beginning of the twentieth century is another reflection of this as we shall see in chapter 4. All of this is to say that as a colonial social science, the sociology of North Africa was decisively shaped by the political and intellectual contexts in which it existed. This drastically weakened its achievements from the beginning, skewing its central paradigms, suggesting false questions, and inhibiting the asking of important ones. The French tradition of the sociology of Islam was thus from the outset significantly inflected by its colonial context.

Already by the 1850s, the central assumptions of French views about the nature of North African society can be observed in the work of such writers as Eugène Daumas, Louis Pein, Charles Richard, and Ismail Urbain.[20] These assumptions included the supposedly anarchic state of precolonial society, the essentially negative and obscurantist role of Islam in North African society, the innate fanaticism of Islam, and the division of the society into dichotomous and mutually exclusive groupings: Arab and Berber, nomad and sedentary, rural and urban. From this it was but a small step to conclude that North Africans were congenitally incapable of independence. It goes without saying that these authors accepted the French civilizing mission and French rule as legitimate. The stereotypes of the colonial gospel provide the connecting thread between the liberal humanitarianism of the Saint-Simonians, the *vae victis* of the settlers, and the positivist social Darwinism of late nineteenth-century ethnologists. That such a set of assumptions had direct political relevance is evident. That it also helped to condition the questions that were asked and not asked, and the answers that were given, is no less true and demonstrable.

Finally, if we consider the characteristic emphasis of French *ethnologues* on certain topics (and not others), we may assert that we are dealing with a tradition. It is the gaps and silences in the French ethnographic record, as much as its preferred topics, that outline its distinctive shape. The two topics that most interested students of Algerian society were the principal manifestations of Islam in the countryside (the *ulama,* and other urban religious institutions more generally, were of little concern), and the structure and role of the tribes in Algerian society. Most of the ethnological literature on Algeria focuses on these topics, including the manners and customs variety of reportage, but also a great many more ambitious treatises.[21] To the two major themes of study contributed by the Algerian literature, the ethnology of Morocco added two more: the study of cities, and the study of the relationship between the tribes (notably the "Lords of the Atlas") and the state administration (the *makhzan*). This last topic was the central motif in Robert Montagne's work on the Berbers of the central High Atlas.[22] But it also informs many lesser efforts. The French sociology of the Maghreb remained fixated on these questions until the eve of decolonization.

At the same time some important questions were never raised, and this helps to define the tradition further. There were no studies of contemporary social change, for example (Robert Montagne's work on the *bidonvilles* of Casablanca dates from only 1951), and the political economy of both the pre-colonial and the colonial Maghreb was neglected.[23] Other important but absent topics were segmentary lineage structures (a British monopoly), the *ulama* (what some have called *ulamology* is a postcolonial phenomenon), the Islamic legal system as it actually operated (as opposed to how orientalists said it should), the roots of resistance (despite numerous insurrections, the topic surprisingly failed to attract scholarly interest), and finally, economic ties between city and country (French sociologists tended to presume economic autarchy). According to the French colonial gospel North Africa lacked a history, as a result of which it was condemned to repeat the same meaningless gestures. A veritable island, the Maghreb was viewed as having no cultural and political links to the outside world. France was the sole source of progress; resistance would bring only disaster.

The French tradition of the sociology of Islam went through four major phases, which may be described as the Egyptian phase (1798–1828), the Algerian phase (1830–70), the West African phase (1880s–1910), and the Moroccan phase (1900–1930). To these four some might add a fifth phase for the Syrian and Lebanese mandates. Of these, by far the most important was the Algerian phase. Inevitably, just as the Indian colonial experience tended to shape the perceptions of British orientalists and anthropologists, so the Algerian experience marked the French image of the world of Islam.[24] Most of the leading French scholars of Islamic societies were formed in Algeria, and even those who were not tended to define themselves negatively with reference to the work of the French Algerian experts. One could do an interesting study, for example, of the efforts of French Africanists to free themselves from the influence of the Algerian paradigm.[25] As we will see, the development of the sociology of Morocco was powerfully influenced by the Algerian model. It was through an Algerian lens that Frenchmen viewed other Islamic societies.

Yet the Egyptian experience did not count for nothing. For one thing, as Edward Said has argued in *Orientalism*, the authors of the *Description* created a textual Orient in their own image, where the Islamic Orient "would appear as a category denoting the orientalist's power and not the Islamic people as humans or their history as history."[26] The European relationship with the Orient inseparably linked the desire for knowledge of the other and the desire for domination over the other. As a result of the Napoleonic expedition, orientalism as a discourse on the Islamic other was born. The *Description de l'Égypte* gave birth to a number of subsequent textual children—later large-scale French projects aimed at mapping out the geographic, geological, scientific, and ethnographic terrain on which French imperialism would operate in Greece, Algeria, and Morocco. They include the five-volume *Expédition scientifique de Morée* (1832–36), the thirty-seven-volume *Exploration scientifique de l'Algérie* (1844–67), and the publications of the Mission scientifique du Maroc (1903–25) that are the focus of our attention in this book.[27]

THE FRENCH TRADITION OF
THE SOCIOLOGY OF ISLAM

A distinguishing feature of at least some of the essays on contemporary Egyptian society in the *Description de l'Égypte* is the care they take to provide precise social documentation. Nothing in French colonial ethnography on Algeria, French West Africa, or Morocco comes close to the effort at statistical documentation of the material life of ordinary Egyptians that is found in the Egyptian essays. Nowhere else is there a major effort to map a particular city street by street, including workshops, mosques, baths, and other public buildings. On the other hand, the authors of the *Description* show little interest in popular Islam as a major theme (especially Sufism) or in orientalist production on the Maghreb. Consequently the Napoleonic forces were shocked when they encountered popular resistance from Sufi groups.[28] Why these differences? Who in fact were the authors of the essays on contemporary Egypt in the *Description?* Mostly, they were recent graduates of the École polytechnique, a central revolutionary institution. Disciplined, scientifically trained observers, they were indoctrinated to believe that national regeneration depended on their putting their training to practical use. The effort to gather social statistics and to map human populations in the *Description* project derives from the same Enlightenment instincts as the desire to inventory the natural resources and appropriate the ancient history of Egypt. Here we encounter a more complex and interesting genealogy than that provided by Said.[29]

The thirty-seven volumes of the *Exploration scientifique de l'Algérie* (1844–67) edited by Edmond Pelissier de Reynaud represent a conscious imitation of this early fruit of French colonial science.[30] Drawn from the same Enlightenment spirit that had informed the *Description de l'Égypte* project, the *Exploration scientifique* sought to compile a thorough inventory of Algerian society. As we'll see later on, a similar inspiration lay behind the construction of the Moroccan colonial archive in the period 1890–1925. It is also intriguing to observe how rapidly the process went. In all three of these cases as well, the job was done within the span of a single generation. The colonial administrators and officials who came afterward for the most part confined themselves to further elaborations of the central themes laid down at this time.

In retrospect, examined in historical perspective, the French tradition of the sociology of Islam consisted of three main strands, the complex patterning of whose interactions over a century and a half constituted the tradition. These three strands represent the contributions of three groups: the Arab Bureaux, the civilian amateurs, and the academics. Attached to real social forces with real interests and perceptions of the society, these three groups are of primary importance in understanding not only the contributions to the intellectual tradition of colonial sociology, but also much of the dynamics of French colonial politics. Inevitably, of course, it is important to recognize that there was considerable overlap in the contributions of the groups.

The Arab Bureaux, which began in 1844 with the appointment of Eugène Daumas (1802–71) as head of a Direction of Arab Affairs, contributed the most important strand. From these administrators, or *Robinsons galonnés,* as Jacques Berque has called them, came a disproportionate share of the canonical works on Algerian society, customs, and religion.[31] Closely involved with the life of the tribes, the native affairs officers of the Arab Bureaux knew from direct observation and experience what the civilians and the academics seldom grasped: the attractiveness of Muslim society, its endless capacities for resistance, its subtleties as well as its vulnerabilities. The social and political consciousness of the officers of the Arab Bureaux, already stimulated by its propinquity to the lives of those they administrated, was also enhanced by virtue of the fact that many of them were graduates of the prestigious École polytechnique. A number were also Saint-Simonians, members of a utopian socialist movement. Their revolutionary commitments and sensitivity to cultural difference gave the analysis of this group a depth lacking in the work of other French observers. At the same time, their participation in the military conquest failed to prevent at least some of them from holding racist attitudes toward Muslim Algerians.

Both the strengths and the weaknesses of the Arab Bureaux as a colonial archive of knowledge about Algerian society derived from its alliance with the tribes. The culture of tribal society, no less than its "moral topography," was first limned by the men of the Arab Bureaux. The model of tribal structure first worked out by Eugène Daumas, Thomas Pein, Charles Richard, and Thomas Ismail Urbain was based on the genealogical structure of the patriarchal family. Techniques of oral investigation, including careful cross-questioning of local informants, made possible Daumas's study of the tribes of the Sahara and Ernest Carette's of those of Kabylia.[32] The application of these methods was later to produce such works as Émile Laoust's *Mots et choses berbères* and Auguste Mouliéras's study of the Rif.[33]

Another early topic of study was popular Islam, especially the role of the Sufi *turuq*. These were widely believed to be deeply involved in Algerian resistance to the French presence. Charles Richard's study of the popular religious roots of the Algerian resistance effort, *Étude sur l'insurrection du Dahra (1845–46),* sought to explore the history and content of popular Islamic millenarianism.[34] While Richard, like many other French observers of the period, viewed Islam through the lens of the religious struggles of the French Revolution, he also saw Muslim popular religious beliefs as a source of spiritual strength and political resistance.[35] François de Neveu's *Les Khouan* was the first inquiry based on responses to an administrative questionnaire that sought to systematize information on Algerian membership in Sufi brotherhoods. The political role of the marabouts (as the leaders of rural saintly lineages were called) was a related topic that stimulated much research. Here the major work was Louis Rinn's *Marabouts et Khouans.*[36] However, following the suppression of the last major resistance movement in 1871, interest in the political power of Islam essentially disappeared. Thereafter, studies of popular religion focused on rural marabouts, saintly lineages, and sufi orders, generally viewed through the lens of an exoticizing orientalism.

The rule in general appears to be the following: the farther from the blood and thunder of military conquest, the less relevant and less reliable the ethnography. Why should this have been the case? A number of reasons come to mind. The first generation had the advantage of being first, and of everything thus being new, fresh, and interesting. Moreover, insofar as many of the early observers were military men or directly tied to the colonial enterprise, they had a vested interest in understanding the society in all its specificity, and in being able to distinguish its chief components. Put simply, lives might depend on it. Later on, as bureaucratic routine took over, officers had only to update the reports of their predecessors. They became increasingly overwhelmed by paperwork, and spent less time in the marketplace or on horseback frequenting their charges. As time went on, the military advantage shifted decisively toward the Europeans. The ability to deploy powerful new military technologies rendered moot errors in political analysis. Confronted with the machine gun, tribal forces, however brave and resourceful, stood no chance. For these reasons, therefore, the early periods were formative.[37]

Accordingly, if we were to plot on a map the successive thrusts of French military advance in North Africa, we would discover a close correspondence with the advance of knowledge about the society. By the end of the Second Empire the ethnographic inventory of Algeria was virtually completed; only the Sahara remained to be explored.[38] For Tunisia, we have good ethnographies only for the southern regions, as only there was a tribal military administration on the Algerian model established.[39] The historical development of French knowledge about Morocco adhered to much the same outline: first the populations of the coastal districts and the central plain, then the cities of the interior, and only later on, the tribes of the Rif, Middle and High Atlas, the Sous, and the Saharan steppe. In Morocco, however, the populations of the Berber areas and the Saharan zones were for the most part the monopoly of the military administrators of the Arab Bureaux, while French civilian researchers (many of them academics) worked on the cities and the plains.

A second group, the civilian amateurs, made contributions to the elaboration of the sociology of Algeria. Men like Camille Sabatier and Henri Duveyrier (1840–92), however, possessed neither the motivation for research nor direct access to the Muslim populations.[40] Therefore their intellectual contribution to the ethnography of Algeria was the weakest of the three groups of researchers. However, if their contribution is assessed in political terms, it emerges as fundamental. Even the few civilians who could speak with real authority on Algerian matters tended primarily to advance views of Muslim society that reflected the interests of French settlers. Indeed, it is this that makes them important. The bitter and unrelenting hostility of French settlers to the Arab Bureaux and the latter's support of the great feudal Arab chiefs provided one of the leitmotifs of French settler politics, and seriously influenced the course of Algerian colonial history. For individuals like Dr. August Warnier, the men of the Arab Bureaux were the real enemies of France in Algeria.[41] Lording it over the tribes, they lived the life of pashas;

their corruption was legendary, and so was their duplicity. The aristocratic origins and royalist sympathies of many of the officers were repugnant to the settlers, who loudly proclaimed their ardent republicanism. Although there can be no doubt that the settlers greatly exaggerated, there was some substance to their charges. Many of the officers were of aristocratic origin; some were royalists. Others, Saint-Simonians for the most part, were sympathetic with many features of Algerian society, and adopted a paternalistic attitude toward the Muslim populations. Some conducted social experiments on the tribes entrusted to their administration.[42] The main reason for the hostility of the settlers, however, was the land question (in this respect Algerian history resembles that of the American West). The Arab Bureaux constituted the chief obstacle to the extension of colonization, civilian rule, and settler domination. So long as a region was under military government, settlers had a difficult time acquiring land there.

To be sure, there were instances of dialogue between these two strands of the French tradition. One such was the collaborative work of Adolphe Hanoteau and Aristide Letourneux, *La Kabylie et les coutumes kabyles* (1872–73).[43] (Hanoteau was *chef de bureau* at Fort National, and Letourneux was an Algiers lawyer.) It was Letourneux who, with his barrister's eye for system and order, processed what had been local oral customary practice into a kind of Berber administrative handbook (the *qanun-s*), a useful instrument for combating the supposed nefarious influence of the sharia. The influence of *La Kabylie et les coutumes kabyles* extended even to Morocco, where it helped to inspire the Berber policy of Lyautey and his successors.[44] Later the same *politique des races* was applied in Syria and Lebanon with regard to the Druse and Alawi minorities during the mandate period, with equally unfortunate results.[45] In general it would seem that the chief result of efforts at collaboration between military men and civilians was to accentuate the tendency already inherent in the tradition of the Arab Bureaux to turn local customary practices into fixed and rigid principles.

The intensification of the debate between settler interests and the Arab Bureaux, the chief protectors of the Muslim populations, led to the increased politicization of French ethnography. The decree of 1863 (a misguided effort at halting speculation in tribal lands) provoked a new interest in Arab society for a time. However, following the collapse of the Second Empire after the Prussian invasion in 1870 and suppression of the Moqrani rebellion (1870–71), French policy perhaps inevitably took on a sharply antimilitary coloration. The ensuing settler backlash led to the dismantling of the Arab Bureaux (which were permitted to continue only in the Saharan region), and the enactment of a series of punitive regulations known collectively as the *code de l'indigénat*.[46] The years that followed, 1870–1900, were disastrous for Algerian Muslims. And they were equally disastrous for the sociology of Algeria. From a quasi-autonomous intellectual by-product of the Arab Bureaux, the ethnography of Algeria became increasingly dominated by the discourse of French colonial politics. No longer a serious threat, Muslims did not have to be taken seriously. As a result, there was little incentive to study them.

THE ALGERIAN COLONIAL GOSPEL

This development found direct expression in the crystallization of the Algerian colonial gospel, a patterned set of stereotypes about the nature of Muslim Algerian society, especially the so-called Kabyle myth, a set of stereotypes on the supposed differences between Arabs and Berbers. Elements of the Kabyle myth can be traced in the writings of Abbé Raynal and precolonial French travelers. What is new about its post-1871 manifestations is the effort, clearly influenced by the racialism of late nineteenth-century social theories, to construct a systematic policy on the basis of these differences. The Berberophilia of the Kabyle myth became fully elaborated in the post-1871 period.[47] The Berber-speaking Kabyle people were believed to be potentially assimilable to French civilization by virtue of the supposed democratic nature of their society, their superficial Islamicization, and the higher status of Kabyle women. Some officers, like Baron Aucapitaine (1832–67), jumped to the conclusion, "In one hundred years, the Kabyles will be French!"[48] For a time a policy of cultural assimilation of the Kabyles was attempted by the French government, but given the uneven results it was soon abandoned (though a few schools were permitted to continue). The most extreme among the settler theoreticians of Berber separatism was Camille Sabatier, whose intellectual nullity was matched only by the extremes of his race-conscious thought, and the credulity of the French Algerian public, whose clamorous support gave Sabatier an influence his ideas were far from deserving. Sabatier observed:

> The unknown Lycurgus who dictated Kabyle *qanun*s [customary law]was not of the family of Mohamed and Moses but of that of Montesquieu and Condorcet. Still more than the skull of these Kabyle mountaineers, this work bears the seal of our race![49]

The persistence of the Kabyle myth was one of the most enduring aspects of the French sociology of Islam.[50] It, together with other elements of the Algerian colonial gospel, exercised a particularly unfortunate impact on French writings on Algeria, particularly in the period leading up to the First World War.

French academics, the third group that contributed to the elaboration of the sociology of Islam, were involved in the study of Algeria from the time of the conquest. But it was not until after 1870 that they emerged as a distinct group. Their new prominence was directly tied to the emergence of the social sciences in France and the reorganization of French higher education after the fall of the Second Empire. And it was Émile Masqueray who, more than any other, endowed the academic study of Algerian society with prestige and legitimacy. As the secretary of Victor Cousin and a brilliant young graduate of the École normale supérieur, Masqueray was well connected in governmental circles and destined to have an important career. His *Formation des cités chez les populations sédentaires de l'Algérie* (1886) shows the influence of the Berberophilia of the time—as well as that of Fustel de Coulanges (whose *Ancient City* was then enjoying a major vogue).[51] Masqueray was at the center of the intellectual currents of his time, rather than on the fringes, like the other Algerian academics. Thus he was able to transcend, even if only partially, the crippling effects of the politicization of colonial sociology, and was entrusted with founding the École d'Alger (from which the Université d'Alger would eventually emerge). Masqueray's doctoral thesis differed sharply from the Algerian tradition in its bold application of the comparative method, and its rigorous attention to the verification of evidence and the testing of hypotheses. It is no surprise that he had no imitators.

Toward the end of the nineteenth century the focus of the French sociology of Islam began to shift away from Algeria. The Muslim societies of French West Africa were the next to attract the attention of French researchers. The study of what would later be called *Islam noir* began in earnest in 1880s, when French native affairs specialists, both military and civilian, turned their attention to the role of the Sufi *turuq* in the West African Sudanic belt from the Senegal to Timbuktu.[52] Since most French West African specialists had previously served in Algeria, they brought with them a concern with the political role of the Sufi brotherhoods and the marabouts. Thus began an abiding concern with West African popular Islam.

In the superheated atmosphere of racism and chauvinism of fin de siècle France, French officials in Algeria became obsessed with the fear of

Pan-Islamic conspiracies, particularly that of the Sanusiya brotherhood (this despite the fact that there was little evidence to support their concern). Unfortunately, this popular psychosis was not limited to colonial Algeria. A preoccupation with the Sanusiya also marked French writing on *Islam noir* in the pre-1914 period. If we look a little closer it is difficult not to see that French fears of popular Islamic uprisings derived from anxieties generated by the church/state struggle in France of the period (then in a phase of heightened tension). Concerns about Algeria are also reflected in the effort after 1900 to develop a native policy for Afrique occidentale française (A.O.F.) aimed at blocking the extension of Islamic law and fostering the spread of the French language. Here we see the influence of the Kabyle myth, which had prompted French efforts in Kabylia to prevent Arabization and Islamization by building schools and law courts employing the French civil code or Kabyle *qanun* law.[53]

No discussion of French studies of West African Islam would be complete without mention of the role of Paul Marty (1882–1938). Born in Algeria, Marty served in A.O.F., Morocco, and Tunisia in the course of his career. One of the last of the military ethnographers formed in the Algerian native affairs tradition, Marty's writings on *Islam noir* constitute an important (and sometimes the only) source on West African Islam in the period 1913–25. His sympathy for the plight of Muslim elites caught in the undertow of history, and his conviction that French colonialism was the vector of progress, made him a sensitive observer of African society. Marty had more than a dozen monographs to his credit, most notably "Les mourides d'Amadou Bamba."[54] His extraordinary productivity (based on the dissemination of questionnaires to local officials throughout A.O.F.) stands alone in the annals of the French sociology of Islam.

FRENCH KNOWLEDGE OF MOROCCO, 1880–1900

In 1900, on the eve of the diplomatic crisis known as the Moroccan question, France possessed little accurate ethnographic knowledge of Morocco other than of the coastal cities and the tribes along the Tangier-Fez "road of the ambassadors." A case could be made that British studies of Morocco at the time were superior. The absence of documentation is surprising, given the political stakes. Yet apart from a few classic works, French policy circles had remarkably little reliable information on Moroccan society.[55] As late as 1900,

British studies of Morocco were still clearly superior.[56] Using the pseudonym Eugène Aubin, Eugène Descos described his predicament in 1901 as he sat down to write *Le Maroc d'aujourd'hui:*

> I naturally took advantage of my long hours of solitude to read most of the works published on Morocco. Aside from historical facts, I scarcely found anything to exploit; for nothing exists, to my knowledge, no book, written in any language, which lays out, for those who might be interested, the mechanism of Moroccan life and the Moroccan government.[57]

Most of what the French knew about Morocco derived from the published and unpublished reports and maps prepared by the members of the French military mission. From 1884 until 1912, French military instructors served the Moroccan government and were charged with training the Moroccan army, much as French instructors had earlier helped train a modern Ottoman army. In practice, the chief purpose of the military mission was spying, which in this case meant gathering the political gossip of the court. Commissioned reports (both published and unpublished) focused more on military and political intelligence than on the main features of Moroccan society.[58] The Berber-speaking groups of the Rif and Atlas Mountains—some 40 percent of the total population—remained virtually unstudied.[59] Topographic maps prepared by the military mission were often of high quality and played a significant role in informing French military planners about the terrain on which they might one day be required to act.[60] Both the official reports and maps were prepared for a restricted audience primarily composed of staff officers charged with preparing and updating contingency plans with regard to Morocco. They did not circulate outside the Ministry of War and played little role in shaping French policy toward Morocco at this time.

Before 1900, France had two additional sources of information about Morocco: confidential reports prepared by the diplomatic corps, which did not circulate outside of Quai d'Orsay circles, and studies by individuals (of which there was a great paucity). However, looming over all these sources is Charles de Foucauld's *Reconnaissance au Maroc: Journal de route.*[61] Incontestably the most important work on Moroccan society published before 1900, it went through numerous editions and served as the vade mecum of several generations of French Morocco hands.[62] At a time when few Europeans dared travel by themselves in the countryside without adopting Moroccan garb, Foucauld decided to travel in disguise, surprisingly opting to dress as a Moroccan Jew and staying only among Jews. In this way he was able to pass almost unnoticed.[63] The publication of *Reconnaissance au Maroc* immediately propelled its author to prominence in colonial circles.[64]

The book itself became an instant classic of the ethnography of Morocco. However, it was an ethnography with a difference, for despite a few brief descriptions of social rituals or of the operation of social institutions, it contains few passages of any length that can be described as ethnographic. Instead, its primary focus is to provide as meticulous a description of the topography of the terrain traversed as possible. In this sense, it is the author's "cartographic eye" (the emphasis being on cartography more than ethnography) that is its most characteristic feature. As a result, subsequent travelers were able precisely to identify each point mentioned and at every moment to locate themselves in the Moroccan landscape. The French military relied heavily on *Reconnaissance au Maroc* in the conquest of Morocco in the first part of the twentieth century, and carried the work everywhere it went.

Foucauld's social observations of Berber-speaking groups in Morocco broke in important ways with the verities of the Kabyle myth. *Reconnaissance au Maroc* contains few of the racist strictures about the alleged differences between Berbers and Arabs that tainted French ethnographic production in this period. Such distinctions, Foucauld believed, should be understood as linguistic rather than racial in character. Why, we might ask, was *Reconnaissance au Maroc* able to transcend the powerful biases of its time? We might begin by locating the book and its author in the French political and intellectual fields. At the time of its publication, Foucauld himself was unknown. While his aristocratic background gave him a certain cachet, he was marginal to the debates that roiled the French political field. Despite the fact that *Reconnaissance au Maroc* was explicitly written to facilitate the French conquest of Morocco, it does not conform to many of the then current stereotypes about Moroccan society or Islam. Morocco was not on the active political agenda in either Algeria or Paris in the 1880s, and thus *Reconnaissance au Maroc* was able to transcend the deforming lens of the political field, at least to a degree. Indeed, the success of the project reflects its dual marginality to both the French intellectual and political fields.

The French government was not the only supplier of information about Morocco, however. The Algerian colonial government (the Gouvernement général de l'Algérie) also had a strong interest in "doing Morocco." It was the principal source of proven experts on North African Muslim societies. The next chapter addresses the Algerian contribution to the ethnography of Morocco.

TWO

The Algerian Origins of Moroccan Studies, 1890–1903

The rapid emergence of Morocco as a French object of study in the period 1900–1912 was in its own way as surprising as the nonexistence of this subject before 1890. The next four chapters trace the complex intellectual genealogy of French studies of Morocco from 1890 until the establishment of the French protectorate in 1912. They examine the institutional and intellectual reworking of research and teaching about North Africa and the multiple contexts in which these changes occurred. In this chapter I chart the emergence of Moroccan studies as a specific field in the period 1890–1902. I begin by tracing the modernization of French orientalism after the Franco-Prussian War as part of the larger transformation of French higher education in the period. Next I survey the advent of the new "scientific imperialism" and the reform of Algerian native policy under Jules Cambon. Finally, I explore the rise of the École d'Alger as the leading center of academic knowledge about North Africa, and its efforts to position itself as the center of expertise in Moroccan studies.

THE NEW ORIENTALISM

The French defeat in the Franco-Prussian War and the emergence of the Third Republic set off an extended period of national soul-searching. Many French people were quick to see the outcome of the war as the victory of the German schoolmaster, for which the remedy was the modernization of French education. The German seminar method was introduced in France, and things German enjoyed a certain vogue in intellectual circles.[1] The modernization of public education had in fact begun under the Second Empire, but it accelerated under the Third Republic.[2] Starting in the 1880s the Nouvelle Sorbonne was constructed. It incorporated the old medieval institution into the massive brick-and-mortar structure on the rue Saint-Jacques we know today. Similarly, the École pratique des hautes études was reformed along lines that reflected new concerns. In this time of intellectual ferment, new disciplines, such as sociology, were established, and old ones, such as classics and history, were set upon a new basis. Older provincial higher schools (*écoles supérieures*) were strengthened, and new provincial universities founded.[3] New journals were launched, new scholarly associations established, and French higher education professionalized. Not everything changed, however. The discipline of *anthropologie* remained largely impervious to change. It was not related to the fieldwork-based discipline of cultural anthropology, which at this time was beginning to develop in Britain (Malinowski) and the United States (Boas). Then there was the discipline of orientalism.

Once regarded as "the science of human society," orientalism had been the principal authorized interpreter of textually based non-Western civilizations. Under Silvestre de Sacy (1758–1838) it had occupied a position in French intellectual life that was unrivaled in the world at the time.[4] As a result of the continuing importance of philology in older humanist circles and among leading politicians, orientalism retained its clout with the Ministry of Public Instruction. The Académie still controlled a number of endowed chairs in oriental subjects at the Sorbonne, the Collège de France, and the IVe section of the École pratique des hautes études.[5] Orientalists continued to enjoy a strong presence in the Académie française through Arabists like Charles Barbier de Meynard, the translator of the *Thousand and One Nights,* and a member of the Académie des inscriptions et belles lettres. The central institution of orientalist learning was the École des langues orientales vivantes (ELOV), on the rue de Lille, known as "Langues O." At ELOV non-Western civilizations were studied through their principal texts (such as the Confucian classics, the Bhagavad Gita and other Hindu manuscripts, the Qur'an and Islamic writings). Surprisingly few Parisian orientalists had traveled extensively in the Middle East, and the study of classical texts dominated to the exclusion of all else, while knowledge of vernacular non-Western languages was systematically denigrated. Islam was regarded with contempt. (To be fair, so too were Middle Eastern Christianity and Judaism in this period of militant *laicité*.)[6] Few French metropolitan orientalists were capable of carrying on a conversation in Arabic dialect, which was regarded as the province of native informants (*répétiteurs*). Ernest Renan's advice to the French government in 1891 is illustrative of this point of view:

> For works of philology and erudition on Arabic literature, there should be no illusions. Such work will always be better done in Paris, London, Leiden, or Berlin than in Cairo or Damascus.... The most learned of the habitués of the mosques have nothing to teach those who have had as their masters our great Arabists of Paris, Leiden, and Leipzig.[7]

When Renan died in 1892, orientalism was intellectually marginal. Viewed from the center of the intellectual French field, Langues O. was widely regarded as lacking in prestige. (Even in the next generation, no less a figure than Jacques Berque, professor at the Collège de France, manifested his resentment of its intellectual marginality.)[8] There's no wonder it was slow to respond to the intellectual challenge of the emergent social sciences—especially sociology, then newly minted.[9]

Around 1900 things began to change. Gaston Maspéro, director of the Institut française d'archéologie du Caire (IFAO) and a professor at the Collège de France, sought to modernize the curriculum at Langues O. He encouraged the introduction of instruction in the colloquial spoken languages of the Middle East, which began (somewhat timidly) under Octave Houdas (d. 1916).[10] Subsequently instruction in spoken Arabic (primarily the Algerian dialect) was encouraged by Hartwig Derenbourg (d. 1908) and his successor, Maurice Gaudefroy-Desmombynes.[11] The first chair of vernacular Berber was established at ELOV in 1913. It emphasized the Kabyle dialect of Algeria (rather than Shawi, or one of the Moroccan Berber dialects).[12] Instruction in the major Eastern Arabic dialects were added as France acquired its mandates over Syria and Lebanon after World War I. The increased attention to vernacular languages may be seen as representing a shift in the conception of the field, as well as a transformation in pedagogical method. It also reflected the opening of a new job market for ELOV graduates. Previously, the majority of them had been employed in the diplomatic corps as translators and interpreters. But with the changes in the curriculum in the early twentieth century, ELOV increasingly sought to place its graduates in the colonial administration and as instructors in the emergent colonial universities (*écoles supérieures*). Chairs devoted to colonial subjects were created at the Collège de France and the Sorbonne. Between 1890 and 1925 a half dozen such chairs were created at the Collège de France. The subjects included the geography of the Maghreb, Muslim sociology, history, and language. New chairs in Islamic and colonial subjects were established at this time at the Sorbonne as well. They were funded by the colonial governments in French Africa and the Maghreb and relevant government ministries. (The chair of colonial history dates from 1892.)

At a time when metropolitan orientalists continued to be deeply invested in philological erudition, those in French Algeria were interested in the study of the living languages and folklore of Algeria (both Arabic and Berber). They also willingly collaborated with the French native affairs administration in projects of practical interest (and thus operated within the colonial political field). Both metropolitan and Algeria-based orientalists tended to share the same political reflexes, notably an ardent republicanism and an essentially racist conception of the field. Their differences derived in part from the institutional context. Here the École d'Alger proved to be more responsive to new intellectual currents because of its less deeply rooted institutional structures and traditions. As the Moroccan question moved to the political front burner, the connections between the intellectual and political fields grew stronger for both metropolitans and "Algerians." By 1900, the existence of an ambitious group at the École d'Alger began to attract attention in France.

"SOCIOLOGIE COLONIALE"

As we have seen, then, France in 1900 had but a paltry understanding of Morocco. Aside from a rudimentary knowledge of Moroccan geography gleaned from transiting the "road of the ambassadors" from Tangier to the capital, and rough estimations of Moroccan military capabilities, no in-depth study of a single Moroccan tribe, city, or social group existed (as was also the case for Algeria). Viewed from Paris, Morocco was an orientalist fantasy of vivid colors and strong emotions, a Tibet on the doorstep of Europe, frozen in time and cut off from the world. But the real Morocco remained singularly out of sight. French policy experts were aware that their knowledge of Morocco was insufficiently detailed to enable them to undertake the conquest of Morocco without provoking massive resistance. If France were to acquire Morocco, they insisted, it would need a far deeper understanding of Moroccan history, culture, and society. But how might this be done? The struggle between orientalism and positivism seemed to have no obvious resolution.

By the 1890s things had begun to change, however. Great power rivalries intensified. The French colonial lobby (a loose coalition of parliamentary, bureaucratic, and business groups) began increasingly to feel its strength, and to cast covetous eyes in the direction of Morocco. Algerian military and commercial interests pressed for the completion of France's North African empire by the conquest of Morocco. Yet these groups faced a serious problem—colonial expansion was unpopular with French voters. It was widely regarded as too costly, as well as an unpatriotic diversion from *la ligne bleu des Vosges* and the prospect of regaining the lost provinces of Alsace-Lorraine from Germany.[13] Fortunately, as some leading French colonialists proclaimed, a remedy was at hand. The acquisition of colonies no longer had to be the sort of bloody and bothersome process that the conquest of Algeria had been. Given the lukewarm public response to a possible French intervention in Morocco, the French public could be induced to support colonial expansion only if it were convinced that it could be done efficiently and cheaply. The new doctrine was slow to gain adherents at first. While there were colonial officials who understood the need for a scientific understanding of the subject populations, they were initially an isolated minority without influence on policy. By the 1890s, however, the colonial group had begun to gather supporters in the bureaucracy and the National Assembly. Key figures such as Auguste Terrier and Robert de Caix, leaders of the main procolonial group, the Comité de l'Afrique française, maintained an active publicity campaign for colonial expansion.

In the new intellectual and political context, French colonialist circles were attracted to the doctrine of "scientific imperialism," which had developed from the comparative study of colonial administrations and a new positivist confidence in social analysis. Through the systematic study of a society, and its religion, institutions, and economy, colonizers could map the society's strong and weak points, the better to exploit them. Only through the comparative study of the experiences of other European colonial powers, it was believed, could France expand its empire without major political misadventure or budgetary and political strife. Paul Leroy-Beaulieu, a leading colonial theorist, concluded that in the absence of a better understanding of colonial societies, France risked wasting its national blood and treasure for no certain advantage.[14] As a result of his work and that of others it was possible to envisage a scientifically based colonialism.

Another student of comparative colonial policy, Joseph Chailley-Bert (1854–1928), noted that in comparison to other European colonial powers (especially British India) France had been slow to see the necessity of a detailed social mapping of the societies under its colonial tutelage.[15] The leader of a major colonial pressure group, the Union coloniale, as well as an expert on Dutch and British colonial policies in South and Southeast Asia, Chailley-Bert saw French Algeria as the symbol of all that was wrong with French colonial policy. French rule in Algeria was hugely expensive and wasteful, and its policies needlessly provoked the natives. The implications for Morocco were clear enough. With the French public more than ever opposed to issuing a blank check for colonial expansion, Chailley-Bert argued, only by adhering to a scientific program of rule would France gain the backing it needed for the Moroccan venture.[16] It was General Joseph Gallieni, whose career spanned French Sudan (1886–88), Indochina (1892–94), and Madagascar (from 1895), who concisely formulated the new teachings: "The officer who has successfully drawn an exact ethnographic map of the territory he commands is close to achieving complete pacification, soon to be followed by the form of organization he judges most appropriate."[17] Gallieni's endorsement of military ethnography became one of the koans of the proponents of scientific colonialism and a vivid framing of the connections between knowledge and power. Louis-Hubert Lyautey first encountered the new military sociology while serving as Gallieni's subordinate in Indochina and Madagascar.[18]

Jules Cambon, who served as governor-general of Algeria from 1891 to 1897, was one representative of the new current of thought. His appointment in Algeria brought to the forefront a key member of the nascent colonial group interested in Morocco. Like his brother Paul, who had earlier been resident-general of Tunisia (1882–86), Jules Cambon viewed the protectorate system of administration as better adapted to the realities of colonial rule than the Algerian system. A student of the British experience in India, he had concluded that the best recipe for stability consisted of low taxes, a non-oppressive police, clear administrative procedures, and a vigorous but intelligible legal system. Cambon denounced the racism and greed of Algerian settlers and the policies that had undermined the influence of the great Arab families, the natural leaders of Algerian Muslim society. In a much-cited retrospective judgment on French rule in Algeria, he stated that as a result of the policies of previous governments "today, we find ourselves confronted with a kind of human dust on which we have no influence. We have no intermediaries between ourselves and the native population."[19] Other influential figures in the Algerian administration who shared Cambon's views included the future Governors-General Charles Jonnart and Paul Revoil as well as senior Algerian native affairs officials, such as Louis Rinn, Nicolas Lacroix, André de Saint-Germain, and Alfred Le Chatelier.

Cambon was a strong believer in the need to modernize French colonial doctrine. For this reason he supported the use of ethnography as a tool of colonial administration. He appointed Nicolas Lacroix, a former officer in the Arab Bureaux, to centralize native policy directly under his authority, and to replace the multiple and competing jurisdictions that had previously characterized native affairs policy in Algeria.[20] Lacroix was charged with devising a coherent policy toward the Sahara and the Moroccan frontier that would permit French expansion without provoking major resistance.[21] Finally, to facilitate the coming conquest of Morocco, Cambon commissioned a four-volume compilation of French knowledge of Moroccan society: *Documents pour servir à l'étude du nord-ouest africain* (1894–97).[22] Written (one is tempted to say "assembled") by H. M. P. de Lamartinière and Nicolas Lacroix, it drew heavily on previously commissioned studies by French military and diplomatic personnel. Lamartinière was a senior French diplomat who had previously served in Morocco. Both men served in Cambon's native affairs cabinet. The preface to the first volume established the prophetic path that the series sought to follow, making available to policymakers precise information about a country "whose destiny will preoccupy our diplomacy." Its publication was a signal that a French campaign to incorporate Morocco into its North African empire was brewing.

The four volumes of *Documents* were very much in the tradition of the *Exploration scientifique de l'Algérie*. They provided a convenient digest of French knowledge about the northern and southern Algero-Moroccan frontier (volumes 1–2) and the Saharan oases (volumes 3–4). Lamartinière and Lacroix's work viewed the diverse tribal populations of this vast zone through the lens of the *fiche de tribu* (the file card that recorded the vital statistics of each tribe). Rather than engaging the complex specificities of the groups studied, difference was flattened so as to locate each group in a statistical chart whose main features included population, names of leaders, and numbers of horses and rifles the group could bring to bear. The oases communities, for their part, were understood as "municipalities," a sign of the intellectual influence of Masqueray's *Formation des cités*.[23] Published in a limited edition primarily for a government audience, *Documents* reflected contemporary anxieties about political turbulence along the Algero-Moroccan frontier in the 1880s (notably the protracted rebellion of the Ouled Sidi

Cheikh after 1864).[24] Insofar as their multivolume compilation contested Moroccan claims to the central Sahara, Lamartinière and Lacroix's work can also be seen as an act of political appropriation. The work's appearance stimulated the serious study of Morocco. More extensive French intellectual engagement with the complex realities of Morocco would have to wait for another time.

Cambon next set about reorganizing the administration of the Saharan territories (which had been divided into three circumscriptions) by placing them under the authority of native affairs officers rather than civilian administrators. But this was too little too late. By this time most of the native affairs officers of the old days had retired. Native policy was now carried out through the military chain of command, with Arab shaykhs treated as local functionaries. In the new top-down system, officers/administrators had less direct contact with the tribespeople under their jurisdiction. Instead they worked through the officially appointed indigenous petty officials. The combination of administrative routine, the privileges of power, and the conviction of being the bearers of progress conspired to distance native affairs officers from their charges. Some took advantage of their situation to oppress the local inhabitants with a host of arbitrary and capricious demands. Young royalist officers, like Lyautey (before he met Gallieni), might imagine themselves as tribal chiefs, swanning about in well-tailored *jellabas,* galloping about the countryside with their retinues by day, and reclining by the fireside of an evening to feasts of roasted mutton provided by the local tribespeople.[25] It was all so seductive. Even for the times, it was all so retro. Thus it was that by the 1890s, the majority of the officers of the Department of Native Affairs were no longer in close touch with the tribes of the High Plateaus. The Arab Bureaux tradition was well on its way to becoming a fossilized remnant. But not all of it.

A few old-time Arab Bureaux officers, men like Colonel André Gaston de Saint-Germain (1850–1913), continued to adhere to a different view of relations with Algerians.[26] Saint-Germain espoused a republican populism as the radical antidote to the aristocratic nostalgia common to the top-down native affairs officers. In this respect he was the transmitter of an older and more egalitarian Arab Bureaux tradition. An anecdote makes clear his point of view. In the 1880s, Saint-Germain was the commanding officer in Bou Saada, a town in the High Plateaus of central Algeria, when a young lieutenant arrived to receive his orientation. Saint-Germain took him aside to explain how things worked. In Ottoman times, he intimated, important visitors had been welcomed by impressive feasts (known as *diffas*) provided by the tribe as a communal obligation. As visitors were occasional and their stay but brief, this placed no great burden on the tribe. However, once French rule was established in the High Plateaus, the *diffa* became an entitlement rather than a freely offered gesture of hospitality. Visiting French dignitaries came to expect it as a matter of right, and the costs rose exponentially. All this might appear dreadfully romantic, Saint-Germain told Le Chatelier. But it was a different story if you understood that the costs fell entirely on the local inhabitants. To provide a *diffa* for an Arab Bureaux officer on his rounds (including his entourage of horsemen, bearers, servants, etc.) might in fact be very expensive. According to Saint-German, just to feed the officer and his entourage would have necessitated the provision of a minimum of four sheep, numerous chickens, and large quantities of vegetables, raisins, and semolina. Then there was the cost of providing food and water for the members of the officer's entourage as well as for their horses and transport animals. Looked at from this angle, the cost of a *diffa* was potentially ruinous. Suitably chastened, the lieutenant resolved never to be so thoughtless himself.[27]

An ontological divide separated the top-down and bottom-up schools of native affairs. The cost of providing a *diffa* was of no concern to those native affairs officers who favored the top-down approach. Administrators in this tradition viewed the tribes as organic entities that might be controlled by the adroit granting and withholding of privileges from their leaders, the shaykhs. The shaykhs, in turn, were believed to be a natural aristocracy whose status and position were sanctioned by time and immemorial custom. For them as well, the Islam of the tribes (including the saintly lineages and Sufi orders) was seen as institutionally cut off from the world. It was impermeable to the destabilizing influence of the ulama, the cities, and the wider world. For the adherents of the top-down school, rural religion was a narcotic that helped render the tribes docile. Nonetheless, while heterodox Sufism and the cult of local saints might reinforce existing indigenous power hierarchies, it was no prophylaxis against the preachings of rural hedge priests and mahdis, against whom a native affairs officer had always to be on guard. To this end, the job of the native affairs officer was to reinforce the power of the marabouts and their conservative values and to oppose those who sought to undermine it. For those like Saint-Germain and Le Chatelier, who held the alternative view, Algerian peasants were seen as entirely logical in their pursuit of individual economic and personal advantage. Given a chance, they believed, peasants and tribesmen were as capable as ordinary Frenchmen of making a better life for themselves. Unfortunately, so Saint-Germain believed, they were obstructed by the dead hand of tradition, personified by the tribal elite and rural Islam. These institutions they regarded as corrupted by power.

Native affairs officers like Saint-Germain tended to be ardent republicans, members of the Parti radical, militant secularists, and economic populists. Strongly imbued with the anticlerical values then common on the French left, they were also sworn enemies of religion. Thus they denounced the superstitious practices of the marabouts and Sufis, whom they viewed as opponents of science, rationality, and the modern world. Logically, by this line of reasoning one might have expected them to support the assimilation of Algerian Muslims into a multiracial society. But here we encounter the contradictions of the colonial world: French democracy was deemed unsuitable for Algerian Muslims. On this, the adherents of the two schools agreed. Both schools viewed the tribe (seen as a homogenous category) as the embodiment of the real Algeria and all that was healthy in colonial Algeria. French policy, they believed, should be dedicated to preserving the tribe from the contaminating influence of the cities (which were prey to evil influences and vices of all kinds). Faced with the contrast between the urban and rural Algerias, it mattered less whether rural society was viewed as the abode of dissolute tribal aristocrats and hedge priests or the home of virtuous peasants. What mattered most was that the tribe be seen as a reservoir of order and stability, uncontaminated by the modern world, and thus a counterweight against change.

THE ÉCOLE D'ALGER, 1890–1900

In 1880 an *école d'enseignement supérieur* was established in Algiers. Under the leadership of Rector Charles Jeanmaire, it grew steadily and by 1895 enrolled 565 students (which ranked it tenth among French provincial universities). From these humble beginnings the Université d'Alger and its schools of law, medicine and pharmacy, letters, and sciences would eventually emerge. By 1902, some 62 students were enrolled for various language degrees, while 325 students overall were enrolled in the programs of the school of letters.[28] The study of Muslim Algerian history and society was based at the École des lettres (also known as the École d'Alger).[29] Under the dean of the faculty of letters, René Basset, whose vision and example did much to shape the school's development, the École d'Alger had by 1900 become a center for the study of Algerian society, language, and institutions.[30] Basset was an indefatigable scholar whose work encompassed Arabic, Berber, and Ethiopic linguistics and folklore. He was also an institution builder with a talent for getting difficult people to cooperate. The École d'Alger group brought together scholars interested in all aspects of contemporary Muslim Algerian society, from dialect studies and folklore to current political trends and the impact of social change, and even informally included lycée instructors like Auguste Mouliéras. By 1900, the École d'Alger was widely acknowledged as the largest group with proven competence in the study of Maghrebi Islam and the language and customs of North Africa.

In Edmond Doutté, the École d'Alger group possessed an important intellectual leader, one who was in touch with the times.[31] Born in 1867 in Chalons-sur-Marne, Doutté studied natural science at a local lycée and then as a student at the Museum d'histoire naturelle. As a young man he was diagnosed as suffering from a hemoptysis (a wasting liver disease of undisclosed origin) that required him to live in a warm climate (according to the medical science of the time). With help from a family friend, Lieutenant (later General) Thomas Pein, Doutté opted for Algeria. He began his Algerian career in the Aurès Mountains as an *administrateur-adjoint de commune mixte,* and soon developed an interest in Algeria and Algerians. Following his transfer to Oran province and already hooked on Algerian religious culture, he met Auguste Mouliéras, then professor at the Tlemcen Médersa franco-arabe. Mouliéras's vast knowledge of Arabic and Algerian folklore and Doutté's growing interest and aptitude convinced him to switch fields and become an academic.[32] Following Mouliéras's appointment to Oran, Doutté was named his temporary replacement. In 1900, he was appointed to the École supérieure de lettres in Algiers, where under the guidance of its director, Henri Basset, his career blossomed.

Strongly influenced by Sir James Frazer's *Golden Bough* and Émile Durkheim's *Elementary Forms of Religious Life,* Doutté sought instead to identify the underlying archetypes that informed Muslim religious practice, an approach that can be observed in his writings in his pre-Moroccan period.[33] Doutté was the author of numerous works on Algerian folk Islamic practices, among them *L'Islam algérien en l'an 1900, Magie et religion dans l'Afrique du Nord* (1908), and *Enquête sur la dispersion de la langue berbère en Algérie* (1913).[34] He was extremely prolific and enjoyed excellent relations with the Algerian native affairs bureau.

Professor of geography Augustin Bernard was another important figure at the École d'Alger. A graduate of the École des lettres (where he subsequently became an instructor), Bernard collaborated on several important government reports with Nicolas Lacroix, an officer in the native affairs office of the Gouvernement général. Among these reports was *L'évolution du nomadisme en Algérie* (1906), the product of an Algerian government inquiry into the status of nomads in the Tellian Atlas and the Sahara.[35] It drew heavily on data collected by French military authorities according to a centrally distributed questionnaire. Whereas earlier French works had seen the existence of nomadic groups as a threat to the security of the settled areas, the authors described a crumbling way of life and the ecological devastation that followed the establishment of French rule. Against the grain of Algerian administrative practices (and republican ideology) the authors argued that the tribe, not the individual, was the base of pastoralist society and that the aim of policy should be to reinforce the tribe and not undermine it. Hitherto, French observers had expressed confidence that the normal course of social evolution was favorable to Muslim society. *L'évolution du nomadisme* was one of the first works to question this assumption. A second report edited by Bernard and Lacroix was *La pénétration saharienne*. It sought to draw up a balance sheet on the living standards of the peoples of the Algerian Sahara. Not surprisingly, considering its sources, the report concluded that on balance the Saharan tribes were better off under French rule than they had been previously. Once again, however, some doubts were allowed to surface.[36]

With the opening of the Moroccan question, Augustin Bernard turned his attention to Morocco. His *Les confins algéro-marocains,* a study of French influence on the populations of eastern Morocco, was published in 1911. Funded in part by the Comité du Maroc, an important colonial lobbying group, it provided detailed information on the population and resources of the region and traced the progress of French penetration.[37] Bernard also wrote *Le Maroc,* perhaps the most important general guide to Morocco of this period. It went through many editions.[38] Augustin Bernard ended his career as director of the Institut de géographie in Paris and professor at the Sorbonne.

The École d'Alger scholars were positivists heavily influenced by the fossilized tradition of the Arab Bureaux and its demands for "product": the *fiche de tribu,* a premasticated and largely deboned statistical presentation of the tribe focused on its demography (human and animal), influential figures, *tariqa* members, natural resources, and oppositional propensities. This was the tribe shorn of its history and its culture, reduced to a skeleton, a series of flash cards (*fiches*) that gave administrators a misleading sense of mastery, even as the changing culture of Algeria was escaping their notice. Thus, for example, the emergence of the protonationalist Young Algerians (Jeunes algériens) after 1900 came as a complete shock. As was the discovery that Algerian Muslims were in touch with currents of Islamic modernism based in Middle East, notably the Salafiyya movement. Symptomatically, French Algerian scholars displayed little engagement with the actually existing Arabic/Islamic literate culture of contemporary Algerians. Instead, they viewed the Islam of the subject Muslim population as "that which must be gotten past" in the dialectic of progress.

While Doutté and Bernard were strongly linked to the "policy-relevant" circles that required the production of statistically based studies modeled on the *fiches de tribu,* other approaches were beginning to emerge. One important development was the study of Kabyle language and culture. The period also saw the flowering of Algerian folklore studies (including the collection and translation of folktales, proverbs, and other manifestations of Algerian popular culture). William Marcais, another prominent member of the École d'Alger, was a folklorist, art historian, and Kabyle specialist. The reputations of both Basset and Doutté derived in part from their folklore studies. Other leading folklore scholars included Auguste Mouliéras, Georges Delpechin, and Joseph Desparmet.

The first study of Moroccan society was Auguste Mouliéras's *Le Maroc inconnu,* a two-volume ethnography of the popular culture of northern Morocco.[39] Mouliéras was professor of Arabic in Oran famed for his remarkable knowledge of spoken Arabic and the Kabyle dialect of Berber. But it was to his formidable knowledge of Algerian popular culture that Mouliéras owed his reputation. Mouliéras had introduced Edmond Doutté to the subject of Algerian folklore when the latter was just starting out. Such was their friendship that after Mouliéras was appointed at Oran, he saw to it that Doutté replaced him for a time as professor at the Madrasa franco-arabe at Tlemcen. Doutté later returned the favor by extolling the virtues of his mentor's book to the Algiers scholarly milieu. *Le Maroc inconnu* was in many ways a tour de force. It afforded readers a stunning portrait of the popular culture of northern Morocco in two volumes (on the Rif Mountains and on the Jabala regions, respectively). Unable to conduct research in Morocco for lack of political contacts and funds, Mouliéras sought instead to make a virtue of necessity. Much of his material came from an Algerian Kabyle informant named Muhamad Ben Tayyib, who had lived in Morocco for five years. Mouliéras systematically trained Ben Tayyib to recall even the tiniest details of his encounters along the trail in feats of memory so extraordinary they still have the capacity to dazzle. While the methodology employed was ingenious and its topographic and ethnographic detail impressive, *Le Maroc inconnu* failed to meet the needs of French planners. In addition, Mouliéras was too isolated from the main intellectual currents of the period for his book to find a readership, and he had the bad luck to study the one part of Morocco that did not become French (it was incorporated into the Spanish protectorate in 1912).

Although neither was closely affiliated with the École d'Alger, two other folklore scholars and teachers at the Madrasa franco-arabes also deserve mention: Georges Delpechin and Joseph Desparmet.[40] The intellectual vogue for folklore studies is clearly linked to the triumph of French colonialism as well as the mechanization of agriculture in the Algerian countryside (and the consequent destruction of the tribe). But it also seems to have been connected to the renewed interest in metropolitan French rural culture just as it was disappearing in France (nowadays we might call this salvage anthropology). French interest in Algerian folklore at this time inscribed itself in a double binary: that between tradition and modernity and that between colonizer and colonized. It assumed that Algerian Muslim society had no politics (or none at least with links to the contemporary world) and that European rule was unproblematic. Both assumptions would subsequently prove to be erroneous.

Thus it was that on the eve of the First Morocco Crisis (1905) the École d'Alger was well placed to dominate research on Morocco based on its ambitions and prior accomplishments. Its members (primarily Doutté and Bernard) had already conducted a series of research trips into the Moroccan interior that were funded by the Comité du Maroc, the Algerian Gouvernement général, and French geographic societies. Their reports had appeared to much acclaim in the pages of the *Bulletin* of the Comité de l'Afrique française. There was every reason to expect that the École d'Alger group would become the uncontested leaders in the emerging field of Moroccan studies. But this is not what happened. Instead, starting in fall 1903, Algerian scholars began systematically to be denied permission by the French Legation at Tangier to conduct research in Morocco. Why was this so? In the next chapter, I consider the struggle between the École d'Alger and its chief rival, the Mission scientifique du Maroc, over research on Morocco, and what it tells us about the place of colonial Algeria in the French political and intellectual power fields.

THREE

The Political Origins of the Moroccan Colonial Archive

IN 1900 THE COHORT OF scholars gathered under the leadership of René Basset at the École d'Alger constituted the largest group of experienced researchers in North African affairs. They were eager to play a major role in the study of Morocco. Moreover, they had already shown promising results in a series of scientific expeditions led by Edmond Doutté, Augustin Bernard, and Auguste Mouliéras and sponsored by the Comité du Maroc in the period 1900–1904 that had begun to fill out the inventory of Morocco begun with the *Documents pour servir à l'étude du nord-ouest africain*.[1] By late 1903, thanks largely to the success of the Doutté study missions funded by the Comité de l'Afrique française, the École d'Alger appeared destined to dominate the study of Moroccan society and institutions in a future protectorate. All the French Algerians asked was the chance to place their knowledge and their patriotism in the service of French colonial aims.

The establishment of the Mission scientifique du Maroc in October 1903 came as a bolt out of the blue. Within days, Algerian scholars began to have problems in obtaining authorizations from the French Legation in Tangier to conduct research in Morocco. Only gradually did it become clear that there had been a major change in Moroccan policy in Paris. The news was received in Algiers with shock and amazement. Were French Algerian scholars to be excluded from the study of Moroccan society? What had gone wrong? This chapter examines the struggle for control of social research on Morocco. The micropolitics of French academia, we will discover, is a good spot from which to observe the connections between the struggle among academics for research terrain, the clash of French political and economic interests, and the potential destabilization of the European alliance system.

ALFRED LE CHATELIER AND THE MISSION
SCIENTIFIQUE DU MAROC

One man who instinctively seems to have grasped the rules of the new game was Alfred Le Chatelier, the founder of the Mission scientifique du Maroc, and the architect of the downfall of the École d'Alger. Le Chatelier was a military intellectual and policy entrepreneur, a man of vision and brilliance. He was also possessed of a domineering personality and a genius for alienating his friends. Born into a wealthy and well-connected provincial bourgeois family of engineers and scientists in 1855, Alfred Le Chatelier was the one who did not fit. He began a military career as an *officier des affaires indigènes* in Algeria in 1876, serving for ten years and eventually rising to be *chef de bureau* at Ouargla. There he was initiated by Colonel André de Saint-Germain into a style of native administration completely at variance with the "top-down" version then currently in vogue. Saint-Germain was a believer in the methods of the old Arab Bureaux in which the *chef de poste* became the administrator, advocate, and judge of the natives in his charge (see chapter 2). Le Chatelier applied these lessons while posted to Ouargla (1882–85). Very much in the style of his mentor, he opened a local school, established a court (*mahakama*), introduced public health measures, had wells dug, and held regular meetings with the elders of the group. A convinced republican at a time in the history of the Third Republic when this meant something, Le Chatelier championed ordinary people rather than the Muslim elites.

A militant secularist in a period when the republic was still under threat from the monarchist and Catholic Right, Le Chatelier opposed the influence of the Sufi orders.[2] In an unpublished autobiographical memoir he recounts that while he headed the post of the Mekhedma tribe in the Sud-Oranais (before his posting to Ouargla), he conducted a "republican propaganda" campaign among the local peasants. They resented being regularly required to provide alms (*ziyara*) to itinerant marabouts of the Awlad Sidi Shaykh Sufi order. Descendants of a saintly lineage considered locally to be powerful intercessors with the divine, the Awlad Sidi Shaykh incarnated the classic Algerian maraboutic group of the High Plateaus. At the time they were just coming off a period of intermittent rebellion against the French authorities (1867–81) and were in a phase of deeply investing in rebuilding the family business. They were actively encouraging credulous peasants to make donations to their shrine. Le Chatelier's republican propaganda coincided nicely with the vulnerability of the Awlad Sidi Shaykh, so his advice to the Mekhedma did not fall on stony ground. A week after receiving the tribal delegation, Le Chatelier's colleagues at the Arab Bureau in Ghardaia several days' ride away informed him that when they opened the door one morning, they discovered several Awlad Sidi Shaykh marabouts lying across the threshold rolled into carpets and tied up. Pinned to them was a collective letter from the Mekhedma stating that since they knew their rights, they no longer wished to be exploited by the Awlad Sidi Shaykh! That is why they were taking the liberty of delivering them to the Arab Bureau.[3] As Le Chatelier was later able to piece together the story, it turned out that these marabouts were the same individuals who had previously come through his area seeking alms.

Like many other Arab Bureaux officers of the period, Le Chatelier loved the Sahara and its people and was greatly interested in the exploration of the Sahara and West Africa. In 1880 he participated in the first Flatters expedition, which had tried (vainly, as it turned out) to traverse the Sahara from north to south. Thereafter his "vagabond spirit" (a term he employs in an unpublished autobiographical note) directed him outward, toward the world of Islam.[4] Between 1886 and 1890, while nominally attached to a regiment in France, he traveled extensively in Morocco, West Africa, Egypt, and Turkey. He wrote a series of privately printed books and brochures for the Section d'Afrique of the État-major général.[5] As a consequence of his travels he became very knowledgeable about Islamic societies not only in Africa and the Maghreb but also in the Middle East. In part, his interest was stimulated by the contemporary French colonial obsession with Pan-Islamic plots. He believed that when the context of the wider world of Islam was considered, there was little basis for these fears. Le Chatelier's writings on African Islam were germinal for the young Paul Marty, the future author of more than a dozen books on aspects of West African Islam (on which see above, chapter 1).

As a young officer Le Chatelier served in the cabinet of Charles de Freycinet while the latter was minister of war (1890–91), in which capacity he was assigned to monitor the debates in the Chambre des deputés. In this role, he met and befriended many up-and-coming politicians and diplomats, especially those interested in colonial expansion. Chief among them were Eugène Étienne, a leading Algerian politician who was to become head of the colonial group in the parliament, and Paul Révoil, a future governor-general of Algeria with a strong interest in devising a more rational native policy. In 1891 Le Chatelier's active military career came to an end, when he resigned after refusing a direct order. He had been ordered to join the second Flatters expedition, but declined to participate because of the organizers' willful disregard of elementary Saharan political realities.[6] Following the massacre of Flatters and most of his men, Le Chatelier's career was at an impasse. Fortunately he had influential friends. Freycinet arranged for him to have a year's leave to continue his studies of Islam in Africa while things cooled down. After sojourning in Dahomey and the French Congo, Le Chatelier returned to Paris and resumed his military career. He hoped to be able to convince the French government to support the type of African policy he had pioneered at Ouargla. When this effort led nowhere, Le Chatelier presented his definitive resignation from the army on April 14, 1893.[7]

Around this time the French colonial African lobby group, the Comité de l'Afrique française, was becoming involved in the recently created French Congo (across the Zaire river from the Belgian Congo). Abandoning for the moment his efforts to develop support for a more coherent French Islamic policy, Le Chatelier threw himself into championing a railroad scheme linking the interior of the French Congo to the coast. As a charter member of the Comité, Le Chatelier hoped to make a financial killing and invested much of his personal fortune in this venture. The political situation, however, favored French colonial investors with greater in-country experience, and stronger clout in the Parisian colonial parliamentary circles. When an adverse governmental decision preferred a scheme headed by his business rival, Harry Alis (a pseudonym of Leon Hyppolite Percher, a founder of the Comité de l'Afrique française), Le Chatelier suffered huge personal losses. In 1895 he provoked a duel with Alis as a result of which the latter was killed.[8] The conflict between two of the founding fathers of the Comité de l'Afrique française split the French colonial lobby and made Le Chatelier an outcast in colonial policy circles.

From 1896 to 1900, now with important enemies in high places and with his reputation tarnished, Le Chatelier withdrew from French colonial politics and devoted himself to private business.[9] His decision was also shaped by his recent marriage to Marie Langlois, a talented Parisian artist. Since she shared neither his interest in African travels nor his interest in Islamic studies, the couple sought a project in which they could both participate. The result was an enterprise dedicated to the revival of French ceramics along modern lines, the Atelier de Glatigny. In the meantime, Le Chatelier stayed involved in the Parisian political scene. Thanks to his being named the executor of the Orgeries estate (the Orgeries were old family friends), he became involved in funding and organizing trans-Saharan expeditions. He provided detailed instructions to the leaders of the 1898 Foureau-Lamy expedition, which was the first to successfully traverse the Sahara. Its organizers were Fernand Foureau, a researcher at the Ministry of Public Instruction, and Captain François Amédée Lamy, who had previously overlapped with Le Chatelier in the Sahara and in the French Congo. The Foureau/Lamy expedition demonstrated that a carefully organized and well-led Saharan expedition could succeed.[10]

By 1900 the political atmosphere surrounding the Moroccan question was increasingly approaching the boiling point. Impatient with the superheated nationalist passions and incoherent political struggle in Paris, Alfred Le Chatelier decided to reenter the debate. He drafted a privately printed brochure, "Lettre à un Algérien sur la politique saharienne" (April 1900), and arranged for it to be distributed to a select list of leading political figures. A realistic assessment of the consequences of intemperate action along the Moroccan frontier at a delicate moment, its purpose was to call for the development of a cautious and determined French policy.[11] Le Chatelier's ideas gained the instant approval of Paul Révoil, who headed the French Legation in Tangier, and Eugène Étienne, a leader of the *parti colonial* in the Chambre des deputés. The power of Le Chatelier's argumentation and political connections as well as his willingness to challenge established orthodoxies soon established him as a force behind the scenes. It was largely Le Chatelier's policy that Révoil sought to apply during his term as Algerian governor-general (1901–3): "What we need on the Moroccan frontier is a minimum of gunshots and a maximum of economic and political activity."[12] Eugène Étienne, the acknowledged leader of the French Algerian deputies, found Le Chatelier's analysis of the Moroccan frontier problem to be compelling. With the backing of Révoil and Étienne secured, the stage was set for the next step in the rehabilitation of Le Chatelier—the creation of a chair at the Collège de France that would enable him to gain a wider audience for his views.

"POLITIQUE MUSULMANE ET AFRICAINE"

To find the origins of the chair in Muslim sociology and sociography at the Collège de France, one must go back to 1888. In that year Alfred Le Chatelier proposed the creation of an *office central de recherches et d'études islamique*s, to be attached to the Section d'Afrique of the État-major général. His increasing disenchantment with the rigidity and lack of imagination of the Armée d'Afrique soon made him seek other sponsors. In 1891, while serving in the cabinet of the minister of war, Charles de Freycinet, Le Chatelier again launched the idea, but lack of funds and bureaucratic rivalries assured that it never got off the drawing board. Already it was clear that what he had in mind went well beyond a clearinghouse of information on the Islamic world. In Le Chatelier's eyes the *office central* would introduce method into the study of Islamic affairs. Better yet, it would establish a set of principles (*corps de doctrine*) that would henceforth determine French policy toward France's Islamic colonial subjects. In 1900, the idea appears to have been dusted off again. Le Chatelier proposed the creation of a documentation center to be attached to the French Legation in Tangier to serve as the foundation for planning a scientifically based native policy in Morocco. His plan also called for the center to intervene in order to guide French opinion and to develop clear principles on Moroccan affairs to which all could refer. But in the absence of a regular funding source, the project languished.

In early 1901, a revised version of the *office central* proposal appeared. This version called for the establishment of a personal chair for Le Chatelier at the Collège de France that would serve as the base from which the other aims of the proposal would be accomplished. But from the outset there were unforeseen problems. The proposed title of the chair, "Politique musulmane et africaine," raised hackles in the Ministry of Public Instruction bureaucracy. Both Louis Liard, president of the Sorbonne, and Louis Bayet, head of the Department of Higher Education at the ministry expressed concerns about the lack of observance of bureaucratic forms. Since the establishment of a chair at the Collège de France came under their authority, they had expected to be consulted. When they were not, they made their unhappiness known. Although neither Étienne nor Révoil found it objectionable, the Department of Higher Education regarded the term *politique* as unduly provocative and unscholarly. Eventually a compromise formula was found. The chair would be named "Sociologie et sociographie musulmane." By appropriating the newly minted term *sociologie,* Le Chatelier could present the chair as scientific and modern. The neologism *sociographie,* he explained some years later to Édouard Michaux-Bellaire, was a way of ridiculing Auguste Comte, "whose writings have always annoyed me." With this double substitution of titles, the opposition of Liard crumbled, and the chair was approved.[13]

Despite the unorthodox way in which the chair was created, the *Réglements* of the Collège de France did in fact authorize the creation of chairs funded from outside sources, even chairs destined for specific individuals. A number of other colonial chairs would be similarly created in the years to come. A striking thing about the Le Chatelier nomination was the direct intervention of prominent politicians to establish a chair that would have, so its founders hoped, considerable political influence in France (rather than merely academic influence). The program traced out in the final prospectus explicitly referred to the need to utilize the chair to generate a *corps de doctrine* in matters Islamic. At the same time, adroitly exploiting the vogue of the term *sociologie,* and invoking the recommendation of Ernest Renan (1823–92) that the Collège continue to be hospitable to new subjects not yet recognized in a university program, the prospectus explicitly emphasized the innovative character of the subject in the minds of its sponsors. According to the prospectus, the chair of Muslim sociology was sought to set the tone of the coming debate about Morocco, to orient French policy toward it, and more generally to guide French policy toward its Islamic colonies.

It is likely that a basic schedule for future action had already been agreed on with Révoil and Étienne when Le Chatelier's nomination to the chair of Muslim sociology at the Collège de France was announced. According to the announcement,the creation of the chair would give rise to a small (nameless) scholarly mission to Morocco. The mission would transform itself into the Mission scientifique. Once the mission's political and budgetary status was secured, it in turn would blossom into a Moroccan Institute, modeled on the Institut d'Égypte, with a dozen full-time staff. The proposed Moroccan Institute would not only publish the ethnographic inventory of Morocco, but also run an *école d'application* (training school) destined to train future members of the Moroccan colonial administration. The establishment of the chair of Muslim sociology was thus but the first step in a program of far-reaching ambition. Given the existence of a large if internally divided colonial lobby in France, such a program could not be openly avowed from the beginning. A more gradual and less overt means had to be employed. The problem of financing, however, was critical. While it was no great thing to raise the 10,000 francs required to fund the chair at the Collège de France, a full-scale institute required a more serious, long-term financial commitment. But where would the necessary funding come from? It should be noted that in 1901 no appropriate rubric supporting French policy in Morocco yet existed in the French national budget. (Not until 1904 would such a budgetary rubric be established.) For both political and financial reasons, therefore, it was best to make haste slowly.

To launch the Mission scientifique a proven researcher and administrator was required, preferably one who was not a member of one of the existing academic factions. Le Chatelier asked Gaston Maspéro, professor at the Collège de France and a major figure in the world of French orientalism, for recommendations. Maspéro suggested Georges Salmon, a brilliant young Arabist. Salmon was a graduate of Langues orientales, where he had been a prize student of Hartwig Derenbourg (1844–1908). Of modest social origins, before discovering his vocation Salmon had worked at the French Post Office (PTT). Discovered by Maspéro, he had been hired as a researcher at the Institut francais d'archéologique orientale (IFAO) in Cairo in 1899.[14] Only twenty-six years old at the time of his appointment, Salmon already was recognized within the field as one of the up-and-coming young French Arabists. He spoke excellent Arabic (although not the Moroccan dialect) and had shown himself to be a disciplined and fluent writer. Moreover, he was endowed with a phenomenal work ethic. While at IFAO he had written two monographs, translated two Arabic manuscripts, and edited a book on Silvestre de Sacy (1758–1838).[15] He was the author of two additional articles, a report on a study mission, and two erudite notes in the *Bulletin* of the IFAO.[16] Best of all from Le Chatelier's point of view, Salmon had no association with the École d'Alger group and thus was not encumbered with unfortunate political baggage.

Recalled from Cairo to Paris by Maspéro, Salmon was interviewed by Le Chatelier and offered the position on the spot—even though no funds had yet been committed by the government.[17] Salmon's actual nomination was an example of bureaucratic deviousness of a high order. He was named *administrateur adjoint stagiaire de commune mixte (hors cadres)* by the Algerian governor-general, Paul Révoil.[18] Then he was detached to conduct a study mission (*mission d'études*) in Morocco under the oversight of Alfred Le Chatelier While Salmon's salary came from the Algerian government, administratively he was under the authority of the chair of Muslim sociology of the Collège de France. The duration of his mission was initially fixed at two years, with a salary of 6,000 francs per year, plus 6,000 francs for expenses, 2,000 for office expenses, and another 4,000 for expeditions into the Moroccan interior.

In fact, the appointment of Salmon was still more devious that even this account might suggest. While negotiations proceeded apace in Paris to obtain a more secure base for the future Moroccan Institute, Salmon was dispatched to Tangier with instructions to keep a low profile and stay out of politics. He arrived there on November 21, 1903, and presented himself initially as being charged with the establishment of a library on Moroccan society, in some vague manner attached to the French Legation. The legation provided him with space in a building in Tangier donated by the French firm of Brunschvig.[19] A modest research library on Moroccan history and society was opened soon thereafter, to which the staff of the legation were given access. The French government contributed a subvention of 75,000 francs to pay employees' salaries and to support the library's activities. Thus set up, Salmon began quietly to prepare the first volume of *Archives marocaines* for publication.

Le Chatelier detailed his instructions and expectations to Salmon in a long letter of October 26, 1903, which concluded thus:

> Don't forget . . . because your studies have been limited till now to Egypt, that your appointment has not been [made] without opposition. You must justify it by avoiding the temptation to proceed too rapidly. . . . If you can leave aside all other preoccupations than sticking to the program laid out for you: organization of the library so that it can provide the services expected of it, rapidly pulling together abundant research materials, and providing personal services to all who seek it . . . , you will rapidly see your situation develop in the direction which I anticipate, through the recognition of a mission that has as its program, not authoritative studies, but the patient, disinterested collection of research materials.[20]

Meanwhile in Paris, Le Chatelier was already pushing on to the second stage of the operation. He announced the establishment of the Mission scientifique du Maroc as a dependency of his chair. Its aims were described as being the preparation of ethnographic studies on Moroccan society, and the creation of a library for the use of members of the Mission scientifique and of the French Legation. Funding was to be provided by the Ministries of Foreign Affairs and Public Instruction. A Conseil de perfectionnement (Advisory Board) was appointed to oversee its operations. The Conseil held its first meeting on December 3, 1903, and reviewed the report on Salmon's activities in Tangier following his arrival.

The establishment of the Mission scientifique du Maroc was a major step in the coordination of French research on Morocco. According to its founding directives, academic studies of pure orientalism were to be forsaken for works of a more practical sort. Research topics were to be selected on the basis of their relevance to the needs of French planners concerned with Morocco. A "scientific" inventory of Morocco would be rapidly generated, thereby enabling policymakers to discover the organizing principles of the Moroccan state and its cultural and social bases. Looking back twenty-five years later, Édouard Michaux-Bellaire, Salmon's collaborator from the earliest days, put it this way:

> The aim in creating *Archives marocaines* was to compile the catalog of Morocco so to speak, its tribes, its cities, its brotherhoods, and to discover the origins, the ramifications, the rivalries and the alliances; to follow them throughout the history of the different dynasties, to study the institutions and the customs, to explore, in a word, in the measure of the possible the terrain on which we might one day be called to operate, to allow us to act in full knowledge and to devise a native policy, without too many errors, without weaknesses as also without useless violence and to create an administration supple enough to apply to the characters of the different tribes without ceasing to be coherent.[21]

The next six months were to be crucial in deciding the destiny of the Mission scientifique. The project had been rapidly assembled—rather too rapidly it soon developed. The sudden replacement of Paul Révoil as Algerian governor-general by Charles Jonnart at the end of 1903 threatened to jeopardize the whole enterprise before it was fully launched. Jonnart did not know Le Chatelier, nor was he au courant with the project of a Moroccan Institute. Through the intervention of Étienne, however, the affair was smoothed over. Jonnart was willing to grant Le Chatelier his total confidence on the basis of latter's reputation as a proponent of a *tache de huile* (oil spot) policy in the Algero-Moroccan border region (a position with which General Lyautey was also identified). More troubling was the funding, which was in fact quite shaky. In order to cover expenses, Le Chatelier had been forced to contribute 8,000 francs of his own money. The contribution of the Algerian government was in fact only 8,000 francs; the Quai d'Orsay had promised 2,000, but could not deliver it until the 1904 budget had been approved; the Ministry of Public Instruction continued to temporize.

In the meantime the nomination of Salmon was beginning to attract heavy fire from both the École d'Alger and Parisian orientalists, both of whom were dissatisfied that one of their number had not been selected. They strongly protested to the director of higher education, Louis Bayet, in an effort to bring pressure to bear to force the modification of the project. Salmon was accused of incompetence—was he not an archaeologist by training? He knew nothing of North Africa, not even the local language.

Moreover, his opponents insinuated he was untried, lacking in experience, possibly even a Jew (the latter on the basis of his having been a protégé of Hartwig Derenbourg).[22] In short, he was thoroughly objectionable, and his nomination to a position of such critical importance for the destiny of France was a scandal! Any number of other established scholars would be preferable—to begin with someone from the École d'Alger.

The opposition to the Le Chatelier program was led by Edmond Doutté, professor of Arab society at the École des Lettres at Algiers. Thanks to his four expeditions to Morocco in 1901–3, his enormous energy, and his ambitious plans for the future, Doutté was Le Chatelier's principal rival at the time. In a series of letters written in 1904 to Auguste Terrier, the general secretary of the Comité de l'Afrique française, Doutté complained bitterly about Le Chatelier. (It is worth recalling that as the head of the Comité de l'Afrique française, Terrier was unlikely to be well disposed toward Le Chatelier. Doutté was therefore assured a good reception.) In a long letter of April 19, 1904, Doutté vented his feelings to Terrier:

> Just as they did for Tunisia, they have tried to confiscate Morocco as an object of study. The author of this confiscation is not unknown to us, it is not necessary that I name him. He aspires to be the head of a school of researchers that will study Morocco. He only lacks one thing to be the head of a school [of thought]—that is, to have disciples. To have disciples one must have trained them oneself, which supposes a bit of work and objectivity, a knowledge that commands recognition, the power to put aside traditions and doctrines, [and] long teaching experience. Lacking these qualities, he has imagined that stealth, money, intrigue, and boldness would be enough, and not having trained any disciples, and for good reason, he thought he could hire them.[23]

These bitter words, and many more besides, give eloquent voice to the extent of the anger generated by the announcement of the Mission scientifique. Doutté's fears that the Salmon mission was directed against the École d'Alger, and ultimately his own ambitions, are manifest from the outset. By June 1904, he was convinced that he was correct in his analysis, as news arrived that the French Legation in Tangier was denying the authorization to conduct research in Morocco to French Algerian researchers. Worse still from Doutté's perspective, funding for expeditions along the Algero-Moroccan border suddenly dried up, and the Algerian governor-general himself seemed won over to the Le Chatelier position.[24] Doutté found further evidence of his fears in recent changes in the native affairs bureaucracy of the Algerian colonial government. Nicolas Lacroix, the longtime head of the native affairs division (an ally of Doutté), was brusquely relieved of his functions. Colonel André de Saint-Germain, Le Chatelier's former boss, was named to replace him. (Shortly thereafter an arrangement between the two relieved Doutté's fears somewhat.)[25] By the end of May, Doutté was writing, "Here the watchword is to disinterest oneself from Morocco."[26]

The counterattack against the Salmon nomination was three-pronged, and it wrought serious damage to the Le Chatelier program. One aspect of it we have already seen: the attempt to damage Salmon's reputation. A second dimension was Doutté's effort to mount a counteroffensive designed to show that the École d'Alger was not in the least discouraged, and that in fact it had very ambitious plans of its own in the works. Already in the above-cited letter of April 19, Doutté confidentially announced his plans to Terrier, seeking the endorsement of the Comité du Maroc.[27] He proposed nothing less than a four-volume continuation of the old Lamartinière and Lacroix series, *Documents pour servir à l'histoire du nord-ouest africain*. Doutté would prepare two volumes, one on Marrakech, the Houz, and the High Atlas, and the second on Fez, its material life, religion, and the *makhzan* (government). Geographer Augustin Bernard had agreed to prepare a volume on Tangier and the Atlantic coast, while orientalist William Marçais was signed up to write a second volume on Fez, focusing on Islamic culture, education, and archaeology. The author of a possible fifth volume on the city of Tetouan and the Spanish presidios remained for the moment undecided.[28]

Doutté's timetable called for him to complete his book on Marrakech rapidly. This would be followed in 1905 by the joint expedition of Doutté and William Marçais to Fez. Doutté claimed to have a signed document from Jonnart authorizing him to proceed with the full series of volumes. He scored a small victory when the December 1904 issue of the *Bulletin* of the Comité de l'Afrique française contained a brief mention of the École d'Alger project. It presented Doutté's plans as having the backing of the Comité du Maroc while omitting any announcement of the establishment of the Mission scientifique du Maroc. In the end, all this scheming was ultimately for naught. Except for Doutté's volume on Marrakech, which came out in 1905, none of the other projected volumes were ever published. In the larger context, Doutté's health situation and the increasing opposition of Moroccans to European researchers of all kinds doomed the projected École d'Alger series in advance. Nonetheless, upon reflection, the French Legation in Tangier was in the end unwilling to continue interdicting French Algerian researchers from Morocco.

A third aspect of the Algerian counteroffensive and ultimately the most damaging was the Paris bureaucratic campaign to cut the appropriations of the Mission scientifique. In addition, the opponents sought to alter the mission's charter by placing it under the jurisdiction of the Ministry of Public Instruction, thereby making it administratively responsible not to Le Chatelier, but to the Academie des inscriptions et belles lettres. As we have seen above, despite his not having acquired secure funding for the Salmon mission, Le Chatelier was compelled to go forward with his project. With the support of Eugène Étienne, he worked out the plan for a Moroccan Institute that was submitted to the Chambre des deputés in the spring of 1904.[29] The resolution proposed by Étienne argued the case for the establishment of an Institut du Maroc:

> Our entire colonial history warns us of the necessity of a complete study of Moroccan society as the essential base of methodically peaceful Moroccan policy. Haven't we fought many times in North Africa, West Africa, [and] Indochina against traditions and parties with which experience has shown that in the end it might have been possible to agree at the outset? We have been led thus to end where we should have begun, in multiplying schools of experts, study missions, local institutes, to rank native sociology first in our preoccupations with native government. But the possibilities of misunderstandings and thus of conflicts between two civilizations that come in contact are numerous. How [can we] avoid them without a deep understanding of the Moroccan milieu ... ?
>
> Colonial experimentation has led us thus to apply the doctrines formulated by the followers of August Comte for whom sociology is to politics as biology is to medicine. We must know how to inspire ourselves in Morocco by the positivist spirit if we wish to perform practical work there. Let's begin where we ended elsewhere: by determining everything about Moroccan society in terms of its ancient and modern evolution, so that we [can] guide it more surely, without friction and blows, toward its future evolution: that of peaceful progress, under the auspices of democratic France.[30]

The budget committee hearings on the Étienne resolution provided the opportunity for which Le Chatelier's adversaries had been waiting. They mobilized their political allies, and forced a series of modifications in the plan. Their chosen instrument was the parliamentary committee charged with reviewing the proposal and chaired by Senator Lucien Hubert.[31] The Hubert committee report completely gutted the original scope of the Mission scientifique and reduced it to an archaeological and philological mission under the Académie des inscriptions.[32] The Conseil de perfectionnement

(Advisory Board), headed by the orientalist Charles Barbier de Meynard, was appointed to oversee the functioning of the Mission scientifique and thereby to lend it creditability. Barbier was a staunch opponent of Le Chatelier. Under his leadership, the Advisory Board intervened to block discussion about the future of the Mission scientifique until the fate of the legislative proposal had been decided.[33] As originally envisioned in the Étienne proposal the Institute project included a budget of 75,000 francs and a staff of eight. The Hubert senate committee suspended consideration of the resolution to establish a Moroccan Institute until the outstanding questions were resolved. Plans for an *école d'application* (a kind of staff college for the future protectorate native affairs administration) were also dropped at this time.[34] The very existence of the Mission scientifique was suddenly placed in jeopardy.

It was only as a result of Le Chatelier's incredible personal efforts that he was able to salvage his proposal. Eventually, through the intervention of Paul Révoil and Eugène Étienne, these bureaucratic obstacles were resolved, and the project was approved in unmodified form. Since the legislation proposed by Étienne specifically claimed that the Moroccan Institute was modeled on the French institutes in Cairo and Hanoi, and since both of those were under the jurisdiction of the Ministry of Public Instruction, either the Moroccan Institute would conform to the legal precedent (which implied the triumph of Le Chatelier's rivals), or it must be abandoned.[35] With a heavy heart, Le Chatelier decided to salvage what was left, and the Moroccan Institute scheme was definitively dropped. Then ingeniously, the substance of it was resurrected by retaining the name Mission scientifique, together with the connection to the Ministry of Foreign Affairs that went with it. Nominal authority was accorded to the Ministry of Public Instruction, while an exchange of letters between the ministers established where the real authority lay. While the Ministry of Public Instruction would provide part of the funds, it would have no control over the operations of the Mission scientifique. The decision regarding the establishment of an *école d'application* was simply deferred until circumstances became more propitious for its resurrection. Finally, the compromise called for the enlargement of the Conseil de perfectionnement to include some of the opposition (including René Basset of the École des Lettres), while the authority of the Délégué générale (Le Chatelier) was confirmed as far as the day-to-day operations of the Mission scientifique were concerned. It seemed a victory snatched from the jaws of defeat.[36]

FOUR

When Paradigms Shift

POLITICAL AND DISCURSIVE CONTEXTS OF
THE MOROCCAN QUESTION

DOES ORIENTALISM HAVE A HISTORY, or only an epistemology? Said's *Orientalism* does not allow for the possibility of a temporary rupture in the discourse of orientalism, since the same essentialist stereotypes about colonial societies endlessly recirculate. Thus in important respects orientalism does not "have a history." Yet, as we have just seen, something very like this occurred with respect to French representations of Morocco during the period 1900–1904. Said's approach to orientalism derived from French theorist Michel Foucault's notion of discourse. Said suggested that as a discourse (and not just a set of intellectual practices) orientalism provided the lens through which Europeans viewed the Middle East, the set of stereotypes that "stood for" the region. In so doing orientalism the discourse summoned "the Orient" into existence while reducing it to a set of reductive binaries. However, Said's appropriation of Foucault's idea of discourse was flawed in important respects.[1] While Said stressed the discursive context (as James Clifford has pointed out), he also sought to restore the preeminent position of the canonical author. Thus Said "fail[ed] sufficiently to historicize the discourse of orientalism," and "relapse[d] into traditional intellectual history."[2] In order to account for the struggle for control of research on Morocco in the period 1900–1904, we must accordingly switch theorists.

This is where the work of Pierre Bourdieu becomes relevant to our inquiry. Bourdieu's sociology of symbolic domination in French life hypothesizes a division between what he refers to as the *political field* and the *scientific field*. As opposed to Said's orientalism, in which history does not exist, Bourdieu's concept of field (*champs*) opens outward toward history and allows for change. It permits us to consider the relationship of individuals and groups to one another as well as to the fields in which they are inserted. For Bourdieu the political and intellectual fields had specific properties that can be ascertained. Bourdieu's theory structured an intellectual field of nested hierarchies, culminating in the so-called *grandes écoles* (among them the École polytechnique, the École normale supérieure, the École des ponts et chaussées, the École des mines, and more recently the École nationale d'administration). But intellectual prestige is only one element of Bourdieu's schema. Attained ranks and job titles are also readily ascertainable in a wider field of hierarchies. Finally, Bourdieu's idea of *symbolic capital* (the symbolic tokens of authority and prestige) determines the place of an individual in a status/honor hierarchy. In Bourdieusian terms, the struggle for control of scientific research on Morocco in 1900–1904 is best understood as a struggle over *symbolic capital*.[3] It was also a competition in which the position of Le Chatelier's followers and those of the École d'Alger in the French intellectual and political fields were actively in play. With this brief excursus, let us return to the dramatic exclusion of Algerian scholars from research on Morocco by the Quai d'Orsay in October 1903.

The battle for the control of social research on Morocco provides a precious window into the operation of the government and institutions of Third Republic France, and the connections between its political and scientific fields. Somehow what had begun as a turf war between a provincial university research group and a politically connected interloper morphed into a pitched battle that split the French government into rival factions representing major political and economic interests. Although conflicts over research are not unprecedented in academia, few have had such far-reaching consequences. The crisis activated activated political fault lines within the French state and the world of French orientalism, greatly magnifying the upheaval. The struggle over the Mission scientifique mobilized political forces in the highest reaches of the French government. The affair was resolved only after the intervention of the foreign minister, Théophile Delcassé, and the head of the *parti colonial,* Eugène Étienne, the heads of key government departments and parliamentary committees, and some of the leading academic figures of the day. Questions of persons, of politics, even of patriotism, were raised. Bitterness, skullduggery, and petty-mindedness wore the masks of scientific detachment, personal altruism, and French national interest. The existence of a discursive crisis is unimaginable in Said's theory. How can this be explained? What can the struggle to control social research on Morocco tell us about the structure and operation of the intellectual and political fields in France at the turn of the century? Let us return to a consideration of the multiple contexts in which the struggle over the Mission scientifique can be situated.

/

THE POLITICS OF RESEARCH

In normal times colonial ethnography was intellectually marginal to the French intellectual field. However, under certain conditions it might assume considerable importance in both the national intellectual and political arenas. That is, the autonomy of the intellectual field from the political field was not fixed, but must be established and not assumed for specific cases. In the superheated political atmosphere of early twentieth-century France, battles over research on Morocco were fought out not only in faculty meetings and private salons, but also in the halls of the establishment itself. Rival research approaches to Morocco in such an environment were inevitably scrutinized not only for what they might yield in the way of scientific advances, but also for the interests and policy options that lay behind them. Let us consider what was at stake from the point of view of the different groups.

The coalition that opposed Le Chatelier and the Mission scientifique was drawn chiefly from the École d'Alger and the orientalists of the Académie des inscriptions and the École des langues orientales, with some support within the Ministry of Public Instruction. While the École d'Alger dominated research on Morocco, their thinking was not fully in keeping with the evolving policies of the Quai d'Orsay and the government as a whole. The latter had to contend with a tricky diplomatic context, and a recalcitrant Moroccan government. A successful French diplomatic offensive in Morocco would require international approval, as well as the acquiescence of the *makhzan*. In the meantime, negotiations continued between France and the *makhzan,* as well as between France and the European powers. In this context the École d'Alger might well have seemed the best research group to undertake the ethnographic inventory of Morocco. The Algiers group shared a positivist self-confidence in the capacity of science to assist in the devising of an appropriate native policy for Morocco. Its leader, Edmond Doutté, claimed for himself the status of sociologist, and was associated with Marcel Mauss and the *Année sociologique* group.[4] The École d'Alger group also had a history of reliable partnership with the Gouvernement général. Moreover, its members had already completed a series of successful study missions to Morocco in the period 1900–1903 that had added a great deal to French knowledge of the Moroccan interior (see chapter 5).

Where the French Algerian scholars disqualified themselves in the eyes of the Quai d'Orsay was the policy option they favored (the "tribes policy"), which promised continual frontier "incidents" and international flare-ups. Until a coherent French policy line was established (in 1904), debate continued between the adherents of the so-called tribes policy and those of the so-called *makhzan* policy. The diplomats on balance favored the *makhzan* policy of working with the Moroccan sultan to introduce reforms and establish order. They were nonetheless sensitive to the risks of instability along the Algero-Moroccan frontier (as well as the opportunities it might present). The Parisian policymakers were primarily interested in obtaining reliable ethnographic and political information without domestic political blowback or international incidents. In retrospect, the kerfuffle over the tribes policy disguised the fact that these distinctions mattered less for the development of Morocco policy than a scan of the opinions of politicians might suggest.

Viewed from Paris, the selection of the École d'Alger as the research entity of the government had a second problematic feature. It exposed the French position in Morocco to the potentially destabilizing influence of colonial Algerian groups and factions, with possible negative consequences for French plans. In the international diplomatic and financial context of the time, the Quai d'Orsay saw nothing but headaches arising from the unleashing of Algerian settler interests on Morocco. What French diplomacy required was stability and accountability. The French Algerians could deliver neither. Algerian settlers and small-time business operations promised to generate crisis upon crisis in Morocco. There was already abundant evidence on this score, including the recent revelation of the connections between Oran business interests and Abu Himara, a rebel based in the Rif mountains near Mellila.[5] Freelance Algerian intervention in Moroccan politics promised to disrupt relations with the Moroccan government, the approval of which was essential to the success of French policy. Insofar as the École d'Alger was connected to Algerian settler interests, granting the former primacy in research in Morocco seemed a risky bet on political grounds, even without entering into the intellectual merits of their contribution.

While allied in their opposition to Le Chatelier and the Mission scientifique project, the Algerians, the Paris orientalists, and the education bureaucracy agreed in their hostility toward Le Chatelier, they differed in their positions on the Mission scientifique. The École d'Alger wanted to supplant it, or failing that, to block it. The Parisian orientalists planned to convert it into a philological and archaeological institute, the better to provide research positions for themselves and their students. In the crunch, the orientalists had the more influential supporters, as an examination of the budget committee's report on the original Jonnart resolution reveals.[6] As important as this was, it was the opposition of the bureaucrats of the Ministry of Public Instruction that further inflamed the crisis. The education bureaucrats viewed the dispute as openly flouting established bureaucratic procedures and threatening the prerogatives of the ministry. Le Chatelier was found to be totally unsuitable for the position because of his lack of university degrees—especially since the bureaucrats of the ministry had not been consulted in advance on the Mission scientifique proposal. Their preferred resolution of the crisis required a reassertion of the established precedents and bureaucratic norms. Once the proper forms were obeyed, the education ministry officials were perfectly willing to cooperate with the Quai d'Orsay. They were little interested in diplomatic struggles or native policy preferences. But the crisis was not limited to the École d'Alger, the Paris orientalists, and the Ministry of Public Instruction bureaucrats.

More redoubtable still was the opposition of the Comité de l'Afrique française. A glance at its monthly *Bulletin (BCAF)* for the period reveals its unwavering support of Doutté and the École d'Alger group. The *AF* editors took advantage of every occasion to praise Doutté and his team, while scarcely mentioning the existence of the Mission scientifique du Maroc. Certainly there was no love lost between Auguste Terrier, the general secretary of the Comité, and Le Chatelier.[7] This did not explain the antagonism of the Comité toward the Mission scientifique, however. Their dispute was not only personal. It reflected a major policy disagreement with Delcassé over French strategy toward Morocco. The Comité supported the policy of military incursions along the Algerian frontier known as the "tribes" policy. It called for regular French military action along the frontier to prevent Moroccan tribes from raiding into Algeria. If these raids led to the piecemeal conquest of Morocco, the Comité would not be opposed. But a frontier clash was precisely what Delcassé and the Quai d'Orsay feared most, since it could lead to an international incident, sabotaging years of careful diplomacy. His policy, known as the *"makhzan"* policy, was based on winning the approval of the Moroccan state for a French reform program. Since Delcassé's diplomatic maneuverings provided no remedy for the insecurity along the frontier, it was unacceptable to Algerian settler interests.

From a Quai d'Orsay perspective, the main alternative source of potential administrators for a future Moroccan protectorate was the Gouvernement général de l'Algérie. The Quai d'Orsay viewed this prospect as having serious liabilities. Not only was the Algerian colonial administration widely criticized for its costs and inefficiency, the tyranny of settler interests had proven itself to be adverse to metropolitan control, and potentially destructive of just the sort of delicate compromises on which French diplomacy depended. For the Quai d'Orsay there were important advantages to having the ethnographic research on Morocco concentrated in a single entity, especially if was under its control. Were a Moroccan Institute to be created, it might not only preside over the creation of a reliable base of information on Moroccan society of use to policymakers, but also assist in the training of French diplomatic and administrative officials for a future Moroccan protectorate. In Le Chatelier, the Quai d'Orsay saw a man of enormous energy and experience who appeared capable of providing the empirical information about Moroccan society that its strategy required. Le Chatelier's proposal for a Moroccan Institute that could take in hand not only policy planning but also the training of future administrators was another advantage.

Eager to avoid having a chance incident upset its careful calculations, and desiring to control all phases of French activities in Morocco, the Quai d'Orsay (both its officials in the Tangier legation and those in Paris) preferred the Le Chatelier project to the École d'Alger. Le Chatelier's espousal of a technocratic position—do your work, and stay out of politics—in his advice to Georges Salmon and the members of the Mission scientifique was reassuring. At the same time, the Quai d'Orsay was delighted to have the information provided by the Mission scientifique. Moreover, the views of Révoil, Étienne, and Le Chatelier on the feasibility of the "peaceful penetration" of Morocco won Delcassé over to a program that would also be the apotheosis of the dreams of the "scientific" colonialists. For the Quai d'Orsay, the prospect of a "scientific" and "peaceful" penetration of Morocco, without the turmoil caused by hordes of French businessmen and speculators of all kinds, seemed persuasive, especially as the pressure of the Comité du Maroc (often allied with Algerian interests) intensified (see below, chapter 6).

THE FIRST CRISIS OF ORIENTALISM

By 1900 French orientalism was in a state of crisis. We can call it (with a nod to Anouar Abdel-Malek) "the first crisis of orientalism." Abdel-Malek was an Egyptian Communist intellectual who had been interned under Nasser for his political views. Following his release from prison he was exiled to France. There he subsequently wrote an article for *Diogenes* called "The End of Orientalism."[8] It was one of the first works to challenge colonial forms of knowledge, and was mentioned by Edward Said as having inspired him in writing *Orientalism.*[9] For Abdel-Malek and other French-speaking Third World militants of the period, the end of the colonial empires and the intellectual ferment that accompanied the Algerian independence struggle (1954–62) had brought about an intellectual crisis in the way Europeans viewed the ex-colonial Third World. Abdel-Malek called the system of ideas about colonized peoples "orientalism." (In 1963 Marxist thought was still dominant in French intellectual circles, and the concept of discourse was not yet available.) We now know that Abdel-Malek was overly optimistic in seeing the end of orientalism. Nonetheless my purpose in invoking the "first crisis of orientalism" is to draw attention to the fact that the critique of colonial forms of knowledge did not begin with Said.[10] Abdel-Malek's article also leads me to wonder, Might there have been other crises of orientalism (that is, of colonial forms of knowledge)? Did the patterned way in which the French thought about North Africa and Muslims have a history? Or was it always and everywhere the same? Might there have been a "first crisis of orientalism" before the "big bang" crisis at the end of European colonial empires?[11] If so, what were the historical limits of this crisis?

As a historian interested in the relations between knowledge and power, I find the concepts of discourse and hegemony that Said borrows from Foucault and Gramsci (respectively) to be inadequate for my purposes. By positing the Orient as other, Said argues, orientalists created the Orient they purported to study, endowing it with essential characteristics that continually reasserted themselves. Orientalism, he insists, was more than the sum of the various intellectual, artistic, and literary images of the other. By its cultural ubiquity and imbrication in the fact of European dominance over the globe, orientalism possessed undeniable power. Indeed, it was a discourse of power, the intellectual grid through which the world was perceived.[12] But what if the deployment of power, and the forms of representation, were contested in their own time? By the lights of Foucault and Gramsci, this cannot be. According to postcolonial theorists, orientalism did not have a history other than the history of power. In their view there is nothing problematic in the unfolding of orientalist representations, or in their congruence with power. But (an objection arises) if power is everywhere, then it is nowhere, and one cannot explain the appearance of nationalism. In postcolonial theory, hegemony produces a world in which orientalism is essentially homogenous and devoid of struggle, politically saturated, yet curiously inert. Counterhegemonic discourses by definition cannot exist.[13]

What if there were "wrinkles" in the smooth surface of orientalist discourse that permitted the emergence of alternative conceptualizations (if only for a time)? How might their existence be understood? More generally, what was the relationship of alternative orientalist understandings to the larger political field within which they existed? This chapter examines the struggle for control of ethnographic research on Morocco in the period 1890–1914 to make a broader argument about power and its complex instantiation. It suggests that on at least one occasion it was possible (if only provisionally) to think outside the box of colonial binaries—the 1904 crisis over control of social research on Morocco.

. . .

By 1900, the legacy of French studies of colonial Algerian society had cohered into an intellectual and policy toolkit that was readily transferable to Morocco. It incorporated protocols and intellectual categories for the study of Algerian Sufi orders and popular Islamic beliefs and practices. But it also included the institutional memory of the conquest and administration of Algerian Muslims. A deep-seated fear of mass insurrections and Pan-Islamic conspiracies underlay French experience of Islam in Algeria and periodically set off intelligence panics. These can be conceived as the reciprocal of ethnographic ratiocinations about the Muslim Algerian other in which we see in its most naked form the ideological component of French colonial ethnography. Together, these aspects of the Algerian experience shaped a distinctive French approach. The prospect for representations of Morocco was more of the same. Instead of this, however, at least for the first few years of French research on Morocco, something else happened. French researchers resisted the colonial binaries in the name of a more circumstantial and complex account of Moroccan society and history. How did their work differ from the stereotypes of the Algerian colonial gospel? What explains the remarkable openness of their pre-1904 studies of Morocco? Unpacking the shifting political and discursive contexts is the subject of this chapter.

Pre-World War I France was consumed with anxiety over religion. Science and rationality were seen as in danger of being undone by the forces of superstition and darkness. For staunch republicans, the republic itself was in danger because of the nefarious activities of religiously motivated plotters. The Dreyfus affair (1894–1906) is one example of this anxiety. Arising from suspicions that a French officer of Jewish origin was a spy for Germany, it morphed into a decade-long wave of political anti-Semitism and fears of alleged Jewish plots that split factions and divided families. A struggle over the so-called laic laws, ostensibly activated by fears on the left of the secret power of the Vatican, pitted the Parti radical and its allies against the monarchist and Catholic Right in a series of increasingly violent affrays. The fear of Pan-Islamic plots belongs in the wider discursive context of fears of social contagion in metropolitan France.

In fact, the atmosphere of crisis was broader still. The "unloved" Third Republic was detested by the monarchist and nationalist Right as "La Geuze" (the Whore). A number of seedy corruption scandals (the 1888 Panama affair was just the biggest) appeared to justify this reputation. Political parties were divided over the colonial question (notably Morocco) as well as the Dreyfus affair and the debate over the separation of church and state. On the parliamentary left, Radical Socialists, Socialists, and others sought to oppose the bourgeois state, but lacked the numbers to do so. Outside of the parliamentary arena things were especially tense. Armed nationalist-royalist street gangs (Action française) confronted worker activists of the Socialist Internationale and the newly founded Confédération générale du travail. Illegal strikes (all strikes were illegal) and work stoppages proliferated, and were ruthlessly crushed by the police and (in some cases) the army. Exterminist thoughts flourished in the shadows. France in 1914 was a stalemated society.[14] The tensions caused by the unresolved Moroccan question served only to exacerbate the overall atmosphere of crisis.

THE PARADOX: EARLY VIEWS OF MOROCCO

In view of the foregoing, one might think that the portrait of Morocco in early French writings on Morocco (1900–1904) would have reflected the verities of the Algerian colonial gospel. However, contrary to all expectations, this is not what ensued. In fact, a review of the early writings by French observers of Morocco reveals that Morocco was depicted as a land where differences were not hard-edged but surprisingly malleable—in other words, quite unlike the image of Algeria in the colonial gospel. The collective image of Moroccan society the French presented contrasted sharply with the binaries of the

Algerian colonial gospel. To exaggerate a bit, we could say that the French portrait of pre-1904 Moroccan society resembles nothing so much as Clifford Geertz's 1971 depiction of it in the *New York Review of Books*.[15] But by the latter date Morocco was independent, and social change had swept most of the old social structures away, so Geertz was describing social reality of the time. The remarkable openness of pre-1904 studies of Morocco is difficult to explain, especially given the reinforcement of the discursive power of French orientalism by the heated nationalist rhetoric surrounding the Moroccan question.

For example, in 1904 neither Doutté nor Aubin viewed Morocco as divided irrevocably between *bled el makhzan* and *bled el siba*. "The expression of bled el-makhzan opposed to that of bled el-siba is incorrect," Doutté wrote in 1901, "for all of Morocco under different forms and to varying degrees undergoes the action of the makhzan." He went on to point out the folly of attempting to draw a map of Morocco with dissident and surrendered zones marked off, because the European notion of the nation-state as linguistically homogenous and marked by boundaries differed profoundly from the Islamic conception of Dar al-Islam. Whereas Europeans thought in terms of territorial limits, Moroccans thought in terms of the ritualized submission of tribal groups to the sultan.[16] This misunderstanding, Doutté continued, was at the root of much of the conflict along the Algero-Moroccan frontier. Aubin similarly portrayed the Moroccan state as a vague federation held together by Islam and the activities of *makhzan* bureaucrats: "Relations [between *makhzan* and *siba* territories] continue even while the battle rages."[17] While a European might interpret the persistent conflict between the *makhzan* and the tribes as mere anarchy, Doutté was of a different opinion: "All this is not disorder, but an order; in this apparent chaos all the living forces ended up by finding an equilibrium: the play of classes and of parties of all kinds resulted in a kind of social stasis that constitutes a durable state, as much in the tribes as in the cities."[18] The final judgment of Aubin was similar: "If there is no government whose organization appears more simple than that of Morocco, there is nonetheless none whose operation is more complicated. It is a veritable group of little autonomous states, toward which the makhzan must proceed according to a diplomacy appropriate for each one."[19] In the end, both men emphasized that the *makhzan-siba* division was inadequate to explain the relationship between the sultan and the dissident tribes, and that as Morocco was an Islamic state, the conception of the nature of the Moroccan empire and of the ruler's authority differed considerably from European notions of territorial sovereignty.

What explains the openness in conceptions of Morocco before 1904, and the rapid imposition of the Moroccan colonial gospel thereafter? The answer to this question has both political and discursive components.

POLITICAL AND DISCURSIVE CONTEXTS

Let us start with the political context *that* frames our understanding of the changing views of Moroccan society. The year 1904 marks an important turning point in the history of French involvement in Morocco. Hitherto, discussions about Morocco in French political circles had always posited French support of the *makhzan* as only one of the ways in which Morocco might be won over. Some groups had favored the tribes policy, by which the piecemeal conquest of Morocco, tribe by tribe, had been envisaged. After the signature of the entente cordiale and the 1904 loan agreement, this strategy had to be abandoned. Whereas the entente cordiale gave France a free hand in Morocco (in return for giving Britain the same in Egypt), the loan agreement gave France a vested interest in the survival of the Moroccan state. Together, the entente cordiale and the loan agreement welded France's Morocco policy to the fate of the *makhzan* (if not to any particular sultan). Henceforth, if France were to have a protectorate in Morocco, it would have to do so with the cooperation (fictive would do, but active would be better) of the Moroccan government.[20] Only via this arrangement could France's objectives be achieved. A piecemeal conquest as envisaged by the supporters of the tribes policy was now viewed as potentially risky to the international legitimacy of France's policy, as well as costly and disruptive of French interests in Morocco.

Before 1904 there were two main rival strategies regarding how France should go about taking over Morocco: the "*makhzan* policy" (which proposed the introduction of reforms in cooperation with the Moroccan government) and the "tribes policy" (which foresaw the gradual conquest of Morocco on a piecemeal, tribe-by-tribe basis starting from Algeria). In fact, the line between the two was not clear, and depending on the context, the government pursued both simultaneously. Nonetheless, at the time, the lines were believed by participants to be sharper than they now appear. While the *makhzan* policy was largely supported by the French diplomatic corps, the tribes policy was backed by Algerian settler and military interests.[21] In 1904 the entente cordiale decided the contest in favor of the *makhzan* policy.

However, to mollify critics in the French Chamber of Deputies, the policy was rebaptized (with unintentional irony) as "peaceful penetration." Under the rubric of peaceful penetration, France would seek to introduce a broad range of reforms in Morocco as an aspect of its cooperation with the sultan and the *makhzan*, and thus achieve a position of dominance.[22] Since the policy called for a compliant Moroccan government, it proved difficult to enact because of persistent Moroccan resistance along the Algero-Moroccan frontier.[23] German intervention in support of the Moroccan position in 1905 temporarily blocked the Delcassé policy and brought about the collapse of his government. Nonetheless, peaceful penetration and cooperation with the *makhzan* remained the official French policy toward Morocco even after the fall of Delcassé. The volatile nature of both the French internal political scene and the international diplomatic front militated against a more overt and aggressive French policy.

A sign of the victory of the *makhzan* policy was its endorsement by the 1906 international conference at Algeciras. It gave France a vested interest in the survival of the Moroccan state (although not necessarily any given sultan). The full advantages of this state of affairs were slow to be appreciated. Characteristically, it was General Hubert Lyautey who was the first to see how it could be exploited. Lyautey, who commanded French troops in Algeria along the frontier with Morocco, found cooperation with the *makhzan* to be too onerous, because of the covert resistance of local Moroccan officials. Instead Lyautey devised a policy for the Algero-Moroccan border that fully satisfied French desires for control of the area without alarming either the sultan's local representative or the *makhzan,* or the European powers, or the French opposition. First conceived in 1904 and enacted during 1905, the Lyautey solution was a clever combination of public assertions of cooperation with the Moroccan government and de facto extensions of French control over selected portions of the Algero-Moroccan frontier. France selected the local officials and forced the *makhzan* to appoint them, then organizing pro-French groups in each tribe, collecting taxes on behalf of the sultan (from which the costs of French administration and the upkeep of local forces were deducted), and developing roads, markets, and medical dispensaries to give the local population a stake in the success of the operation.[24]

Best of all, by substituting itself for the *makhzan,* France put itself in a position where it could dismiss any resistance on the part of the tribes as the traditional dissidence of *bled el-siba,* rather than as a politically significant response. Moroccan patriotic opposition was recast as the actions of a recalcitrant and obstreperous group of dissidents, and Moroccan resistance recoded as the expected opposition of *siba* tribes to *makhzan* authority. By redefining resistance France could pursue the piecemeal conquest of Morocco without making it vulnerable to international objection.[25] The same general strategy was subsequently followed in the 1907 Beni Snassen campaign, the French intervention in the Chaouia of the same year, and the 1911 relief of the siege of Fez. Each intervention led to the further extension of French control over Moroccan territory. Since France carefully collected taxes, respected the local religion and customs, and worked with local *makhzan* officials, European powers and French domestic opinion were persuaded to accept this as a testimony of the government's good faith.

A second major factor affecting the discursive options was the 1904 loan agreement by which French interests were redefined as identical with the interests of the Compagnie marocaine, the cartel created by the French government to preside over Moroccan economic development.[26] The primary actors in the Compagnie marocaine in turn were the Banque de Paris et des Pay Bas (a Franco-Belgian banking conglomerate) and the Compagnie Schneider (a French industrial giant). A creation of the high capitalist world of finance and industry of the period, the Compagnie marocaine was authorized to invest in Morocco's mineral resources (should any of consequence be discovered) as well as to make major land acquisitions. The Compagnie marocaine radically restructured the existing Moroccan economy, in effect dealing Moroccan landholders out of the game (unless they were adroit enough to agree to serve as associates), and condemning the peasantry to a marginal existence. Any arable land not spoken for was potentially available for French settlers. What the new economic arrangements did not do, at least outside of the coastal plains, was to call into question preexisting tenure arrangements, or to confiscate tribal lands (as in Algeria). Well-placed Moroccan landed elites were therefore grandfathered into the protectorate economic deal in advance, but only if they kept on their best behavior.[27] France's economic stake in Morocco therefore differed profoundly from that in Algeria or even Tunisia where settler colonialism was encouraged.

The political and economic consequences that flowed from the entente cordiale and the 62.5-million-franc 1904 loan agreement gave France a vested interest in the *makhzan*. It also led to a major discursive shift in how Moroccan society was perceived by French and European observers. The political and discursive conditions that had made it possible to imagine Moroccan society in complex and historically situated ways reached its pull-by date. When they did, the discursive window slammed shut, and the hegemony of colonial discourse on Morocco was reestablished.

THE MOROCCAN COLONIAL GOSPEL

The consequences of this discursive shift were dramatic. They can be seen in the post-1906 views of Edmond Doutté and Édouard Michaux-Bellaire, as well as in the writings of pundits and policy makers in France like Eugène Étienne, the head of the colonial lobby in the Chamber of Deputies. A crucial determinant of the colonial gospel image of Morocco was the Eurocentric conceptual framework on which it was based. Instead of starting from the premise that Morocco, as an Islamic state, possessed a rather different notion of sovereignty than that which European countries adhered to, such concerns were pushed aside in favor of the new knowledge/power calculus. Thus Étienne could claim in 1904: "The sultan is only a great religious leader. He has only one-third of the surface of Morocco under his direct and immediate authority. This is the territory to which is given the name bled el-makhzan, 'the land of government'; the other two-thirds of Morocco bears the name bled el-siba, that is, 'the land of independence.'"[28] Explorer René de Segonzac, in a passage devoted to demonstrating how the *makhzan* and its agents had destroyed the democratic assemblies of Berber notables, referred to the "theocracy of the sultan, emperor, and pope."[29] Multiple citations of this sort from the French writings on Morocco between 1904 and 1912 exist.

While it is not surprising that a politician like Étienne should have viewed Moroccan society through the binaries of the colonial gospel, it is somewhat startling to find Michaux-Bellaire expressing sentiments of a similar nature. Improving on the *makhzan/siba* dichotomy, Michaux-Bellaire proclaimed in 1908 that Morocco was divided into two segments, or "organisms": these were the "makhzan organism" and the "Berber organism." Moroccan history, he claimed, was stuck between two contradictory impulses:

> The situation of the makhzan vis-à-vis this national organism [the Berber organism] is about the same as that of the ancient Phoenician and Roman conquerors; like them, it is incapable of finishing its conquest and organizing it, and it has been unable to absorb for its benefit the Berber vitality, to assimilate it; all that it can do is to resist it, to contain it within its limits and to declare itself responsible for its actions vis-à-vis Europe in order to justify an authority which it is moreover incapable of exercising by its means alone.[30]

Michaux-Bellaire concluded with the pious hope that some day the two organisms would be fused into one by France, whose benevolent rule would unify Morocco once and for all. By equating Arab and *makhzan,* Berber and *siba,* in a vivid formula, Michaux-Bellaire only reproduced in a scholarly article what had been repeated endlessly by less talented writers in plain and simple prose. Michaux-Bellaire's "L'organisme marocain" became a classic statement of the Moroccan colonial gospel.

A third element of the Moroccan colonial gospel was the representation of Moroccan Islam. From the late nineteenth century French observers were struck by the role of religious personages, sharifs, and saints, and their followers, in Morocco. Their local or regional influence often rivaled that of the sultan himself. In the pre-1904 period French supporters of the tribes policy proposed that instead of backing the *makhzan,* France should seek to win over the most influential religious notables and use them to favor French colonial penetration.[31] This was linked to the conception of the sultan as pope and emperor, in a version of the two swords theory of medieval kingship, in which his spiritual and temporal authority could be distinguished analytically from one another. According to this interpretation, the authority of the sultan as emperor (i.e., his temporal authority) extended over only the *bled el-makhzan,* while his authority as pope (i.e., his spiritual authority) was recognized in the *bled el-siba.* The tribes of the *bled el-siba* might respond to the spiritual appeals of the sultan, but they refused to accept his temporal authority and refrained from paying taxes or providing military contingents. From this one might infer that the *siba* populations were somehow not fully Moroccan—a conception that Lyautey was to utilize fully along the Algero-Moroccan frontier.[32]

The 1908 overthrow of Abd al-Aziz by a coalition of rural magnates in favor of his brother, Abd al-Hafiz, led to further changes in French views of Islam. Scholarly detachment and abstention from value judgments about Islam gave way to angry and bitter denunciations. In this new chauvinistic mood, even distinguished scholars like Doutté and Michaux-Bellaire asserted that Islam was the cause of the stagnation of Moroccan society, weighing "the entire country" down, in Doutté's words, "like a leaden mantle."[33] The study of Islam could only confirm its violence and hostility to civilization and progress: "Among the characteristics of Islam which most strike us, fanaticism is certainly in the first rank."[34] This attitude of fear and hostility gradually became the new orthodoxy.

By this point most of the main elements of the Moroccan colonial gospel had emerged. It consisted of three interlocking binary formulations. First,

Morocco was conceived as divided into two realms: one where the Moroccan central government (the *makhzan*) was supreme, taxes were collected, governors governed, and laws were respected; and a second, where the central government was impotent, and unruly tribes devoted their time to feuding and banditry. Under the rubric of *bled el-makhzan* and *bled es-siba* (the "land of government" and the "land of insolence"), a portrait of a regime emerged in which neither side was able to gain the upper hand.[35] Closely interwoven with the division of Morocco into two realms was a second binary division according to way of life. In this formulation Morocco was divided between its sedentary and its nomadic populations, neither of which was able to impose its will on the other. Finally, there was the split between the Arabic- and Berber-speaking populations. Moroccan history was portrayed as the eternal struggle between Arab *makhzan* forces and Berber *siba* dissidents.

The apotheosis of the Moroccan colonial gospel can be found in Henri Terrasse's 1950 classic, *Histoire du Maroc*.[36] For it is here that the different elements of the Moroccan colonial discourse were brought together in their final form. A central element in Terrasse's orientalist vision was the division of precolonial Moroccan society into *bled el-makhzan* and *bled el-siba*. Terrasse's formulation is the classic one. The *bled al-makhzan* is portrayed as constituting "neither a firm bloc nor a coherent force; it was only the coalition, maintained by force, of the directing and profiting elements—the makhzan and the guich (Ar. jaysh, or military) tribes—in passive resignation."[37] *Bled el-siba,* on the other hand, is viewed as profoundly divided by the ancient rivalries of clans, tribes, and *leffs* (moieties), marked by feuding and incapable of presenting a coherent resistance to the *makhzan*. According to Terrasse, before the arrival of the French, Islam was unable to supply the "moral unity" that would have enabled the sultans to bring about the political unity of the country.[38] Instead Moroccan politics was marked by the ceaseless efforts of the *makhzan* to impose its authority on the rebellious tribes of *siba*-land, and the latter's constant defense of their independence.[39] Even today, the image of a Morocco divided between *makhzan* and *siba,* Arab and Berber, and nomad and sedentary persists. A tentative conclusion from this brief review is that far from dating from time immemorial, the history of the Moroccan colonial gospel itself has a history.

Until 1912 the composite set of stereotypes that composed the Moroccan gospel remained incomplete in one respect: no stereotype of the Berber had taken root. In part this was because relatively little was known about the Berber-speaking populations of Morocco until after the establishment of the protectorate. No doubt in part it was also because the bulk of French energies and attention was absorbed by the task of fending off European rivals and solidifying French control. Since most Berbers lived outside the Atlantic coastal zone, which was the chief focus of French attention, there was little reason to think much about them.

FIVE

Tensions of Empire, 1900–1912

THE MOROCCAN COLONIAL ARCHIVE EMERGED under multiple auspices—intellectual, political, and institutional. Initially relatively open and undogmatic, it was attentive to social and historical complexity, and above all to the differences between Morocco and other parts of the Islamic world. But this fresh start for the study of Maghrebi societies was soon followed by an increasingly narrow and dogmatic conception of the field. From the start, however, the ethnographic study of Moroccan society was inextricably tangled in the passions aroused by the Morocco crisis. As the field became progressively more deeply inflected by the political context, the discursive possibilities of thought and action were drastically abridged. This chapter explores the parallel accomplishments of the Mission scientifique du Maroc and the study missions sponsored by Comité de l'Afrique française, which together shaped a new subject, Moroccan Islam, as well as a new discursive modality, Ethnographic Morocco.

THE MOROCCAN COLONIAL ARCHIVE IN ITS
MULTIPLE POLITICAL CONTEXTS

While little known or acknowledged, a Moroccan resistance movement constituted an important obstacle in the path of a French protectorate. Moroccan resistance helped shape both the representations of Moroccan society and the discursive lens through which they were perceived. In the absence of sustained resistance, the contours of the Moroccan colonial archive (not to mention Moroccan history) would have been quite different. Only by more completely historicizing the creation of the Moroccan colonial archive (including considering the impact of Moroccan resistance) can we can grasp the ways in which the political and the intellectual fields interacted.[1]

The unfolding of the Moroccan question began with the 1899 death of Ba Ahmad, the aged grand vizier and regent. Seeking to take advantage of temporary Moroccan disorganization, the French government sent troops into the Touat oasis in the Algerian Sahara. Since Morocco had long regarded the oasis as Moroccan (as they also did Saharan territory extending to Timbuktu), when the *makhzan* acquiesced in this fait accompli, a portion of the Fasi ulama dissented vigorously.[2] Divisions within the Moroccan elite over the correct strategy toward French agression persisted until 1912. The French occupation of Touat also attracted the attention of British diplomacy. It soon provoked the formulation of a British reform plan that consisted of several elements. Among these were the adoption of a new land tax, the *tartib,* and plans for the construction of telegraph and railroad links between Fez and the coast. But when these reforms were incompetently handled, they succeeded only in provoking resistance along the Fez-Rabat corridor.[3]

As the atmosphere of tension increased in 1901 and early 1902, a series of kidnappings and several attacks on British citizens ensued. Things came to a head in 1902 when a British doctor, David J. Cooper, was set upon and killed in the streets of Fez by a crazed individual.[4] While the *makhzan* temporized, a rebellion erupted, led by Abu Himara (1902–9), a former *makhzan* employee. Despite the *makhzan*'s best efforts to suppress it, the revolt spread to the nearby tribes. Abu Himara managed to elude capture and to remain at large in northeastern Morocco (with the suspected connivance of Oran-based Algerian colonial interests) until 1909. Meanwhile the Quai d'Orsay put the finishing touches on a comprehensive reform program to be presented to the Moroccan government. By 1904, international rivalries between Britain and France had reached their peak even as Morocco appeared on the verge of political chaos.

At this point events moved into uncharted territory. First came a diplomatic thunderbolt—the announcement of the signing of the Cambon-Lansdowne agreement on April 8, 1904. The centerpiece of foreign minister Delcassé's diplomatic strategy, the Anglo-French entente removed the main obstacle to a French protectorate. By its terms, Britain agreed to recognize French priority in Morocco, and France renounced its claims to Egypt. (Spain and Italy had previously recognized French priority in Morocco.) Not having been previously informed, the Moroccan government was livid. But its margin for maneuver was slight.

A second major development then intervened. It was the conclusion of a major loan agreement between the *makhzan* and a consortium of banks headed by the Banque de Paris et des Pays Bas on June 12, 1904. The 62.5-million-franc loan obligation completely changed the old financial game, according to which the *makhzan* had played its creditors off one another. With the diplomatic path to a protectorate cleared, and now holding the financial upper hand, the Quai d'Orsay announced in December 1904 its intention to present a major reform plan to Abd al-Aziz.

The French declaration immediately put things on the political boil. The Moroccan government reply was to summon an assembly of notables at Fez to consider the terms of the French reform plan and provide its advice. Meanwhile it sought diplomatic support for its position from Germany and the Ottomans. The March 21, 1905, landing of the German kaiser, Wilhelm II, at Tangier to support the Moroccan position astonished the French and set off a new phase of the Moroccan question. After prolonged and acrimonious negotiations it was agreed that an international conference should be convened at Algeciras on January 16, 1906, to hear the dispute. When the delegates to the conference failed to support the Moroccan position and proposed a set of reforms to be adopted, pending which the French would be permitted to have their way, the stage was set for a dramatic increase in political tension in Morocco.

While French Morocco experts sought a reliable source of research on Morocco, it was by no means clear where such an initiative would come from. While the Algerian scholars were ambitious and under Edmond Doutté had a plan, they lacked a reliable source of funding and were politically compromised in the eyes of the Quai d'Orsay because of their close links to the French colonial lobby. What was needed was a concerted research strategy, one in tune with the ideas of the new scientific imperialism. In the eyes of French policymakers, Le Chatelier's proposal for the establishment of the Mission scientifique du Maroc appeared more likely to generate useful knowledge and to avoid provoking incidents. Instead, what emerged was a de facto (but unintended) collaboration between the Mission scientifique du Maroc and the Comité de l'Afrique française. To understand why this was so, we need to acquire a deeper sense of the types of colonial knowledge each group produced, as well as the institutional contexts in which it was generated.

The Mission scientifique du Maroc (MSM) was the foremost producer of research on precolonial Morocco, Between 1904 and 1934 its journal, *Archives marocaines* (*AM*), published thirty-three volumes comprising more than 10,000 pages, most of which appeared before 1912. The MSM provided a stable institutional context for studying Moroccan society. In the conception of its founder, Alfred Le Chatelier, its purpose was to provide systematic and reliable information on Moroccan society for French policymakers and interested parties. The journal was edited by Georges Salmon and Édouard Michaux-Bellaire, whom we have encountered in previous chapters. Together they were able to produce a journal of Moroccan history and culture that quickly established itself as the gold standard for reliable information on Morocco. After Salmon's untimely death in 1905, Michaux-Bellaire took over as editor, and the frequency of publication increased.

In the first phase of its existence (1903–6) *AM* published translations of Arabic documents, brief ethnographies of Moroccan social and political institutions, and ethnohistories of northern Moroccan communities.[5] This represented a move away from the *fiche de tribu* approach represented in Le Chatelier's earlier conception of the journal's role. Thereafter, the mix of types of articles gradually changed. Translations of Moroccan Arabic books and manuscripts increased, to accommodate the major acquisition of Arabic materials in Fez by Salmon and Michaux-Bellaire in 1905, while the proportion devoted to ethnography declined—perhaps a reflection of the changing political circumstances. The focus of *AM* on the written Arabic culture of Morocco stood in sharp contrast to the field research strategy adopted by the Comité du Maroc, discussed below.

The establishment of the MSM coincided with the ascendancy of sociology among French policymakers. In the international struggle over Morocco, French expertise on Maghrebi culture and society constituted a decisive advantage for France. Practical knowledge of social and political institutions counted more in the ·eyes of policymakers than did philological erudition. Only a scientifically informed imperialism, it was asserted, had the potential to save French lives and to avoid major expense. This is clear from Le Chatelier's 1903 instructions to Georges Salmon: "The studies undertaken until now on Morocco are of two sorts: those purely scientific and the others more particularly statistical. I would like to see you apply yourself to introducing scientific research in the study of questions which are generally statistical in nature."[6] To today's reader, Le Chatelier's distinctions may appear a bit murky. By "statistical" he seems to have meant the tradition of the *fiche de tribu* in which he had been trained. In this sense for Le Chatelier "scientific" appears to have been a synonym for "modern," an equally vacuous term. In other contexts it seems to mean what contemporary social scientists might call "ethnographic" or "thick description."[7] His use of the term is frankly confused.

Georges Salmon arrived in Tangier in the late fall of 1903 and immediately set to work. Initially his staff included just Édouard Michaux-Bellaire and a rotating group of translators seconded by the French diplomatic mission in Tangier. Working intently, they soon had enough material for the first several volumes, and elements of two additional volumes were well advanced. Meanwhile in Paris, Le Chatelier sought to retain the funding he had been promised and to hold off the challenge of the École d'Alger and its supporters. The first volume of *AM* appeared early in 1904 and immediately proved its worth to policy planners.[8] It included a study of the Moroccan administration in Tangier (a revelation in its careful documentation of the complexities of the *makhzan* administrative organization), the first full-length ethnographic study of a Moroccan tribe, the Fahçya. The same issue included trailblazing studies of Moroccan property tax law, translations of Arabic manuscripts, as well as studies of local Tangier manners and customs. Since the European diplomatic representatives all resided in Tangier rather than in Fez, the Moroccan capital, it was especially important for them to possess accurate information on the structure and operation of the *makhzan* bureaucracy. Although most of the articles bear the signature of Salmon, they reflected the work of both men.

The first issues of *AM* revealed to its readers the existence of a previously unknown Morocco, one endowed with its own complex political heritage, institutional structures, and literate culture. The energy with which Salmon and Michaux-Bellaire produced *AM* still has the capacity to astound. How were they able to accomplish so much so rapidly? Most important was the selection of Georges Salmon to head the MSM. When recruited in Egypt in 1902 by Gaston Maspéro, Salmon was already an established orientalist with numerous publications. While not a specialist on North Africa, he was a brilliant Arabist. Moreover, he had shown an instinct for finding important manuscripts, as well as an ability to manage several projects at once, and a work ethic to bring them to a successful conclusion.

But Salmon was not alone in bringing about the success of *AM*. His colleague, Édouard Michaux-Bellaire, had a deeply informed understanding of

Moroccan society and culture based on his twenty-year residence in Morocco, most of it in the countryside around al-Qsar al-Kabir and also at Tangier. Previously unknown to Le Chatelier, Michaux-Bellaire appears to have been recommended by someone in the French Legation. His vast knowledge of Moroccan culture and society, his many personal contacts with Moroccans, together with his prodigious work ethic made him an excellent match for Salmon, the accomplished Arabist and academic. A merchant interested in Moroccan society, Michaux-Bellaire spoke Moroccan Arabic fluently, wore Moroccan clothing, and lived in al-Qasr. His deep immersion in matters Moroccan enabled him to produce a series of ethnohistorical studies of particular local communities notable for their historical complexity and depth of analysis. Had there been no Michaux-Bellaire, the critics who objected to Salmon's lack of Moroccan experience might have found more of an audience. In the event, the regular appearance of *AM* soon put an end to all such caviling.

The relationship of the two men seems to have clicked from the beginning. In 1904 Salmon went to El Ksar to spend a month at the Michaux-Bellaire's country home. What he saw astonished him: "Mr. M-B is truly a precious guide. He has lived here for many years and knows everyone. He lives entirely à la marocaine, wearing Arab [dress] and speaks Arabic sufficiently well to fool many Moroccans. Thanks to him we will obtain a great deal. Yesterday we spent all day questioning students about [the availability of] local manuscripts. We're sure we'll obtain them."[9] (The problem of obtaining loans of Arabic materials was not so easily conjured. It turned out that an interpreter at the French Legation had absconded with a manuscript after promising to return it. The experience of such one-sided cultural "borrowings" continued to bedevil relations with Moroccans.)

The early issues of *AM* provided detailed information about Moroccan cultural and legal realities of interest to French businessmen as well as to diplomats and the military. Salmon's discovery that tribes in the area around Tangier enjoyed private and transmissible rights to land was immediately seen by knowledgeable French readers as providing a point of entry for French investors interested in acquiring property in Morocco. Also, studies of land ownership and Islamic pious endowments (Ar. *waqf*) included in volume 1 provided readers with reliable information on local property law—in sharp contrast to Algeria, where the French had been very late to grasp the nuances of Islamic property law.[10] In another example, policymakers noted with interest that quasi-feudal landholdings (*azib*) of Moroccan marabouts enjoyed tax-exempt status hedged about by supernatural sanctions.[11] Similarly, a study of the administrative structure of the Tangier municipality was keyed to French political and commercial interests. The early articles' disproportionate focus on northwestern Morocco reflected Michaux-Bellaire's long residence in the region.

The topic of the Moroccan tax system, a mystery to most Europeans at the time, was taken up in the first issue of *AM*. According to Michaux-Bellaire (and contrary to received European opinion), Morocco had a functioning tax system that had to be taken into consideration when doing business there or in planning the modernization of the country's fiscal structure. The article provided examples of the amounts of the taxes and the different categories of Moroccan land law under international treaties (including the Madrid Convention of 1881). It concluded with an analysis of the *tartib* of 1901 (which had established a new general tax on agriculture) and its likely impact on Europeans owning property in Morocco. Michaux-Bellaire's approach was practical, not theoretical—the very opposite of the erudite studies of Paris orientalists or the Algiers folklorists and native affairs consultants.

Salmon's translation of an Arabic manuscript by Ibn al-Tayyib al-Qadiri on the Idrisi shurafa, also in the first volume of *AM*, provided an abundance of empirical information about the main sharifian groups in Morocco and their current descendants.[12] In it, Salmon took up many questions of interest to French policymakers: What were the origins of the Alawite dynasty? What was its relation to other sharifian lineages in Morocco, in particular to its main rival, the Idrisi-s, who traced themselves to Mawlay Idris, the founder of Fez?[13] Might the latter be an alternative royal line, if things went badly with the Alawites? Which branches of sharifism were still politically potent in Morocco? The article was a revelation to French policymakers.

An excerpt from the *Hulal al-Bahiya,* an Arabic manuscript written by an anonymous Fasi author, appeared in the third issue of volume 1 of *AM*.[14] Its publication opened a window onto Moroccan responses to the 1899 French conquest of the Touat oasis in the central Sahara. It constituted a rare French acknowledgment of the existence of a Moroccan claim to the Saharan oases (which remains an impediment to a comprehensive settlement of the Algero-Moroccan frontier today).[15] French policy planners might not have been quite so surprised at Moroccan reactions to their policies had they taken the existence of Moroccan political responses more seriously.

While Tangier was a good base for the MSM, in view of the latter's dependence on Arabic books and manuscripts, a study mission to Fez was necessary. It is there that the court resided and the leading religious and educational institutions were to be found. Although Fez, its institutions, and leading figures remained largely unknown, unraveling its mysteries had never appeared more important. Salmon and Michaux-Bellaire set about planning a trip to Fez in early 1904. Its purpose was to acquire the documentary basis for a study of Moroccan written culture (religion, law, history) by purchasing as many Moroccan Arabic books and manuscripts as possible. The publication of Arabic texts in initial issues of *AM* had already had a dramatic effect. The sharpened focus on the literate culture of Morocco helped move French attention to law, history, and religious doctrine. It also implicitly strengthened the hand of the French government in its insistence that Morocco was a sovereign state with a complex culture—the basis of its *makhzan* policy. By the same token it undermined the perception that Morocco was a mere assemblage of superstitious tribesmen, as the supporters of the tribes policy contended. The focus on Arabic written culture would allow French planners to more fully understand Moroccan realities without putting French researchers at risk in the field.

With the British no longer an obstacle thanks to the entente cordiale and financial control of Morocco assured by the 1904 loan agreement, the French deemed that the time was ripe to present their long-deferred reform plan to the Moroccan government. Thus it was that Georges Saint-René-Taillandier, the French minister at Tangier, announced his intention to travel to Fez in January 1905. The timing of the Saint-René mission threatened to compromise the MSM expedition before it could set out. After consulting with his ministers, Abd al-Aziz declared his opposition to the proposed French reform plan, which he saw (not entirely unreasonably) as a disguised protectorate treaty. Since Saint-René was keen on having Salmon and Michaux-Bellaire accompany him, the MSM mission threatened to become entangled in the poisoned atmosphere of the Moroccan question. But to join Saint-René's embassy would almost certainly have compromised its integrity, which depended upon good relations with Moroccans.[16] While Le Chatelier intervened in Paris to protect the MSM, Salmon engaged in lengthy discussions with Saint-René. Eventually he was able to make the latter understand that close association with the diplomatic mission threatened to sabotage his own. Finally the plan was agreed. Salmon wrote to Le Chatelier: "I'll leave three weeks [after Saint-René], hire a good *fqih* to help with [acquiring] manuscripts, while relations with [*makhzan*] officials will be organized by Ben Ghabrit." In concluding, he requested that Le Chatelier urge the Quai d'Orsay to issue an authorization to Salmon to consult the archives of the French Legation in Tangier as well as French consulates in Morocco.[17] Salmon and Michaux-Bellaire then bided their time until after the departure of the French diplomatic mission in early January. Only in March 1905 did they set forth. Their objective: to gather Arabic manuscripts as well as oral testimonies on the operation of the Moroccan government, the role of the ulama and the bourgeoisie of Fez.

No sooner arrived in Fez than Salmon was able to see for himself how adversely the French diplomatic mission had affected the political environment. As popular sentiment in Fez grew more anti-French by the day, Sultan Abd al-Aziz had convened an assembly of notables to rule on the suitability of the reforms. The main aim of the Salmon mission had been to purchase Arabic books from local booksellers and private individuals. In the highly politicized context, Moroccan dealers were unwilling to sell books and manuscripts directly to Europeans.[18] In order to get around this problem, Salmon decided to work through a Moroccan intermediary. Here the role of Michaux-Bellaire and the legation's Algerian translator Si Kaddour Ibn Ghabrit proved invaluable. Their optimism, however, was misplaced. Once it became clear for whom he was working, the *talib* they had hired as an intermediary was attacked and savagely beaten by an angry crowd. The *talib* was lucky to get away with his life. In the eyes of the citizens of Fez, book buying was viewed as a form of espionage.

Nonetheless the Salmon expedition was a huge success. It brought back to Tangier some 163 lithographed Arabic books (only 50 existed in all the libraries of Europe at the time), as well as 30 original Arabic manuscripts and abundant additional written documentation. (For a complete list of the books acquired by the Fez mission of Salmon, see Le Chatelier's account in *AM*.)[19] These purchases secured the future of the MSM, which quickly became *the* source for authoritative documentation on Morocco, much consulted by all European (not just French) diplomats and policy advisers. Even the hitherto skeptical *Afrique française* was impressed with the vast amount of documentation recovered: "Thanks to his hard work in Fez, he [Salmon] managed to pull together in a few months sufficient documentation to occupy him for several years of research and translation works. To these works must be added moreover the numerous volumes that Salmon, this young scholar of 30 years of age, has already produced on Moroccan manners and customs."[20]

The euphoria surrounding the success of the Fez mission dissipated rapidly, however, when Salmon died on August 22, 1905, from the effects of dysentery contracted during his last week in Fez. His passing brought to an end the first phase in the history of the MSM.

In the first phase of its existence the MSM made a vital but little known contribution to furthering French ambitions in Morocco through its role at the Algeciras conference. However, following the German intervention in 1905 the political context changed dramatically. The convening of an international conference at Algeciras, a Spanish port just across the Strait of Gibraltar, provided the occasion for demonstrating the expertise of the MSM to the diplomatic corps. To obtain the international backing of the conference, it was crucial that French diplomats demonstrate their superior understanding of the Moroccan dossier. Thus the stakes were high when the delegates met in Algeciras between January 16 and April 7, 1906, to consider possible reform plans to be introduced to Morocco. Looking back on the conference, Paul Révoil, the head of the French delegation to Algeciras, asserted that French ethnographic authority gave France a crucial advantage:

> As of now, the *Archives marocaines* has rendered a precious service to our Moroccan policy, independently of the progress that its example has imposed on all other studies of Morocco. It is easy to understand this [point] from the role of the Mission at Algeciras where it was represented by widely distributed [copies of] the *AM* to the different missions—as well as the additional services it will render in Morocco. This [occasion] was practically of the same order [of magnitude] as M. Salmon's intervention in the discussions (at the preparatory sessions in Tangier the previous year) relative to expropriation under Moroccan law—which the Moroccan delegates claimed to be contrary to the sharia, and of which he was able to demonstrate the legitimacy sanctioned by use.[21]

Révoil went on to state: "The MSM is thus one of the most justified institutions of our Moroccan policy. One can say that it has imposed itself even upon our most informed experts." It is nonetheless important to add that while Révoil believed in the importance of the MSM in presenting the French case at Algeciras, he came to this position late in the game. Before the conference it had required a personal letter from Le Chatelier to George

Louis of the Ministry of Foreign Affairs to get Révoil to include the MSM in the French delegation.[22] Révoil had also been reluctant to make use of Eugène Aubin, despite the fact that he was the best-informed French diplomat on Moroccan affairs at the time. Mysteriously, Aubin was not included in the French delegation at the last minute.[23]

From the perspective of Franco-Moroccan relations, the Algeciras conference marked a major turning point in the dynamics of the Moroccan question. It coincided with the application of reforms that were mandated by the 1904 Franco-Moroccan loan agreement, among them the establishment of an international debt commission (Controle de la dette), on the model of the debt commissions established earlier in Egypt and the Ottoman Empire.[24] As European officials took up positions in Moroccan ports to oversee the collection of customs revenues, their presence stoked Moroccan resentment. When the reforms agreed on by the powers at the Algeciras conference were rolled out in 1906 they occasioned much anger and resentment. One particular source of conflict emerged: the formation of an international police force in Moroccan port cities. Comprised of European-trained Moroccan units (*tabors*) under French and Spanish officers, the port police were charged with maintaining order. Although popular anger in the ports was already palpable, no thought was apparently given to the likely feedback caused by instituting so many reforms simultaneously. Moroccan reactions appear to have caught European observers completely by surprise, though in retrospect such a response should have been predictable. As French researchers began to encounter popular hostility, they became the object of violence, and two Frenchmen (Alfred Charbonnier, Émile Mauchamps) were killed by angry mobs.[25] By late 1906, field research in the Moroccan interior had become impossible. The second phase of social research on Morocco had begun.

THE COMITÉ DE L'AFRIQUE FRANÇAISE

The Comité de l'Afrique française (CAF) and its subsidiary, the Comité du Maroc (CM), were the leading nongovernmental sponsors of study missions to Morocco between 1900 and 1912.[26] In fact, the CAF supported study missions throughout French colonial Africa, and not just in Morocco. Its purpose was to energize the colonial lobby, specifically the members of the CAF (and especially the major donors). It also made available documents and research reports to enable informed citizens to intervene in public debates in support of colonial expansion. With its wide contacts, the CAF was able to involve other interested donors—matching up government ministries, colonial governments, geographical societies, and private funding sources with specific projects. The CAF/CM "seal of approval" was vital to assembling and funding research missions. Sometimes the CAF role was limited to obtaining prior ministerial approval for the publication of excerpts from official reports likely to be of interest to readers of the *Bulletin* or its monthly supplement, *Renseignements coloniaux* (*RC*). In other circumstances, the CAF might take the initiative in launching particular missions without the direct participation of the French government, as a way of assisting the latter in maintaining "plausible deniability."

Unlike the MSM, the CAF was not a publicly funded research institution. Its Moroccan expeditions and study missions were not the expression of a coherent research strategy. Rather, they were commissioned piecemeal in response to individual proposals from academics, military officers in the field, and unaffiliated explorers. The CAF in turn passed them on to the Ministry of War and other agencies of the French government. Over the period 1900–1912 (according to published records), the CAF/CM dispensed in excess of 300,000 francs for Moroccan study missions and expeditions. A 1907 published partial accounting noted that the expenses of the Tangier office alone totaled 58,500 francs. Of this sum, 4,000 francs were spent on four study missions, with another 6,000 francs being used to pay informants and to gather information.[27] (In fact, it is impossible to come up with an accurate accounting of CAF-funded missions given the vague criteria regarding what constituted CAF backing.)

Over the period 1900–1912 the CAF sponsored more than fifty study missions to Morocco (see table 1). While some of the grant recipients were faculty members at the École d'Alger, others were not. Researchers communicated directly with Auguste Terrier, the secretary-general of the CAF. The missions had various origins, objectives, and funding sources, ranging from months-long field research expeditions to short junkets for French businessmen. For example, how should one count the more or less permanent hydrographic mission headed by Commandant Alfred-Henri Dyé that systematically mapped the rivers of Morocco in the period 1904–7.[28] Although *Afrique française* lists some of the Dyé expeditions, its accounting is almost certainly incomplete. Should his hydrographic mission be counted as one long study mission, or as a series of individual ones? In the end, I have decided not to count the Dyé missions, since their ethnographic content is minimal. Finally,

TABLE 1 French Research Expeditions to Morocco, 1899–1912
Sponsored by the Comité de l'Afrique française

1899	De Segonzac (Rif Mountains)
1900	De Segonzac (southern Morocco Berber areas) Brives (southern Morocco) Moulieras (Fez)
1901	Brives (southern Morocco/western High Atlas) Doutté (southern Morocco plains) De Segonzac (Sous)
1902	Doutté (Houz)
1903	Brives (W. Atlas)
1904	Bernard (northern Morocco) Brives (southern Morocco/western High Atlas) Doutté (Ihahen) Lemoine (western High Atlas) De Segonzac, Gentil & Buchet (southern Morocco/western High Atlas) Gentil, Buchet, de Flotte de Rocquevaire (Sous)
1905	Gentil & de Flotte (Sous) Gentil (southern Morocco) de Flotte (southern Morocco) Brives (southern Morocco)
1906–7	Brives (southern Morocco)
1907	Gentil (Atlas Mountains)
1908	Gentil (southern Morocco)
1909	Gentil (Chaouia)

NOTE: In most cases, summary reports of the above expeditions were published in *Afrique française* and/or its monthly supplement, *Renseignements coloniaux*. Some had multiple sponsorships. In addition, some resulted in monographs and articles.

EXPEDITION LEADERS: Augustin Bernard made multiple trips; Auguste Brives made five trips to Morocco (see his *Voyages au Maroc, 1901–1907* [Algiers: A. Jourdan, 1909], Dec. 3, 1901–Feb. 25, 1902, July 23–Oct. 7, 1903, Jan. 3–May 30, 1904, Aug. 15–Oct. 10, 1905, Nov. 10, 1906–July 24, 1907); Edmond Doutté made multiple trips (four); René de Flotte de Rocquevaire had multiple itineraries in 1905; Louis Gentil made seven trips and traveled with Louis Buchet in September 1904 and participated in the February 1910 Segonzac mission in Chaouia; René de Segonzac made multiple trips (four?).

there were the CAF study missions that sought to introduce French business-men and opinion makers to Moroccan realities in the period 1911–12. Should these be counted as officially sanctioned study missions, since their value to science was approximately nil? Or were they junkets for lobbyists? Such distinctions, while making clearer the complex problems of an attempt to identify the ethnographic missions, are beside the point, and not of interest to us in this book.

But which ethnographic missions are of interest? In the end I have decided to focus on the contributions of the twenty-five highest-profile study missions financed by the CAF between 1900 and 1907. These missions range from the high-profile expeditions of Edmond Doutté and René de Segonzac, each of whom led five study missions, to that of Auguste Mouliéras, who led but a single ill-fated study mission (discussed in chapter 8).[29] In addition, it seems plausible to include the geological missions of Louis Gentil (five total) and Abel Brives (also five) as well as those of geographers Augustin Bernard and Paul Lemoine (one each), since they also gathered a great deal of political intelligence on Moroccan society. In effect these seven individuals accounted for all twenty-five CAF ethnographic/political missions to Morocco during the period.

Because of the difficult political environment, the ethnographic missions were carefully organized. The researchers traveled in disguise, were heavily armed, and depended on interpreters and native informants. They covered as much territory as possible as rapidly as possible. Funds were scarce, and university vacations brief. Together these individuals added greatly to French knowledge of the populations of southern Morocco, especially the *tashelhit*-speaking Berbers of the High Atlas Mountains. The rest of this section reviews the specific contributions of the CAF/CM study missions to the Moroccan colonial archive. The CAF study missions to the Moroccan interior came to an end following the 1907 murder of Émile Mauchamps in Marrakech.[30]

The most important contributor to the ethnographic study missions was Edmond Doutté, whose impressive organizational skills and deep interest in North African folklore and religion made his study mission of particular interest. Doutté was enthralled by the details of popular religion: saint cults, belief in magic, curing rituals, all situated against the background of James Frazer's *Golden Bough* and Durkheimian sociology.[31] Despite his sometimes fragile health, Doutté's work ethic was phenomenal. In addition, the erudition of his work from this period was remarkable.[32] His earlier (non-Moroccan production) has been discussed in the previous chapter. Doutté's Moroccan expeditions in the period 1900–1905 were intended to expand his comparative sociology of popular Islam in North Africa by adding Moroccan examples. His second (1901) and third (1902) expeditions moved through the southern Moroccan countryside, collecting detailed information on popular religion and saint cults.[33] This research was later deployed in his 1905 book, *Merrakech,* a work of scholarly erudition that focused on cultural survivals, magical aspects of Sufism, and superstitions.[34] The book must have been a disappointment to French experts because of the dearth of politically relevant detail. The fourth expedition (summer 1904) is the only one to which scholars still refer. It focused primarily on the political structures and folk beliefs of the Ihahen Berbers in the region between Mogador (Essaouira) and Marrakech.[35] One of the first examinations of a Berber tribe and its relationship to the *makhzan,* it merits comparison with Michaux-Bellaire's ethnohistorical studies of the tribes of the Gharb published in *AM.*

In addition to his scholarly work, Doutté periodically advised the French government about its Morocco policy. His confidential reports show him in a different light—as a provider of intelligence to imperial policymakers. His 1900 report has been discussed in the previous chapter. In 1907 Doutté was called on to evaluate the political situation in southern Morocco in the midst of the Hafiziya insurrection. This secret report remained unpublished but was circulated within the French bureaucracy.[36]

Another important figure (although not an academic) was René de Segonzac (1867–1962). A French aristocrat and veteran of the Armée d'Afrique who came late in life to exploration, Segonzac led five expeditions to Morocco in the period under study, all of them funded by the CAF. His peregrinations charted broad swaths of the mountainous regions of Morocco from the Rif to the High Atlas, adding greatly to French geographical knowledge. Like Charles de Foucauld (on whom he modeled his approach), he undertook his arduous journeys disguised as a Moroccan (the disguises varied) and without the official authorization of the *makhzan.* An 1899 expedition to the Sous Valley was subsequently published in 1901 under the title *Excursion au Sous.*[37] A second book, *Voyages au Maroc (1899–1901),* incorporated his travels through the Western High Atlas, the Middle Atlas, and the Rif.[38] *Au Coeur de l'Atlas,* the book for which he is best known, was supported by grants from the CM and a host of other institutions.[39] It included more than two hundred pages of geographical information and hundreds of photographs.

The CAF/CM also sponsored a number of geological and geographic missions in the period, which while primarily scientific also collected ethnographic and political intelligence. For this reason they are of interest to us here. Among the most important were those of Abel Brives (1868–1928) and Louis Gentil (1868–1925), which mapped the geology and geography of the Western High Atlas Mountains.[40] In mapping the mountains, Brives and Gentil surveyed the terrain for future military action (including the attitudes of local tribes toward the French). Brives, a French Algerian geologist, conducted a total of five expeditions into the Moroccan interior in the period 1901–7. His *Voyages au Maroc (1901–1907)* provided a baseline for measuring subsequent accounts. Gentil's *Dans le Bled es Siba* summarizes his expeditions in the period 1905–6. Gentil was the first European to describe the *qanat* (filtration gallery) irrigation system of the Marrakech plains region. He recorded that everywhere he went, the local inhabitants manifested a "very marked animosity to the *roumis* [Europeans] who have come to spy upon the Bled es Siba."[41]

The findings of the CAF geological expeditions made possible the publication of the first modern map of Morocco.[42] Louis Gentil's *Le Maroc physique* (1912) was the first scientific account of the geology of Morocco It was Gentil who discovered the junction point of the three major Moroccan geological plates during a 1909 expedition in the territory of the Zaer, southeast of Rabat.[43] Otherwise French geological discoveries in this period were meager. Despite the fact that Morocco had been an important producer of silver and copper in medieval times, the geological expeditions produced no economically important mineral discoveries. More embarrassing still, French geologists failed to discover the mineral resource for which modern Morocco is known: the massive phosphate deposits of Ouen Zem were discovered only after the establishment of the protectorate.[44] Before the advent of artificial fertilizers, mineral phosphates were a basic component of modern high-input agriculture. Today Morocco is the dominant producer of phosphates in the world.

THE REORGANIZATION OF THE MISSION SCIENTIFIQUE DU MAROC

The question of who would succeed Salmon at the MSM was quickly decided. Under the circumstances, there was only one real choice: Édouard Michaux-Bellaire (1857–1930). But who was he? Despite his importance to the history of Morocco and the origins of Moroccan social science, even today relatively little is known about Michaux-Bellaire's life or what originally brought him to Morocco at the age of twenty-seven.[45] According to one source, he dressed in Moroccan clothing and adopted a Moroccan lifestyle while living with a Moroccan woman.[46] The little we know of his French political beliefs puts him squarely in the mainstream of the French republican Left of the period.

A testimony of how he was regarded was his election as head (*doyen*) of the French community in Tangier and president of the Comité de la mission laïque.[47] He also served as honorary vice-consul in El Ksar in the 1890s and even briefly as interim vice-consul in Fez. His deep knowledge of Moroccan culture and Moroccan Arabic made him an obvious choice as Salmon's replacement.

Nonetheless, the reorganization of the MSM took more than a year to accomplish. Michaux-Bellaire's selection seemed obvious to well-informed observers, though his lack of academic degrees or training provoked the opposition of the Ministry of Public Instruction. Already critical of Le Chatelier, the ministry tried to force on him the appointment of an archaeologist who did not know Arabic.[48] Then there was the question of putting the MSM on a more stable administrative footing. From the beginning the operation of the MSM had depended on ad hoc arrangements with the French Legation for personnel to translate its Arabic documents. This situation too was addressed in the reorganization.

By the end of 1905, the MSM found itself in a new building with a spacious new library housing 40,000 books and manuscripts (many in Arabic) (making it by far the largest library devoted to Moroccan studies in the world). Its staff of five included Michaux-Bellaire, one translator-interpreter, and three translator-interpreter interns. (The latter were recent graduates of the École des langues orientales, hired for a year as interns with the guarantee of jobs at the French Legation thereafter.) This arrangement gave the MSM the stability it needed, and proved attractive to potential interns as well. The interns were assigned to translate the Arabic documents and manuscripts brought from Fez. The results (thirteen issues of *AM,* more than 5,000 printed pages in three years) spoke for themselves.

Once confirmed as head of the MSM, Michaux-Bellaire was able to reorganize the staff, produce quality copy, meet deadlines, and maintain the publication schedule. With the aid of the intern translators, Michaux-Bellaire was able to produce a dozen volumes from the materials gathered at Fez over the next several years. Here we see the solidity of the system put in place by Le Chatelier and Salmon. Under Michaux-Bellaire's stewardship, *AM* shifted away from shorter articles, translated documents, and in-depth ethnohistorical studies of its beginnings. Instead it exploited the rich trove of Arabic manuscript materials gathered at Fez. Evaluating its contributions, Paul Révoil asserted: "This publication fills, in consequence, a lacunae often mentioned for Algeria and Tunisia, where, in the absence of social studies of the same order undertaken and carried out systematically, the causes of misunderstandings multiplied between our government and that of the natives." [49]

Years later, looking back on the early days of the MSM, Michaux-Bellaire remarked on the importance of Le Chatelier's system:

> The work of Le Chatelier . . . is considerable. . . . He took part in all the work, issued directives, made plans, often helping us to get past difficulties [by] putting things back on track when they seemed to go astray, [and by insisting on rewriting] that which appeared to him poorly written. In a word, it is to him that the Mission scientifique owed not only its creation but also its production and it is always in conformity with his methods that the Section sociologique operates today.[50]

Le Chatelier's vision of the MSM as a clearinghouse for ideas and policies, together with his instinct for selecting ideas and colleagues, were vital to its success. Le Chatelier drew on his years as a native affairs officer in Algeria, and his subsequent career as a military intellectual working for the Ministry of War, to hone his editorial and organizational skills. From his time in the Arab Bureaux he learned to organize field data drawn from many sources.[51] In writing his monographs *Mémoire sur le Maroc* (1890) and *L'Islam dans l'Afrique Occidentale* (1899), he developed a system for organizing collaborative writing projects that he drew on in editing *AM*.[52] For each issue of *AM* he would select the topics of the essays to be written by Salmon. Working jointly, Le Chatelier and the MSM team would next develop an outline for each essay and assign work tasks and deadlines to each collaborator. Initially, Le Chatelier made available his extensive personal database of *fiches de tribu* on Morocco. It goes without saying that without Le Chatelier's Paris political network, the MSM would have had no chance of surviving the attacks of its enemies nor would its message have received so favorable a response.

. . .

This chapter has traced the emergence of the discourse on Moroccan culture and society, "Moroccan Islam," and a new discipline, Moroccan studies. The MSM and École d'Alger were anchored in different institutional contexts and tended to recruit researchers from different intellectual milieus—École des langues orientales vivantes in the case of MSM, and the École d'Alger for CAF/CM. The fruit of divergent initiatives and intellectual approaches, the MSM and the École d'Alger provided an uncertain basis for the consolidation of a coherent vision of Moroccan studies. Of the two, the MSM offered the sounder intellectual legacy and the stronger institutional structures. Its main publication, *AM,* was noted for the high quality of its articles on Moroccan ethnography and history, such that by 1912 its intellectual hegemony was unrivaled. However, the rural studies of the early years had largely ceased by 1906. Thereafter *AM* was primarily known for translations of Arabic documents and manuscripts. While the valorization of Moroccan written culture was unprecedented, it was not social science. In contrast, the study missions sponsored by the CAF were politically provocative, their funding unstable, and their research product of variable interest to policymakers. The MSM and the CAF-sponsored missions did not share a common intellectual vision. After 1906 both research groups became increasingly contaminated by the ambient fears and phantasms of the period. As a consequence, the discursive parameters of Moroccan studies were shaped less by academic intellectual/disciplinary pressures than by the French political context, and the growing importance of Moroccan resistance.

Academically proven, with well-established links to metropolitan centers, French Algerian scholars constituted the largest—indeed the only—alternative source of academic expertise on North African history and culture to the MSM. They dominated the study missions funded by the CAF in the pre-1912 period. Their published and unpublished reports and studies added greatly to French knowledge of southern Morocco, particularly its Berber inhabitants. However, the Algerians lacked institutional structures and protocols for deciding which ideas to valorize and which not to valorize. As we have seen above, by 1900 Algeria had entered a phase of intellectual growth and dynamism marked by a renewal of the study of local dialects and Algerian folklore. French Algerian scholars, among them Edmond Doutté, sought to draw on the growing prestige of the social sciences in France, and the political ascendancy of scientific imperialism, to enhance their authority vis-à-vis their rivals. But despite his ambition and dynamism, Doutté failed to found a school, in the sense of a group of collaborators who could carry forward his intellectual projects.[53] He was undone in part by his fragile health, but even more so by the fact that he was not the head of the École d'Alger during the period. That person was René Basset, a linguist and folklorist whose interests were resolutely focused on Kabyle language and folklore. Thus Durkheimian sociology was slow to penetrate the structures of the Université d'Alger.

Le Chatelier's response to the intellectual provincialism of Algeria was to invoke the social engineering logic of fin-de-siècle scientific imperialism. The title of his chair (*sociologie et sociographie musulmane*) asserted (somewhat disingenuously) a claim to the modern social sciences. Here Le Chatelier's opportunistic effort to capitalize on the label "sociology" mirrors his cynical lack of engagement with the field itself. The intellectual position of the MSM was shaped not only by Le Chatelier's political and intellectual baggage, but by the skills and talents of its first editors, Georges Salmon and Édouard Michaux-Bellaire. Encouraged by Le Chatelier to provide empirical knowledge to French strategists of empire, the MSM initially produced thick descriptions of Moroccan social worlds remarkable for their relative lack of ideological loading, together with translations of important legal and religious texts. Institutionally this left the MSM on the margins with respect to the French intellectual field, as exemplified by the École d'Alger. But by virtue of its alliance with the Quai d'Orsay it was able to implant itself successfully in Tangier and enjoyed institutional continuity, even as *AM* continued to be favorably received by those in power. The interpenetration of the political and intellectual fields continued to shape the destiny of the MSM after 1912.

A reflection of the self-consciously social scientific moment in which it emerged, by 1912 the Moroccan colonial archive constituted the most important social science record of any Islamic society compiled in the colonial period. Colonial studies of Islam in Algeria, British India, and the Dutch East Indies (the main rivals) were lacking in various respects. Most of the writings on Algeria were deeply flawed by partisanship, or lacking in rigor. While the Indian colonial archive was the envy of French colonial theorists, little of it focused specifically on Muslims.[54] However, as this chapter has suggested, while impressive in certain regards, Moroccan studies was deeply imbued with the colonial binary stereotypes of the Algerian colonial gospel. The next chapter examines how, following the establishment of the protectorate, Moroccan studies became more complexly woven into its fabric.

PART TWO

Native Policy Morocco

The officer who has successfully drawn an exact ethnographic map of the territory he commands is close to achieving [its] complete pacification, soon to be followed by the form of organization he judges most appropriate.

GENERAL JOSEPH-SIMON GALLIENI, *Trois Colonnes au Tonkin, 1894–1895* (PARIS: R. CHAPELOT, 1898), 154

[Real] peaceful penetration consists of putting a thousand with rifles against a hundred fellows with pop-guns.

COMMANDANT FARIAU, QUOTED IN AUGUSTE FÉLIX CHARLES DE BEAUPOIL, COMTE DE SAINT-AULAIRE, *Confession d'un Vieux Diplomate* (PARIS: FLAMMARION, 1953), 123

SIX

Social Research in the Technocolony, 1912–1925

AFTER THE MAY 1911 RELIEF of the siege of Fez (see chapter 2), French troops occupied the land corridor between Rabat and Fez and imposed French authority on the refractory tribesmen. With no further resistance in the months that followed, the path to a French protectorate seemed smooth. Economically Morocco had long since lost its independence. The Moroccan public debt belonged to a consortium of French banks, and the Compagnie marocaine, a consortium of French industrialist businesses, was busily acquiring Moroccan land and mineral rights with *makhzan* approval.[1] French policymakers had reached a consensus about the future of Morocco. It would become a protectorate juridically similar to Tunisia with a resident-general who would report administratively to the Quai d'Orsay. The protectorate's native administration would be modeled on the Tunisian system of *controleurs civils,* while the French army's role would be limited to putting down rebellious tribes where necessary. All that remained was for the French to obtain Abd al-Hafiz's signature on the protectorate treaty.

BEFORE "THE REVOLUTION"

It was in this context that Edmond Doutté was commissioned by the Quai d'Orsay in January 1912 to provide a confidential assessment of the political situation, and make suggestions regarding native administration under the protectorate.[2] Doutté recognized that the political situation was dicey and that what he called Moroccan xenophobia was widespread. Yet despite resistance to French rule, he postulated, Moroccans were ready for progress. Doutté began by making a basic point. Unlike Algeria, Morocco was not "une poussière de tribus" (a tribal dust heap)—a reference to Paul Cambon's pronouncement regarding late nineteenth-century Algeria.[3] Instead Morocco had a social division of labor (which as a good Durkheimian, Doutté saw as a sign of progress).[4] Running down his checklist, Doutté asked, Had the *makhzan* not provided Morocco with a literary language, a religion, a legal system, a measure of security, equal justice among the tribes, freedom of trade, and the emancipation of the individual from the guardianship of the tribe? These were major achievements, he insisted.[5] Staking out a position in the future policy debate, he denounced those poorly informed individuals who had succumbed to the myth surrounding the "Lords of the Atlas." What some call Moroccan feudalism, he stated, "does not exist." There was no example in Moroccan history, he insisted, of a great chief who had been able to transform his governorship into hereditary rule. He insisted that the great *qaids* posed no threat to French rule. The events of the next months were to demonstrate just how optimistic this account was.

Doutté's proposal for the native administration of the Moroccan protectorate reflected the political realities of winter 1912 (at least as viewed from Paris). It was based on the distinction between areas of military rule (where the tribes had only recently surrendered to French authority) and areas of civilian rule. Doutté took care to specify that the protectorate should be erected "behind the screen of the makhzan." In order "to avoid creating a native aristocracy, as we did in Algeria where it required enormous effort to destroy after having created it with our own hands." Instead (no doubt well aware of what the Quai d'Orsay intended to do) he proposed a native administration on the Tunisian model, in which local districts would be placed under *makhzan* control. While local Moroccan officials would be appointed to assist French civilian officials as "the sultan's delegates," all the power would be in the hands of their French "advisors." Direct contact with the tribal populations should be restricted to native affairs officers, while Moroccans in districts under civil rule would be under the authority of consular officials. Reflecting contemporary Algerian thinking about the errors of French Kabyle policy, Doutté suggested that Arabizing the Berbers would be a mistake. Instead, he urged that Berber populations be governed by non-Muslim intermediaries (he seems to have meant the *controleurs civils*). He also recommended breaking up large tribal confederations and banning private vengeance and the feud. He summarized his policy line as follows: "Apply a makhzen policy to the bled el makhzen, and a tribes policy in the Bled siba." Doutté's policy line here echoed the tribes policy he had publicly supported in 1904.[6] In an aside, he suggested that the École d'Alger be granted control over social research on Morocco.

Matters did not proceed according to expectations, however. In a stunning development, the signature of the Treaty of Fez on March 30, 1912, was followed not by the installation of a new French order, but by the mutiny of Moroccan troops against their French instructors on April 17. The mutiny instantly obviated all prior prognostications. It is hard to imagine the degree of chaos that ensued. Caught by surprise, the French government had to revise its plans on the spot. Ambassador Henri Regnault, a career diplomat, had been sent to Fez to obtain the sultan's signature on the protectorate treaty with the expectation that he would be named resident-general. In the confusion that followed the mutiny, it became clear to French policymakers that Morocco required a different approach. The idea of organizing Morocco along the lines of the Tunisian protectorate also had to be abandoned, at least for now. Only a military general with experience in the new methods of colonial governance could restore order. Regnault was informed that he would have to step aside. Within a few weeks his replacement was selected: Louis Hubert Gonzalve Lyautey (1854–1934).

Lyautey's appointment dramatically altered the situation and set the Moroccan protectorate on a different track. Soon after his arrival in Fez on May 24, Lyautey found himself confronted with an even bigger crisis: that very night the city came under sustained and coordinated siege from a coalition of nearby tribes, in league with inhabitants of the city. Simultaneously, the nearby cities of Meknes and Sefrou also came under attack. While French politicians and experts dithered, Lyautey's judgment was clear:

> Those who know this country have never noticed a rise of fanaticism and xenophobia so deep and so generalized ... it's that there are two Moroccos, that prior to the events of 17 April and the proclamation of the Protectorate, and that after them, there is a historic gulf, a Revolution, and this is what France does not see.[7]

The persistence of Moroccan resistance throughout the summer tied down French military forces in the Fez-Meknes region. A national resistance movement was taking shape.

The ability of the French government to arrange a smooth transfer of power to a new sultan of its own choosing was thwarted by Sultan Abd al-Hafiz's refusal to resign. In the meantime, other crises threatened in central and southern Morocco. By July there were credible reports that

Marrakech was in danger of falling into the hands of supporters of Mawlay Ahmad Haybat Allah (known as El Hiba), a millenarian Saharan leader. Simultaneously came reports from the southern Middle Atlas that the Zaian, a powerful Berber confederation, were organizing. Their leader, Moha ou Hamou, was alleged to be in contact with the Fez area insurgents, El Hiba, and more problematically, Abd al-Hafiz. In the summer of 1912, Lyautey was confronted with all of these crises at once. By the end of September the insurgents in the Fez-Meknes region had been temporarily dispersed, El Hiba had been vanquished, Marrakech was occupied by French troops, and Sultan Abd al-Hafiz had been forced to abdicate and go into exile. The building of the protectorate could finally begin. However, the legacy of "the Revolution" proved more resilient than French policymakers imagined.

· · ·

This chapter considers the transformations of Moroccan Islam following the establishment of the French protectorate. New institutional imperatives were engaged, and the achievements of the MSM and the École d'Alger were reevaluated in terms of their relevance to the needs of the colonial state. The enthusiasm of the formative years faded in the face of the complex demands of building the protectorate. In the meantime, the tendency for the stereotypes of the Algerian colonial gospel to assert themselves became irreversible. The decisions taken in the early years of the protectorate shaped the development of its institutions.[8]

THE MOROCCAN PROTECTORATE
AND BRITISH INDIA

Consideration of the establishment of the French protectorate as a world event is central to rewriting Moroccan colonial history. If we accept that Morocco was but one of many countries that underwent the experience of colonialism, we are able to move away from a binary colonizer/colonized narrative toward a more complex, dynamic, and multicausal world historical narrative. After all, it was not foreordained that Morocco would become a French protectorate, or that the protectorate would take shape as it did. Nor was Lyautey destined to become its resident-general. Awareness of the multiply contingent character of the French protectorate is a central feature of

Daniel Rivet's magisterial *Lyautey et l'institution du protectorat français au Maroc* (1988) The decisions made by individuals and groups, and the sequence in which events unspooled, shaped the available alternatives for all actors, opening some possibilities and forestalling others. In the light of these considerations Moroccan precolonial protest and resistance were key in shaping French and Moroccan options in 1912

Upon closer inspection, the French protectorate appears to have been shaped by the chaotic collision of multidimensional political forces, rather than being the product of carefully designed French policies. In this sense, the early Moroccan protectorate represented not the triumph of the "Lyautey method" or of French scientific spirit, but rather what the French call "Système D" or "muddling through." It is only retrospectively that the origins of the protectorate appear as the systematic application of a previously devised plan. In fact there was a plan; it was the attempt to apply the principles of what was then called "scientific imperialism"—that is, Lyautey's attempt to apply the lessons of British India to Morocco. But, as we will see in this chapter, this plan was systematically thwarted by developments both in Morocco and in France.

An expression of the new positivist confidence in social analysis, the doctrine of scientific imperialism was based on the comparative study of colonial administrations. That it also reflected the widening gulf between European and colonial societies is an insight that is available to us only now. Leading French policymakers and colonial officials had long wished to organize the Moroccan protectorate in accordance with the contemporary theories of scientific imperialism. Louis Hubert Lyautey, who had first encountered the new military sociology while serving as Gallieni's subordinate in Indochina and Madagascar, was a strong backer of the policy of scientific imperialism. Morocco provided a new context for the conduct of ethnographic research on the British model, one that was more purpose-driven, and more closely linked to the needs of the conquest. Although Lyautey sought to adopt the approach of the new scientific imperialism in the months that followed these events, that dream was soon rendered unfeasible. But let us consider what was at stake, and why the protectorate did not follow this path.

Inspired by Joseph Chailley-Bert, Lyautey looked to British India for models of what worked. The French problem, colonial theorists agreed, lay not in military pacification (at which the Gallieni/Lyautey system had proven its effectiveness), but in the domain of colonial governance. What Morocco required, the theorists agreed, was a system of colonial governance inspired by the best practices of other colonial powers, notably the British in India. Lyautey had considerable experience in colonial warfare (Algeria, Indochina, Madagascar) and was a strong supporter of Chailley-Bert's approach to comparative colonial administration. (Lyautey offered this terse comparison of the British and French approaches: "British power, unified conception, continuity in design, governmental stability, inflexible method, instantaneous execution, practical sense, tenacity, flexible adaptation to countries and climates. In a word, everything we're not.")[9] Lyautey believed that the French protectorate in Morocco would do well to consider the British example. Central to his strategy was the establishment of an administrative staff college for the training of native affairs personnel, the Bureau politique. The graduates of the Bureau politique would be rigorously schooled in Moroccan languages (Arabic and Berber), as well as in Moroccan history, politics, and culture and the main elements of Moroccan law (both sharia and customary law).

But what was the British system of rule in South Asia? According to historian Clive Dewey, Indian colonial governance consisted in the gathering of knowledge about colonial populations and governance and its implementation by a highly trained core of officials. After the 1856 mutiny, India was ruled by the Crown via the senior Indian Civil Service (I.C.S.). Indian Civil Service officers were the most powerful officials in the empire, if not the world.[10] A tiny cadre, only 1,200 strong that governed more than 300 million Indians, the Indian Civil Service directed all the activities of the Anglo-Indian state. Each civilian (as they were called) ruled over an average 300,000 subjects, and each civilian penetrated every corner of his subjects' lives.[11] Known as "the steel frame of empire," the officials of the Indian Civil Service were recruited via a rigorous meritocratic examination (for which, until the late nineteenth century, no Indians could apply).[12]

By comparison, training and recruitment of French North African administrators were lacking. Lyautey regarded Algerian experience as especially problematic. The corruption and partisanship of the civilian officials, and the high-handedness of the officers of the Arab Bureaux, were legendary. While the Tunisian system had been created to avoid the excesses of the military rule of the Arab Bureaux, its standards of recruitment were low (there was no entrance examination and knowledge of Arabic was optional), and candidates tended to be appointed based on whom they knew, rather than what. Since he was eager to establish a modern, professional native administration in Morocco, Lyautey looked toward British India for models of what worked.[13]

In India, the local I.C.S. administrators were tasked to provide information on South Asian societies, customs, and history in response to official questionnaires. The results were collated and published in provincial and local gazetteers, whose purpose it was to introduce newly arrived officials to the locales to which they had been posted.[14] Nothing like the provincial gazetteer existed for any part of the French empire. Multivolume compendia like the *Description de l'Égypte* and the *Exploration scientifique de l'Algérie* had their origins in the Enlightenment project of Diderot's *Encyclopédie*. Their scientific taxonomies lacked the local detail and applicability that colonial officials required. Lyautey believed that Morocco needed its own versions of the British Indian handbooks and gazetteers. It is here that the French doctrine of scientific imperialism became relevant.

The May 1912 revolution galvanized a French effort to develop the governmental capabilities of the protectorate. Morocco was to be an example of the technocolony, a conservative monarchy where respect and homage was accorded the Moroccan crown and religious and social hierarchies while real power lay with French agents of authority. A Moroccan sultan who was seen but not heard was the perfect complement to an omnipresent French protectorate administration, with its insatiable needs for social documentation and control. The Moroccan protectorate gave Lyautey an opportunity to put theory into practice with the establishment of institutions of surveillance and control. Who knew? Morocco might even serve as a pilot project for a restored French monarchy.

In Lyautey's Morocco, questions of governmentality and the ordering of the state were to be keyed to the rational apprehension of the population in its statistical manifestations, the manipulation of social hierarchies and groups, and the coercive deployment of instruments of power. Symbols of authority were theatrically deployed in an effort to bring about the willing consent of Moroccan subjects in the colonial enterprise. Every detail of the organization of the protectorate would be rationally conceived and ordered in the function of the whole. Morocco would develop a modern agricultural and mineral-extracting economy in alliance with the Compagnie marocaine, whose holdings dwarfed all other economic players in Morocco.[15] Small-stake settlers and businessmen would be permitted to establish themselves, but only at the sufferance of the Residence générale. A settler democracy on the Algerian model was to be avoided at all costs. More specifically in the present context, the new Morocco would be based on the establishment of a modern system of native government based on systematic intelligence and scientific observation of the indigenous population by trained administrative personnel. That, in any event, was Lyautey's plan. The reality turned out to be somewhat different.

THE COLONIAL ARCHIVE INSTITUTIONALIZED

The April mutiny and the coordinated insurgency of May 21, 1912, seriously compromised the launch of the protectorate.[16] Not only did "the Revolution" (as Lyautey referred to it) call into question the wisdom of having a diplomat serve as resident-general; it also rendered obsolete the plan to have native governance performed by the consular corps. The political unrest in Morocco and the inability of French policymakers to get a handle on Moroccan resistance made evident the need for a strong native policy–planning department. The implications of the new situation were not lost on Alfred Le Chatelier, the founder of the Mission scientifique du Maroc (MSM) and editor of the *Revue du monde musulman,* who was an important backstage participant in the struggles for a scientifically based native policy. This is where matters rested until the fall of 1912.

With the military/political situation in Morocco relatively stable, Lyautey returned to Paris and immediately plunged into discussion with political and military leaders about the future of the protectorate. Eager to set up a native affairs research and training administrative unit, he also had a series of previously little known meetings with Le Chatelier in Paris and Vichy. As a result of these meetings, Le Chatelier drafted a lengthy letter to Lyautey on January 10, 1913, summarizing their discussions. He began by laying out his vision of how the MSM might be restructured under the protectorate.[17] Le Chatelier began by urging the establishment of a native affairs staff college (the Bureau politique), and the printing of works modeled on the handbooks and gazetteers of British India, as well as more scientifically grounded publications such as *Archives marocaines* (*AM*).[18] He provided a cost estimate for each of the proposed items.[19] In reply, Lyautey wrote expressing his belief that the MSM's proven record of competence made it an excellent choice for this task: "We are agreed on the essentials, on the need for an intensely active policy with a solid scientific basis, agreed also on the shape of procedures—documentation, publication and the use of political agents."[20] Leaving aside the question of the political bureau, Lyautey added that he would very much like to appoint as central political agent someone who would serve as Le

Chatelier's delegate to the Residency General, and as his main liaison with the regional political agents. Perhaps Michaux-Bellaire would be suitable?[21] It is clear from reading this exchange that Lyautey's plan drew heavily on Le Chatelier's earlier proposal for an *école d'application*.[22]

On March 31 the revised proposal was sent to the ministers of foreign affairs and war. It called for the establishment of an administrative staff college to be called the Political Agents of the Protectorate. Charged with the training of native affairs officers, it would report directly to Lyautey.[23] He began with a brief presentation of the necessity of funding and rethinking the mission of the MSM under the protectorate:

> At the moment we begin the heavy task of the organization of the protectorate, I very much want to be able to make a broad appeal for the assistance of the Mission scientifique du Maroc under the authority of its General Delegate. I completely share the views of M. A. Le Chatelier on the need to provide Morocco rapidly with a native policy strongly based upon science and sociology, and I have already received major contributions from him. It seems especially important to me that it [the Mission scientifique] be enabled to continue [its collaboration] with me without delay, a measure to which I attach a great interest. I submit it to you at the moment of my departure without waiting for the proposals that I'll make to the Minister of Foreign Affairs.[24]

Before broaching the subject of the Bureau politique, Lyautey laid out his view of colonial governance. He began with a frank assessment of the political situation in Morocco: "The natives are distanced from us by the psychological factor of hatred. They must be drawn toward us by the psychological factor of [personal] advantage." The new *makhzan* must stand for justice and avoid identifying with the old *makhzan* traditions of exploitation: "When a lying vizir is publicly, 'noisily' executed, when a *qaid* who collects taxes without providing receipts is punished in front of everyone, we can reduce the occupation forces by 20%. But it is crucial that repressive justice be exercised with certainty and publicly with pomp and circumstance." Summing up his views, he stated: "It is imperative that a native knows, understands, that there is material profit in our domination."[25]

In the same letter Lyautey suggested that Charles René-Leclerc (then the *delégué générale* of the Comité du Maroc in Tangier) be assigned to encourage native agriculture and commerce. Urban trade fairs, exhibits, and Berber festivals should also be encouraged. "Don't take land away [from the natives], encourage agricultural development," he said. By the same token, Lyautey called for the establishment of schools and medical dispensaries. While it is hard to affect people's ways of thinking, he insisted, Moroccans were more capable of rapid evolution than Algerians. In the conclusion to this letter (perhaps signaling growing tensions), he defiantly stated that until the Ministry of Foreign Affairs and the Ministry of Public Instruction agreed to fund this project, he would no longer correspond directly with either minister.[26]

A key aspect of Lyautey's plan was the establishment of a staff college on the model of the I.C.S. This would be accomplished by converting the MSM from a research unit into an agency charged with training political agents for the protectorate: "The Mission scientifique will intervene to recruit, train and direct the political agents from the technical point of view."[27] According to the Le Chatelier plan, the political agents would select either a military or an administrative career path, and then be assigned to govern a local district. The MSM would also provide informational briefings to the Bureau politique and the resident-general, but would otherwise have no decision-making authority. Civilian political agents were to be recruited primarily from the graduates of the École des langues orientales and the École d'Alger—since these were the chief places providing training in Arabic interpretation. Once selected, they would serve a three-year internship at the MSM before being sent into the field. Simultaneously Lyautey established a new administrative unit, the regional political agents, whose charge was to assist in centralizing the collection and dissemination of information about the populations in each region. The existing regional military intelligence libraries were to be centralized at the Bureau politique of the Résidence générale in Rabat. At first, it looked as though everything was on track.

That summer the outlines of Lyautey's proposal circulated in the corridors of the Quai d'Orsay. On August 27 the foreign minister, Stephen Pichon, wrote requesting a full proposal, along with Lyautey's justifications for the establishment of a new agency.[28] In his reply, the resident-general evoked the volatile political situation he had inherited and the need to limit the expenditure of blood and treasure. He reviewed his arguments for the creation of a body of political agents of the protectorate, asserting that his method was cheaper in the long run. Such a policy was delicate, requiring suppleness and a perfect knowledge of which arguments to use, when, and with what likely effects. Only in this way would it be possible to gradually persuade Moroccans to accept the protectorate authorities. "Nothing in Morocco," he stated, "enabled me to design such a policy. The scientific basis was almost entirely lacking due to the nature and essentially closed character of the country."[29] The Political Agents of the Protectorate alone could provide the necessary scientific basis for organizing a native policy, he asserted. Previous historians have largely ignored the efforts of Lyautey and Le Chatelier to impose a radically different native policy regime on Morocco, one grounded in social research and a trained corps of native affairs personnel.

Under Lyautey's proposal the Political Agents of the Protectorate would not be directly involved in administration. Rather they would focus on gathering the scientific documentation required for rational policy planning. Their role would be advisory and consultative, not administrative. While nominally under the authority of the regional military commanders in Morocco, they were ultimately under the authority of the Residency General (Résidence générale), via the Directory of Political Affairs (Direction des affaires politiques). Whereas the Dutch in Indonesia and the British in India had developed an administrative structure of political agents charged with the administration and documentation of native peoples, neither *controleurs civils* (as in Tunisia) nor *agents de renseignements* (as in Algeria) were comparable. Moreover, they lacked the required prior experience and training in native affairs, and their other duties precluded their having the necessary time to undertake such studies. The question of who would fund the new agency (the Residency General or the Quai d'Orsay) was left pending. Lyautey concluded his proposal with a call for its immediate endorsement.[30]

Perhaps predictably, the proposal was summarily rejected by Pichon, under whose authority the Moroccan protectorate ultimately lay. Pichon's summary dismissal of the Lyautey plan opens for inspection a central contradiction of the Moroccan protectorate: the continuing struggle between the Residency General and the Foreign Ministry. From the start, the Quai d'Orsay had never wanted a military man to be resident-general. Indeed until the April 17 uprising, career diplomat Henri Regnault had expected the job to be his. In the confusion following the uprising, any thoughts of a smooth transition of power had to be abandoned. Regnault had been compelled to withdraw. However, while the Quai d'Orsay had been compelled to acquiesce in Lyautey's appointment, it battled to retain its administrative control over Morocco. From the outset the Residence générale found itself caught in a struggle with the Quai d'Orsay over who was in charge. Even the naming of the native policy–planning bureau came under close scrutiny. Anything that smacked of the Arab Bureaux was rejected by the Quai d'Orsay as being too military, and thus a challenge to its authority. In the end, the native affairs office was called the Service de renseignements—a nomenclature selected for its vagueness. (Only after the departure of Lyautey in 1926, was its name officially changed to Services des affaires indigènes.)

A sign of the situation of divided rule was the establishment of the Moroccan *controleurs civils* on July 13, 1913. Unable to prevent their creation, Lyautey sought Quai d'Orsay agreement that candidates for the *controleurs civils* would have to undergo rigorous training and pass an Arabic proficiency examination before their appointment. However, he was unsuccessful in placing the selection and training of future *Controleurs civils* under the authority of the Residency.[31] Had Lyautey's plan for a training school for native affairs officials and for the establishment of a Bureau politique been enacted, it would have granted the resident-general close control over native administration and the training and appointment of local French officials, and produced a much more "British"-style colonial administration. Right up to its final days the Moroccan protectorate bore the imprint of the division between military and civilian control. The conflict raised major questions about native policy, the formation of intellectual disciplines, and even the nature of the Moroccan state. The evolution of social research on Morocco was thereby closely interwoven with the struggles over the early protectorate's administrative structures. New debates were provoked in the process.

THE NEW ROLE OF THE MISSION SCIENTIFIQUE

Despite the Foreign Ministry's rejection of the Lyautey/Le Chatelier proposal for a native affairs agent training school, other elements of the British Indian colonial repertoire proved easier to adopt. These included the redefinition of the role of the MSM and the launching of a new publication series, Villes et Tribus du Maroc. The decisions made in this period consolidated the place of the MSM in the protectorate administration, while also distancing it from the new academic field of Moroccan studies, which was emerging in Rabat.

At the center of Lyautey's new native policy team was the political agent who would serve as his delegate to the Résidence générale. Édouard Michaux-Bellaire, editor of *AM,* was selected to fill this position. As Lyautey wrote to Le Chatelier, "[He] will be your constant representative to me, will incarnate your doctrine and [thus] make possible the best interface with the regional [political] agents. He'll be my direct advisor, working ceaselessly in your name with my political service." The question of where to locate the offices of the MSM proved to be more difficult to resolve. In the end Lyautey favored keeping its offices in Tangier (the base of the MSM since its foundation). This would better safeguard its special character and enable it to keep an eye on things in that city, which was fated to come under international jurisdiction (being incorporated into either the French or the Spanish protectorate). The alternative choice, Salé, was located across the Bou Regreg River from Rabat. By opting for Tangier, the decision was inevitably interpreted as a deliberate distancing of the MSM from the corridors of power.

In the same letter Lyautey stated his preference that the MSM be confined to the production of research for the protectorate government. Implicitly this meant it would not be excluded from the emerging academic field of Moroccan studies as well as from research on Berber studies.[32] While this was presumably not what Le Chatelier expected, he was delighted that most of his proposals had won favor. He quickly sent along draft decrees intended to clarify the role of the MSM.[33] Lyautey's reply could not have been more reassuring: "I attach a high price to seeing the development of individual initiatives for the establishment of sociological studies aimed at completing the rest of our [knowledge of Morocco]."[34]

In the new division of labor, *Archives marocaines,* the chief publication of the MSM, was endowed with a new mission. The early issues of *AM* had contained many striking ethnographic essays (most of which had been written by Michaux-Bellaire and Salmon) that together demonstrated France's commitment to scientific imperialism. After 1912, the focus of *AM* shifted to the production of authoritative translations of important Arabic works. With Michaux-Bellaire seconded to native affairs, the new emphasis maximized the talents of the editorial staff, which consisted primarily of young translators on loan from the French Legation in Tangier. The Arabic documents were invariably well selected and translated, and their publication enabled the French to gain a better understanding of the complexities of the Moroccan cultural scene. They included, for example, Ahmad b. Khalid al-Nasiri's chronicle, *Kitab al-Istiqsa.* In its new format *AM* was reduced to two issues per year. It continued to have a ready audience among French native policy intellectuals in the protectorate.

One bureaucratic oddity was that the Mission scientifique remained a budgetary dependency of the Ministry of Public Instruction (as it had been from the outset), rather than of the protectorate, at the annual rate of 30,000 francs. Only following the retirement of Lyautey (1925) and Le Chatelier (1926) was it possible to redefine the role of the MSM (and funding sources). At this point it was renamed the Mission sociologique du Maroc and became a budgetary responsibility of the protectorate. These changes also marked an important transformation of the protectorate itself, since France by this time was deeply involved in the Rif war against Abd al-Krim al-Khattabi (1921–26), where the Lyautey methods were widely believed to have failed.[35] From a deeper perspective, the new name also signified that the MSM had become more routinized and less in touch with the always shifting bureaucratic realities.

VILLES ET TRIBUS DU MAROC

The launching of a new MSM publication series, Villes et Tribus du Maroc, was another sign of the influence of British colonial India. The new series was intended to make available a systematic ethnohistorical survey of Morocco (on the model of the provincial gazetteers). The idea for the series derived from the ill-fated 1907 French military intervention in the Chaouia (Ar. Shawiya), which had been experienced by the French military as a massive intelligence failure. The administrative history of this project is deeply interwoven with the attempts to win approval of the Bureau politique and to reorganize the MSM. In 1907 the Chaouia campaign had provoked embarrassing questions from French politicians and the press.[36] The French higher command, especially those in tune with the new scientific imperialist dogma, were startled that things could go so wrong so fast. The protectorate could not be built on ethnographic confusion.[37] The Ministry of War ordered Lyautey to Rabat to prepare an official report on the Chaouia campaign (though he never appears to have done so). It also commissioned the collection of oral histories and *fiches de tribu,* but otherwise nothing was done.

For Le Chatelier the existence of the Chaouia intelligence data represented an opportunity for the MSM. In early 1913 he wrote to Lyautey proposing that the MSM staff edit a series of volumes to be called Villes et Tribus du Maroc. The first two volumes would focus on Casablanca and its region and would be based on the previously collected information. Lyautey, seeing an opportunity to develop a Moroccan equivalent of the British gazetteers of India, was an enthusiastic supporter. He announced to the foreign minister, Pichon, that the new series was in preparation.[38] Simultaneously he informed Le Chatelier that he had ordered relevant documents and maps to be made available to the MSM for this purpose. Lyautey's support for the Villes et Tribus series could not have been more emphatic. Although the two men were agreed on the development of the Villes et Tribus du Maroc series, they disagreed over its contents and had rival conceptions of its purpose.

Authorized by an administrative decree of October 18, 1913, the Villes et Tribus series sought to provide agents of the native affairs administration with detailed local information on Moroccan regions. It specified that

> all notices produced in the different regions [of Morocco] bearing upon the ethnographic, historical, sociological, economic and administrative condition of the cities and tribes of Morocco, works of any nature, emanating from officials of the Protectorate, having a sociological character or of interest to native policy, that the Resident General may deem useful to publish will be gathered in a documentary collection published under the auspices of the Residency General by the Mission scientifique du Maroc.[39]

The fruit of a sustained collaboration between the MSM and French native affairs agents, the Villes et Tribus series was placed under the general editorship of Édouard Michaux-Bellaire. The writing of the volumes was organized according to Le Chatelier's system of subdividing complex editorial tasks, which assigned achievable goals to subordinates. Le Chatelier suggested to Michaux-Bellaire that one member of the MSM staff be tasked to prepare each of the Casablanca and Chaouia volumes. "Prepare a draft, then send a specialist to verify the facts on the spot," he wrote. With this editorial system in place, it was possible to maintain an ambitious publication schedule. Although the plan for the Villes et Tribus series had Lyautey's support, it soon encountered resistance elsewhere.

In Le Chatelier's original conception, the Villes et Tribus du Maroc series had included volumes on Rabat and its region; the south Atlantic coast (Azemmour, Safi, and Mazagan and their region); Meknes and the Middle Atlas Berber tribes; Fez and its hinterland; the Tadla region; Marrakech and the Hawz; the region around the port of Mogador; Figuig and the tribes of the Guir valley; and Oujda and the tribes of the Moulouya River valley. In retrospect, the vast ambition of the series assured that it would never be completed. That said, it is striking is how much in fact was accomplished (for a list of volumes published in the series, see table 2).

TABLE 2   Mission scientifique du Maroc
Villes et Tribus du Maroc: Documents et Renseignements
11 volumes (1915–1932)

Casablanca et les Chaouia	
Volume 1	*Casablanca et les Chaouia* (Paris: Ernest Leroux, 1913)
Volume 2	*Les tribus* (Paris: Ernest Leroux, 1913)
Rabat et sa région	
Volume 3	*Les villes avant la conquête* (Paris: Leroux, 1918)
Volume 4	*Les villes après la conquête* (Paris: Leroux, 1918)
Volume 5	*Les tribus* (Paris: Leroux, 1918)
Volume 6	*Le Gharb (Les Djabala)* (Paris: Leroux, 1918)
Tanger et sa zone	
Volume 7	*Tanger et sa zone* (Paris: Leroux, 1921)
Tribus berbères	
Volume 8	Commandant Léopold Victor Justinard *Les Aït ba Amran* (Paris: Honoré Champion, 1930)
Volume 9	Général Georges Spillmann *Districts et tribus de la Haute Vallée du Dra'* (Paris: Honoré Champion, 1931)
Région du Doukkala	
Volume 10	*Les Doukkala* (Paris: Honoré Champion, 1932)
Volume 11	*Azemmour et sa banlieue* (Paris: Honoré Champion, 1932)

Casablanca et les Chaouia consisted of two volumes—the first on the history and ethnography of Casablanca and its immediate hinterland, and the second on the tribes of the Chaouia province. Each tribe was discussed separately, starting with its history, basic sociological and ethnographic characteristics, economic promise, and the names of its chief leaders and groups. In effect the editors of *Casablanca et les Chaouia* merged the categories of the *fiche de tribu* with more modern sociological and economic categories of analysis. Unlike the journalistic accounts produced at the time, the editors sought to identify the motives of the Casablanca protesters and to understand why the French intervention had spun out of control. They provided a remarkably clear-eyed account of the social roots of the Chaouia *siba* and all that ensued. Nothing in the literature of French colonial Morocco approaches the level of historical detachment in these two volumes.

As might have been expected in the case of two such strong-minded individuals, Lyautey and Le Chatelier soon fell out over editorial control of the *Casablanca et les Chaouia* volumes. Their disagreements, which took various forms, had begun in 1912. From the outset, Le Chatelier was determined to restrict the focus of the two volumes to the Moroccan tribes of the Chaouia at the time of the uprising, whereas Lyautey wanted to enlarge the coverage to include material on post-1907 colonial society in the Chaouia province. While the publisher was already printing the manuscript, Le Chatelier sought to excise this material, or at least to place it in an appendix. There were huge cost overruns. When Le Chatelier made these known, Lyautey requested a detailed list of the contents.

Lyautey's micromanagement extended to the cover and title page. Le Chatelier insisted that it should say only "Résidence générale de la France au Maroc," whereas for Lyautey it was imperative that it say "Bureau politique," referring to the administrative body that had just been scrapped by the Quai d'Orsay. For Le Chatelier this formula made it appear as though the MSM was integrated into the military chain of command, and therefore signified the appropriation of the MSM by the native affairs department. In response Lyautey claimed that the rubric "Bureau politique" was just a transitory formula (although in fact it was the very symbol of his dream of organizing the administration of Morocco on the model of British colonial India). In an effort to resolve the dispute, Le Chatelier requested that the publisher, Ernest Leroux, print different proof versions of the cover and send them to Lyautey.[40]

The two men had a more substantive disagreement over the contents and purpose of the Chaouia volumes. Le Chatelier wanted them to contain only ethnographic information, modeled on the *fiche de tribu* of colonial Algeria. Lyautey wanted them to be much more inclusive, so that by reading them a political agent arriving in Morocco would know all he needed to know in order to function. In a letter of December 11, 1913, to Le Chatelier, Lyautey argued that the aim of the Villes et Tribus series was to create a "body of knowledge," that is, "anything connected to the geography, the colonization [of the land, or] the economic condition of the country." He insisted that if this material were relegated to an appendix (as Le Chatelier proposed), this would insure that it would not be read. Lyautey insisted that the political agents needed to be informed not only about native society and culture but also about the Moroccan economy. At one point in the dispute, Lyautey proposed that the volumes have several tables of contents, not just one. Finally, in an effort to accommodate Michaux-Bellaire's concerns, Lyautey agreed that the cover refer to the volumes as having been produced by the Bureau de renseignements rather than the Bureau politique.[41]

Le Chatelier's introduction to volume 1 noted the considerable quantity of reports and studies provided to the MSM (the better no doubt to assert the civilian auspices under which the series was prepared, and to implicitly deny that it was a military project). Along with the observations and replies gathered during the editing of the volume, a vast quantity of source material was collected and subsequently listed in the "Pièces annexes." A published list of the names of all French military officers and *controleurs civils* who had served in the Chaouia over the period 1907–14 was also included. This jumble of materials underscores the lack of consensus between Le Chatelier and Lyautey. (Subsequent volumes would not suffer from this confusion.) Information was carefully cross-checked with the officers in the field (and Michaux-Bellaire and his assistant Marcel Graulle were sent to the Chaouia to verify facts in dispute). The final manuscript was completed on July 14, 1914, but the printing was delayed to the following spring because of the outbreak of World War I. This timing ensured it would never be read.

The focus on cities in the Villes et Tribus series was an important innovation. Except for the Algerian city of Constantine (whose protracted resistance had provoked the interest of administrators) the French had neglected the study of North African cities.[42] But by the time the first volumes of the series appeared, there was no political urgency to analyzing the Moroccan urban scene. The image of Moroccan cities in the rest of the Villes et Tribus series are timeless and largely devoid of politics. Here the statistical method of the Algerian Arab Bureaux has triumphed, and the innovative social historical ethnographies of the early volumes of *AM* have been pushed aside, leaving dutiful lists of leading inhabitants. *Casablanca et les Chaouia* lacked a connected historical account of events.

Taken together, the two volumes of *Casablanca et les Chaouia* were intended to provide basic information for administrators, organized according to standardized categories. Less obviously but nonetheless significantly, they made possible the writing of an alternative history of the Casablanca landings and the Chaouia campaign (1907–8). To obtain this overview, one must assemble it piecemeal from the individual tribal and clan accounts spread over both volumes.[43] A forensic history it is not.

This insight opens up a larger critique: by the time of the publication of the two volumes, French power had completely transformed the dynamics on the ground, making lists of clans, horses, tents, rifles, and so on irrelevant. The machine gun and the howitzer (not to mention the appropriation of Moroccan land) had already drawn a line underneath the supposed political/ military potency such lists purported to describe. When the population of Casablanca reached 35,000 people, its precolonial cityscape had become unrecognizable. By 1918 Casablanca's international trade had begun to stitch the country and city together in new ways, giving advantages to those groups and individuals able to play the French card. The city limits had expanded well into the interior, the surrounding lands purchased by French settlers or by large-scale business interests like the Compagnie marocaine. Landless peasants and their families flocked to the city to seek work as manual laborers, petty tradesmen, colonial soldiers, domestic workers, sex workers, or in rare cases employees of the emerging protectorate government.[44]

The question thus arises, knowing that the worlds described were no longer extant, why did the protectorate government continue to publish the Villes et Tribus series? Surely its value to bureaucratically overburdened and increasingly incurious native affairs officers was close to nil. The chief value of the series lies elsewhere. Its publication must be seen as part of a media campaign to demonstrate that Morocco was in good hands. The first two volumes of the series represented an effort to market the accomplishments of the Lyautey system (just two years into the experiment), and the statistical information they contained was intended to reassure readers of the mastery of the protectorate administration. Thus they were never the "how to" manuals for the colonial administrator that they purported to be (any more than the Indian Civil Service's handbooks were). Finally, the more cynically minded might say that the series was a screen to divert the gaze of observers away from what was happening on the ground—the large-scale appropriation of the land and resources of Morocco.

The Villes et Tribus du Maroc series remains a monument to the dream of a scientific native policy. Both Lyautey and Le Chatelier benefited from the series. It legitimized furhter Lyautey's approach to colonialism (and his image as a technoroyalist), and attested to Le Chatelier's continued relevance to colonial policy. As a result of his role as general editor of the series, Michaux-Bellaire became indispensable to the native policy brain trust of the protectorate, eventually becoming the voice of pre-protectorate Morocco to future generations of native affairs agents.

THE INSTITUT DES HAUTES ÉTUDES MAROCAINES

The CAF/CM-sponsored Moroccan study missions' academic reputation and links to major Parisian educational centers created new opportunities for colonial Algerian scholars in the Moroccan protectorate. These included the launching of an institution of higher education, the École supérieure des lettres, in Morocco, as well as a research unit, the Institut des hautes études marocaines, and *Hespéris,* the first academic journal of Moroccan studies. With the MSM confined to political intelligence, native administration under the protectorate was primarily populated by military administrators and scholars drawn from colonial Algeria. Given Lyautey's well-known antipathy to colonial Algeria, what explains the choice of French Algerian scholars?

The École supérieure des lettres et de la langue berbère was launched in 1915. Although its mission was described as promoting the study of Moroccan history, culture, and institutions, the only academic position listed was a chair of Berber languages. Simultaneously a new research institution was established, the Institut des hautes études marocaines (IHEM), which would share personnel with the university. It was to publish a journal, the *Bulletin de l'Institut des hautes études marocaines et d'études berbères.* At this stage the decision to establish both institutions remained largely theoretical, as other matters of greater importance preoccupied the administration. Nonetheless, a glance at the title of the institute's journal reveals a lack of clarity in the delineation of the institutional relations between the IHEM and the native policy division. By 1917 some of these concerns were resolved, when the journal was retitled *Archives berbères* (in obvious counterpoint to *Archives marocaines*). But the question remained, Would Berber studies be part of the emergent university faculty or an organ of the native policy bureau? The editorial board of *Archives berbères* included a mix of military men and academics, a sign that the institutional lines of authority remained blurred. The editor was Colonel Henri Simon, director of the native affairs section of the Bureau politique, while Mohamed Nehlil, an Algerian Kabyle who taught Berber language in Algiers, was listed on the editorial board. Thus the Algerian academic tradition was merged with that of the Arab Bureaux, but within a far narrower political compass.

The establishment of the École supérieure conformed to the general transformation of French higher education in the pre-1914 period. The politics behind the decision to establish the IHEM and the École supérieure showed Lyautey's political and institutional lucidity. The École d'Alger, while it had no reason to expect favoritism from Lyautey (whose views of the French Algerian mentality were well known), held a major card: it alone could supply the Moroccan protectorate with qualified personnel. Moreover, the personal connections of Doutté and his colleagues with key individuals in the Parisian university world and the Comité de l'Afrique française ensured that the École d'Alger had clout. In the emergent division of labor between native policy management and academic institutions, the MSM was assigned a central role as the clearinghouse of information on Moroccan society, and allocated a provisional mission to train the native affairs personnel of the protectorate. While Le Chatelier may have cherished thoughts of influencing the development of Moroccan studies in the new protectorate, he was poorly placed to bring it about, being neither an academic nor an official. The establishment of the IHEM and the École supérieure represented an implicit statement that by virtue of its monopoly of Moroccan studies France alone among European states was qualified to govern Morocco. In this respect knowledge of Morocco went hand in hand with French power over Morocco, the one being the justification of the other.

The establishment of the IHEM and the École supérieure des lettres in 1921 marked the inception of the academic discipline of Moroccan studies. For Lyautey, the purpose of the École supérieure and the IHEM was to consolidate the accumulation of information about Moroccan society begun by the MSM. As a sign of its new professionalism, the title of the IHEM's journal was changed to *Hespéris,* a Greek name for Morocco.[45] In the years that followed, *Hespéris* was to become the principal space in which expertise on Morocco was fostered, especially in the fields of history and archaeology. Moroccan scholars whose expertise was based on their deep knowledge of Arabic sources were marginalized, creating a de facto racial division of labor. The annual IHEM conferences were attended not only by academics, but also by protectorate officials (sometimes Lyautey himself) and even occasionally by Moroccan scholars (at Lyautey's insistence). The emergence of talented French scholars such as Évariste Lévi-Provençal and Émile Laoust quickly gave the new field an aura of respectability.[46] The new field of Moroccan studies was essentially a French monopoly, with international scholars reduced to the role of observers. From this point onward the history of the social sciences diverged from the humanistic disciplines, as the MSM was incorporated into the Bureau des renseignements. Finally, by a Lyautey decree the Section historique du Maroc was established under the direction of Henry de Castries. Its main role was to publish *Les sources inédites de l'histoire du Maroc,* a series of volumes of European archival documents on the relations of different European countries with Morocco starting in the fifteenth century with the Saadian dynasty.[47] As a result of these developments, the professionalization of Moroccan studies was well under way by the end of World War I.

· · ·

This chapter has focused on the institutionalization of the Moroccan colonial archive after 1912. The structures within which knowledge about Morocco was created, preserved, and diffused were often crucial in determining which ideas were deemed important and therefore worthy of preservation, and which were not. Institutional structures fostered and preserved particular currents of thought, while those lacking an institutional support tended to disperse rapidly. As the deployment of French power changed, so too did the nature and function of orientalist representations in the colonial state. The division of labor was driven less by formal achievements than by personal and institutional connections. In retrospect it is perhaps not surprising that the MSM became the intellectual brain trust for the policy division of the native affairs office, or that the scholars of the École d'Alger dominated the new university and its research branch. Conjunctural developments such as interbureaucratic rivalries and the nature and extent of Moroccan resistance were also significant in shaping the development of the discourse on Moroccan Islam. By historicizing the intersection of the fields of power and knowledge one can trace the links between the evolution of social research on Morocco and the outcomes of policy debates. After 1912, the discourse on Moroccan Islam developed a number of new modalities: Moroccan studies (a new academic discipline), native policy Islam (the application of Moroccan Islam to local governance), and governmental Morocco (the discourse on the colonial state). Together they generated an important part of its legacy to contemporary Morocco.

SEVEN

Berber Policy

TRIBE AND STATE

WHEN THE PROTECTORATE WAS ESTABLISHED, the French had no prior knowledge of the *thamazight*-speaking pastoralist Middle Atlas Berber groups. Ignorance of these groups contributed to a major debacle in the period 1912–14, when French measures to introduce security provoked instead a series of major rebellions. Gradually the French came to realize that there were crucial differences between the *tashelhit*-speaking groups of southern Morocco, the *tarifit* speakers of northern Morocco, and the *thamazight* speakers of the Middle Atlas.[1] Whereas the former two were hierarchically organized sedentary agriculturalists, the latter were acephalous (having no permanent leaders) pastoral transhumants. After several significant military reverses, French control over the Berber areas gradually solidified. But when the French sought to establish a native policy in Morocco in 1930 modeled on the stereotypes of the Algerian Kabyle myth, this transparent effort to play divide and rule provoked the first large-scale expression of Moroccan nationalist indignation. Thereafter French Berber policy, having prematurely been hailed a success, became a persistent weak point of the protectorate government.

THE ORIGINS OF LYAUTEY'S BERBER POLICY

The inability of French troops to suppress the resistance of the *thamazight*-speaking Berbers of the Middle Atlas constituted a vexatious and dangerous situation in the early protectorate. The lack of a coherent French understanding of the diversity of Middle Atlas Berber societies and cultures signaled a failure in French policy and set off a major struggle in native policy circles.

Lyautey's initial willingness to rely on the Mission scientifique du Maroc (MSM) as the official source of policy analysis was challenged by both the officers in charge of suppressing Middle Atlas resistance and the Algerian experts charged with launching the École supérieure des lettres in Rabat. This chapter begins with two questions: Why was it was so difficult for the French to develop a workable analysis of the complex world of Moroccan Berber societies? What light does this failure shed on the relationship of knowledge and power in colonial Morocco? The answers, we will discover, lie in a consideration of interconnections between colonial representations, ethnography, and native policy.

The image of Berbers in pre-protectorate Morocco was remarkably slow to cohere. Frenchmen familiar with the Berber-speaking Kabyles of Algeria tended to assume that Moroccan Berbers were essentially similar to their Algerian cousins. In addition, they had trouble reaching agreement about basic facts concerning Berber societies. For example, there are passages in Charles de Foucauld's *Reconnaissance au Maroc* that describe the Berbers of the Atlas Mountains in terms of the stereotypes of the Algerian Kabyle myth, while others employ a more nuanced language that suggested the folly of dichotomous formulations. The Marquis de Segonzac, on the other hand, expressed negative, indeed frankly racist, views about the *thamazight*-speaking Moroccan Berbers in his account of his 1907 expedition. The striking thing about Berber groups, he asserted, was their religious intransigence, political anarchy, and immorality, not to mention their ugliness and brutality.[2] Indeed, he implies these characteristics can be found among all Moroccan Berbers. However, his views were unusual at the time, perhaps because the French lacked knowledge and experience of Morocco's Berber groups. In contrast, Eugène Aubin was mostly mute on the subject of the Berbers of *bled el-siba,* for example, having traveled little among them.[3] Prejudice did not necessarily interfere with empirical observations. For example, Edmond Doutté took pains to disassociate himself from the Kabylophilia of the period. But instead of insisting on the distinction between Arabs and Berbers in Morocco in 1901, Doutté minimized it: "As much in Morocco as in Algeria the ethnic division of natives into "Arabs" and "Berbers" is a vain distinction, because no criteria can be invoked on which to base this distinction."[4] Just as one could find Arab speakers who used to speak Berber and vice versa, he insisted, nomadic and sedentary populations could be found who spoke both languages:

The word "Berber" has no precise sense except a linguistic one, where it designates a group of dialects closely allied by common character. . . . One can thus, if one wishes, divide [North] Africans into Berberophones and Arabophones; into nomads and sedentaries; into numerous anatomical types; but the ethnic classification into Arab and Berber corresponds to no concrete fact capable of being singled out.[5]

Doutté's more nuanced and empirically grounded view helps set off his position from those expressed in Algeria at the time, which tended toward the dichotomies of the Algerian colonial gospel. Nonetheless, it should be noted that Doutté (here perhaps displaying his Algerian colonial roots) frankly disliked Arabs, and feared the results of the Arabization of the Berbers: "This arabization, at least in the limits of our present field of observation, generally coincides with a recrudescence of fanaticism in religious sentiment and with a considerable lowering of morality."[6] Nonetheless, his distinction between Arabs and Berbers remained founded primarily on linguistic evidence. He restrained his impulses to wax enthusiastic in favor of the supposed superior virtues of Berbers over Arabs. Later students of Moroccan Berbers would not be so scrupulous.

Perhaps because ethnographic observations of Moroccan Berbers in the pre-1912 period varied, the French failed to devise a coherent policy line based on the supposed distinctions between Arabs and Berbers. One who urged the adoption of a pro-Berber policy was the secretary-general of the CM, Robert de Caix [de Saint-Aymour]. But his was far from being the majority view at the time. More typical was the attitude of Augustin Bernard:

As for the attitude of Berbers and Arabs toward French penetration, it doesn't differ as much as is sometimes imagined. Doubtless there are differences between them that can and must be taken into account, but we should give up building a policy on it, any more than one was built in France on the Celtic, Germanic, or Roman origin of the inhabitants, even supposing it [to be] known. The Arabs and the Berbers are too mixed, their social state especially is too similar, for one to be able to radically oppose them against one another, as we used to believe could be done.[7]

Lyautey did not find the differences between Berber and Arab to be relevant to native policy at the time either.[8] The conclusion seems clear: in the pre-1912 period there was no Moroccan "Kabyle myth," nor was there a French Berber policy for Morocco.

However, differences can be found between French representations of Moroccan Berber society found in *Archives marocaines* (*AM*) and those published in the *Bulletin* of the CAF. At the time the focus of *AM* was primarily if not exclusively on the Arabic culture and history of Morocco. Neither Georges Salmon nor the succession of interpreters on loan to the MSM from the French Legation in Tangier had any knowledge of Berber language or culture. Édouard Michaux-Bellaire had lived among the Arabic-speaking groups of the Lukkus River valley, and spoke no Berber. As for experience with Berber populations, he had but a limited amount. By 1912, the MSM scholars had produced not a single study of a Berber tribe. In sum, *AM* was of limited utility to French policymakers interested in "Berberistan."

In contrast, the study missions of the CM had focused on the Berber-speaking regions of southern Morocco. Nonetheless, its research reports, when assessed in terms of ethnographic yield, show few significant studies of Berbers. This is perhaps not hard to understand, since (with the exception of sociologist Edmond Doutté) most of the other leaders of these expeditions were geographers and geologists with no prior experience in Morocco. While their missions led to a vastly improved understanding of Morocco geology and topography, they produced not a single study of the political organization of a *tashelhit*-speaking Berber tribe. The exception was Doutté's important ethnographic study of the Ihahen, previously discussed. The geologists further accredited the belief in the "feudal" origins of powerful Berber chieftains of the High Atlas—the so-called great *qaids*—but their observations lacked ethnographic detail. At no point was the *Berberité* of the great *qaids* made central to an analysis of their power. Paul Lemoine's 1905 suggestion that France ally itself with the great *qaids* appears to have gone unheeded. Similarly, Lemoine's discovery of the importance of *leffs* (village-based factions) in the politics of the High Atlas, which formed a crucial basis for later French policy, excited no interest at the time.[9]

The conclusion that emerges from this survey of pre-1912 French ethnographic writing about Moroccan Berbers is therefore mixed. Although some authors urged France to pursue a policy that took advantage of the alleged differences between Arabs and Berbers, others no less insistently denied the differences on which a policy might be based. French efforts to devise a policy grounded in the Berber ethnicity of the Lords of the Atlas would have to await the establishment of the protectorate. Even then, as we shall see, the adoption of a Berber policy was met with stout opposition.

The stubborn resistance of the Middle Atlas Berbers in the period 1911–15 exposed a significant gap in French knowledge of Moroccan society. The Aith Ndhir, whose territory lay to the south of Meknes, can serve as a model of what went wrong. The Aith Ndhir had played a leading role in the siege of Fez and Meknes during the 1911 rebellion, and subsequently in May 1912 again led the tribes of the Meknes area in a much larger challenge to French authority. After being forcibly subdued by French forces toward the end of 1912, they rebelled a third time in the spring of 1913. For the ensuing six months they and their allies were able to threaten communications between Fez and Rabat.[10] None of the policies attempted by protectorate authorities were successful. French efforts to introduce tribal councils (*jama'at*), which had worked in Kabylia, came to naught. So too did efforts to purchase the loyalty of the chiefs, a tactic that had worked in southern Morocco with the great *qaids*. Nothing seemed to apply to the social realities of the Middle Atlas. As the Middle Atlas Berbers were pastoral transhumants, their seasonal migrations rendered them largely immune to policies such as interdicting known hostile elements from access to local markets. Because of their acephalous structure there were no chiefs to bribe.

By 1913, faced with a native policy disaster, the need for a planning group specifically focused on the Middle Atlas groups was clear. But who should lead it, how should it be organized, and where should it be based? The debate over Berber policy tended inevitably to become a debate over ethnographic knowledge. But the unknowns were many, and not only empirical. As we will see, contending policy groups each had significant bureaucratic and political points of attachment, and the debate threatened to expose serious rifts in the protectorate administration.

But where should a Berber study center be established, and who should run it? The stalemate led to the emergence of several rival projects. But as late as 1914 no resolution seemed at hand. Lyautey and his policy staff were unable to focus on the Middle Atlas because the continuing political instability in the Marrakech region after 1912 took priority. Until it was resolved, no troops could be diverted to the Middle Atlas. Moreover, the early protectorate was plagued by bureaucratic confusion and tangled lines of authority. Every major decision provoked enormous in-fighting between the Résidence générale, the Foreign Ministry (which had oversight responsibility for the Moroccan protectorate), and the Ministry of War (which controlled the troops in the field). On several occasions Lyautey offered his resignation in frustration, before being persuaded to withdraw it. In fact, the Middle Atlas Berber question was not yet ripe for solution. Too little was understood about the history and customs of these groups, or the roots of continued resistance. In addition, officers and men with knowledge of the Middle Atlas were lacking, while troop levels were stretched thin. As a result, it was well into 1914 before it was possible to begin to devise a comprehensive strategy.

A frontal attack on the French post at El Hadjeb in March 1913 by elements of Aith Ndhir and the surrounding tribes provided the necessary catalyst.[11] Within weeks, a major uprising engulfed the entire region, as groups previously uninvolved began to show signs of restiveness. Faced with disaster, Lieutenant Colonel Henrys, the regional commander, was finally able to get the attention of the policy experts in Rabat. With a coalition of Middle Atlas tribes threatening communications between Fez and the Rabat coast the French applied massive force. But they failed to gain the upper hand in the months that followed. As French efforts faltered, they exposed the underlying confusion about how best to deal with the *thamazight*-speaking Berber pastoralists.

Seeking to take advantage of the situation, Le Chatelier wrote to Lyautey in the fall of 1913, proposing that the MSM refocus on producing ethnographic studies of the Middle Atlas Berbers. As late as December Le Chatelier still believed that the MSM would soon be transferred from Tangier to Meknes and be formally incorporated into the protectorate administration and charged with the training of all native affairs personnel (a resurrection of his *école d'application* proposal). He even informed Michaux-Bellaire that the MSM would receive carte blanche to conduct ethnographic research in the Middle Atlas.[12] But over the ensuing months the MSM remained in Tangier, while its incorporation into the protectorate administration encountered unforeseen delays. In fact, the struggle for the control of ethnographic research that pitted the École d'Alger against Le Chatelier had flared up once again. But this time Lyautey concluded that the MSM lacked the required expertise for the job. Neither Michaux-Bellaire nor any of his colleagues had direct knowledge of the Berbers of the Middle Atlas region or knew the *thamazight* dialect. Indeed the conclusion was more far reaching. What was required was research targeted to the needs of native policy planners, not ethnographic studies of Middle Atlas Berbers. By January 1914 the question of research on the Middle Atlas was well and truly posed.

But now there was a new player: the native affairs bureaucracy, which distrusted academic researchers and was filled with confidence in its abilities to chart native policy for the new protectorate. But it too was divided. On the one hand, there was the Rabat-centered native policy planning bureau headed by Colonel Henri Simon (which reported to Lyautey). On the other hand was the Meknes-based operations staff (under the command of Lieutenant Colonel Henrys). While Le Chatelier dreamed of the transformation of the MSM into a Berber policy shop, Henrys was finalizing his own proposal, which was nothing less than the establishment of a Berber studies center at Meknes.[13] It sought to place Berber policy on a solid documentary base—at once scientific and applied. Only an organized research center, he maintained, could gather knowledge about the Berbers from a practical and specifically Moroccan point of view. Its research and teaching would especially benefit French military officers trained in Algeria and called to serve in Berber areas in Morocco. It would complete their education about Moroccan culture and society.

Concretely, the center envisioned by Henrys would have three chairs, with professors of Berber civilization, the Middle Atlas Berber dialect, and customary law under a capable director, and endowed with a library and archives.[14] It would provide the fruits of its research to protectorate officials assigned to Berber districts. Other specialists might be added later, including professors of agronomy, botany, native art, and so on. Finally, the center would publish a new journal, *La revue des questions berbères,* as well as a monograph series. Henrys's plan called for Algerian scholars Edmond Destaing to do ethnographic studies of Middle Atlas Berbers, and Alfred Bel and Émile Laoust to be charged with running the section training teachers for schools in Berber communities; Noyrigat, a soldier who spoke both Arabic and Berber, would coordinate documents in the center. Destaing was charged with dispensing instruction in the rudiments of the *thamazight* Berber dialect, which would be indispensable for officers, teachers, and functionaries.[15] Funding was to be provided provisionally by Henrys from his own budget, although later it would require a line in the protectorate budget.

Henrys carefully sought to position his center by distinguishing Moroccan Berbers from Algerian Kabyles. Whereas the tribal *jama'a* (council) in the Middle Atlas was a living organism, he noted, in Algeria the Kabyle *jama'a* had become a fossilized remnant of a former time. Henrys concluded his proposal by quoting Augustin Bernard to the effect that Berber societies from one end of Morocco to the other had a strange family resemblance to one another, while their differences were more a matter of nuance than strong contrast.

In reply, Lyautey insisted that while he strongly endorsed the idea of a Center for Berber Studies, it should not be located in Meknes, but in Rabat, as part of the central administration of the Residency General, since the Berber question involved all of Morocco, and not just the Middle Atlas. Based in Rabat, the center would have access to the expertise of the faculty of the École supérieure de langue arabe et de dialectes berbères, which had been in de facto operation for two years, even if its formal opening had been delayed by the war. "It is indispensable that the central administration be impregnated by the importance of the Berber question and the means of dealing with Berber populations," wrote Lyautey.[16] Anything as sensitive as Berber policy was best kept under the control of the central administration. It could not be delegated to a regional commander.

Lyautey next had to give Le Chatelier the bad news that the MSM would not be assigned to study the Berber populations of the Middle Atlas.

> To gain a deeper knowledge of the Berber population upon whose territory we have significantly intruded, I have been led to create a Comité d'études berbères in Rabat composed of the civil and military officials of the protec-torate who appear to me to be the best qualified. The mission of this commit-tee is to gather all studies of Berbers done in Morocco and to make them the object of a real investigation [aimed at] providing us with the bases for the policy to pursue toward these populations. These studies would be published in the *Bulletin* edited in Rabat, where all persons interested in Berber ques-tions might find helpful directions.[17]

Lyautey concluded by saying that he would send Le Chatelier the first issue of the *Bulletin* soon, and hoped that he would lend it his full support. Henrys's proposal (and Lyautey's response) suggests that as late as March 1915 neither Le Chatelier nor Michaux-Bellaire was aware of the creation of the Comité d'études berbères, nor of the launching of a new journal, *Archives berbères,* that focused on Berber affairs. This seems inconceivable, but the documentation available does not support a different conclusion.

Unprepared for this news, Le Chatelier mobilized his friends to provide letters of support. General Franchet d'Esperey wrote to Lyautey praising the work of the MSM and stating that as a sign of his eagerness, Le Chatelier was willing to consider moving the MSM from Tangier to Meknes.[18] But the campaign was too little too late. Since the experts on Berber language and customs who staffed both the new center and the École supérieure in Rabat were mostly drawn from Algerian Kabyle specialists, Lyautey's decision amounted to a complete victory for French Algerian experts—a point not lost on François Domergue, who noted with pleasure that most of articles in the first issue of *Archives berbères* were signed by graduates of the École des lettres of Algiers, who "for a long time have been prepared to produce studies that are more methodical and more scientific than many of those previously published."[19]

From a broader perspective, the unexpected resolution of the debate over Berber policy research reveals the existence of a de facto alliance between French military intelligence experts and Algerian Berber specialists. How did it come about? What were the consequences of this alliance for French policy and research on Moroccan Berbers? What were its implications for policy toward Berber populations of other parts of Morocco?

BERBER POLICY AND THE BERBER MYTH, 1912–1919

Thanks to the study missions sponsored by the CM, there was greater awareness of the Berber bloc of southern Marrakech and the role of the great *qaids*. But the lens through which the High Atlas Berbers were apprehended placed little emphasis on their "Berber-ness." Instead it emphasized the role of the picturesque Lords of the Atlas, the great *qaids*. The capture of Marrakech in August 1912 by the forces of el Hiba had emphasized the urgency of developing a comparable analysis of southern Berber societies. One might therefore have expected that southern Morocco would have been the staging ground for the development of Berber policy. But this was not the case. Instead, the native policy adopted for the Atlas was straight out of the playbook of the Algerian Arab Bureaux: deals were cut with the leading great *qaids* on how much autonomy they required, cash was distributed, and the French protectorate administration agreed to stand aside. French policy in southern Morocco was thus a kind of indirect rule *à l'anglaise*, with the Lords of the Atlas standing in for Indian princes. Under this alliance, entire swaths of southern Morocco were governed not by the sultan, the official ruler of Morocco, but by favored local potentates. Whatever the policy was, it certainly did not depend on the supposed Berber qualities of the inhabitants of the High Atlas.

Lyautey's romantic royalism and paternalism (as well as the desperate need for a quick solution) certainly predisposed him to favor the great *qaids*. On his first visit to Marrakech in 1912, he observed, "I am living here for the past ten days in total fairyland: there is no orientalist painting which reaches the brilliance of my arrival in Marrakech." Further along he noted, "One must remark that in the persons of the grand *qaids* of the South, we are dealing with true feudal barons, masters and lords of their lands, having at their disposition warriors, citadels, and prisons."[20] It was a useful fiction. Only after the publication of Robert Montagne's *Les Berbères et le makhzen dans le sud du Maroc* (1930) did the French learn of the late nineteenth-century origins of "Moroccan feudalism."[21] The protectorate presented itself as a system of indirect rule in which the great *qaids* were invested with authority by the protectorate government (and not the sultan). But as the great *qaids* died off, they were replaced by more tractable individuals, and authority gradually returned to French control. Daniel Rivet's summation captures the situation nicely:

> The policy of the great *qaids* was in the beginning an association of reciprocal services and benefits undertaken by halves and composed of innuendos. In exchange for the restoration of their power, until then instable and revocable, the great *qaids* rented out to the protectorate their capacity to undertake military expeditions and their deep knowledge of how to manipulate the complex springs of the society.[22]

The Middle Atlas presented a different social landscape. Instead of the great *qaids* it was home to transhumant Berbers riven by feud but fiercely devoted to the preservation of its customs and way of life. It was the inability of French military columns to install a durable peace in the region despite yearly expeditions that made a well-documented ethnography imperative. From a different perspective, the threat posed by *thamazight*-speaking Middle Atlas Berbers to the orderly administration of the region by the *makhzan* was a failure of the ethnographic imagination. It turned out that in 1912 only one French officer, Maurice Le Glay, had any knowledge of the tribes of the region or their language, and that not one study of the language, customs, or institutions of any Middle Atlas tribe existed.[23] Because the periodic revolts jeopardized the French position in northern Morocco, something had to be done, and rapidly. French military commanders could hardly afford to wait several years until the tribes of the region had been fully studied before undertaking their conquest. Making policy on the fly was a recipe for disaster. In the absence of detailed ethnographic studies, a solid understanding of Middle Atlas Berber political and social organization was required if previous errors were to be avoided.

When the Aith Ndhir (also known in Arabic as Beni Mtir), a transhumant tribe whose lands stood astride the Meknes plain and the foothills of the Middle Atlas, began to attack French posts in the region in the spring of 1913 the nonapplicability of the Lyautey system to the Middle Atlas groups became evident.[24] French observers might have been aware of oppositional tendencies of this tribe, since the Aith Ndhir had been among the leaders of the failed 1911 insurrection against Sultan Abd al-Hafiz. After the 1911 revolt was suppressed, a French military garrison was established at El Hadjeb, the chief settlement in Aith Ndhir territory. However, in the spring of 1912 the Aith Ndhir once again rebelled and attacked El Hadjeb in the spring of 1912 while other tribes (both Arab and Berber) were laying siege to Fez. French attempts to buy the loyalties of self-proclaimed leaders came to naught repeatedly, as defeated groups among the Aith Ndhir quickly disowned their supposed leaders. By spring 1913, the tribe once again went into opposition and began to ally itself with the other tribes of the area to attack the French posts. French experts were alarmed by their continuing failure to get the upper hand. Finding a solution to the Aith Ndhir problem was given top priority, and a special military command, the Cercle des Beni Mtir, was created within the Meknes region. Lieutenant Colonel Henrys, one of Lyautey's most trusted officers, was given special powers to bring the situation under control.[25]

The difficulties French military commanders experienced in the conquest of the Middle Atlas Berbers depended only partly on their ignorance of *thamazight* society. It also derived from weaknesses in the Lyautey method of pacification as developed along the Algero-Moroccan frontier between 1903 and 1908. The Lyautey system (which should be distinguished from the *makhzan* system of administration discussed above) depended on a clever mixture of political action and force to obtain the surrender of a hostile tribe. French commanders would seek out the most influential tribal leaders and marabouts and then, through the liberal application of bribes and threats, obtain the submission of the entire tribe. In this manner a tribe could often be brought under control without a shot being fired. In practice, of course, it rarely worked out that way, and a certain amount of force generally had to be employed to convince the last recalcitrants. One of the most characteristic features of the Lyautey system nonetheless remained its reliance on influential notables in the pacification process.[26]

Beyond this shift in style of governance, a more complete ethnography of Middle Atlas Berber society was clearly required to provide the basis for a more adequate policy. It is here that Adolphe Hanoteau and Aristide Letourneux's three-volume classic, *La Kabylie et les coutumes kabyles,* became relevant, exerting a powerful influence on the orientation of French research on Middle Atlas Berbers.[27] Two aspects of Hanoteau and Letourneux's findings seemed particularly relevant to the situation of the Middle Atlas Berbers. The first was the role of the *jama'a* (pl. *jama'at*), or council of elders, in deciding the most important questions facing the life of the group. Although the *thamazight*-speaking groups of the Middle Atlas were without permanent chiefs, French analysts influenced by the Kabyle myth argued that, as in Kabilya, groups like the Beni Mtir were in fact governed by a *jama'a.* In effect, they were democratic societies. A great error of the *makhzan* policy, Henrys proclaimed, was that it had sought to impose *qaids* on groups that had never previously accepted them, when in fact "the real authority remained in the hands of the *jema'a* and the elders."[28]

The absence of established chiefs was only one aspect of the problem. Henrys became aware that the Aith Ndhir saw the terms of their surrender as representing formal acceptance of the political authority of the sultan, as well as *makhzan* administration, including *qaids, qadis* (judges), and sharia law. It thus represented a direct threat to their customs, institutions, and way of life. Soon Middle Atlas Berber tribes increasingly began to refuse to accept any surrender terms that required their recognition of *makhzan* jurisdiction. To address this issue, Henrys and his staff modified the language of the formal surrender agreement. Instead of being asked to surrender to the *makhzan,* the new formula specified that the tribe surrender to the *dawla* (literally, the state; in practice the colonial state), and that the *dawla* guarantee the exercise of customary law to the tribe. For example, Henrys ordered "the use [among the Zaian] as was done among the Beni Mtir and the Beni Mguild of the word *dawla,* which the mountain-folk will learn in course to respect as soon as they see the difference between the *dawla* of today and the *makhzan* of yesterday."[29] This new formula proved to be successful when applied to the Beni Mtir and Gerrouan in 1913, and it was extended to the other Berber tribes of the Middle Atlas in the years that followed. In the same vein, the local French official in the Middle Atlas was called a *wasita* (go-between), a more acceptable verbal formula than *qaid.* Other minor changes in terminology were made to encourage the belief in French respect for the specificity of Berber society.[30]

A second influence of Hanoteau and Letourneux was Henrys's conviction that Middle Atlas Berber society (like Kabilya) was governed by Berber customary law (*izerf*) rather than the sharia, Islamic law. Henrys insisted that *izerf* was the key to regulating the internal life of the community, just as it was in Kabilya. *Izerf* was the collective province of the tribal elders and served as the basis of tribal customary law, the *qanoun*. As a result of this highly interested reading of Hanoteau and Letourneux, French policy toward the Berber-speaking groups of the Middle Atlas strongly favored *izerf* and the authority of the *jama'a* as the central features of these societies.[31] However, there was a basic error in the French analysis. They failed to recognize that Algerian Kabyle society was composed of sedentary arboriculturalists, whereas the *thamazight* speakers of the Middle Atlas were pastoral transhumants who migrated seasonally with their flocks and herds.

Lyautey and his chief collaborators on native affairs prided themselves on their empirical and nonideological view of Morocco. Like other members of the Lyautey *zawiya* (as the coterie of officers around Lyautey was known), Lieutenant Colonel Henrys was a convinced critic of what he regarded as the French native policy blunders in Algeria.[32] Certainly, if one examines the track record of French Algeria, there is much that might have justified his feelings. Nonetheless, he and other French policymakers were heavily influenced by the romantic stereotypes of Kabyle myth then dominant in colonial Algeria. The absence of Middle Atlas social organization and political functioning remained troubling. From the start, most of the early French experts on Moroccan Berber society and customs had been trained in Algeria. Thus Paul Henrys, Henri Berriau, and Henri Simon had all begun their careers in Algeria and had all worked with Berberophone groups. While there was much about the Algerian administration they disliked (its bureaucratic inefficiency and the nefarious influence of the *colons* for openers), the Kabyle myth was not one of those things. Much the same is true of the French civilian scholars who played a role in the formation of Moroccan Berber policy. Berber linguists Émile Laoust, Émile Biarnay, and Mohamed Nehlil, law professors like Henri Bruno and Louis Milliot, and human geographers like Louis Gentil and Augustin Bernard all formed their ideas about the Berber language, society, and customs in colonial Algeria and were strongly influenced by the racist stereotypes about Berber society of the Kabyle myth. They were not slow to find these traits among the Middle Atlas Berbers of Morocco.

French experts claimed to see broad continuities with the supposed history of the Kabyles. Thus they claimed that Middle Atlas Berbers were the original inhabitants of Morocco and had steadfastly resisted Arab invasions while remaining largely independent of the *makhzan*.[33] Moreover, they were at best superficially Islamicized, or if not, schismatics who refused to have anything to do with sharia law.[34] As evidence they asked how else to explain the preservation of the customs, rituals, and superstitions of their earlier faith under a veneer of Muslim beliefs and practices? Had they not fought bitterly against the imposition of sharia law in place of their customary law?[35] Moreover, the same experts claimed that Middle Atlas Berbers had an instinctive distrust of personal power. It was this democratic spirit that enabled them to resist the *makhzan* and the emergence of powerful chiefs, they claimed.[36] Like Algerian Kabyles, they were able to resolve most important problems through their *jama'at*. On questions that dealt with the honor of the group, they asserted, the *jama'a* was incapable of resolving the dispute. However, "to thoroughly understand the role of the *jama'a*, it would be necessary to look at Berber family institutions and to examine the veritable sovereignty that the chief of the patriarchal family possesses, as in ancient Rome."[37] Finally, the Berber political system was saved from anarchy only by the strong Berber sense of independence against outsiders.[38] The customary laws that regulated the internal life of the group, as in the case of the Kabyles, were often written down in the form of *qanouns*. These customs "are more often in harmony with the spirit of our [French] code than the laws of Islam." In their social life, the Berbers were marked by a certain roughness of manner, but "Berber mores are distinguished from Arab mores because they don't have the religious base of the Koran."[39] Also (in another echo of the Kabyle myth) Moroccan Berber treatment of women was alleged to be much closer to European practices than to Arab ones, since Quranic prescriptions relative to women, their place in the family, and their rights were not observed by Berbers. Indeed, these experts asserted, their attitude was the exact opposite of Moroccan Arab Muslims.

From this analysis of Berber society a number of policy implications can be deduced, which tended to emphasize the necessity of preserving the central institutions of Berber society (or what were regarded as such at the time) from Arabization and Islamicization; they were applied only gradually by the protectorate government. The initiatives taken between 1913 and 1919 that can be seen in retrospect as marking the origins of the Berber policy came into full flower only later. By 1919 the essential traits of the Berber myth and the Moroccan colonial gospel were already in place. By 1919 as well essential policy decisions had been made on which the completed edifice would be erected between the two wars.

The French promise that the laws and customs of the surrendering Berber tribe would be respected, and that *qaids, qadis,* and sharia law would not be imposed on the group, contained the seeds of a Berber policy. In order to make such a promise, however, French agents had to have a more complete idea of just what these laws and customs were. Accordingly, one of the first acts in the matter of Berber policy was a circular of July 30, 1913, sent out by Lyautey, that ordered native affairs officials to inquire on the extent to which Berber-speaking groups under their jurisdiction practiced customary law, "in order to better fix the 'formula' which is appropriate to these populations."[40] The need to give at least some legal justification to the practice already followed in the submission of the Beni Mtir and Guerrouan in 1913, and the Beni Mguild in 1914, however, soon led to the promulgation of a decree before the results of this study were widely known. The official *dahir* (decree) of September 11, 1914, set forth the principle that tribes judged "de coutume berbère" would be permitted to keep their own judicial regime, and that further decrees would elaborate the exact terms under which customary law would be administered.[41] Initially, tribes classed as "de coutume berbère" included the Beni Mtir, Beni Mguild, Zaian, and Guerrouan. Others were added to the list in the years that followed. No further laws were promulgated to clarify the exact legal position of the customary law regime under the protectorate until the decree of May 16, 1930 (the infamous "Berber *dahir*"). The conclusion is clear: the road to the Berber decree began in the early days of the protectorate.

In order to facilitate policy decisions about the Berbers, it was imperative that as much accurate information as possible about Berber society should be gathered as soon as possible. The Lyautey circular of July 30, 1913, was the first step in the systematization of research on Berbers in Morocco. Already Henrys had convened Maurice Le Glay, Émile Laoust, and Mohammed Abès to serve as a kind of brain trust on Berber problems on an ad hoc basis. At the initiative of Henrys, a special Berber study center was set up at Meknes in 1913, and things began to take a more organized form. The reports produced by this group formed the basis for Henrys's recommendations to Lyautey. These in turn resulted in the *dahir* (decree) of September 11, 1914.[42] Fairly soon it was understood that the *thamazight*-speaking Berbers of the Middle Atlas were only one of the three major groups of Berber speakers in Morocco. A broader effort to centralize information on Berbers was required. As a result, on June 15, 1914, Lyautey ordered that a further questionnaire be sent to all military posts in Morocco specifying the points on which further data were needed.[43]

From the beginning, French commentators on Moroccan Berber policy were concerned to avoid the mistakes that had been made in Algeria. In this list of errors they included the delay in recognizing the specificity of Kabyle society, the inadvertent favoring of the spread of the Arabic language and of Islamic law, and the unreasonable haste to assimilate the Kabyles to French civilization once a Berber policy had been adopted.[44] To insure that the Arabic language would not be unwittingly encouraged in Berber territory in Morocco, and to facilitate carrying out a flexible Berber policy, Berber-speaking French officers were assigned to each military post. To attract applicants for the position of entry-level *contrôleurs civils,* the salary of native affairs officials who knew Berber was increased by a special allowance.[45] In this manner it was hoped that qualified individuals would be attracted, so that native affairs officers would no longer have to utilize Arab interpreters and secretaries. (In practice, however, there were never enough Berberophones for the purpose.) In order to limit the Islamicization and Arabization of the Berbers, records were kept in French, rather than in Arabic, following the colonial Algerian practice. By keeping the records in French, the protectorate government sought to exercise control over affairs within each Berber tribe.[46]

Much of the thinking about the Berber policy adopted in this period drew on the Algerian example.[47] This approach was motivated by a desire to encourage the gradual assimilation of the Berbers to French civilization instead of facilitating their Arabization. At the root of this feeling lay a sharp awareness of the demographic imbalance between colonizers and colonized. If France were successfully to maintain its position in Morocco over the long run, the assimilation of some the indigenous population was necessary.[48] But this assimilation should be a very gradual process. The unfortunate results of undue haste were all too evident in the Algerian example and must be avoided.

How might assimilation best be accomplished? After a lot of discussion within the protectorate administration, it was agreed that the establishment of French schools in Berber-speaking Middle Atlas districts provided the model. Once again there was an Algerian model: the *écoles franco-arabes.*[49] A preliminary decision to establish French schools appears to have been reached before 1919.[50] From a 1914 memorandum by Augustin Bernard, we know that the protectorate administration commissioned Émile Laoust, Alfred Bel, and Charles Bertschi to produce studies on the education question. All concluded in favor of the establishment of French schools among the Berber tribes and strongly supported the assimilation of Moroccan Berbers to

French culture and civilization. But in his report Bernard unfortunately gives no idea of what decisions, if any, were taken on this recommendation. However, a policy study of 1948 referring to this earlier period notes: "By a directive from Lyautey dated November 18, 1920, the creation of schools was begun. In 1923 five schools were opened in the Middle Atlas (at Sefrou, Ahermoumou, Azrou, Imouzzer, and Ain Leuh). Each was to receive one hundred students. Instruction was by French teachers. This system lasted until 1946."[51]

Since most French observers regarded it as unlikely that the Berbers would choose to learn Arabic when the prospect of learning French was available, they felt that there was no need to rush things. The inevitability of assimilation appeared unquestionable even to such pragmatic observers as Augustin Bernard:

> Neither the Berber language nor law can subsist in the presence of a superior organism. It will thus be necessary to give them our language and our law. In the same fashion, since they have no chiefs, or chiefs without authority, the native affairs officer will be the real chief. This consequence should not frighten us; however, it is appropriate to mention it.[52]

The contrast between this view and Bernard's previous opinion, cited above, is too eloquent to require comment.

THE COLONIAL GOSPEL COMPLETED

By 1919 the stereotypes of the Moroccan colonial gospel were locked in place. These included representations of the Moroccan state as well as of the place of Berbers in Moroccan society. By 1919, the binary opposition between Arabs and Berbers, *makhzan* and *siba,* and between the political and religious authority of the sultan, had fused into a single mutually supporting discourse. The Berber myth that crystallized between 1912 and 1919 derived its principal features from the romantic stereotype of Berbers that had been developed earlier in Algeria. The ultimate goal of French Kabyle policy had been the assimilation of the Berber-speaking Kabyles into French culture and civilization. Similarly, the Berber policy that emerged in Morocco between 1912 and 1919 aimed at the eventual assimilation of Moroccan Berbers. Since the process was considered to be a long one, the Berber policy that was followed in Morocco focused on keeping the Berbers from becoming Arabized and Islamicized and shielding them as much as possible from the anti-French feelings that were beginning to affect the Arab populations. By serving as guardian of the customs and traditions of the Berber-speaking populations of Morocco, the French sought to guide them toward a future that would be neither French nor Arab.[53]

After 1919 the goal of assimilation gradually faded away when it was discovered that most Moroccan Berbers were just as attached to their religion as the Arabs were. Nonetheless, the policy of shielding them from incorporation into Arabic civilization persisted.[54] Following the emergence in the 1920s of the first stirrings of the nationalist movement, the contradictions of carrying out this policy were not long in appearing. They burst into flame in 1930 with promulgation of the Berber *dahir*. The Berber decree ignited immense opposition all over Morocco and marks one of the first successes of the young nationalist movement.[55] By 1930 the time had long since passed when a romantic and paternalistic image of Berbers would be quietly accepted by Moroccans.

Although the Middle Atlas was the crucible in which French Berber policy was elaborated, no integrated Berber policy was ever developed. While some (but not all) Middle Atlas Berbers were under the jurisdiction of a French-invented customary law, Berber speakers in other parts of Morocco remained under the jurisdiction of the sharia courts, rather than customary law. While the "Lords of the Atlas" exercised power over their vassals (with French approval), they remained under the authority of the sultan.

EIGHT

Urban Policy

FEZ AND THE MUSLIM CITY

The nineteenth-century French quest for vivid colors, pungent odors, and intense emotions that might relieve the oppressive grayness of bourgeois existence looked to the Orient (in this case, the Maghreb) to provide the necessary diversions. As enshrined in the paintings of Eugène Delacroix and the books of Pierre Loti, one city above all loomed in the French imagination as the apotheosis of all that was most captivating, most mysterious in the Orient. It was the Moroccan city of Fez, the "setting sun of Islam." That is to say, a certain image of Fez did—as for the realities, little of a systematic or reliable sort was known about the city until the beginning of the twentieth century.

The contrast between the long period of romantic misinformation about Fez and its society, and the sudden appearance of a more scientifically grounded view, corresponds to the brusque acceleration of the pace of change and the onset of the French colonial offensive in Morocco after 1900. There is no doubt that the Frenchmen whose studies of Fez did so much to transform Western understanding of the city, being good positivists, were convinced that they had accomplished therein a victory for science and rationality. That they also helped lay the foundations for the triumph of French imperialism in Morocco was an unstated source of great satisfaction to them. Today, we are less inclined to vaunt uncritically the virtues of "science" and "progress," and a study of the work of the first generation of French students of Moroccan cities, in particular their work on Fez, raises the question of whether their image of the city differed substantially in its assumptions from that presented by Loti.

This chapter takes up the ethnographic literature on the city of Fez during the period that runs roughly from 1894 until 1925, especially the precolonial period, during which the major outlines of what became the standard view were elaborated. The French ethnography of Fez serves as a kind of touchstone of the concerns of French urban ethnography in Morocco, more generally: the same categories were employed, the same assumptions made, and the same political axes were ground.[1] By studying Fez, we get a sense of the preoccupations of the first generation of French ethnographers. The line of analysis they pursued established the general outlines of French urban studies during the protectorate (1912–56), which lasted until the appearance of the studies of the Casablanca *bidonville* (shantytown) done by Robert Montagne and André Adam.[2] The route to a more adequate sociology of the Maghreb necessarily passes through a reconsideration of the colonial literature. It is not certain that the work of the earlier generation of colonial ethnographers will be diminished by such an inquiry.

AN ORIENTALIST IN FEZ

In February 1900 Auguste Mouliéras arrived in Morocco on an official mission funded by the Ministry of Public Instruction. Charged with studying "the functioning of the University of Fez and native education," he reached Fez on March 1, 1900, and set to work.[3] With his Arabic skills and rapport with Moroccans, he was a skilled field-worker. During his month-and-a-half-long stay he compiled a great deal of information on popular culture in Fez, to be included in his book *Fez,* published in 1902. One chapter of his book on the city was presented originally as a lecture to the Geographical Society of Algiers in 1901.[4] However, the consequences of proceeding straight to Fez without first obtaining the authorization of the *makhzan* soon became clear to him. Without official authorization, no member of the Fasi ulama would talk with him.[5] Eventually Mouliéras was reduced in desperation to paying money to speak with a supposed *alim* (scholar) who in the event turned out to be a fraud. Faced with the failure of his mission, Mouliéras redoubled his efforts. Although eventually he found people with whom he could to speak, none were members of the Fasi ulama. His interviewees included an aged Middle Atlas Berber, whom he encountered in the street; the British vice consul, James McIver MacLeod, about whom he had many misgivings: and representatives of the Jewish community of Fez. (Mouliéras's book contains one of two discussions of the contemporaneous Jewish society of Fez written by a non-Jewish author.)[6] But all these individuals and groups were marginal to Fasi Muslim society. While Mouliéras's *Fez* contains many remarkable flights of orientalist erudition (see, for example, his discussion of the different theories regarding the origins of the name of the city, the origins of the different Moroccan dynasties, or the origins of the *istiksa* prayer), he could have written them without leaving his study.[7] It is as an ethnographer that he falls down.

Initially, Mouliéras managed to establish a rapport with the Moroccans he encountered, but he became increasingly frustrated by his inability to find viable interlocutors among the Fasi ulama. Over the course of his stay, his militantly antireligious and anti-Islamic attitudes came to the surface, drawing him into violent arguments with Moroccans time and again.[8] Evoking the alleged homicidal cruelty of Moroccan rulers, including Abd al-Aziz, the then incumbent, he denounced them as "vampire sultans," implying thereby a genetic trait common to the dynasty, if not to Moroccans generally. Later, he bitterly deplored "the leaden cloak of Islam, bearing in its folds, wherever it exists, silence and darkness." Succeeding at one point in being invited to a performance of the celebrated young Fasi female singer Brika, once she began singing he was quickly disabused by her voice: "The marvelous larynx of the biggest star of Fez still rings in my ears a year later, and it is likely that the hoarse and cracked voice of Brika will remain in my memory as the archetype of human mooing in its ugliest explosion."[9] The last part of his book abounds in impassioned denunciations of Moroccan culture, a veritable bestiary of orientalist prejudices. By the end of his stay he could not wait to leave in what he seems to have come to regard as the fieldwork experience from hell. Thus Mouliéras's *Fez* is the record of an ethnographic and personal failure. Undone in part by his irascibility, prejudice, and impetuosity, he would never again be entrusted with a study mission to Morocco.

The brevity of Mouliéras's stay (barely six weeks) and the fact that he proceeded in defiance of Moroccan regulations calling for all researchers to apply for an official authorization no doubt helped shape the final outcome. More consequential was his orientalist obscurantism, a trait that links his work to the rest of the École d'Alger. Although Mouliéras's work ethic and the ingenuity with which he interrogated his informants are genuinely impressive, in the end his work failed to make its knowledge accessible in a form in which it could be put to use, and thus failed to command the respect of policy planners. Neither empiricist in the manner of the Bureaux arabes (which sought to quantify numbers of tents, people, horses, rifles, etc.) nor sociological after the fashion of the Durkheimians (who sought to link "facts" to a theoretically guided interpretive scheme), from a policy planner's point of view Mouliéras's work was simply illegible. Full of literary flourishes, personal asides, *obiter dicta,* and feats of pure erudition, Mouliéras's *Fez* (and his *Le Maroc inconnu*) reflected the mentality of a French provincial *société savante* (learned society) more than that of a modern sociological inquiry. While we do not know how the Ministry of Public Instruction (which funded his research in *Fez*) responded to Mouliéras's report on his fieldwork, it is doubtful that French policymakers found it of much utility. Despite or because of its idiosyncratic aspects, Mouliéras's *Fez* thus provides us with a stick by which measure the work of other French observers.

For a number of reasons, urban studies constituted the core around which the interests of the early students of Moroccan society tended to gravitate. Fez in particular, because of its religious and commercial importance, excited a great deal of attention. Other cities studied were Tangier, Tetouan, Rabat, El Ksar el Kebir, Marrakech, and the coastal cities of Casablanca, Mazagan, Safi, Mogodor, and Oudjda. French policymakers were convinced that mastery of the cities was key to the eventual establishment of a protectorate. After 1912, this interest was carried forward in a series of volumes under the collective title Villes et Tribus du Maroc, which were prepared by the native affairs section of the protectorate administration. Cities of course were more easily studied than the perennially fractious tribal populations (which were mostly off-limits to French observers in the period 1900–1912). Finally, there was a French intellectual school of urban studies that traced its roots to Fustel de Coulanges's *La cité antique* (1864). Émile Masqueray's important thesis on Algeria, *La formation des cités chez les populations sédentaires de l'Algérie* (1886), played an important role in stimulating research on Maghrebi cities.[10]

Given these concerns, it is no surprise that the French should have been vitally interested in obtaining precise information about Fez. The city had long been regarded as one of the essential keys to Morocco, since it was the political and religious capital of the country, as well as a center of trade and commerce of national scale. Yet if Morocco in general was only dimly known in 1900, Fez itself was a riddle of great proportions, and its merchant class and intransigent ulama made it a real threat to French diplomatic strategy. Before 1902, few Europeans had visited Fez, save for diplomats on brief missions to the royal court. French consular representation at Fez was only permitted in 1892. The difficulty of communications with the coast and the fragility of government control over the nearby tribes helped to delay

European penetration. From 1897 until 1902 the sultan resided in Marrakech, and there was a hiatus in French interest in Fez. Not until March 1902, when the court once again took up residence at Fez, did the city return to the spotlight.

The French ethnographic literature on Fez before 1904 (if the term *ethnographic* is not too grandiose—perhaps we should speak of proto-ethnography) was limited to a few travel accounts (including one by a French doctor[11]) and works of folklore by Georges Delphin and Auguste Mouliéras.[12] None of these works could lay claim to serious scientific status, although to this day they retain a certain musty charm. A more systematic study of the city was evidently called for. An excellent beginning was made in 1904 with the publication of a series of articles in the *Revue de Paris*. They were the work of an experienced French diplomat writing under the pseudonym of Eugène Aubin.[13] The following year saw the appearance of Henri Gaillard's *Une ville d'Islam: Fez,*[14] as well as a series of articles by Charles René-Leclerc on the economy of Fez,[15] and the first of a series of articles in *AM* devoted primarily to the role of Islam in the life of the city.[16] By 1912, the picture was all but complete: thereafter the literature largely fills in the blanks, adding detail and color rather than developing new categories of analysis. The relatively short time required for the elaboration of an ethnography of Fez (the same is true of Morocco more generally) is quite striking. So too is the development of certain topics, and the neglect of others. The only significant opening of a new topic was the emergence of studies of the artisan craft guilds of Fez, beginning with the work of Louis Massignon.[17] Seen against this background, Roger Le Tourneau's *Fès avant le protectorat*[18] stands as a fitting capstone to a tradition of urban ethnography and social history that began in 1904 with the work of Aubin.

An important aspect of the research on Morocco before 1912 is the explicitly political context in which it developed. The unleashing of the French colonial offensive coincided with the first publications on Morocco. The establishment of the Comité du Maroc and the Mission scientifique du Maroc (MSM) in 1903 signaled an upsurge of interest in Morocco in French colonial circles. French preoccupation with the Moroccan question has much to do with the questions French colonial circles asked and the categories of analysis they developed. The ethnographers of Fez thus embarked on their researches with one general purpose in mind—to further the development of French interests in Morocco, at the expense of European rivals. What this boiled down to was the search for the key to Moroccan society, the secret or secrets that, once known, would enable Frenchmen to plan policies regarding Morocco with the least possible disruption of Moroccan society, and the least expense of blood and treasure on the part of France. The utilitarian concept of ethnography had a number of important consequences for their analysis, influencing what they chose to treat and what they left out, as well as shaping the general context into which they sought to fit their picture of Fez.

Who were the ethnographers to whom we owe the very impressive list of works outlined above? One of the first things to be observed about them is that with only two exceptions, all were diplomats. That is to say, they were drawn from the ranks of French diplomatic personnel in Morocco, although not all of them continued to pursue such a career. Career diplomats like Henri Gaillard and Eugène Aubin [Coullard-Descos],[19] consular officials like Édouard Michaux-Bellaire,[20] and interpreters like Louis Martin and Léon Pérétié[21] were among the major contributors to the emerging ethnographic literature on Fez. Only Georges Salmon,[22] the young head of the MSM, and Charles René-Leclerc,[23] head of the Tangier office of the CM, can be excluded from this generalization. In the absence of French academic experts on Moroccan society, this in itself is not too surprising: where else could the necessary expertise have come from?

A second observation about the background of these men also suggests itself. None were trained ethnographers (the field was little developed in France at the time), and only a few of the authors discussed here had prior experience in an Arabic-speaking country. The ethnography of Fez (and to a large extent that of Morocco as well) in the period was the work of nonprofessional observers (some of whom had decades of in-country experience). Here one must distinguish between those who came before 1902, and those who came after. Michaux-Bellaire and Gaillard had lived in Morocco since the 1890s and had an intimate knowledge of the language and customs there. Gaillard was the French vice-consul at Fez from 1900 and had served previously in other posts in Morocco. Michaux-Bellaire had briefly served as acting vice-consul at Fez in 1895–96, otherwise living in Tangier and El Ksar for a prolonged period.

Another striking feature of the work of the ethnographers of Fez is the fact that the academics worked not as individuals, but as part of research teams. The MSM is perhaps the clearest example of this tendency. As we have seen in previous chapters, *Archives marocaines* published a series of articles all derived from Salmon's 1906 research trip.[24] It is the division of labor pioneered by the MSM that most resembles the operations of a contemporary social science research team. Even seemingly individual achievements such as the works of Gaillard and Aubin turn out upon examination to be based on the collaboration of a number of assistants and local informants. In Aubin's case, Kaddour Ben Ghabrit (1873–1954), the counselor on Muslim law of the French Legation at Tangier, provided vital assistance. An Algerian Muslim born in Sidi Bel Abbes and a graduate of the Médersa franco-arabe of Tlemcen, Ben Ghabrit was perfectly at home in French drawing rooms and the homes of the Fasi bourgeoisie. He was able to exploit his position to make himself an essential intermediary between the French and the Moroccan elite. At this point in his Moroccan career, Ben Ghabrit was still developing the ties that he would later exploit to such advantage.[25] Already his knowledge of Fasi society was legendary. Aubin's *Morocco Today* quickly became an essential reference for Europeans interested in Morocco.[26]

The early generation of French ethnographers was interested first in the role of Islam in the life of the city. A great deal of attention was devoted to exploring its complexities. In particular, there was considerable interest in the role of the shrine of Mawlay Idris, the founder and patron saint of Fez. In addition, the sprawling interrelated and very influential Idrisi sharifian families also excited attention. A motivating factor in this choice may well have been the influence of Fustel de Coulanges's *Cité antique,* with its discussion of ancestor cults.[27] But there were clearly other important reasons for their concern. One was the prevalent opinion that Moroccan Islam represented the greatest obstacle to the establishment of a French protectorate, representing a badge of nationality and a nucleus around which resistance might crystallize. Thus a careful understanding of Moroccan Islam, and especially the religious institutions and classes of Fez—given the importance of Fez and the Idrisi sharifs elsewhere in Morocco—was essential for French policymakers. (On Moroccan Islam see chapter 10.) The MSM research group took the lead in exploring these topics. Together with Aubin and Gaillard, they sought to focus attention on the role of the religious brotherhoods (Ar. pl. *turuq*) in Fez, and on the chief mosques and madrasas of the city. In particular the role of the Qarawiyin mosque university was stressed. Finally, they outlined the importance of the Fasi religious scholars and sharifs in forming public opinion in the city, and throughout Morocco. The major families of sharifs were delineated, their genealogies studied, and their present-day influence assessed. In keeping with the flavor of the times, these studies emphasized the religious intolerance of the Fasi ulama toward Europeans.

A second major subject of interest to the ethnographers of Fez were the notables (Ar. *a'yan*). Not really a class, not exactly a caste either, the notables were the wealthy merchants, local officials, and others who dominated the political and economic life of the city. French scholars were interested in the social composition of the *a'yan,* the distinctive traits of the Fasi bourgeois mentality, and the uneasy relationship between Old Fez (Fas al-bali) and New Fez (Fas al-jadid). Much of this illustrated the "manners and customs" variety of reportage so characteristic of early ethnography: the collection of social traits, rituals, and beliefs, rather than the analysis of the structure of kinship, or of the symbolic religious structures. Aubin, for example, presented the first convincing portrait of that complex of genteel customs, language, and dress that marked off the bourgeoisie from the artisans and workers of Fez, and distinguished the urban population from the people of the countryside. Both Aubin and Gaillard underscored the role of the *a'yan* in resisting the centralizing efforts of the *makhzan*.[28] Michaux-Bellaire, writing in 1922 with the benefit of a decade of hindsight, notes:

> Only Fez presents the particularity rather rare in Morocco of having a real bourgeoisie composed of wholesalers, merchants, and artisans. The head of the principal commercial establishments had under their sway not only the less wealthy members of their own families, but also a numerous clientele of employees, workers, and those in their debt: they were real merchant princes, who recall the patricians of Carthage, or more recently, of the Italian republics.[29]

Since the opposition of the *a'yan* could be dangerous to French plans, a major focus of French policy during the pre-protectorate period was determining how the *a'yan* might be won over to the French cause, or effectively neutralized.[30] The portrait of the Fasi notability in the pages of the French ethnographers is one of a proud, suspicious, and cultivated merchant class, not unaware of the balance of forces in the world, but imprisoned by its avarice and its fears of rural unrest.

The Fasi economy was a third major focus of French interest. Since Fez occupied a position of great importance in the economy of Morocco, and Fasi merchants constituted an important group of potential intermediaries, knowledge of their business methods and their situation at Fez might be useful. Potential French investors and merchants were naturally interested in knowing more about their Muslim business partners. The research of Charles René-Leclerc, head of the Tangier office of the *CM,* into the economy of Fez was published in 1905 in *Renseignements coloniaux,* a monthly supplement to *Afrique française.*[31] Relying on statistical information provided by Gaillard, as well as on materials gathered locally by his network of informants, René-Leclerc was able to specify for the first time how the merchants of Fez had been able to exploit their privileged position to become the single most important group of economic middlemen in Morocco. He produced the first general portrait of the extent of Fasi trade with Europe, Africa, and the Near East, and examined in detail the circumstances of the production, pricing, and marketing of goods at Fez—all items of concern to French business interests. Finally, he provided an important glimpse into the structure and operation of the artisan craft guilds of Fez. (It might be remarked parenthetically that the economy of Fez was of little interest to the MSM group, who were far more fascinated with religious matters, and that the best study on the subject was written by the local agent of the French colonial lobby.)

A final area of concern of the early researchers on Fez was the structure, internal functioning, and composition of the Moroccan government, the *makhzan.*[32] Since the court resided at Fez more or less continuously from 1902 until 1912, and the bureaucracy was staffed by the graduates of the madrasas of Fez, no study of Fez could be complete without detailed treatment of the *makhzan.* It was Aubin who provided the most detailed and convincing description of the operations of the *makhzan.* Together with Gaillard, Aubin subjected the manners, customs, and recruitment of *makhzan* officials to scrutiny, and underscored the interpenetration of the *makhzan* elite and the notability of Fez. Gaillard and Aubin noted the traditional rivalry between the two major sections of Fez: the city of the government, Fas al-jadid, and the old city of Fez, Fas al-bali. Since the French government from 1904 onward pursued a policy of close collaboration with the *makhzan,* detailed knowledge of the habits of the bureaucracy was obviously important. If France were to be able to establish a protectorate, such information would be at a premium in the planning of policy.

The French ethnographic literature on Fez produced between 1904 and 1912 remains to this day an enormously impressive achievement. As a portrait of Fez on the eve of the protectorate, it is notable for its amplitude and detail. Without it, subsequent scholars would have had a much more difficult time. From the vantage point of the postcolonial present, however, the image of Fez as it emerges from this collection of diverse materials was based on a number of questionable assumptions, to which we now turn.

French ethnographers tended to assume that Morocco was somehow immune to the forces that were in the process of transforming the rest of the world. The assumption was especially tempting, since according to the tenets of the evolutionary views then in favor in anthropology, "survivals" were to be expected, and Morocco seemed a particularly clear example of such a survival.[33] If Morocco were assumed to be unchanging, then Fez could easily be viewed as a traditional Islamic city, somehow miraculously preserved into the twentieth century. The high walls that surrounded the city, its narrow winding streets and bustling *suq*-s, all reinforced the impression of archaism. Only later was it discovered how far wrong this judgment was. Research by historians such as Roger Le Tourneau (whose *Fès avant le protectorat* remains the reference point by which all else is measured) and Jean-Louis Miège has demonstrated that the colonial assumptions of an unchanging Morocco are erroneous.[34] Already well before the protectorate, Fasi society had undergone far-reaching social and economic change. Much the same is true in the cultural sphere, as the research of Évariste Lévi-Provençal and Abdullah Laroui has demonstrated.[35] Fez (and Morocco more generally) was undergoing a literary renaissance of important dimensions before 1912. Fez was thus neither unchanging nor cut off from the currents of thought that were in the process of transforming the Arab and Muslim world.

The assumption of ethnographers of Fez that the urban notables were the key to winning the city has already been touched on. If France could secure the support of key *makhzan* officials, religious leaders, and wealthy merchants, they believed, then Fez could be easily controlled. Behind this assumption of the dominance of the notables, it now seems clear, there stands an additional, more theoretical assumption—namely, that Moroccan society was an organic entity in which the various parts were integrated into one another, and that there was an identifiable "head."[36] This head, our observers theorized, was the *a'yan*. This assumption in turn, in the minds of at least some of the ethnographers, may have been connected to the Durkheimian notion of organic solidarity. While this assumption was not totally unwarranted (and in fact Lyautey was later to erect a native policy on the assumption of the primacy of the notability in Fasi politics, together with the assumption of an unchanging Morocco), it misled French ethnographers into an almost fatal misjudgment of the people of Fez's capacity for resistance.

Time and time again, French experts were taken by surprise by the outbreak of urban unrest and political resistance to French colonial aspirations. In 1904–5 a coalition of *makhzan* officials, religious scholars (ulama) and secular notables succeeded (with German support) in blocking a French protectorate. This opposition had not been foreseen. While the outcome of the Algeciras conference (1906) restored French claims to predominance in Morocco under an international mandate, Moroccan resistance had by no means ended. Indeed, it merely intensified. Again, the role of Fez was critical to the outcome. In December 1907 and January 1908, a series of violent riots and popular disturbances (also unforeseen by French observers) broke out at Fez. The ulama were compelled by the mob to depose Abd al-Aziz as sultan and name his brother, Abd al-Hafiz, to the throne on a platform of militant resistance to the French. Again in 1911 Fez occupied center stage, when a rural insurrection made common cause with popular forces in the city, and almost succeeded in overthrowing Sultan Abd al-Hafiz. Finally, in April 1912, a mutiny of Moroccan troops against their French instructors at Fez sparked a major urban revolt, which was only repressed with heavy loss of life on all sides.[37] In each of these instances, French Morocco experts had been wrong in their predictions. Given the considerable sophistication of their analysis of Fasi society, the question naturally arises, How could this have happened?

Several answers suggest themselves. One is that French Morocco experts were incorrect, or only partially correct, in their conclusions that the *a'yan* controlled Fez. The resistance to the French reform program in 1904–5 was largely the result of the political intervention of the *a'yan* and ulama of Fez. According to the prevailing theory the notables' role in the struggle might have been predicted, since it agreed with the paradigm of notable dominance. But the popular movements in 1907–8, 1911, and 1912 did not conform to this paradigm. Instead the social turmoil and resistance efforts were directed against the *a'yan* themselves, as well as against the French. In each of these instances, while some notables and ulama became involved with the movement, it was popular forces based in the city and the adjacent countryside that took a major role in determining the course of events. It is perhaps understandable that the French ethnographers of Fez should have been quite unprepared for the possibility of an initiative from below. The social origins of most of the ethnographers were impeccably bourgeois, and this gave them a natural sympathy for their Moroccan counterparts. In French society before World War I, moreover, the preponderance of notables at all levels of society was marked, and social forces were only beginning to emerge. Not for nothing was the Third Republic popularly known as "La République des notables." Thus it was natural that French ethnographers should leave the lower classes of Fez out of their equation. Still, in the face of events that did not accord with the paradigm, one might think that their previous understanding would have been revised. It was not.

The individuals who made up the 1905 MSM research team on Fez were not unaware of the political and intellectual ferment. Their articles bear witness to their thoroughness, if not their perspicacity. But their assumption that Moroccan Islam was unchanging was so deeply rooted that they simply did not grasp the significance of the facts. Instead they sought to explain the popular unrest of 1907–8, 1911, and 1912 as the result of Moroccan anarchy and xenophobia. These traits were allegedly characteristic of Moroccan national culture and were the natural response of an archaic social organism when confronted with one of greater complexity and a higher level of development. Thus reasoned our ethnographers. In this way they managed to avoid dealing with the question of whether Moroccans were influenced by ideologies and currents of thought other than those presumed to derive from the so-called traditional character of their society. Blinded by orientalist stereotypes, the French never seem to have noticed the existence of Moroccan national sentiment. Nor did they ever focus on the political role of the Moroccan ulama in the pre-protectorate period. Yet as several recent studies have shown, the social movements of these years cannot be explained except through reference to the roles of the *a'yan* and the ulama.[38] Despite the major role in the important events at Fez in the period played by Muhammad ibn al-Kabir al-Kattani, an *alim* and leader of an important religious brotherhood at Fez with a sizable lower-class clientele (to cite just the most striking example), no serious French study of the role of his role, or that of his *tariqa,* the Kattaniya, exists.[39] Such gaps in the literature were more than mere oversights, and a recognition of the context in which French ethnographers worked can help us to understand the real significance of such omissions.

Most French experts were convinced that there was little or no connection between the city of Fez and the rural populations living in its environs. This left many unexplained lacunae in their portrait of the economic ties between Fez and the surrounding tribes. One assumption was that the tribes were autarchic. A second related assumption was that the goods manufactured in Fez were intended either for the consumption of the court or for export. Events like the tribal involvement in the popular uprisings of 1907–8 and

1911, which might have cast doubt on this belief, since they revealed the close collaboration of urban and rural insurgents, remained unexplainable anomalies. One person who grasped the significance of the connection between Fez and its hinterland was Michaux-Bellaire, and even he was not always consistent in this regard.[40] In 1922 he characterized it this way:

> The relations of the Berber tribes who supplied it with merchandise and from which it received the products required for its food and its industries made Fez the true market for Berbers of the central and eastern regions of Morocco. This resulted in a political bond based on a community of interests that often allowed the Fasi bourgeoisie to stand up to the *makhzan* and even to plot against it thanks to the support of the Berber tribes.[41]

More recent studies have emphasized the close connections between Fez and the surrounding countryside, the constant flow of men and goods into and out of the city from nearby areas, and the multiplicity of relationships between the two.[42] It is at this point that the wider political and intellectual context in which the studies of Fez took place becomes relevant, for, in fact, the assumptions that were made about the nature of Morocco and Moroccan society were widely shared at the time. These assumptions in turn appear connected with both the circumstances of French political involvement in Morocco, and the set of stereotypes about Morocco that accompanied it. Beginning in 1904, with the signing of the Anglo-French entente, France acquired a vested interest in Morocco, and with it in the continued existence of the *makhzan*. To cloak French colonial ambitions in a mantle of respectability, and thereby preserve the government from either international criticism or domestic political opposition, French policy emphasized close cooperation between the French government and the Moroccan government in the institution of needed reforms. This policy of peaceful penetration depended on the tacit acquiescence of the Moroccan government. In this way France could expand its influence in Morocco and eventually substitute itself for the *makhzan* without risking either a major war of conquest or the inevitable delays that it would have occasioned. The patriotic resistance of Moroccan tribes was recoded as the traditional opposition of *bled el siba* to the authority of the *makhzan*.[43] As long as France enjoyed a clear military superiority there was no need for an alternative explanation based on a reanalysis of the social setting and the roots of resistance.

The emergence of this *makhzan* policy coincided with a sudden change in the way French ethnographers depicted Moroccan society. As we have seen above, before 1904, French ethnographers emphasized the openness, flexibility, and absence of sharp cleavages in Moroccan society. But starting in 1904, when France acquired a vested interest in the *makhzan,* this nuanced and balanced portrait gave way to one based on a series of dichotomous images, including the supposed opposition between *makhzan* and *siba,* Berber and Arab, and city and country. These stereotypes dominated French ethnography right to the end of the protectorate. Thus French policy during the period of the Moroccan question, and the image of Morocco that crystallized during this period, were mutually reinforcing. By seizing on a few aspects of the society and paying less attention to others that were no less important, French ethnographers and politicians helped to generate a series of stereotypes about Morocco that lasted well beyond the lifetime of the protectorate. Such a stereotypical image of Morocco survived because it best seemed to explain the peculiarities of pre-protectorate Morocco, and at the same time provided a convincing rationale for French colonial dominance.[44]

FEZ: THE REVOLUTION AND AFTER

The occupation of Fez in June 1911 by the French caught the city's population completely off guard. The long siege of the city by the tribes had placed peoples' nerves on edge. Food supplies were low, and the possibility of a riot was never far from the minds of the upper class. At first, the merchants and notables of Fez were initially surprisingly willing to accept the French occupation. The restoration of order, they reasoned, would be good for business, and would no doubt soon lead to the improvement of communications between Fez and the coast. This also promised to work to their advantage. Unfortunately for them, what transpired in the months that intervened between the occupation and the signing of the protectorate treaty was a prolonged period of economic stagnation. The presence of the French army, in fact, tended to drive prices up, and there were constant incidents of jostling in the crowded streets of the city between townspeople and French troops. Clumsy administrative decisions by the Fez Native Affairs Bureau further aggravated the situation. The French native affairs officers, moreover, had no previous Moroccan experience. Many of them spoke no Arabic, and even those who did carried over their habits of rough treatment of natives acquired in service in Algeria and Tunisia.

By March of 1912, not only the artisans and common people but also increasingly many of the notables were feeling alienated from the French. The news of the signing of the protectorate treaty, accordingly, arrived in this political atmosphere with all of the effect of a bomb. The mutiny of *makhzan* troops against their French instructors on April 17 soon spread to the population of the city and led to several days of rioting and looting, primarily at the expense of the hapless Jewish population whose quarter of the city, the *mellah,* was looted and burned to the ground. The widespread unrest at Fez posed an immediate political problem for the new resident-general, Hubert Lyautey. Given the importance of Fez in the political life of the country, reassuring the notables and ulama of the city was crucial. One thing was certain: the policies adopted by Lyautey's predecessors were a complete failure. Lack of foresight, lack of experience, and a complete insensitivity to the pride and aspirations of the notables of Fez, together with lack of firm direction from above, were all in varying proportions responsible for the debacle. Under the circumstances a new analysis and a new policy were clearly needed. What had gone wrong?

French assumptions about the nature of Fez and Fasi society were entirely consonant with the stereotypes of the Moroccan gospel. The Fez revolts of 1907–8 and 1911, while offering warning signs that these understandings were defective, did not lead to a reevaluation. The mutiny of *makhzan* troops at Fez in March 1912 and the siege of the city that followed a month later soon changed French views. The suddenness and violence of the upheaval demonstrated the inadequacy of French ethnography of Morocco as well as the limitations of French power. Nothing in the Moroccan gospel prepared the French for the close alliance of rural and urban groups during the four-day siege. Nor could it explain the active participation of Fasi notables in the revolt. The 1912 popular upheaval at Fez cleared the way for a new French analysis of Fez and of Moroccan society.

Once order had been restored in and around the city, Lyautey turned to the task of setting the relations between Fez and the new protectorate government on a solid footing. He decided to try a new approach. The Fez Native Affairs Bureau, which dealt with the internal affairs of the city, was drastically overhauled, and its personnel changed. A brilliant young Arabist officer, Captain Georges Mellier, was placed in charge.[45] He organized a series of meetings between Lyautey and representative groups from different segments of the population of the city. Lyautey made an effort to put the notables at ease by assuring them that France had no intention of interfering with the religious freedom of Moroccans, and by strongly implying that it would be much more advantageous for them to cooperate with France than to oppose it. The new resident general spoke with a slightly different emphasis to each group. For example, he promised a group of students from the madrasas of the city that their annual rations (*mouna*) would regularly be paid and even increased, leaving unstated but clearly understood that the students had best stick to their books and keep their noses out of politics. Through the good offices of the British consul, James McLeod, Lyautey sought out Mawlay Idris ibn Abd al-Hadi, an influential uncle of the incumbent sultan, to reassure him as to French intentions and to seek his advice in the current situation. Such meetings and interviews went far to regain for France some degree of trust. In addition, and perhaps most importantly in the short run, Lyautey saw to it that the repressive measures instituted following the mutiny of April were withdrawn, or greatly reduced. As an act of clemency, many of the prisoners arrested following the mutiny were released, and the fines that had been imposed on the notables of Fez were canceled. Orders were given to French troops billeted outside the city to refrain from offending the city's inhabitants with such arrogant acts as riding at a gallop through the narrow, crowded streets. French officers were instructed on the potential dangers of unrestrained displays of French pride, such as elaborate victory ceremonials, flag raisings, and the like. Henceforth, French officers were to observe model decorum in their relationships with the citizens of Fez.[46]

While steps were being taken to lower the French profile in Fez, a daring new policy was in the process of being formulated and approved by the resident-general. It called for the establishment of an elective municipal council with control over the budget of the city, as well as an elected municipal government. The impetus for the project came from the French consul at Fez, Henri Gaillard, who had been engaged in working out the scheme since the French occupation of Fez in June 1911. The bitter feud between the diplomats and the military (a rivalry in which the military seemed to have the upper hand) had until then kept Gaillard's scheme in the background as an essentially Quai d'Orsay initiative. Lyautey was himself too much of a diplomat and too much of a pragmatist to allow such a dispute to interfere with policy planning for the new protectorate government. Especially in view of the dramatic failure of previous French policy toward the population of Fez, and the necessity of restoring order and regaining the political trust of the Fasi elite, the risks entailed in adopting so liberal a policy would be more than compensated for were it to be successful. If the policy were to fail, the degree of alienation of the notables of Fez could hardly be greater than it was already. Drawing on his almost twenty years of experience living in Fez, Gaillard possessed an unrivaled knowledge of the Fasi bourgeoisie. He was well aware of their sensitivities and pride and had already proven his understanding of the intricate web of patronage and genealogy that constituted the core of the political system of the city. Gaillard's knowledge of *makhzan* and palace circles rendered him all but irreplaceable in the present instance. In matters of native policy he was known as an admirer of British rule in Egypt, especially of the administration of Alexandria instituted under Lord Cromer. Lyautey was thus exercising shrewd political judgment in deciding to allow Fez to have a measure of municipal self-government.

In addition to the influence of Gaillard, Lyautey leaned heavily on the advice and experience of another old Fez hand, British consul James McIver McLeod. It was McLeod who advised him of the adverse political effects of the repressive failures instituted by Lyautey's predecessor, General Moinier. Some of the oldest and most influential Fasi merchants were British protégés, and McLeod enjoyed access to other segments of Fasi society that remained out of reach for the French. During the summer of 1912, McLeod found himself much occupied in filling the role of mediator between the new protectorate government and the Fasi notability. It was through the efforts of McLeod that the French were able to transform what had been in June a singularly embittered and suspicious Fasi elite into one willing to take part in an experiment in municipal self-government.

There were in fact several precedents for the establishment of the Fez municipality. One was the convening of a council of the leading members of the Moroccan elite, known as a *majlis al-a'yan,* to consider the 1904 French reform proposals.[47] A second was the ad hoc system of rule known as *shaykh al-rabia,* by which Fez governed itself during the civil war in 1907–8 and the 1911 siege.[48] Each quarter of the city selected by popular acclamation one or more prominent notables who would serve as guarantors of the security of their quarter. The selected notables in turn assembled in common and co-opted from among their number one or more individuals to serve as overall leaders of the city during the time of troubles. A ritual exchange of turbans and *silhams* (cloaks) among those selected, as in the case of other ad hoc alliances in Morocco, known as *'ar,* meant that the participants were constrained under threat of a spiritual kin bond to work together to maintain order.[49] An individual so selected was called a *shaykh al-rabia.* With these proto-representative institutions to build on and a strong sense of Fasi municipal pride, the French architects of a Muslim-Arab municipality for Fez were on relatively solid ground.

The *majlis al-baladi* (municipal council) was established by a decree (*dahir*) of September 2, 1912, addressed to the pasha of Fez.[50] It consisted of fifteen members, with the pasha of Fez serving as president. Seven of the members served ex officio as members of the municipal administration (the pasha and his three *khalifas* [chief assistants], the two *muhtasibs* [provosts of the market] of Old and New Fez, and the *na'ib* [deputy] of the *majlis,* serving as secretary). Eight additional elected members were selected for two-year terms from among the notables of Fez, two for each of the four voting districts of the city. Finally, two additional members of the municipal council were appointed who served in a purely advisory capacity and possessed no vote. They were the *amin al-mustafad,* formerly the treasurer of the city revenues, and the secretary-interpreter, charged with preparing the minutes of the meetings. The French chief of municipal services was an ex officio member. An alternate member was elected in each of the voting districts in the event of the illness or incapacity of one of those officially elected.[51]

Considerable pains were taken by the French to ensure that eligible notables cast their votes in the elections. Following the establishment of lists of eligible electors, discussion and amendment to the lists presented were allowed. Voting districts were created following the traditional divisions of the city, with New Fez counting as one district, and Old Fez being divided into the municipal quarters of Lemtiyine, Andalousiyine, and Adwa. A total of 374 notables were eligible to vote, and, of that number, 258 actually did so. Elections took place over the four-day period stretching from September 8 to 11, and a second ballot was held in one of the quarters because of a tie vote for the alternate. The results were an impressive testimony to the openness of the elections: of the twelve men elected, only one was a French protégé and included were five other protégés—three British, two Italian, and one German. Considering that the vote was held in the early forenoon of the first day of the Muslim month of Ramadan, the voting turnout was quite good. The ages of those elected ranged from 28 to 44, apparently on the principle that younger men, better acquainted with the ways of the West, would be more successful representatives in the new council. Several elderly merchants, who expected to win election automatically, discovered to their chagrin that they received only their own votes. In fact, since the seven ex officio members were all French appointees, the election of one French protégé was enough to tip the balance within the council to the French.[52]

Having badly misjudged the situation in Fez in the spring, the French seemed eager to atone for past errors. The elections to the *majlis al-baladi* and the appointment of Captain Mellier to head the Fez Arab Bureau persuaded the Fasi notables that Lyautey now understood that he could not take the cooperation of the Fasi ulama and the *a'yan* for granted. In the new political calculus, good relations with the Fasi *a'yan* and ulama required more than just a show of consultation. At first, the Fez *majlis* functioned well. Elections were held biannually for staggered terms, and the number of participating notables steadily increased.[53] Soon, however, delegates to the *majlis* found themselves systematically thwarted by the Fez Arab Bureau in their ability to vote on certain issues.[54] By 1914 the experiment of municipal self-government was clearly losing its steam. The successors to Captain Mellier came from colonial Algeria and brought with them their colonial attitudes toward the natives. Although Lyautey had wanted to make the Fez *majlis* a model for the rest of Morocco, he was forced to recognize that this form of municipal administration was unlikely to work in the coastal cities that were under the influence of French settlers. Instead mixed municipal councils were created, in which the French delegates freely exerted their authority over the Moroccan representatives. A final blow was the establishment of separate European *villes nouvelles,* which led to the withdrawal of funds from the Arab medinas. By the end of Lyautey's tenure as resident-general in 1924, a social gulf separated the French and the Moroccans in all Moroccan cities (including Fez by this time).[55]

In 1922 Édouard Michaux-Bellaire, the head of the MSM, the analysis division of the Native Affairs Bureau, was commissioned to evaluate what had gone wrong. In a confidential memorandum he reviewed the history of the *majlis al-baladi*. After a good start, things had begun to go sour. The Fasi bourgeoisie were cruelly disappointed. They had expected to play the same influential role in Morocco under the protectorate as they had before 1912, and at first they had. But after the transfer of the administration of the city of Fez to civilian control (*controle civil*), it was clear to the Fasi bourgeoisie that their opinions were no longer taken into account. Instead they were informed of administrative decisions after the fact. At the same time a host of discriminatory regulations and petty municipal taxes were imposed without their input. Taken together with their unfulfilled economic hopes, the result was that French legitimacy was seriously undermined. Michaux-Bellaire contrasted the attitude of the pre-1912 *makhzan* toward the Fasi elite with that of the 1920s protectorate administration. Before the protectorate the government had "always treated Fez with understanding . . . [and] always *took account of* the bourgeoisie of Fez and . . . refrained from governing them like a Bedouin population . . . it didn't treat them like natives [*bicots*]."[56]

In retrospect the inauguration of the *majlis al-baladi* at Fez in September 1912 was the turning point that did not turn. Although the old orientalist paradigms had failed either to predict or to explain the April/May 1912 uprisings, and a new analysis of Morocco and of Fasi society seemed required, one might have expected a discursive shift in French understandings of Morocco. But this did not occur. Because of France's enormous military superiority, the opinions of Moroccans, even the opinions of the Fasi elite, were superfluous. The need for collaboration with the Fasi elite faded with each French victory. The discursive power of the Moroccan gospel and the entrenched institutional culture of the colonial military bureaucracy proved more than a match for the forces for change. The replacement of Arab Bureau officers by civilian *contrôleurs civils* and the division of Moroccan cities into modern (predominantly French) *ville nouvelles* and traditional (and entirely Moroccan) medinas after the war completed the reassertion of the old paradigms. Except in moments of crisis, when the *majlis al-baladi* at Fez was still useful as a kind of political thermometer, by 1919 it had become a fossilized appendage of the native affairs bureaucracy.[57] For a critical understanding of the postwar context, we turn again to Michaux-Bellaire:

> In politics, you can't do [Pierre] Loti [an author of orientalist fantasies]. The muezzin's chants, the minarets, the old mosques, and the veiled women are tourism or art or poetry, sometimes even love or at least desire, but they are not administration or even organization. The Muslims do not love us, especially not here; they can have sympathy for a few [Europeans] who love them and who defend them against us; but it is perfectly unbearable to them that we govern them.[58]

Why did the new approach to native policy and applied sociology fail to take hold? We can rephrase our understanding of what happened in the language of Pierre Bourdieu as the reassertion of the power of the political field over that of the intellectual field.[59]

PART THREE

Governmental Morocco

Pierre von Paassen, a prominent early twentieth-century journalist, encountered Marshall Lyautey while both were visiting the Musée de l'armée de terre at the Château de Vincennes in the late summer of 1930. A sudden downpour stranded them together for a period, in which an impromptu interview occurred.

Von Paassen began by asking Lyautey the following question:

"Monsieur le Maréchal, you were proconsul of the French Republic in Morocco as Pontius Pilate was the proconsul of Rome in Judea. How would Your Excellency, if I may ask, have dealt with a man like Jesus?"

"Ah," Lyautey laughed, "that's an interesting question! I have thought of it myself sometimes. There is indeed a certain analogy in our positions, and I can tell you at once that Pilate, to my way of thinking, acted correctly as Roman proconsul, when he apprehended the Galilean. His task was to maintain the Pax Romana. What else could he do but put Jesus out of the way, the man who threatened law and order? It has always seemed strange to me that he waited three full years before he had him arrested. There must have been something wrong with the proconsul's intelligence service. . . ."

After discoursing on other topics, Marshall Lyautey continued: "Any man who can gather a crowd in the East should be watched—that has always been my view. During my term as resident-general in Morocco I was always kept informed of what these itinerant mullahs and ulemas and holy men were telling the people.

After a lengthy interlude, Von Passen was able to ask his final question: "Your Excellency would not have acted in the same way under the circumstances?"

To which Lyautey responded: "Parbleu, non! I would not have waited until He had infected the crowds of the capital with his seditious poison. I would have had Him put before a firing squad in his home province, up north in Galilee."

PIERRE VON PAASSEN, Days of Our Years (NEW YORK: HILLMAN-CURL, 1939), 144–49

Somewhere in this exchange lies the Lyauteyian theory of the protectorate.

NINE

The Invention of Moroccan Islam

THE HISTORY OF MOROCCAN ISLAM began with a relatively open first phase (1900–1906) focused on studies of "Islam in Morocco," which under the influence of the laws of colonial entropy gradually morphed into a disciplinarily defined but discursively policed new field, "Moroccan Islam." The open and historically grounded studies of Georges Salmon and Edmond Doutté in the early 1900s gradually became a bestiary of colonial stereotypes of Islam. The appearance of Édouard Michaux-Bellaire's 1909 "L'organisme marocain," the *summum* of colonial knowledge about Moroccan Islam, tells us all we need to know about the possibilities of achieving discursive escape velocity. The ideologically polarized political context prohibited original thought. As a consequence, the French failed to produce a functional analysis of the cultural sources of Moroccan resistance, ignored the role of the ulama, its links to the countryside, and to Islamic centers in the Middle East. Would better thinking about Islam in Morocco have yielded a better policy? Accepting this idea would be to fall into the trap of scientific imperialism— that there exists an Archimedean point removed from the world from which policy can be enacted.

By 1912, French ethnographers had produced a comprehensive inventory of Moroccan social groups and institutions: the *makhzan,* the Arab tribes of the south Atlantic plains, and the Berber groups of the High Atlas.[1] In the space of little more than a decade the books, journals, and articles on Morocco written in French had swelled to an impressive total. If the extent of the bibliography were an index of expertise, then the French could claim to be experts on Morocco. But if one looks at it another way, one might wonder about the utility of "scientific imperialism." For example, French analysts had neither predicted nor explained any of the major anti-French uprisings of the period. Why, one might ask, were there no studies of the Kattaniya, Aynayniya, and Darqawa—the Sufi *turuq* that led the anti-French resistance? Why was there so little interest in the Hafiziya, the movement that came closest to ending French dreams of acquiring Morocco? More generally, why were French Morocco watchers so unprepared for the social movements that repeatedly challenged their policies between 1900 and 1912? Might there be a link between the success of French ethnographers in mapping Moroccan realities, and their inability to perceive Morocco's politics? This chapter explores the question of why a self-consciously social scientific venture went so seriously astray.

To understand the reasons why the French failed either to foresee or to understand Moroccan resistance, we need to shift our attention to French representations of Islam in Morocco, a topic that we have reserved for discussion here. The invention of "Moroccan Islam" as a complex of stereotypes sought to explain Moroccan cultural realities and justify the French conquest. The discourse on Moroccan Islam provided the explanatory lens through which French and subsequent researchers perceived Moroccan culture. It was shaped by the general limitations of colonial knowledge systems and more specifically by the defects of the Algerian colonial legacy. As a consequence it contained hidden blind spots that inhibited the ability of the French to understand the sources of Moroccan resistance. To be sure, the tabula rasa on which the French began the study of Moroccan history and culture in 1900 also played a role. Finally, "Moroccan Islam" was shaped by the discursive context of pre-World War I French politics.

INVENTING MOROCCAN ISLAM

The French discourse on Moroccan Islam gradually took shape between 1904 and 1912. As a system of explanation, it brought together previously loosely integrated preexisting conceptual/ ideological subdiscourses on Sufism, popular religion, sharifism, and the role of the ulama. The first two were components of the Algerian intellectual toolkit imported with some modification (given the proliferation of Moroccan folk religion and its political potency) for the study of Moroccan Islam. By contrast, the study of sharifism and popular religion, which had been relatively undeveloped in Algerian scholarly writings, became in the hands of Doutté and his followers the main trends in the ethnography of Morocco. Like the light of a dying star that continues to diffuse through the heavens long after its actual extinction, the colonial discourse on Moroccan Islam has continued to radiate outward in the postcolonial era, providing a lens through which observers (both expatriate and Moroccan) continue to perceive Morocco.

By 1900 the French experience of Islam in colonial Algeria had cohered into an intellectual toolkit that was readily transferable to Morocco. Drawing on the French institutional memory of the Algerian conquest and the administration of Algerian Muslims, it consisted of a series of intellectual protocols and investigative modalities that reproduced French ambient secularist fears about religion (and not just Islam). Initially, Algerian Sufi orders and millenarian movements were at the center of French preoccupations. By the end of the century they had been replaced by the deep-seated fear of Pan-Islamic conspiracies.[2] Periodic intelligence panics about Muslim uprisings were the reciprocal of ethnographic ratiocinations about the Muslim Algerian other. In them we see in its most naked form the ideological component of French colonial ethnography.[3]

French studies of Algeria were generationally sedimented, with studies of Islamic millenarianism preceding works on Sufi *turuq,* and the study of popular beliefs occurring only toward the end of the nineteenth century. This sequence corresponded to the phases of the French conquest. Historically the anti-French resistance in Algeria had been led by the Sufi orders, notably the Qadiriya, which under the leadership of Amir Abd al-Qadir fought with considerable success for more than a decade. Following his defeat in 1847, resistance continued in the countryside, led by the Rahmaniya and the Darqawiya, regionally based *turuq* that posed less of a threat. As a result of this history, it was predetermined that the French would identify the Sufi orders as an object of study. The methodology they developed called for the head of the Arab Bureau to list the Sufi brotherhoods under his jurisdiction, along with their leaders and members. As a result of the leadership of the Rahmaniya *tariqa* in the Moqrani rebellion (1871–72), police files were opened on Rahmaniya adepts all over Algeria. Other Algerian brotherhoods known for their anti-French activities—the Darqawa, for example—were also closely watched. By 1890 Sufi brotherhoods were no longer much of a political threat to the French, and their study had become highly routinized and bureaucratized along the lines of Octave Depont and Xavier Coppolani's *Les confréries religieuses musulmanes* (1897). The regular census of Sufi orders, their leadership, and membership was a task assigned to the native affairs officers of the local Arab Bureaux. By then the military balance had begun to shift decisively toward the French. Still, as late as the end of the nineteenth century, panics over suspected Sanusiya conspiracies prompted further recurring episodes. The underlying mentality can be accessed in André Servier's *Le péril d'avenir*.[4] It is worth noting, however, that such fears received no support from Doutté, who stated in 1901: "The religious brotherhoods are not secret societies. . . . They come in all forms. . . . In reality the brotherhood is simply the common form of social organization in the Maghreb." He was even willing to acknowledge that mistakes had been made in the past:

> It is possible that in Algeria we have ourselves contributed to giving the brotherhoods a bit of a character of secret societies. This would be a very natural evolution following our domination, even as it is also quite natural that these associations provide refuge for fanatics appalled by contact with unbelievers. We don't consider them dangerous in the current state of things.[5]

In the course of the conquest, the French learned that not all Sufi orders were opposed to them and that they could take advantage of the micropolitics of inter-*tariqa* relationships to win their support. A case in point was the Tijaniya brotherhood. Based at Ain Madi in the Algerian Sahara, the Tijaniya had been rivals of Amir Abd al-Qadir's Qadiriya order well before the French conquest. When Abd al-Qadir became the leader of Algerian resistance in 1834 the Tijaniya refused to join his movement. Instead they approached the French, seeking an alliance. After Abd al-Qadir's defeat in 1847, the Tijaniya were able, with French backing, to cement their position in the High Plateaus and the Saharan oases of Oran province.[6] In Tunisia the local branches of the Tijaniya proved willing collaborators with the French. But French dreams of employing their influence elsewhere in Africa failed. Although the Tijani *zawiya* in Morocco appeared ready to support French policy, in the end it refused to cooperate.[7] But the biggest disappointment was West Africa, where the leaders of the Tijaniya adopted an anti-France stance.[8] These failures reveal a faulty analysis of the Tijaniya, which, instead of having a centralized structure, was comprised of semiautonomous local franchises.

A second example dates from the 1880s. Finding themselves challenged by growing British influence in Morocco, the French cast about for influential Moroccan figures whom they might use to counter their rivals. Having little or no regular access to the Moroccan court or the *makhzan* (where Britain was strong), the French sought to identify Sufi *turuq* and rural elites with whom it might be possible to ally. A promising candidate was soon identified: the sharif of Wazzan, Mawlay al-Ahmad al-Wazzan. Based in the northern city of Wazzan, the Wazzaniya had great influence throughout Morocco. The sharif was regarded as a quasi-divine personage by his followers. The fact that, like the Tijaniya, the Wazzaniya had branches in colonial Algeria no doubt attracted the French as well. The Quai d'Orsay gave the sharif a regular stipend, and accorded him protégé status, which exempted him from local Moroccan taxes and other civic obligations. However, when the French minister, Ladislas Ordega, sought to use the influence of Mawlay Ahmad in 1884 to persuade Sultan Mawlay al-Hasan to accept a reform package, it provoked a major crisis that led to the abandonment of the reform plan and the withdrawal of Ordega in disgrace. This incident appears to have galvanized the ulama and notables of Fez, who opposed to the superstitious practices of Sufi orders like the Wazzaniya. The sharif's influence declined steadily thereafter, and his successors failed to carry his legacy forward.[9] To add to this policy debacle, the Algerian branch of the Wazzaniya proved hostile to French rule and refused to cooperate.

Early studies of Moroccan *turuq* tended to follow the Algerian precedent in listing the numbers of adherents of Sufi orders in each village, the name of the local *muqaddam* (leader), and other relevant features.[10] Given the delays between the compilation of the data and its publication, such studies were obsolete before they were printed. Indeed, the study of Moroccan Sufi orders was never a high priority for French policymakers. One sign of this is that a survey of Moroccan brotherhoods along the lines of Depont and Coppolani's study was published only in 1951 as the protectorate entered its final days. Its author was Georges Spillmann, a career native affairs officer (rather than a civilian).[11] By this date, the *turuq* had long since ceased to have political weight in Moroccan politics. In a last-ditch effort to save the protectorate, French authorities sought to enlist Abd al-Hay al-Kattani, head of the pro-French Kattaniya *tariqa,* to demonstrate in favor of the puppet king Ben Arafa—an action that only reinforces this judgment.[12]

In the elaboration of the discourse on Moroccan Islam, studies of rural folk religion were a second focal point of research.[13] As exemplified in the approach of researchers like Doutté, the study of marabouts, saint cults, curing practices, and spirit possession provided the larger frame for the construction of the discourse on Moroccan Islam. For Doutté, the intellectual task was to locate Moroccan religious beliefs and practices in an evolutionary scheme and link them to Frazerian symbols. Writing about Morocco in a 1901 research report, he states, "No country is more amenable to the study of the survival of old religions than Mohamedanism: springs, trees, especially stones still play an important role in popular religion." While such cults were fascinating in themselves, Doutté and his colleagues regarded them as fossilized relics, throwbacks to the early days of Islam. They firmly believed that Moroccan superstitious beliefs were incapable of change, which in their eyes made them the best possible remedy against the preachings of anti-French prophets. However, neither studies of Sufism in the tradition of the Arab Bureaux nor studies of popular Algerian religion à la Doutté were calculated to shed much light on the cultural sources of Moroccan resistance.

Sharifism (lineal descent from the family of the Prophet) was also a focal point in the discourse on Moroccan Islam. The principle of sharifism was central to Moroccan politics, and sharifian lineages proliferated widely. Local Sufi leaders and marabouts (living saints) commonly claimed sharifian origin. Sharifism provided believers with alternative access to the divine. Nonelites as well as members of well-established families might claim sharifian descent. The ruling Alawi dynasty's claim of descent from the family of the Prophet served as a guarantee of its authority and legitimacy. However, rival sharifian lineages also existed. These included the Idrisis (who first brought Islam to Morocco) and the Sa'dians (the previous dynasty) as well as lesser sharifian lineages like the Sharqawis. Given the plethora of individuals and groups asserting sharifian descent, French observers found it difficult to grasp the significance of the assertion of a sharifian origin to Moroccan politics. Recalling the history of French dynastic struggles, they calculated the chances that a collateral branch of Moroccan sharifs might be encouraged to make a bid for power in the event the Alawis failed to cooperate. The French diplomat who used the pseudonym Eugène Aubin sought to put to rest such obscure fears in his *Le Maroc d'aujourd'hui* (1904). Drawing on the insider knowledge of Kaddour Ben Ghabrit, an Algerian Muslim in the employ of the French Legation, his book provided one of the earliest and clearest explanations of the role of sharifs in the Moroccan polity.[14] More authoritative (because it was based on Arabic manuscripts) was a 1904 article by Georges Salmon in *Archives marocaines* (*AM*) that described in detail the different sharifian lineages in Morocco, and their relationships and rivalries.[15]

Another component of the discourse on Moroccan Islam was the belief that magico-religious practices, such as the belief in *baraka* (blessing), could inhere in lesser saints and Sufi leaders, as well as in the sultan. Sharifism and *baraka* were intimately linked to popular Islamic practices more generally (the sharif of Wazzan, for instance, was also widely reputed for his *baraka*). *Baraka* was not something one could claim for oneself; rather, it was accorded by popular attribution. French observers were slow to appreciate the enormous significance of *baraka,* its multivalent spiritual power, and its quixotic character in Moroccan culture. Doutté was the first French observer to appreciate the importance of *baraka.*[16] The Swedish ethnographer Edward Westermarck (1862–1939) was the first to write about the role of *baraka* in Moroccan culture.[17] Nonetheless, *baraka* was assigned a central role in the discourse on Moroccan Islam only following the establishment of the protectorate. It became the cultural feature that best distinguished Moroccan culture from that of other Muslim societies.

Unlike Algeria, Morocco was not part of the Ottoman Empire, nor had Moroccan cities suffered the devastation that the French conquest had brought to Algerian Muslim urban institutions (mosques, madrasas, and *waqf*). Moreover, following the French conquest, many of the Algerian ulama fled to Fez, Tunis, Cairo, and Damascus. As a result, the role of the Algerian ulama failed to attract the interest of French scholars. By contrast, the Moroccan ulama retained an autonomous intellectual and political authority unknown in colonial Algeria. Thus they were able to play a crucial role in galvanizing Moroccan opposition to the French in the period under study. In 1904, members of the Fasi ulama were actively involved in the Fez *majlis al-a'yan.* They also led the December 1907 movement to depose Abd al-Aziz and to swear allegiance *(bay'a)* to Abd al-Hafiz in January 1908. Despite this history of ulama activism, French researchers displayed little interest in them. The Moroccan ulama inspired no book-length studies and only a few articles, most of which insisted on their superstitious and backward nature, rather than the bases of their political authority. Nor in the period that concerns us here were there studies of the premier institution of higher learning in Morocco, the Qarawiyin mosque university of Fez. The absence of studies of the ulama, especially those in touch with Middle Eastern currents of reform, left French Morocco specialists without a means of understanding some of the most important challenges their policy would confront. The one significant exception was Aubin's *Le Maroc d'aujourd'hui.* Aubin was among the first to stress the political and intellectual heterogeneity of the Fasi ulama, and to recognize their links to currents of political and religious reform originating in the eastern Mediterranean.[18] This was a rare perspective for the time. Until the end of the colonial empires, European researchers on Islamic societies (not just Morocco) comfortably regarded the ulama as unworthy of study. The heyday of what is sometimes called "ulamology" (the study of the ulama) lay well in the future.[19]

By 1904, many of the elements of what would become Moroccan Islam were present, yet the discourse on Moroccan Islam had not yet cohered. The first to draw together the various elements into a persuasive whole was Édouard Michaux-Bellaire. His 1909 article, "L'organisme marocain," wove together aspects of Moroccan history and culture in ways that emphasized the existence of a specifically Moroccan style of Islam. Doutté had previously spoken of a Moroccan organism (*l'organisme marocain*) but not with this specific meaning. Organismic thinking was common in French social thought of the period, and Doutté's use of the term *organisme* should be read as an attempt to establish a link to French social thinkers such as Henri Bergson, August Comte, and the latter's disciples and rivals (including Émile Durkheim).[20] For Michaux-Bellaire, the term "Moroccan Islam" appears to have referred more to the Berber component in Moroccan identity than to its Muslim sources.[21] The content of the Berber field, however, remained to be filled in only after 1912 (see chapter 7). By 1912, the term "Moroccan Islam" was regularly used as a shorthand to signify the distinctive characteristics of the Moroccan polity.

The invention of "Moroccan Islam" marked an important innovation in the field of French orientalism. Although rooted in Algerian colonial culture and the larger political and intellectual culture of France, Moroccan Islam distinguished Morocco from Algeria and Tunisia as an object of study. It enabled specialists on Morocco and Moroccan society to assert their expertise against those with credentials forged elsewhere. Moroccan Islam, by delimiting a specifically Moroccan ethnographic terrain, also shaped the French understanding of Moroccan politics throughout the protectorate period. It brought elements of French knowledge about Sufism and popular Islam together with the more explicitly Moroccan elements of sharifism and *baraka*. The realm of the ulama was regarded as traditionalist, and obscurantist, as was the realm of the marabouts, whom Alfred Bel called "les hommes fetiches," miracle-working thaumaturges.[22] By emphasizing the superstitious religious beliefs and practices that allegedly characterized Moroccan culture, the discourse on Moroccan Islam provided an explanation of Moroccan backwardness, and hence its "colonizability." In so doing it also implied that only France had the knowledge and experience to assist Morocco along the path to progress without causing major upheavals. By definition, "Moroccan Islam" excluded investigation of contemporary Muslim belief and practice in Morocco and the world. It pertained to a timeless Morocco.

The discourse on Moroccan Islam was based on a number of cultural assumptions that bear further examination. One was the image of Morocco as a land that time had forgotten, an outdoor museum of archaic customs and beliefs, the abode of tradition. For the generation of Doutté, Morocco appeared as a survival from another age, its religious scholars stuck in an outdated cultural groove. The portrait of Morocco as a place without history was convenient, for it allowed the French to portray themselves as the bearers of progress to a benighted land.

It is not that Doutté and the other researchers exaggerated the popular religious beliefs and practices of fin de siècle Morocco. Doutté was a splendid ethnographer of popular religion. He was right to invoke Frazer's *Golden Bough* as a lens through which to see Morocco. But his enthusiasm for seeing Morocco through this lens blinded him to the fact that the Morocco of his research was already eluding his categories. (Or perhaps the opposite: that his predetermined categories created a "research Morocco" frozen in time, even though part of him knew that it was not the actually existing Morocco.) In many respects, of course, precolonial Morocco was indeed rich in ethnographic beliefs and practices that looked as though they came straight out of the pages of *The Golden Bough*.[23] The collected books and articles on the Moroccan colonial gospel amply document this fact. But the idea that Morocco was immune to the winds of change was deeply misleading.

A second disabling assumption of the French colonial gospel was that Morocco had no real politics. Instead, there was the eternal Sisyphean struggle between the forces of *bilad al-makhzan* and the supporters of *bilad al-siba*. Occasional spasmodic outbursts were seen by the French as unavoidable, but were devoid of political meaning. In coming to this conclusion French researchers were looking in the wrong direction. What interested them were rural folk religion, marabouts, saint cults, curing practices, spirit possession, and other signs of a decaying but once vital culture. But none of these groups played a significant role in opposing the French. Despite a few notable exceptions (the Kattaniya, Aynayniya, and Darqawa, among others), the main Sufi brotherhoods or *turuq* were politically quietistic in the early twentieth century. Although the pre-1912 period was replete with struggles among rival princes, government factions, *grands qa'ids,* peasants, and tribesmen, none were of significance in the European scheme of things (the only one that counted). Thus French policymakers assumed the actions of Moroccans were devoid of political meaning and could safely be disregarded. But if the French ignored the extent of the politicization of Moroccan society, they did so at their peril.

Why was this the case? One answer is that the military balance had shifted dramatically in favor of the French by the early twentieth century. While Algerian resistance had been a major theme for Arab Bureaux officers in the first half century of French rule, the last significant anti-French jihad in Algeria was the 1871–72 Moqrani rebellion.[24] It was clear to Morocco experts that while France might be inconvenienced in Morocco, there was little danger that it could be militarily defeated. As a result, with but a few exceptions (Alfred Le Chatelier and A. G. P. Martin come to mind), most French Morocco specialists were slow to become concerned when things began to go badly. By 1900 Algerian Islam was widely if erroneously perceived as moribund.[25] This is one explanation of why ethnographers like Doutté turned to the study of popular religious belief.

From this it was but a small step to assume that Morocco was isolated from the rest of the Muslim world, that it was a land without history.[26] Research on Moroccan folklore à la Doutté provided an accurate if partial portrait of Moroccan popular culture and its superstitious beliefs and practices. But to conclude from this that Morocco was a cultural island was a mistake. The culturalist approach of researchers like Doutté and Michaux-Bellaire missed many of the key determinants of Moroccan resistance. If we wish to transcend the Moroccan colonial gospel, we need to locate Moroccan political culture in the larger regional, civilizational, and global contexts in which it existed. French blindness to Moroccan connections with the Arab East and the world at large meant that the French had little awareness of the larger context of Moroccan actions, or of their political meaning. This lacuna repeatedly jeopardized the position of the French in Morocco. While Le Chatelier's broad vision at least implicitly recognized the importance of "offstage" factors in the evolution of Moroccan politics, neither he nor anyone else sought to place events in Morocco in the wider context of world history.

The paradox of Morocco in this period was that it was simultaneously in the embrace of multiple cultural influences. Some Moroccans (especially younger ones) had traveled through Europe and the Mediterranean, read newspapers, and were in touch with the historical trends of the period. Some were even well traveled, and a few subscribed to the Arabic press of the Middle East (as well as. in a few cases. the French press). Literate and aware, their voices counted in the world of urban notables, ulama, and *makhzan* officials. Many among the Fasi ulama were staunch modernist scripturalists in direct touch with the universities of the Middle East.[27] Largely unseen by the French, Moroccan notables were in sustained contact with Ottoman authorities as well as with Pan-Islamic circles that spanned the globe. They sought to forge an alliance with the Ottomans, including not only diplomatic support but also the use of Turkish military instructors. Others, seeking more potent remedies, activated Pan-Islamic connections with the Middle East and beyond. The Egyptian newspaper *al-Muayyad* played a key role in forging ties between Moroccan activists and *al-ittihad al-maghrabi* (Maghreb Unity), a Cairo-based Pan-Islamic organization whose main goal was to support anticolonial resistance in Arab North Africa.[28] There is also evidence that South Asian Muslims contributed to the support of the Moroccan resistance in the pre-1914 period.[29] They strongly opposed a French protectorate and were willing to do what they could to stave it off.

Peasants and tribesmen might have been less able to calibrate the global balance of forces, or to understand events outside of the framework of religious belief, but many of them were nonetheless opposed to the prospect of foreign rule, which they saw as the source of the changes that were undermining their way of life. While deeply conservative, they were also critics of an old order that in increasingly alarming ways appeared to have lost its way. Caught in the middle, they were uncertain which way to turn. Finally, there were those who remained loyal to Abd al-Aziz. Betting on the survival of the old order, they refused to join the Hafiziya, or to participate in the struggle to depose Abd al-Aziz. Insofar as French views came from their connections to these old regime loyalists, the French were deprived of access to the great political earthquake that was the Hafiziya (as the national movement to install Abd al-Hafiz as sultan was called).

While for Doutté Moroccan Islam was a Frazerian survival, if we look more deeply, we see that it was religion (and not just Moroccan Islam) that was the true "survival" even for European contemporaries. One of the most significant drivers of cultural warfare in Third Republic France was the recrudescence of the struggle between church and state. Its modern history goes back to the French Revolution, which saw the seizure of church lands by the revolutionary assembly, and the requirement that the clergy swear an oath of allegiance to the republic. Opposed at the time by the higher clergy and most of the aristocrats, it continued to fester even after relations were regularized by the Napoleon. Under the Concordat (1801), the papacy acquiesced in allowing the French state to name Catholic bishops, in return for which the clergy became salaried state employees and were authorized to provide primary education. This historic compromise went down poorly with partisans on both sides. It offended both the Jacobins on the French Left, and the ultramontane Catholics and royalists on the right. Nonetheless, until the advent of the Third Republic (1872–1940) church-and-state relations continued along the lines laid down by the Concordat.

The Third Republic got off on the wrong footing because the monarchists were in the ascendancy and the republicans were divided. But soon they reversed positions. The alliance of the French church with the monarchists and the Right stoked the political fires on the left. The hostility of Pope Leo XIII to the republic and to modernity in all its forms only exacerbated the situation. While not explicitly about church-state relations, the Dreyfus affair activated this political fault line. In an effort to disrupt the monarchists, the *parti radical* (the main left-wing political grouping) and the French Masonic orders began to push for the legal separation of church and state. Things came to a head in 1901, when the rising tide of anticlerical fervor in France led to the passage of the first of a series of laws that eventually culminated in the legal separation of church and state. After a prolonged and bitter debate, the 1905 law separating church and state was passed. It abolished the Concordat and required the Catholic Church to submit to the administrative regulation of the French state. The state would no longer provide salaries to the clergy, but undertook to pay the upkeep of religious buildings. Had things remained on this plane, the compromise might have held. But the anticlericals saw a chance to twist the knife. They inserted a clause into the law requiring the state to verify the value of churches and other religious structures and their contents, if necessary by deploying police to enforce the law. When French officials were sent to churches to take inventory of the vestments, altar plate, and other valuables this provoked angry demonstrations and fighting, including at least one death.[30]

The violent passions aroused by the clerical/anticlerical struggle in this period underscore the embattled feelings of both sides. Anticlerical forces saw themselves as the inheritors of the legacy of the Revolution, and anticlericalism as the ideological core of the Jacobin tradition. For militant secularists, especially members of the Radical Party, religion was seen as a holdover from another age. Through its institutional power and hold on the minds of the faithful, the church posed a major obstacle to the advance of science and progress in general. In response, anticlericalists proposed a highly charged, emotional defense of the Third Republic against its enemies: monarchy, medievalism, obscurantism, and papism. Only if the church and its allies were crushed could the good news of the revolution finally flower. As the chief defender of the anticlerical position, the Radical Party felt itself to be embattled. Algeria was juridically a part of France in which the Radical Party was especially strong. It regularly sent six deputies to the French parliament, all of whom were *Radicaux* or *Radicaux de Gauche*. In colonial Algeria religion was daily on view, the marker of the ethnicity of Muslims (who were legal subjects but not citizens of France) and Jews (who had become citizens in 1870 with the Crémieux Decree). Insofar as Algerian Jews retained their distinctive customs and dress, their recalcitrance was increasingly taken by militant secularists as a sign that the work of the Revolution remained undone. The anti-Semitic crisis of the 1890s stemmed in part from this perception.[31] While the Catholic Church in Algeria was weaker than in other parts of France, prelates such as Cardinal Lavigerie (1825–92), the archbishop of Algiers, had ready connections with the higher circles of the French Right. In sum, there was much in the colonial Algerian setting to motivate Radicals. More specifically, at the University of Algiers, whose politics were strongly marked by the struggle over religion. Doutté and many of his colleagues personally regarded religion as profoundly retrograde. Doutté wrote from a position of great confidence in the success of the modernist project in Algeria. His fascination with popular Islamic religion is perhaps but a sign of his concern about the continued baleful influence of religion more generally. If we would understand Moroccan Islam we need to reflect on the militant laicité of Doutté and his colleagues.

RESEARCH MOROCCO: CULTURAL AND POLITICAL CONTEXTS

For French Morocco specialists, Moroccan Islam (and the Moroccan colonial gospel more generally) was a relic of a former age. This "research Morocco" was a product of both the cultural moment (and the dominance of organismic thinking in French social thought) and the political context (the apex of anticlericalism). It led researchers to emphasize the political salience of cultural features that no longer drove events in Morocco (though they once may have done so). Other features that in retrospect might have attracted their interest (the political turbulence generated by French policies) remained outside their field of vision. Their failure to understand the importance of the Hafiziya revolution of 1907–8 is instructive in this regard. In sum, while the success of the "research Morocco" in elaborating on existing intellectual paradigms added to the prestige of French *science* and the reputations of individual scholars, from another point of view (given its dismal record in explaining or predicting events) it could equally have been considered a scandalous waste of intellectual energy.

Of course in the end French ignorance was functional. After the 1904 signing of the entente cordiale and the first major loan agreement, France acquired a vested interest in the existence of the *makhzan*. Loudly trumpeting the virtues of "peaceful penetration," the French claimed that by collaborating with the Moroccan government, reforms would be rolled out, Moroccan police would be trained, and Moroccans would acquire, with French tutelage, the ability to govern themselves. This way of framing Morocco permitted the French to portray Moroccan protest and resistance as devoid of political meaning, merely the spasmodic response of primitive tribes, always averse to paying taxes or recognizing the authority of the *makhzan*. Given the level of resistance generated by French policy (Moroccans came close to expelling the French from Morocco no less than five times in the period), it is remarkable that the French and international publics never raised the issue. The discursive power of the Moroccan colonial archive allowed France to claim expertise against all doubters. Indeed it was essential to the prosecution of French policy. Given the narrow political margins in the French parliament on colonial questions (governments rose and fell two or three times a year), and the level of opposition and scrutiny French policy inspired internationally, the French claim to expertise on Moroccan affairs constituted a crucial card in their hand. So there could be no official admission that anything was amiss in France's Morocco venture.

The Hafiziya revolution occasioned only one published analysis of what went wrong. It was Doutté's 1909 public lecture series "Les causes de la chute d'un sultan. A tired rehearsal of the author's views on Moroccan Islam, it appeared in *Afrique française* two years after the event. The entire lecture series was redolent of the trait-collecting mania of James Frazer's *Golden Bough* and displayed not the slightest engagement with its ostensible subject.[32] The six lectures were keyed to topics in which Doutté had previously established expertise: Moroccan Islam and marabouts, anti-Christian fanaticism, sharifianism, sacrifice, messianism, and jihad. Dazzling in their erudition, these lectures sought to link Moroccan cultural traits to Frazerian cultural archetypes ("sacral kingship," for example). Although Doutté identified some of the causes of Abd al-Aziz's overthrow (for example, why the 1901 *tartib* tax reform proved so polarizing) and displayed an acute knowledge of Moroccan factional politics, he failed to identify the social origins of Moroccan resistance. A deeply orientalist and narrowly political reading of the Hafiziya revolution by a leading Morocco expert, Doutté's lectures make one reconsider not only his seriousness, but that of French policy planners in general.

Despite its impressive achievements, the Moroccan colonial archive remains shadowed by the cloud of orientalist stereotypes that occluded the ability of ethnographers to perceive actually existing Moroccan society. In this sense the Moroccan colonial archive is a record of a systematic intelligence failure. Although numerous powerful rural rebellions marked the precolonial period, none were forecast by the French. The 1900–1912 period was replete with urban insurrections, yet the urban working classes and artisanal guilds excited little interest among French researchers. Nor, despite the continual French military debacle, was there a detailed study of urban/rural connections. Although rural revolts were numerous and important, they prompted no reassessment of the sources of Moroccan resistance. Major French military blunders in the Middle Atlas in 1911, 1912, and 1913 were swept under the rug. Not until 1914 were the first studies of the Middle Atlas Berbers published. Of course, there was no interest in the role of women, an almost inconceivable research topic at the time. Finally, other than a few studies by Nahum Slousch published in *AM*, there was little research on the small but important Moroccan Jewish minority.[33]

In the larger perspective, the Moroccan ethnographic archive was summoned into existence as part of a systematic French effort to gather information (*renseignements*) about Morocco, the better to dominate and control it. Thus there can be no doubt about the ultimate purpose for which this information was gathered. Certainly it is no great feat to discover that colonial forms of knowledge were colonialist. What else could they have been? There is no alternative epistemological space from which celestial ethnographers might have produced uncontaminated knowledge of Moroccan society. Historians are taught that sources always bear the stigmata of the time and place of their production, including the personalities of their authors, the nature of their intended audiences, and the contexts in which they sought to intervene. Sources must therefore be carefully cross-questioned, and all sources are to a certain degree contaminated. Human attachments to the world inevitably make this so. Our sense of superiority toward earlier generations—that we know so much now that they were unable to perceive—is thus deceptive, since we too labor under the same conditions of time-boundedness.

TEN

_____

From the Ethnographic State
to Moroccan Islam

THERE WAS NO DISCOURSE ON Moroccan Islam before colonialism. Nor was Morocco an integrated national territory. Rather, the discourse on Moroccan Islam was reinvented at each major turn of the wheel, as Morocco itself was remolded from 1900 onward. Before the establishment of the protectorate, Moroccan Islam—both the French discourse, and the national myth of modern Morocco—was very much a work in progress. Moroccan Islam emerged as an object of study in response to the political and intellectual struggles surrounding the Moroccan question. Under the French colonial gaze Morocco's distinctive society, culture, and institutions were inspected by the lens of power, inventoried, and pathologized. As a result of the work of a generation of French scholars, the Moroccan colonial archive (all French writings on Moroccan culture, society, and history) gradually took shape.

The discourse on Moroccan Islam corresponded to two apparently contradictory impulses. At once deeply modernist in its efforts to organize and govern while profoundly Eurocentric and racist in its assumptions about humanity, it represents a kind of apotheosis of fin de siècle French colonial thought and action. This chapter provides a retrospective examination of the discourse on Moroccan Islam, and the three modalities that it launched: research Morocco, native policy Morocco, and governmental Morocco. It concludes with some reflections on the historical significance of this sort of colonial cultural engineering to the modern history of Morocco.

THE DISCOURSE ON MOROCCAN ISLAM:
IMPERATIVES AND LIMITATIONS

In 1900 France had little systematic knowledge about modern Moroccan culture, society, and institutions. But soon things began to change. By 1906 French knowledge was already sufficient to provide France with undisputed ethnographic authority at the Algeciras conference. By 1912, when the French protectorate was established, the Moroccan archive had become impressive in both its range and its depth. As a result of the publications of the Mission scientifique du Maroc and the study missions sponsored by the Comité de l'Afrique française, the Moroccan colonial archive came into being. It comprised studies of the workings of the societies of northwestern Morocco, Fez, and the tribes of the southern Morocco coast and plains. Until after 1912 relatively little was known about the Berber populations of the Atlas Mountains. Nonetheless, by that date an impressive bibliography had been created. Under the aegis of the protectorate government, the compilation of the Moroccan colonial archive proceeded apace.

A major political dynamic during the period of the Moroccan question was the disruptive feedback between the colonial, metropolitan, and international spaces. Before the launching of the protectorate in 1912, the tensions of empire deriving from the unresolved issues of the Moroccan question twice led France to the brink of war with Germany. These issues threatened the stability of governments, and brought about far-reaching shifts in political alignments. In the atmosphere of continual crisis that characterized Third Republic France, the struggle over Morocco was one of the more significant. In this context it is therefore perhaps not so surprising that a quarrel between research groups over the control of research on Morocco in the period 1900–1904 could open hitherto unsuspected splits between political groupings, bureaucratic factions, and academic rivals.

Under the French protectorate the new academic discipline of Moroccan studies was established, distinct from native affairs, along with a specialized research unit, the Institut des hautes études marocains, an academic periodical, *Hespéris,* and a new university, the École supérieure des lettres de Rabat. Moroccan Islam was reinvented a fourth time in the 1960s and 1970s by a group of British and American researchers as part of the academic debates over modernization theory. A fifth reinvention is currently in progress under Muhammad VI.[1] In each of these transformations of the discourse on

Moroccan Islam, its content and role were altered to fit the new circumstances via the creation of new modalities.

This study has attempted to view the development of the French discourse on Moroccan Islam through the lens of Moroccan responses. In retrospect it is extraordinary how little the French doctrine of "scientific imperialism" had to say about the social and cultural roots of Moroccan anticolonial resistance. Several reasons may be advanced as to why this was the case. First, the discursive authority of Moroccan Islam tended to drown out the voices of both Moroccan resisters and French anticolonialists. Despite the overwhelming military superiority enjoyed by the French, Moroccan resistance was robust and persistent. On multiple occasions it narrowly missed throwing French plans into jeopardy. In the highly charged and shifting political contexts, the discursive context that shaped what researchers could think and write changed constantly.

Exploiting a wrinkle in the larger French discursive frame, interesting and complexly historicized work was produced between 1900 and 1905 that contrasted sharply with the nostrums of the Algerian colonial gospel. But the context shifted after the entente cordiale and the Franco-Moroccan loan agreement of 1904. The de facto French alliance with the *makhzan* rendered inconvenient more complex and nuanced views about Moroccan society. So too did the heightening of political tensions and the emergence of increasingly widespread anticolonial resistance. The laws of discursive gravity being what they are, this led to more historically grounded views being discarded in favor of the binaries of the Moroccan colonial gospel—*makhzan/siba,* nomad/sedentary, and Arab/Berber. After 1907, study missions into the Moroccan countryside became impossible to sustain because of increased resistance, and the discourse on Moroccan Islam became increasingly stultified.

While the binaries of the Moroccan colonial gospel were poor ethnography, they were skillful discursive politics. By asserting that Morocco was riven by the supposed cultural encoding of endless fighting between supposed opposites, the Moroccan colonial gospel sought to justify French presence. In portraying Moroccan anticolonial resistance as merely spasmodic anti-*makhzan* revolts, the colonial gospel ensured they would lack political legibility. Only France (the discourse on Moroccan Islam suggested) could prevent Moroccans from killing one another. By the same fearful logic some Moroccans were provided with a cultural peg on which to hang their willingness to collaborate with the protectorate.

This book has argued for the need to more fully historicize our understandings of colonial forms of knowledge, the case in point being the creation of the Moroccan colonial archive. But since colonial forms of knowledge continue to shape the ways in which we contemporaries apprehend the post-9/11 world, the continual transformation of the discourse on Moroccan Islam provides useful lessons about the connections between knowledge and power. The critique of colonial forms of knowledge has far from exhausted its potential.

ANGLO-AMERICAN REPRESENTATIONS

The transformations of Moroccan Islam did not end with French colonialism. During the period 1965–70, British and American social scientists took up Morocco as an object of study. Most were anthropologists, attracted by Morocco's mixture of tribalism and popular religion. The tone was set by Ernest Gellner, an intellectually combative British philosopher and social anthropologist, and Clifford Geertz, a leading American cultural anthropologist, and his students. Strongly influenced by Karl Popper, Gellner was a critical rationalist who opposed neo-Kantian historicist thinking. Geertz was a champion of symbolic anthropology who had gained his reputation as the result of prior work in Indonesia. Both were deeply grounded in philosophy and committed to anthropological fieldwork. Both had interests that extended far beyond Morocco. Their careers encompassed many phases and are not readily summarized here. Both made notable contributions to theorizing the relations between Islam and the Moroccan state.

The image of Morocco projected by Ernest Gellner in his 1969 book, *Saints of the Atlas,* reaffirmed elements of the French colonial gospel while it changed the emphases.[2] Gellner's polemical style (honed in the philosophy wars in 1950s Britain) and abundant self-confidence enabled him to forcefully criticize French social science views on Morocco.[3] He conducted research among isolated tribes in the central High Atlas with a high propensity to engage in feuding behavior. He argued that their disputes were mitigated by the mediating role of local holy men/marabouts. His collection of essays, *Muslim Societies,* sought to apply his theoretical approach beyond Morocco to the rest of the Muslim world.[4] Thick on argument and thin on fieldwork, Gellner's eruption into the Moroccan intellectual field created a sensation, especially coming as it did at the end of French hegemony. Two aspects of Gellner's approach merit mention here.

First, Gellner viewed Moroccan tribes though the spectacles of then current British social anthropology on segmentary lineages elsewhere in Africa, in which the prevalence of feud risked splitting the tribe as different segments took sides based on their position in the genealogical hierarchy. Moroccan tribes, in Gellner's analysis, were always threatened by a complete breakdown of political order. But such moments of rupture were rare. This could be attributed, he argued (in the second part of his approach), to the role of marabouts, who utilized their spiritual power (*baraka*) to mediate disputes. In an early article, "How to Live in Anarchy," Gellner proposed that the political world of the (presumptively Berber) Ait XX was threatened by Hobbesian propensities toward all-engulfing violence.[5] Yet despite the absence of a state, violence was contained through the mediation of the marabout, and society continued to function. In many respects the world of the Ait XX appealed to Gellner because it authorized him to perform an elegant bit of philosophical jujitsu, scattering both his anthropological and his philosophical rivals by suddenly swapping disciplines in mid-demonstration. His most important accomplishment was reimagining the tropes of Moroccan Islam for an Anglophone and postcolonial world. Before Gellner, *baraka* had not been an important aspect of the French colonial model of Morocco. By showing how *baraka* worked to tamp down violence at the local level, Gellner suggested that it was a feature of the Moroccan political system at all levels. In other essays Gellner claimed that it governed the response of Moroccan rural populations to the king. By importing British segmentary lineage theory from Africa and linking it to *baraka,* Gellner helped rehabilitate the discourse on Moroccan Islam.

The appearance of anthropologist Clifford Geertz's *Islam Observed* (1968) marked his transition from Indonesia to Morocco.[6] Over the years Geertz would return to the comparison of these two quite different societies.[7] Previously the author of four brilliant works on Indonesia, the best known of which was his *Religion of Java* (1960), Geertz began his fieldwork in Morocco in 1964–65.[8] Strongly influenced by American pragmatism in the mold of Henry James, and by British language philosophy à la Gilbert Ryle, Geertz was suspicious of Continental philosophical fashions.[9] His interpretive anthropology challenged the then fashionable structural functionalism of the 1950s social sciences. In *Islam Observed* he developed a stimulating comparison of Morocco and Indonesia based on his early fieldwork and readings of the French colonial literature. His depiction of the eternal struggle of tribe and town reflected the influence of Édouard Michaux-Bellaire's canonical "L'organisme marocain," while his view of Moroccan leaders as a series of variations on the theme of warrior-saint showed the influence of Alfred Bel (1873–1945).[10] In particular, in Geertz's discussion of *baraka* in the spiritual powers of the warrior-saint we see the influence of Gellner (and once again Bel), for whom the figure of the powerless saint endowed with awe-inspiring spiritual powers provided a metaphor for Moroccan society. Geertz's work on Morocco is characterized by its diffidence in the face of the changing political enthusiasms of the moment, and its efforts to identify a core Moroccan identity. While Geertz's views continued to evolve, the clarity and appeal of his early formulations provided an indelible template for Anglophone scholars of Moroccan Islam, in which the influence of the colonial discourse is readily detectable.

Political scientist John Waterbury's *Commander of the Faithful* (1970) provided an influential interpretation of the politics of postindependence Morocco.[11] Borrowing from Gellner (and American anthropologist David M. Hart), Waterbury sought to apply British anthropological theory of African segmentary lineages to the Moroccan case.[12] Waterbury grounded Moroccan politics in its deep cultural history, but transposed the operation of segmentary politics from the High Atlas to the Moroccan parliament. In the 1950s and 1960s political scientists emphasized the role of political parties in post-Liberation Western Europe and newly independent Africa. In the hands of Robert Rezette, Douglas E. Ashford, and I. William Zartman, Moroccan politics looked almost European because it was largely shorn of its cultural specificity.[13]

Written at a time when the bloom was already off the rose of democracy in newly independent Africa, as evidenced by books with titles like *The Role of the Army in Politics,* Waterbury's book offered a clear alternative. He viewed the rise and fall of Moroccan political parties as reflecting not the appeal of party platforms to an electorate, but a game of musical chairs with the king in the role of umpire, and royal patronage as the chief motivator. As "Commander of the Faithful," the king was able to play on differences between political factions, distributing or withholding ministerial portfolios and by continuously changing the rules of the parliamentary electoral game. In this way the monarch was able to establish himself as the leader of the political game and to destabilize all of the parties. (Here Waterbury's *Commander of the Faithful* drew on contemporary studies of patronage politics and factionalism in Fourth Republic France rather than the emerging literature on modernization in the former colonies.)[14] Drawing on the French colonial archive, Waterbury stressed the continuity between pre- and postcolonial Morocco almost to the point where the colonial period disappeared.

The stereotypes of Moroccan Islam were paramount in shaping Waterbury's approach. His first chapter, "The Makhzan as a Stable System of Violence," sets the tone. It derived its understanding of Moroccan politics from the reign of Hasan I (1873–94). After sketching the ways in which Hasan I sought to deploy both force and *baraka* (charisma) to retain control over the often fractious tribes, and a brief discussion of the role of the *shurafa* and *murabits,* Waterbury switched gears. Citing Gellner and Terrasse, he completed his portrait with reference to the role of the *murabit* as mediator, and of the system of stable violence that allegedly was precolonial Morocco. Here we find ourselves deep in the thickets of Moroccan Islam. Where Waterbury's approach differed from the French colonial authors was in his sharp understanding of the centrality of the king in deploying material incentives for the "waltz of the ministries" in postcolonial Moroccan politics, and in his use of segmentary theory to explain it. At a time (1970) when the Vietnam War was still raging, and the American (and Moroccan) intellectual fields were being shaped by Marxist critiques of imperialism and of modernization theory, the recourse to colonial discourse is especially striking. A deeply conservative and cynical interpretation of Moroccan politics, *The Commander of the Faithful* was a flattering portrait of the political skills of Hasan II, its main subject. Partially correct (in its assessment of the dominance of Hasan II), but incorrect as well (in its essentialist collapsing of a much more complex history), *The Commander of the Faithful* was at best a partial success. Somewhat surprisingly, *The Commander of the Faithful* was quickly translated into French and avidly read by Moroccan Marxists of the period, who claimed to be able to see themselves in the mirror it held up.[15] It remains the most influential book on Moroccan politics of the last half century. One could not imagine a more total victory for the colonial discourse on Moroccan Islam.

Anthropologist Dale Eickelman's *Moroccan Islam* (1976) explored the world of a rural pilgrimage center (Boujad) in central Morocco. Eickelman sought to identify changing conceptions of Islam and religious identity among inhabitants of the city over the past century.[16] *Moroccan Islam* was heavily influenced by French accounts of the role of sharifism and maraboutism in Morocco as well as by Geertz's person-centered conception of society as a constellation of personal ties. Yet despite its title, *Moroccan Islam* was also profoundly immersed in Moroccan history. It provided a historically grounded account of the progressive transformation of sharifism and maraboutism in a small town from the precolonial period to the 1970s. At the time of its publication, Edward Said's *Orientalism* (1978) had not yet appeared, and the critique of colonial forms of knowledge was neither well developed nor well theorized.[17] Eickelman explicitly took issue with French formulations of a timeless Morocco, and disputed Bel's idealist merging of popular Sufism and Berber tribalism as the fundamental characteristic of Moroccan Islam.[18] Instead Eickelman provided a historical explanation of cultural change, in which local beliefs in the power of the saints and the local Shaqawi sharifian lineage became unstuck in the 1930s partially in response to the attractiveness of the ideas of Salafiyya Islam, and partially as a result of the transformation of Moroccan society. He suggested that the transformation of the institutions of Moroccan Islam under the protectorate was linked to the congruence between Moroccan religious institutions and French aims and objectives. But while recognizing that the protectorate was a major watershed in Moroccan history, Eickelman found no space to chronicle the violence of the conquest or the massive disruptions and dispossessions that ensued. Moroccans understandably had a different perspective, but were no less ensnared by the discourse on Moroccan Islam.

INTELLIGENCE AND EMPIRE: NATIVE POLICY MOROCCO

Colonial empires depended on the systematic gathering of intelligence about their subject populations in order to function. In his *Empire and Information* historian Chris Bayly examines types of information gathered by the British Indian empire and how it informed the decisions of the colonial state.[19] Whereas for Bayly the Indian native policy was all about caste, French policy in Morocco was closely linked to the discourse on Moroccan Islam. Bayly's book demonstrates the extent to which the British co-opted preexisting Mughal intelligence networks and information retrieval systems. Sharifian Morocco relied on a similar array of informants: *rakkas* (runners who delivered the mail), kif-smoking Hedawa Sufi *shaykh-s,* itinerant peddlers, and minor officials.[20] During the nineteenth century, Bayly suggests, the relationship of the British colonial government to Indian society underwent important changes. Whereas initially, British officials took the trouble to learn Indian languages, adopted Indian lifestyles (including the joint family), by the 1830s, British colonial officials no longer knew Indian languages, and had begun to bring their wives from Britain instead of intermarrying locally.

The transformation from British mastery of Indian culture in the eighteenth century to the racially inflected social distancing of the nineteenth century, with its reliance on Indian *babus* and colonial phrase books, can be understood as the shift from "the command of language to the language of command," in the words of Bernard S. Cohen.[21] As a result of these changes the Raj became cut off from information gathered from native sources. The atrophy of traditional information-gathering systems entailed a break with the Mughal past. *Empire and Information* documents the consequence: the British failure to foresee the 1857 Indian Mutiny, which caught the colonial state unawares. It provoked an intelligence panic that overrode more cautious responses, and stoked a violent racialized British repression, directed especially against South Asian Muslims and other perceived Indian enemies of the colonial state. The interdependence of sociology and surveillance, empire and intelligence, was therefore important in determining the stability and functioning of empire.

In some respects Bayly's book can be seen as a response to Said's 1978 work *Orientalism*.[22] Whereas Said contended that orientalism was totalizing discourse that fused knowledge and power, Bayly's study implicitly asks, If orientalism was a totalizing system and the British colonial state was hegemonic, why did the British state not anticipate the impending Indian mutiny? If knowledge is power, then surely it should have been able to do so. Or, more importantly, why did it fail to conduct a proper postevent forensic analysis of what went wrong?[23] More importantly, how can the existence of anticolonial resistance be explained under a regime of hegemonic domination? For Bayly and other members of the so-called Cambridge school, British imperial strategy in South Asia was dictated by the subcontinental vastness of India and the relative paucity of British administrators and military. Since the British Empire persisted in India over two centuries, they suggest, it must have enjoyed the cooperation of Indians of all social classes and castes, if not a measure of legitimacy in the eyes of at least some Indians. In addition, Bayly insists that far from being unique, the history of the British in India was part of a worldwide phenomenon: the rise and eventual fall of European colonial empires. British colonialism in India was always dependent on the collaboration of Indian elites to make the colonial enterprise work. Since the nationalists arose from this class of collaborators, nationalist historians tended to see postcolonial South Asian history as continuous with its precolonial past, the better to avoid discussion of the colonial period.

Historians of Morocco have similarly tended to emphasize continuities with the precolonial past, instead of seeing the colonial period as a sharp break from the past.[24] Long after the demise of the French protectorate, the mesmerizing influence of Moroccan Islam continues to shape perceptions, diverting attention away from its discursive domination. Ultimately the history of the French in Morocco (like that of the British in India) was part of the worldwide phenomenon of the rise and eventual fall of European colonial empires. The discourse on Moroccan Islam therefore possesses no special magic enabling it to avoid confronting its colonial past.

Referring to the contents of the British colonial archive of India, South Asian subaltern historian Ranajit Guha speaks of "the prose of counter-insurgency."[25] More specifically here we can speak of French colonial ethnography as explicitly and self-consciously counterinsurgent, a tool of colonial social engineering. In this respect the Moroccan protectorate was an ethnographic state. A high modernist project, the French protectorate was supremely confident of its ability to defeat insurgencies, incorporate former rivals, or make them pay dearly. Joseph Gallieni's views about the importance of ethnography to colonial governance have been discussed above. In accord with his vision of the relationship of knowledge and power, Lyautey and the colonial officers around him fiercely opposed the metropolitan military mind-set, and instead looked to a small, ethnographically attuned group of officers led by one of their number, who were able to intervene knowingly in particular contexts with well-chosen modalities. They also opposed premature military interventions. Here the early Chaouia (1907–8) campaign stood out as an example of what not to do. The Lyauteyian ethnography of counterinsurgency was composed of several elements. It began with the standard statistical tool of the Arab Bureaux, the *fiche de tribu,* which listed the numbers of leaders, households, guns, and horses of each tribe. In the Villes et Tribus volumes, this essentially demographic approach was combined with brief histories of each tribe's connections to the rest of Moroccan society, and their responses to French actions.

In the case of Morocco, Lyautey created an ethnographic state in which the structures of the state allegedly derived from the advice of trained native policy practitioners. French "militant ethnography" was central to the Lyautey system, and Morocco was the primary example of an intelligence state among France's colonial possessions. But there is good reason to discount the claims of omniscient social engineers quietly going about their business. In reality the Lyautey style of "peaceful penetration" was as oxymoronic as "painless dentistry." It should not suggest images of social bodies etherized upon the table. Not for the last time did delusions about socially informed warfare and surgical strikes seek to structure a spectator's battlefield so as to deemphasize the real costs borne by colonial populations (and metropolitan taxpayers).

This becomes clear when we examine the historical record. In *The Conquest of Morocco,* military historian Douglas Porch provides his assessment of Lyautey's much-touted Beni Snassen campaign of 1908 (widely seen as a model of the Lyautey system in action): "As an academic organization drawing up ethnographic studies it was a great success. As a spy service it was largely a flop."[26] Porch goes on to ask why the myth of the peaceful conquest of Morocco continued to be so influential. His explanation is devastating: "'Hearts and minds' was more a public relations exercise than a workable military formula. As in all guerrilla wars, the problem for Lyautey was to deprive the determined handful of warriors of the support and sympathies of the noncombatant population." For Porch, the Lyautey doctrine was a failure both in practice and as military theory: "If Lyautey continued to retail 'hearts and minds' it was for reasons connected far more with the political situation in France than with that in Morocco."[27] Equally critical is the assessment of William A. Hoisington Jr. (another historian of the Lyautey period) of the conquest of Morocco: "In Morocco, the ultimate testing ground of the Lyautey method, pacification came everywhere through armed and bitter contests with resistant townsmen and tribesmen. Pacification was war, not peace."[28]

Although Lyautey claimed that the structures of the Moroccan protectorate were shaped by "scientific imperialism"—that is, applied sociology—the realities were far different. Instead, native policy Morocco was a high modernist project that claimed derivation from the colonial archive. French policies derived not from the advice of ethnographically trained policymakers but from the racist binaries of preexisting (mostly Algerian) stereotypes about North African culture and society. There was thus considerable slippage from colonial science to the verities of the Moroccan colonial gospel. In the end, native policy was carried out by soldiers, not social scientists. Complex sociological understandings only got in the way of fighting and governing Moroccans. Science (ethnography) did not drive Lyautey's native policy. Despite the earnest belief of many of its proponents, a scientifically driven native policy was more of a marketing device than a reality.

In his *Empires of Intelligence* Martin Thomas speaks of the "intelligence states" of Britain and France in the Middle East.[29] He postulates that all states require intelligence about their subjects, and as technologies modernize, the aspiration for total surveillance does as well. The primary task of colonial officials was the systematic study of colonized societies, the better to ward off potential trouble. The better informed the state, so the theory went, the better able it would be to ward off danger. The premises of the colonial intelligence state, Thomas shows, were derived from the experience of European police intelligence in the nineteenth century.[30] The realities, however, were far different. In fact, colonial states placed less emphasis on the veracity of political intelligence than on its use in advancing political control. Indeed, Thomas contends, the weight attached to intelligence information was likely to increase in inverse proportion to the specialist knowledge of administrators. As a consequence, the intelligence regimes he describes failed to understand the appeal of nationalism, or for that matter of Marxism. Assertions by colonial officials that they possessed specialized knowledge were often little more than the dressing up of rumor or racial stereotype, the deployment of what Thomas calls "past precedent." Given this history, one might better think of "intelligence states" as unintelligent states. Thomas's expose provides a lens through which to examine Lyautey's Morocco, with its pretentions to scientific imperialism.

MOROCCAN ISLAM: A DISCOURSE OF GOVERNMENTALITY

Under the protectorate, French bureaucrats made a show of respect for the royal person and the principles of indirect rule. Nonetheless, the real decisions were made by French officials. Morocco was never an example of indirect rule. With the independence of Morocco in 1956 the discourse on Moroccan Islam was reimagined once again to fit the realities of an independent modern Morocco. Muhammad V abandoned the (by this time folkloric) title of sultan following his 1944 meeting with U.S. president Roosevelt in Tangier, and began to style himself king. In so doing he signaled his refusal to continue to play the role of rubber-stamp monarch envisioned by the French and his desire to be seen as a modern nationalist head of state. With the end of empire, Moroccan Islam was yoked to support a postcolonial governmental Morocco. It proclaimed the power of the monarchy in the service of a specifically Moroccan Islamic nation.

If we are to resituate our understanding of the colonial period and the historic bargain under which the protectorate was launched, we must think in terms of the deep history of the Mediterranean region.[31] For reform-minded Moroccan elites, as for their Middle Eastern cousins, the protectorate provided a substitute for the self-strengthening movement (the Ottoman *tanzimat*) they had been unable to provide themselves. Under French colonial tutelage the same reforms were introduced to Morocco as elsewhere around the Mediterranean: Napoleonic law, French administrative organization, education, medicine, railroads, telegraphs, roads, and port construction. The package of reforms called "French modern" provided systems of discipline and order, while opening the society to the outside world.[32] Europeans were the first to benefit economically from colonial reforms (it was a colonial state after all), although this changed over the course of the protectorate. In the shadow of the colonial state a Moroccan bourgeoisie emerged: commercial, professional, and administrative. It provided the intellectual leadership of the nationalist movement, although not without some misgivings. Despite clear discriminatory patterns of enforcement, the French security and internal policing eventually benefited at least some Moroccans (especially the elite).

Under the protectorate (1912–56), Morocco became French, and the meanings and functions of the discourse on Moroccan Islam underwent modifications. French claims to superior understanding of Moroccan Islam acquired the capacity to express, organize, and make legible the diverse components of Morocco's political identity. French power summoned into existence a timeless Morocco in which some Moroccans could find a measure of meaning and a simulacrum of legitimacy. This Morocco was Lyautey's greatest achievement. The discourse on Moroccan Islam gained a new life with Moroccan independence. A remarkably successful exercise in the invention of tradition, Moroccan Islam still provides the central discursive prop of the Moroccan monarchy today.

The end of the nationalist struggle proved a key moment in the forging of a new national myth. With the nationalists split several ways, King Muhammad V was able to mobilize support in the countryside among mostly Berber-speaking populations, who were less closely linked to the world economy. Muhammad V discarded the colonial alliance with the great *qaids* and Sufi orders, now irrevocably tarnished in the quixotic French effort to depose him and to impose Moulay Ben Arafa, the quizzling sultan. Instead Muhammad V artfully played urban modernists off against rural conservatives while generating support among Berber-speaking rural elites. The nationalist Right, headed by Alal al-Fasi and the Istiqlal Party, made the best of a bad thing and joined the government. Finding themselves on the losing end of the new political arithmetic, the nationalist Left (many of whom favored a modern republic) was forced to compromise with the Crown. Thus the discourse on Moroccan Islam was once again reimagined to shore up the sagging legitimacy of the state.

The Lyauteyian protectorate institutionalized social engineering discursively based on a high modernist form of the Moroccan gospel. It steered around the structures of old Morocco such as the *makhzan,* and the religious institutions, while infusing them with new meanings. In so doing it created the appearance of a seamless transition from precolonial to colonial Morocco. Thus the discourse on Moroccan Islam as a tool of rule was established. Moroccan Islam structured the transition to postcolonial Morocco, so that both Moroccan and expatriate historians can write as if the colonial period were but a brief interruption in a continuous narrative. So successful was Lyautey's invention of Moroccan Islam that it disguised the extent to which the protectorate in many ways continued after independence, not only institutionally (in developing the lineaments of the modern state) but also in terms of the reinvention of political culture in which old cultural symbolic systems like sultanic *baraka* and despotism were given currency. Faced with the capacity of the monarchy to co-opt all sources of opposition, the development of popular democracy has been stunted, and protest delegitimized. Faced with the technologies of power available to the state, rebellion has not been an option until now.

The cultural power of the Lyautey policy on Moroccan Islam had several elements. One was the *politique des égards*—that is, Lyautey's insistence that protectorate officials observe Moroccan customs when dealing with the sultan, *makhzan* officials, or the urban elites. This was no doubt reassuring and made it easier to get the elite to accept the protectorate. Measures such as banning Europeans from entering mosques are to be understood in this context. Arguably more important but less studied was the gradual transformation of courtly ritual under the protectorate and the redeployment of its symbolic power. The image with which this book began, of Lyautey holding the Moulay Youssef's stirrup so that the latter could mount, symbolized for most Moroccans the role of the protectorate. But how did the enthronement ritual come to Lyautey's attention? Who suggested it to him? Someone may have invoked Aubin's text, the best-known description of the ritual. Perhaps it was Aubin's informant Si Kaddour bin Ghabrit, who, moreover, was chief of protocol in the early protectorate. Or Henri Gaillard. The broader conclusion is that under the early protectorate the courtly ritual was rein-vented so that it would be legible to European eyes, but also so that it could appeal to large numbers of Moroccans. Although the selection process took place in private, the rituals were public. Until now this process has not found its historian.

Under the aegis of Moroccan Islam political bargains were struck that were crucial in cementing the connection between the French and Moroccan elites. They begin with the French pragmatic alliance with the great *qaids* (who secured southern Morocco), and the flattery and little attentions paid to the ulama and merchants of Fez (which got them to modulate their oppo-sition to the protectorate). To them must be added French discreet support for selected Sufi brotherhoods that secured the political backing of the coun-tryside for the colonial state. When the French eventually were compelled to grant Moroccan independence, these colonial political bargains were can-celed. But new ones were struck.

As late as 1946 there was nothing inevitable about the survival of the mon-archy. Nationalists on both the left and the right were to varying degrees opposed to it. The 1934 "Plan des reformes" issued by a group of young Moroccan nationalists (among Muhammad Lahbabi and Muhammad al-Wazzani) explicitly called for a republic. On the right, the Istiqlal (Independence) Party, headed by the dynamic Alal al-Fasi, viewed the monarchy as a pawn of the colonial administration. Although Mohammad V's break with the admin-istration over the 1930 Berber decree was greatly appreciated, he was not regarded by the nationalists at the time as a reliable ally, because the monarchy was viewed as co-opted by the protectorate. When in 1944 Mohammad V took the un-Islamic title of king (and discarded the title of sultan) many Moroccans, including Istiqlal Party militants, were scandalized. Meanwhile, on the left, militants of the emergent labor confederation, the Union marocaine de travail (UMT), regarded kings as a feudal remnant. The boldness of Mohammed V in asserting his role as the leader of the nationalist movement in the 1940s and 1950s, together with French miscues (he was exiled to Madagascar at the height of the crisis of 1955), guaranteed the centrality of the Crown in an independent Morocco.

In postcolonial Morocco the discourse on Moroccan Islam was reshaped, becoming a powerful enforcer of political loyalties. In newly independent Morocco to even hint that the monarchy had flaws was to risk being identi-fied as disloyal, perhaps even un-Islamic. While the royalist model of Moroccan nationalism continued to come under criticism from the Left in the years that followed, it did not result in the expansion of their political base. Indeed quite the opposite occurred. The discourse on Moroccan Islam was especially successful in delegitimizing the opposition. The point of this rapid survey of the postcolonial political history of modern Morocco is to underscore the structural reasons for the success of the Crown. While the specific groups and individuals that had sustained the protectorate were banned from politics in independent Morocco, its rural and less modernized urban constituencies became the base of the monarchy as well. But this essentially instrumentalist rationale for the success of the reinvention of Moroccan Islam is only part of the explanation.

Under the French protectorate the king had not been ideologically central, even if his sacral character was put forward. Instead French colonial discourse emphasized the special nature of Morocco, with its long history of Islamic monarchy, its folkloric emblems of power, and the presence of a large Berber minority. By establishing a political system centered on the monarch King Mohammed V refashioned the discourse on Moroccan Islam to emphasize the centrality of the role of the king/sultan as "Commander of the Faithful." No longer the spiritual axis around which all revolved, politically, everything depended on him as well. He became the chief distributor of patronage, and his support was crucial for all projects above a certain level, while his enmity toward actual or suspected opponents was implacable.

A study of the iconography of royal ritual and ceremony in the twentieth century might provide a better understanding of the ways in which the Moroccan crown sought to broaden its appeal by encoding new rituals and ceremonies. Jocelyne Dakhlia's study of the history of the parasol as a symbol of royalty in Morocco provides a glimpse of how tradition was modernized.[33] She has examined all verbal and iconographic depictions of the rituals of Moroccan royalty (and specifically the parasol as a royal symbol) going back to Saadian times. Dakhlia comes to a number of tentative conclusions. First, Moroccan royal ritual was slow to crystallize into a coherent whole. Not until the late nineteenth century were the elements of courtly ritual, the implements of authority, and costume standardized. Dakhlia also suggests that the emergence of a more codified Moroccan royal ceremonial practice derives from Moroccan interactions with Europeans. Her study focuses on the preprotectorate period, although it includes a glance at what occurred after 1912. Over the years, choices were made that reinvented the courtly ritual so that it would be legible to European eyes, as well as appeal to large numbers of Moroccans. The selection process took place in private, although the rituals were public. Dakhlia notes that the imperial parasol appears to have become noticeably more visible in photographs of the 1920s on the occasion of royal processions.[34] She notes the transformations of representations of Moroccan royalty in the 1930s, following the withdrawal of the Berber decree: "With the reign of Mohammed V (1927–1961) the religious component of sultanic power finds a new consecration in the hearts of his subjects, and contributes to reaffirming . . . his full political legitimacy."[35]

Moroccan subjects responded strongly to the modernization of the symbolic language of power in Morocco. Here is where the instrumental approach ceases to maintain traction. Once Mohammed V had broken with the protectorate authorities over the Berber decree, he focused increasingly on courtly ritual and symbols as part of his self-presentation to his people in an effort to enhance the appeal of nationalism. He also received an overwhelming response from Moroccans from all walks of life. The lesson of this attention to detail in the presentation of the royal person on public occasions was not lost on his son and successor, King Hasan II. His successor, Mohammed VI (1999–present), continues the tradition. Although the appeal of the monarchy cannot doubted, Moroccan Islam is not a primordial essence encoded in the DNA of Moroccans, just waiting to be tapped. Rather, it was the consequence of complex historical processes over the course of the modern history of Morocco. The invention of Moroccan Islam and its successive transformations led to the forging of a powerful political discourse that still has currency. But for how much longer?

ABBREVIATIONS

AB   *Archives berbères*

AF   *Bulletin du Comité de l'Afrique française*

AM   *Archives marocaines*

CHEAM Centre des hautes études sur l'Afrique et l'Asie moderne

FAT   Fonds Auguste Terrier (Bibliothèque de l'Institut de France)

FO   Foreign Office archives, Kew

MAE   Ministère des affaires étrangères, Paris

Nantes   Centre des archives diplomatique de Nantes

RC   *Renseignements coloniaux* (monthly supplement to AF)

RMM   *Revue du monde musulman*

SHAT   Service historique de l'armée de terre, Chateau de Vincennes

NOTES

INTRODUCTION

1. Eugène Aubin [Collard-Descos], *Le Maroc d'aujourd'hui* (Paris: A. Colin, 1904), 473–474.

2. Daniel Rivet, *Lyautey et l'institution du protectorat français au Maroc, 1912–1925* (Paris: Harmattan, 1988), 1:172 n. 133.

3. Mohammed Daadaoui, *Moroccan Monarchy and the Islamist Challenge: Maintaining Makhzan Power* (New York: Palgrave Macmillan, 2011).

4. John Waterbury, *Commander of the Faithful: The Moroccan Political Elite—a Study in Segmented Politics* (London: Weidenfeld and Nicolson, 1970).

5. On the religious attributes of the sultan, see Aubin, *Le Maroc*, 133–136.

6. On sacral kingship the locus classicus is James Frazer, *The Golden Bough: A Study in Magic and Religion* (New York: Macmillan, 1947).

7. Lucien Febvre, *Le problème de l'incroyance au XVIe siècle, la religion de Rabelais* (Paris: A. Michel, 1942).

8. John H. R. Davis, *People of the Mediterranean: An Essay in Comparative Anthropology* (London: Routledge and Kegan Paul, 1976). Also Carleton Coon, *Caravan: The Story of the Middle East* (New York: Holt, 1958).

9. Rahma Bourquia and Susan Miller, *In the Shadow of the Sultan: Culture, Power and Politics in Morocco* (Cambridge, MA: Harvard University Press, 1999); Abdellah Hammoudi, *Master and Disciple: The Cultural Foundations of Moroccan Authoritarianism* (Chicago: University of Chicago Press, 1997); Elaine Combs-Schilling, *Sacred Performances: Islam, Sexuality, and Sacrifice* (New York: Columbia University Press, 1989).

10. Eric Hobsbawm and Terrence Ranger, eds., *The Invention of Tradition* (Cambridge: Cambridge University Press, 1983).

11. David Cannadine, "The Context, Performance and Meaning of Ritual: 'The British Monarchy and the Invention of Tradition,' c. 1820–1977," in Hobsbawm and Ranger, *Invention of Tradition*, 101–164.

12. David Cannadine, *Ornamentalism: How the British Saw Their Empire* (Oxford: Oxford University Press, 2002).

13. Bernard S. Cohn, "Representing Authority in British India," in Hobsbawm and Ranger, *Invention of Tradition,* 165–210.

14. On the Indo-Saracenic turn, see Thomas R. Metcalf, *An Imperial Vision: Indian Architecture and Britain's Raj* (Berkeley: University of California Press, 1989).

15. Jocelyne Dakhlia, "Pouvoir du parasol et pouvoir nu: Un dépouillement islamique? Le cas de la royauté marocaine," *Bulletin du Centre de recherche du château de Versailles* 2 (2005), http://crcv.revues.org/233.

16. Edmund Burke III, *Prelude to Protectorate in Morocco: Precolonial Protest and Resistance, 1860–1912* (Chicago: University of Chicago Press, 1976).

17. Michel Foucault, *The Archeology of Knowledge & the Discourse on Language* (New York: Harper & Row, 1972), chap. 5.

18. Bernard S. Cohn, *Colonialism and Its Forms of Knowledge: The British in India* (Princeton, NJ: Princeton University Press, 1996).

19. For an example, see John Gordon Lorimer, *Gazetteer of the Persian Gulf, 'Omān, and Central Arabia* (Calcutta: Superintendent Government Printing, 1915). Also Henry Miers Elliot, *Memoirs on the History, Folklore, and Distribution of the Races of the North-Western Provinces of India,* rev. John Beames (London: Trubner and Company, 1869); and Alfred Lyall, *Asiatic Studies, Religious and Social,* 2nd ed. (London: J. Murray, 1884).

20. For an overview, see Edmund Burke III, "France and the Classical Sociology of Islam, 1798–1962," *Journal of North African Studies* 18:1 (2007): 1–7. For some critiques, see Philippe Lucas and Jean-Claude Vatin, *L'Algérie des anthropologues* (Paris: Maspero, 1975); and Abdelmajid Hannoum, "Colonialism and Knowledge in Algeria: The Archives of the Arab Bureau," *History and Anthropology,* 2001, 343–379.

21. Steven Lukes, *Émile Durkheim: His Life and Work* (London: Penguin, 1975); and Terry Clark, *Prophets and Patrons: The French University and the Emergence of the Social Sciences* (Cambridge, MA: Harvard University Press, 1973).

22. Donald Ray Bender, "Early French Ethnography in Africa and the Development of Ethnology in France" (PhD diss., Northwestern University, 1964).

23. André Adam, *Bibliographie critique de sociologie, d'ethnologie et de géographie humaine du Maroc* (Algiers: SNED, 1972).

24. Frederick Cooper and Ann Laura Stoler, eds., *Tensions of Empire: Colonial Cultures in a Bourgeois World* (Berkeley: University of California Press, 1997); Ann Laura Stoler et al., eds., *Imperial Formations* (Santa Fe: School for Advanced Research Press and James Currey, 2007); Frederick Cooper, *Colonialism in Question: Theory, Knowledge, History* (Berkeley: University of California Press, 2005); Nicholas Dirks, *Castes of Mind: Colonialism and the Making of Modern India* (Princeton, NJ: Princeton University Press, 2011); James P. Daughton, *An Empire Divided: Religion, Republicanism, and the Making of French Colonialism, 1880–1914* (Oxford: Oxford University Press, 2006); Alice Conklin, *A Mission to Civilize: The Republican Idea of Empire in France and West Africa, 1895–1930* (Stanford, CA: Stanford University Press, 1997).

25. On which point I agree with Cohn, "Representing Authority," 4.

26. Edmund Burke III, "Theorizing the Histories of Colonialism and Nationalism in the Arab Maghrib," in *Beyond Colonialism and Nationalism in North Africa: History, Culture, and Politics,* ed. Ali A. Ahmida (London: St. Martin's Press, 2001), 17–34.

27. See also Bryan S. Turner, *Marx and the End of Orientalism* (London: Allen & Unwin, 1976).

28. Edmund Burke III and David Prochaska, "Introduction: From Postcolonial Theory to World History," in *Genealogies of Orientalism: History, Theory, Politics,* ed. Edmund Burke III and David Prochaska (Lincoln: University of Nebraska Press, 2008), 2–73.

29. James Clifford, *The Predicament of Culture* (Cambridge, MA: Harvard University Press, 1988), chap. 11.

30. Cooper and Stoler, *Tensions of Empire.*

31. Walter B. Harris, *The Morocco That Was* (London: Blackwood & Sons, 1921).

32. Moumen Douiri, *À qui appartient le Maroc?* (Paris: Harmattan, 1992).

33. Earl F. Cruickshank, *Morocco at the Parting of the Ways* (Philadelphia: University of Pennsylvania Press, 1935).

34. Figures cited in Burke, *Prelude,* 24 n. 27, from Jean-Louis Miège, *Le Maroc et l'Europe* (Paris: P.U.F., 1961–63).

35. Discussed in Burke, *Prelude,* chap. 3.

36. Abdelahad Sebti, "Colonial Experience and Territorial Practices," in *Revisiting the Colonial Past of Morocco,* ed. Driss Maghraoui (London: Routledge, 2013), 38–56.

37. Janet Abu-Lughod, *Rabat: Urban Apartheid in Morocco* (Princeton, NJ: Princeton University Press, 1981).

ONE · FRANCE AND THE SOCIOLOGY OF ISLAM

1. Clifford Geertz, "In Search of North Africa," *New York Review of Books,* April 22, 1971.

2. The term *sociology* is used here in something like its broad nineteenth-century sense. It is not limited to, although it includes, the academic discipline of sociology.

3. *Description de l'Égypte, ou recueil des observations et des recherches qui ont été faites en Égypte pendant l'expédition de l'armée francaise, publié par les ordres de sa majesté Napoléon le Grand,* 23 vols. (Paris: Imprimerie impériale, 1809–28).

4. Henri Jean François Edmond Pelissier de Reynaud, ed., *L'exploration scientifique de l'Algérie pendant les années 1840, 1841, 1842, publié par l'ordre du gouvernement,* 39 vols. (Paris: Imprimerie royale, 1844–67).

5. On this point, see Roger Owen, "Studying Islamic History," *Journal of Interdisciplinary History* 4:2 (1973): 287–290. See also Maxime Rodinson, "Situation, acquis, et problèmes d'orientalisme islamisant," in *Le mal de voir: Ethnologie*

et orientalisme; Politique et épistemologie, critique et autocritique, ed. Henri Moniot (Paris: Union Générale d'Éditions, 1976), 242–257; and Edmund Burke III, "Islamic History as World History: Marshall Hodgson, The Venture of Islam," *International Journal of Middle East Studies* 10 (1979): 241–264.

6. Michel Foucault, *The Order of Things: An Archeology of the Human Sciences* (New York: Pantheon Books, 1970). Cf. Pierre Bourdieu, *Esquisse d'une théorie de la pratique* (Geneva: Droz, 1972); for Bourdieu, the equivalent term is *doxa*.

7. Maxime Rodinson, "The Western Image and Western Studies of Islam," in *The Legacy of Islam,* ed. Joseph Schacht and C. E. Bosworth (London: Oxford University Press, 1974), 49–50.

8. Daniel Reig, *Homo orientaliste: La langue arabe en France depuis le XIXe siècle* (Paris: Maisonneuve & Larose, 1988).

9. *Cent-Cinquantenaire de l'École des langues orientales vivantes* (Paris: Imprimerie nationale, 1948); esp. Regis Blachère, "Arabe littéral (1795)," ibid., 50.

10. E. F. Gautier, *Le passé de l'Afrique du nord: Les siècles obscurs,* 2nd ed. (Paris: Flammarion, 1937), subsequently reprinted many times.

11. See, for example, André Gide, *Si le grain ne meurt* (Paris: Gallimard, 1931); Gustave Flaubert, *Voyage en Égypte* (Paris: Grasset, 1991); and Isabelle Eberhardt, *Œuvres complètes* (Paris: Grasset, 1988).

12. Edward W. Said, *Orientalism* (New York: Pantheon Books, 1978).

13. Jacques Berque, *Arabies* (Paris: Stock, 1978).

14. Edmund Burke III, "Orientalism Observed: France and the Sociology of Islam, 1798–1962" (unpublished manuscript).

15. David Prochaska, personal communication, October 1994.

16. A basic point that appears to have eluded many of the authors of essays in the otherwise excellent volume *Napoleon in Egypt,* ed. Irene Bierman (Reading, UK: Ithaca Press, 2003).

17. Edmund Burke III and David Prochaska, "Orientalism from Postcolonial Theory to World History," in *Genealogies of Orientalism: History, Theory, Politics,* ed. Edmund Burke and David Prochaska (Lincoln: University of Nebraska Press, 2008), 2–73.

18. The judgment is that of Berque. See Jacques Berque, "Cent-vingt-cinq ans de sociologie maghrebine," *Annales, E.S.C.,* 11:3 (1956): 320. On the general subject of the development of French colonial sociology, see Donald Ray Bender, "Early French Ethnography in Africa and the Development of Ethnology in France" (PhD diss., Northwestern University, 1964).

19. Charles-Robert Ageron, *Les Algériens musulmans et la France (1871–1919)* (Paris: P.U.F., 1968), 1:67–78.

20. Eugéne Daumas, *Exposé de l'état actuel de la societé arabe, du gouvernement, de la legislation qui la régit* (Algiers: Imprimerie du gouvernement, 1844); Daumas, *Moeurs et coutumes de l'Algérie: Tell, Kabylie, Sahara* (Paris: Hachette, 1853). Also Louis Pein, *Lettres familières sur l'Algérie: Un petit royaume arabe* (Algiers: Jourdan, 1893); Charles Richard, *Du gouvernement arabe et de l'institution qui doit l'exercer* (Algiers: Bastide, 1848); and Thomas Ismail Urbain, "Algérie. Du gouvernement des

tribus. Chrétiens et musulmans. Français et Algériens," *Revue de l'Orient et de l'Algérie* 2 (1847): 241–259.

21. Berque, "Cent-vingt-cinq ans," 320. Cf. also Philippe Lucas and Jean-Claude Vatin, *L'Algérie des anthropologues* (Paris: Maspéro, 1975).

22. Robert Montagne, *Les Berbères et le makhzen dans le sud du Maroc: Essai sur la transformation politique des Berbères sédentaires (groupe chleuh)* (Paris: F. Alcan, 1930).

23. Robert Montagne, *Naissance du prolétariat marocain, enquête collective exécutée de 1948 à 1950* (Paris: Peyronnet, 1952).

24. For a comparison of the British and French traditions, see Edmund Burke III and David Prochaska, "Rethinking the Historical Genealogy of *Orientalism*," *History and Anthropology* 18:2 (2007): 135–151. On the British experience, see Roger Owen, "The Influence of Lord Cromer's Indian Experience on British Policy in Egypt, 1883–1907," in *St. Antony's Papers,* no. 17, ed. Albert Hourani (London: Oxford University Press, 1965), 109–139.

25. David Robinson, *Paths of Accommodation: Muslim Societies and French Colonial Authorities in Senegal and Mauritania, 1880–1920* (Athens, OH: Ohio University Press; Oxford: James Currey, 2000).

26. Said, *Orientalism,* 85.

27. Numa Broc, "Les grandes missions scientifiques françaises au xixe siècle (Morée, Algérie, Mexique) et leurs travaux géographiques," *Revue d'histoire des sciences* 34:3–4 (1981): 319–358. The Morée mission (1829–31), Algeria (1839–42), and Mexico (1865–67) were self-consciously organized with the Egyptian expedition in mind, and involved some of the same individuals (Bory de Saint-Vincent participated in the Baudin and Morea expeditions before being named head of the Algerian one).

28. Juan Cole, *Napoleon's Egypt: Invading the Middle East* (New York: Palgrave-Macmillan, 2007).

29. Burke, "Orientalism Observed."

30. De Reynaud, *Exploration scientifique de l'Algérie.*

31. Jacques Berque, *Le Maghreb entre les deux guerres* (Paris: Seuil, 1962), 124. Many of the judgments in this paragraph are borrowed from Berque, "Cent-vingt-cinq ans."

32. Eugène Daumas, *Le Sahara algérien: Études géographiques, statistiques et historiques sur la region au sud des établissements français en Algérie* (Paris: Fortin, 1845); and Ernest Carette, *Études sur la Kabylie proprement dite* (1848), published as vols. 4–5 of *Exploration scientifique de l'Algérie.*

33. Emile Laoust, *Mots et choses berbères: Notes de linguistique et d'ethnographie; Dialectes du Maroc* (Paris: A. Challamel, 1920); and Auguste Mouliéras, *Le Maroc inconnu: Étude géographique et sociologique* (Paris: A. Challamel, 1902).

34. François de Neveu, *Les Khouan: Ordres religieux chez les musulmans de l'Algérie* (Paris: A. Guyot, 1845); and Charles Richard, *Étude sur l'insurrection du Dahra (1845–1846)* (Algiers: A. Besancènes, 1846).

35. On this topic, see Edmund Burke III, "The Terror and Religion: Brittany and Algeria," in *Colonialism and the Modern World,* ed. Gregory Blue, Martin Bunton, and Ralph Croizier (White Plains, NY: M. E. Sharpe, 2002), 40–50.

36. Louis Rinn, *Marabouts et Khouans: Étude sur l'Islam en Algérie* (Algiers: Jourdan, 1884).

37. This was also the case for the ethnography of Morocco. See André Adam, *Bibliographie critique de sociologie, d'ethnologie et de géographie humaine du Maroc* (Algiers: SNED, 1972).

38. Benjamin Claude Brower, *A Desert Called Peace: The Violence of France's Empire in the Algerian Sahara, 1844–1902* (New York: Columbia University Press, 2009).

39. Gianni Albergoni and François Pouillon, "Le fait berbère et sa lecture coloniale: L'extrême sud tunisien," in *Le mal de voir,* ed. Henri Moniot Collection 10/18, Cahier Jussieu/2. (Paris: Union Générale des Editions, 1976), 349–396.

40. Camille Sabatier, *Études sociologique sur les Kabyles* (Algiers, 1881); and Henri Duveyrier, *Les Touaregs du nord* (Paris: Challamel, 1864).

41. Auguste Warnier and Jules Duval, *Bureaux arabes et colons* (Paris: Challamel, 1869). Also Auguste Warnier, *L'Algérie et les victimes de la guerre* (Paris: Duclaux, 1871).

42. Marcel Emerit, *Les Saint-Simoniens en Algérie* (Algiers: Les Belles Lettres, 1941).

43. Adolphe Hanoteau and Aristide Letourneux, *La Kabylie et les coutumes kabyles,* 3 vols. (Paris: Imprimerie nationale, 1872–73). On the circumstances of the collaboration of the two authors, see Gen. Maurice Hanoteau, "Quelques souvenirs sur les collaborateurs de *La Kabylie et les coutumes Kabyles," Revue africaine* 64 (1923): 134–149.

44. Edmund Burke III, "The Image of the Moroccan State in French Ethnological Literature: A New Look at the Origin of Lyautey's Berber Policy," in *Arabs and Berbers,* ed. Ernest Gellner and Charles Micaud (London: Duckworth, 1972), 192.

45. See Edmund Burke III, "A Comparative View of French Native Policies in Morocco and Syria," *Middle Eastern Studies* 9 (1973): 175–186.

46. John Ruedy, *Modern Algeria: The Origins and Development of a Nation,* 2nd ed. (Bloomington: University of Indiana Press, 2005).

47. Charles-Robert Ageron, "La France a-t-elle eu une politique kabyle?" *Revue historique* 223 (1960): 311–352; Patricia Lorcin, *Imperial Identities: Stereotyping, Prejudice and Race in Colonial Algeria* (London: I. B. Tauris, 1995).

48. Henri Aucapitaine, *Le pays et la société kabyle* (Paris: A. Bertrand, 1857), cited in Ageron, *Les Algériens musulmans,* 1:270.

49. Camille Sabatier, *Essai sur les berbères* (Algiers, 1882). Ageron reports a particularly outrageous example of Sabatier's academic findings: "The Iberians are Berbers who came from Berberistan (between Kabul and Herat)." Ageron, *Les Algériens musulmans,* 1:275.

50. See Ageron, "La France a-t-elle eu une politique kabyle?"; also Lorcin, *Imperial Identities.*

51. Émile Masqueray, *La formation des cités chez les populations sédentaires de l'Algérie (Kabyles du Djuradjura, Chaouias de l'Aurés, Beni Mzab)* (Paris: Leroux, 1886). On Masqueray, see Fanny Colonna and Claude Haim Brahimi, "Du bon

usage de la science coloniale," in *Le mal de voir* (Paris: Union Générale d'Éditions, 1976), 221–241. See also Fustel de Coulanges, *La cité antique* (Paris: Hachette, 1864).

52. For an overview, see Jean-Louis Triaud, "Islam under French Colonial Rule," in *The History of Islam in Africa,* ed. Nehemia Levtzion and Randall Pouwell (Athens, OH: Ohio University Press, 2000), 169–188. Also David Robinson, *Muslim Societies in African History* (New York: Cambridge University Press, 2004); and Vincent Monteil, *L'islam noir: Une religion à la conquête de l'Afrique* (Paris: Seuil, 1980).

53. On French fears of the Sanusiya, see Jean-Louis Triaud, *La légende noire de la Sanusiya,* 2 vols (Paris: Maison des sciences de l'homme, 1995).

54. Paul Marty, "Les mourides d'Amadou Bamba," *Revue du monde musulman* 25 (1913): 1–164.

55. H. M. P. de La Martinière and Nicolas Lacroix, *Documents pour servir à l'étude du nord-ouest africain,* 4 vols. (Algiers: Gouvernement générale de l'Algérie, service des Affaires indigènes, 1894–97).

56. For an introduction to British studies on Morocco, see the writings of J. E. B. Meakin: *The Moorish Empire* (London: S. Sonnenschein, 1899); *The Land of the Moors* (London: Sonnenschein, 1901); *The Moors: A Comprehensive Description* (London: Sonnenschein, 1902); and *Life in Morocco* (London: Chatto & Windus, 1905). See also Walter B. Harris, *The Land of an African Sultan* (London: Samson, Low, Marston and Rivington, 1889); and Harris, *The Morocco That Was* (London: Blackwood & Sons, 1921); Robert B. Cunninghame Graham, *Moghreb el Akca: A Journey in Morocco* (London: Duckworth, 1898); and Arthur Leared, *A Visit to the Court of Morocco* (London: Low, Marston, Searle and Rivington, 1879).

57. Eugène Aubin [Léon Eugène Aubin Collard Descos], *Le Maroc d'aujourd'hui,* 8th ed. (Paris: Armand Colin, 1913).

58. For example, Jules Erckmann, *Le Maroc moderne* (Paris: Challamel, 1885).

59. Charles de Foucauld, *Reconnaissance au Maroc, 1883–1884: Journal de route* (Paris: Challamel, 1888); 2nd ed. (Paris: Société d'Éditions géographiques, 1939).

60. The French military mission is discussed in Wilfred Rollman, "The New Order in a Pre-colonial Muslim Society: Military Reform in Morocco, 1844–1904" (PhD diss., University of Michigan, 1983). Today found in Série C of the French military archives (Armée de Terre) conserved in the Château de Vincennes in Paris, they constitute an important auxiliary body of French knowledge about Morocco.

61. Vicomte Charles de Foucauld was born in 1858 in Strasbourg of an aristocratic family, educated at St. Cyr, and served in the Armée d'Afrique from 1880 to 1882. After his exploration of Morocco (1883–84), he experienced a spiritual crisis as a result of which he became a Catholic priest and eventually a missionary to the peoples of the Sahara. He was killed in Tamanrasset in 1916 by the Touareg, who viewed him with some justification as a spy.

62. Foucauld, *Reconnaissance au Maroc.*

63. One wonders nevertheless just how successful he was in this regard. At several points he is unmasked only to have his interlocutor become more rather than

less candid. It is also worth noting that Foucauld scarcely ever manifests a liking for (or indeed expresses much of an interest in) the Moroccan Jewish families with whom he stayed.

64. Daniel Nordman, "La Reconnaissance au Maroc," in *Profils du Maghreb: Frontières, figures et territoires (XVIIᵉ et XIXᵉ siècle)*, Publications de la Faculté des Lettres et des sciences humaines de Rabat (Casablanca: Imprimerie Najah el Jadida, 1996), 141–180.

TWO · THE ALGERIAN ORIGINS OF MOROCCAN STUDIES

1. Jean Digéon, *La crise allemande de la pensée française, 1870–1914* (Paris : P.U.F., 1959).

2. Theodore Zeldin, *Emile Ollivier and the Liberal Empire of Napoleon III* (Oxford: Clarendon Press, 1963).

3. Fernand Braudel, "Personal Testimony," *Journal of Modern History* 44:4 (1972): 448–467; François Dosse, *New History in France: The Triumph of the Annales,* trans. Peter V. Conroy Jr. (Urbana: University of Illinois Press, 1987).

4. Henri Dehérain, *Orientalistes et antiquaires: Silvestre de Sacy, ses contemporains et ses disciples* (Paris : Geuthner, 1938) ; and Dehérain, "Les établissements d'enseignements et de recherche de l'orientalisme à Paris," *Revue internationale de l'enseignement* 5 (July 15, 1939), 125–148 and (October 15, 1939), 222–238. For more on de Sacy, see Daniel Reig, *Homo orientaliste: La langue arabe en France depuis le XIXᵉ siècle* (Paris: Maisonneuve & Larose, 1988); and Edward Said, *Orientalism* (New York: Pantheon, 1978).

5. For more on Barbier de Meynard (1827–1908), see Reig, *Homo orientaliste,* 99–100. Also see the obituary in *Journal africaine,* ser. 12 (1908): 338–351.

6. Daniel Schroeter, "Orientalism and the Jews of the Mediterranean," *Journal of Mediterranean Studies* 4 (1994): 183–196.

7. Rapport de M.E. Renan, 6 XII 1881 (pp. 22–25), Archives nationales, Série F/17, No. 13 052.

8. Jacques Berque, *Arabies* (Paris: Stock, 1978) ; and Berque, *Memoires des deux rives* (Paris: Seuil, 1989).

9. On the history of ELOV, see *Cent Cinquantenaire de l'École nationale des langues orientales vivantes* (Paris: Imprimerie nationale de France, 1948). Also Paul Boyer, "L'École nationale des langues orientales vivantes," In *La vie universitaire à Paris,* ed. Boyer (Paris: A. Colin, 1918), 194–205; Henri Cordier, *Un coin de Paris : L'École des langues orientales vivantes* (Paris: E. Leroux, 1913).

10. While primarily known as a translator of Arabic texts, Houdas (who had spent twenty years in Algeria) also taught spoken Arabic based on Maghrebi examples. Among his translations were 'Abd al-Rahman ibn 'Abd Allah al-'Sadi, *Tarikh es-Soudan,* 2 vols. (Paris: E. Leroux, 1898–1900); Muhammad ibn Isma'il Bukhari, *Les traditions islamiques,* 4 vols. (Paris: Imprimerie nationale, 1903–14); and Abu al-Kasim al- Zayani, *Le Maroc de 1631 à 1812* (Paris: E. Leroux, 1886).

11. On the history of Arabic instruction at ELOV, see Régis Blachère, "Arabe litéral (1795)," in *Cent Cinquantenaire,* 47–55; and G. S. Colin, "Arabe vulgaire," ibid., 95–112. Maurice Gaudefroy-Desmombynes, although known primarily as a student of Muslim institutions, was by training a comparative Semiticist and was also much interested in ethnography and folklore. His *Manuel d'arabe marocain* (1913) played a vital role in the training of the first generation of native affairs officers and administrators of the Moroccan protectorate. Gaudefroy-Desmombynes was the first to apply the new linguistic science to the teaching of Arabic at the École des langues orientales.

12. *Cent Cinquantenaire.*

13. A French law of 1900 required that the colonies be self-supporting. French politicians were well aware of public resistance to costly colonial ventures. For this reason colonial governors sought to support infrastructure projects with local taxes. Jacques Marseille, *Empire coloniale et capitalisme française: Histoire d'un divorce* (Paris: Albin Michel, 1984).

14. Paul Leroy-Beaulieu, *De la colonisation chez les peuples modernes* (1874; Paris: F. Alcan, 1908). See also Henri Brunschwig, *French Imperialism, 1870–1914: Myth and Realities* (New York: Praeger, 1966); Fr. original, 1960.

15. Joseph Chailley-Bert (also known as Joseph Chailley) was the leading French authority on comparative colonial policies, and the head of a colonial pressure group, l'Union coloniale. Among his many influential writings are *Java et ses habitants* (Paris: A. Colin, 1900) and *L'Inde britannique: Société indigène, politique indigène, les idées directrices* (Paris: A. Colin, 1910).

16. Joseph Chailley-Bert, *Dix années de politique coloniale* (Paris: A. Colin, 1902), chap. 4, argues for the pursuit of native policies based on the tradition of the Algerian Bureaux arabes. On the defects of the Algerian experience, see also Paul Leroy-Beaulieu, *L'Algérie et la Tunisie* (Paris: Guillaumin, 1887).

17. Paul Rabinow, *French Modern: Norms and Forms of the Social Environment* (Cambridge, MA: M.I.T. Press, 1989), 147.

18. Louis Hubert Lyautey, *Lettres de Tonkin et de Madagascar (1894–1899)* (Paris: A. Colin, 1921).

19. In a speech on June 18, 1894, as cited in Charles-Robert Ageron, *Les Algériens musulmans et la France, 1871–1914* (Paris: P.U.F., 1968), 1:518–519.

20. On the role of Cambon, see Ageron, *Les Algériens musulmans,* chap. 9.

21. Jules Cambon, *Le Gouvernement Général de l'Algérie* (Paris: E. Champion, 1918), ix-xxi.

22. H. M. P. de La Martinière and Nicolas Lacroix, *Documents pour servir à l'étude du nord-ouest africain,* 4 vols. (Algiers: Gouvernement générale de l'Algérie, service des affaires indigènes, 1894–97).

23. See the introductory essay by Fanny Colonna to the 1988 reprint edition of Masqueray's *Formation des cités chez les populations sédentaires de l'Algérie* (Paris: Edisud, 1988).

24. For reviews, see Pierre Vidal de la Blache, *Annales de géographie* 6:28 (1897): 357–363; and Augustin Bernard, in *Bulletin de la Société de géographie et d'archéologie d'Oran* 17 (1897): 243–252.

25. Lyautey's delight in the color of tribal life is well known. See his letters published in André Le Reverend, *Un Lyautey inconnu: Correspondance et journal inédits 1874–1934* (Paris: Perrin, 1980).

26. The role of André de Saint-Germain merits further examination. See the biographical notice on him in Raymond Peyronnet, *Livre d'or des officiers des affaires indigenes, 1830–1930*, 2 vols. (Algiers: Imprimerie l'Algérienne, 1930).

27. Draft autobiographical fragment, account of Bou Saada visit, no date, 29 pages, Le Chatelier Papers, Dossier A.

28. On the history of the University of Algiers, see *Cinquantenaire de la Faculté des lettres d'Alger (1891–1931)* (Algiers: Société historique algérienne, 1932). Also Jean Mélia, *L'épopée intellectuelle de l'Algérie: L'histoire de l'Université d'Alger* (Algiers: La Maison des Livres, 1950), esp. 163–164 (for enrollment history).

29. On the École d'Alger, see Henri Massé, *Les études arabes en Algérie (1830–1930)* (Algiers: Société historique algérienne, 1933); also published in *Revue africaine*, nos. 356–357 (1933). Also Mélia, *L'épopée intellectuelle;* and *Cinquantenaire de la Faculté des lettres.*

30. On René Basset, see the obituary notice by Ismael Hamet, *Académie des sciences coloniales* 2 (1925): 257–259.

31. On Doutté, see Dr. J. G., "Edmond Doutté 1867–1926," *Académie des sciences colonials: Compte rendus des séances* 8 (1926–27): 531–535.

32. George R. Trumbull IV, *An Empire of Facts: Colonial Power, Cultural Knowledge, and Islam in Algeria, 1870–1914* (Cambridge: Cambridge University Press, 2010), 82–84.

33. James G. Frazer, *The Golden Bough: A Study in Magic and Religion,* 2nd ed., 3 vols. (London: Macmillan, 1900); and Émile Durkheim, *Les formes élémentaire de la vie religieuse, le système totémique en Australie* (Paris: F. Alcan, 1912).

34. His major works from this period included a major bibliographic essay, "Bulletin bibliographique de l'Islam maghrébin," *BSGAO* 19 (1899) : 37–123, as well as two books: *Notes sur l'Islam maghribin, les marabouts* (Paris: E. Leroux, 1900) and *L'Islam algérien en l'an 1900* (Alger-Mustapha: Giralt, 1900). An ethnographic brochure, *Les Aissaoua à Tlemcen* (Chalons-sur-Marne: Martin, 1900), also dates from this period.

35. Augustin Bernard and Nicolas Lacroix, *L'évolution de nomadisme en Algérie* (Paris: A. Challamel, 1906).

36. Augustin Bernard and Nicolas Lacroix, *La pénétration saharienne* (Algiers: Imprimerie Algérienne, 1906).

37. Augustin Bernard, *Les confins algéro-marocains* (Paris: E. Larose, 1911).

38. Augustin Bernard, *Le Maroc* (Paris: F. Alcan, 1911).

39. *Le Maroc inconnu* was originally published in two volumes: vol. 1, *Le Maroc inconnu: L'exploration du Rif* (Paris: J. André, 1895; vol. 2, *Le Maroc inconnu: L'exploration du Djebala Maroc Septentrional* (Paris: Challamel, 1899). With the opening of the Moroccan question the two volumes were combined and republished under the title *Le Maroc inconnu: Étude géographique et sociologique* (Paris: A. Challamel, 1902).

40. Desparmet's published works total more than two hundred articles and books.

1. On the *Documents pour servir,* see chapter 2.

2. Autobiographie, 2e état, no date, Le Chatelier Papers, Dossier A.

3. Ibid.

4. Ibid.

5. Le Chatelier's books from this period include *Les confréries musulmans du Hedjaz* (Paris: Leroux, 1887); *Les Médaganat* (Paris: Jourdan, 1888); *L'Islam au XIX-ième siècle* (Paris: Leroux, 1888); *Questions sahariennes: Touat-Chambaa-Touareg: Mission dans le sud algérien* (Paris, 1890); *Mémoire sur le Maroc: Situation actuelle de la France au Maroc, programme politique, questions économiques; Voyage au Maroc d'octobre 1889 à mars 1890* (Paris: Privately printed, 1890); *L'Islam dans l'Afrique occidentale* (Paris: G. Steinheil, 1899). An extensive (although still incomplete) listing of his publications can be found in Raymond Messal, *La genèse de notre victoire au Maroc: Un précurseur, Alfred Le Chatelier (1855–1929)* (Paris: Dunod, 1931), 331–336.

6. ALC to Eugène Etienne, Juan les Pins, 3 août 1913, Note autobiographique, p. 18, Le Chatelier Papers, Dossier A.

7. On the circumstances of his resignation, see Messal, *La genèse de notre victoire,* 142–144. It appears that the resignation was not formally accepted by the Ministry of War until April 21, 1899. "Notice autobiographique," Le Chatelier Papers, Dossier A.

8. Robert A. Nye, *Masculinity and Male Codes of Honor in Modern France* (New York: Oxford University Press, 1993), 211.

9. The history of the Alis/Le Chatelier duel in 1892 was for a long time suppressed. It was a major scandal in colonial circles, as a result of which Le Chatelier , a founder of the Comité de l'Afrique française, was compelled to resign. On his Congo activities, see Messal, *La genèse de notre victoire,* chap. 6.

10. The Foureau/Lamy expedition eventually ended badly as well when several years later, in an effort to link up with other French expeditions in Tchad, Lamy was killed by Touareg on April 22, 1900. This, however, was a separate mission in which Le Chatelier was not involved.

11. Messal, *La genèse de notre victoire,* 165–192.

12. Chambre des Deputés, Session de 1904, No. 1893, Projet de Résolution ayant pour objet de créer un Institut marocain, presenté par M. Eugène Etienne, Deputé, Annexe au process verbal de la 2e séance du 8 juillet 1904.

13. ALC to Michaux-Bellaire, January 2, 1927, Le Chatelier Papers, Dossier A. In 1912 Le Chatelier wrote the German orientalist Martin Hartmann in a similar vein. See Martin Kraemer, "Arabistik and Arabism: The Passions of Martin Hartmann," *Middle Eastern Studies* 25:3 (1989): 283–300.

14. "Les obsèques de Georges Salmon," *Dépêche de Tanger,* no. 125 (Aug. 25, 1906), in which we learn that Salmon began to study Arabic at age thirteen.

15. Georges Salmon, *Études sur la topographie du Caire: La Kal'at al-Kabch et la Birkat al-Fil* (Cairo: Imprimerie de l'Institut français d'archéologie orientale, 1902); Salmon, *Notes d'épigraphie arabe* (Cairo: Imprimerie de l'Institut français

d'archéologie orientale, 1902); Salmon, trans., *Un texte arabe inédit pour servir à l'histoire des Chrétiens d'Egypte* (Cairo: Imprimerie éditions de l'Institut français d'archéologie orientale, 1906); Salmon, trans., *L'introduction topographique à l'histoire de Bagdadh d'Abou Bakr Ahmad ibn Thabit al-Khatib al-Bagdadhi* (Paris: E. Bouillon, 1904); Salmon, ed., *Silvestre de Sacy (1758–1838),* 2 vols. (Cairo: l'Institut français d'archéologie orientale, 1905).

16. "Notes sur la flore de Fayyoum d'après An-Naboulsi," *BIFAO,* 1901, 25–28; "Répetoire géographique de la province du Fayyoum d'après le Kitab Tarikh al-Fayyoum d'An-Naboulsi," *BIFAO,* 1901, 29–77; "Le nom de Babidj dans la géographie égyptienne," *BIFAO,* 1901, 235–239; "Rapport sur une mission à Damiette," *BIFAO,* 1902, 71–89; "Notes d'épigraphie arabe," *BIFAO,* 1902, 109–112.

17. Maspero to Delcassé, October 17, 1904, Private, MAE, Maroc, Questions Culturelles et Religieuses I (1902–7), N.S. 405. In his letter of recommendation Maspero wrote about Salmon, "The remarkable abilities and the exceptional gifts which he has already displayed so brilliantly in particular since his arrival in Morocco are for us the best guarantee that his authority will rapidly be affirmed."

18. The English translation of his title is "deputy administrator in training of commune mixte (unattached)."

19. For the early history of the MSM, see Édouard Michaux-Bellaire, "La Mission scientifique du Maroc," *Archives marocaines,* 1925. On the financing of the project, see Eugène Étienne, "L'Institut marocain," *Renseignements coloniaux,* 1904, 194–195. (*Renseignements coloniaux* was a supplement to *Bulletin du Comité de l'Afrique française;* hereafter it is cited as *RC.*)

20. ALC to Salmon, October 26, 1903, Le Chatelier Papers, Dossier A.

21. Édouard Michaux-Bellaire, "La Mission scientifique du Maroc," *Archives marocaines,* 1925, 1–22: "Il s'agissait, pour créer les *Archives marocaines* de faire pour ainsi dire le catalogue du Maroc, de ses tribus, de ses villes, de ses confréries, d'en retrouver les origines, les ramifications, les luttes et les alliances; de les suivre dans l'histoire à travers les différentes dynasties, d'en étudier les institutions et les coutumes, de reconnaître, en un mot, dans le mesure du possible le terrain sur lequel nous pouvions être appelés à opérer un jour, pour nous permettre d'agir en toute connaissance de cause et de faire de la politique indigène, sans trop d'erreurs, sans faiblesses comme sans violences inutiles et de créer une administration assez souple pour pouvoir s'appliquer aux caractères des différentes tribus sans cesser cependant d'être une."

22. Members of the École d'Alger believed that Salmon was Jewish because he had briefly been the assistant of Hartwig Derenbourg (who was a well-known French Jewish orientalist) at the ELOV. Coming as they did just a few years after the anti-Semitic riots in Algiers in 1899–1900, their views are perfectly in accord with the time. See Le Chatelier to Étienne, Paris, January 19, 1904, Archives d'Outre-Mer, Série 4H A. On the fin de siècle anti-Semitic crisis in Algeria, see Charles-Robert Ageron, *Les Algériens musulmans et la France, 1871–1919* (Paris: P.U.F., 1968), vol. 1, chap. 22.

23. Doutte to Terrier, April 19, 1904, Parc Stephane, Mustapha, Terrier MS 5897, Correspondance VII, BIF.

24. Ibid.

25. Ibid.

26. "Ici le mot d'ordre est de se désintéresser du Maroc." Doutté to Terrier. May 27, 1904, Parc Stéphane, Mustapha, Terrier MS 5897, Correspondance VII, BIF.

27. Doutte to Terrier, April 19, 1904, Parc Stephane, Mustapha, Terrier MS 5897, Correspondance VII, BIF.

28. Ibid.

29. MAE, Maroc, N.S. 405, Questions culturelles et religieuses, 1902–15. Dossier 1, "Écoles, missions scientifique, 1902–1907," Enclosing Chambre des Deputés, Projet de Résolution No. 1893, Lucien Hubert, "Institut marocain."

30. Étienne, "L'Institut marocain," 194–195.

31. MAE, Maroc, N.S. 405, Questions culturelles et religieuses, 1902–15. Dossier 1, "Écoles, missions scientifique, 1902–1907," Enclosing Chambre des Deputés, Projet de Résolution No. 1893, Lucien Hubert, "Institut marocain."

32. ALC to Direction politique, Ministère des affaires étrangères, November 7, 1904, Le Chatelier Papers, Dossier A.

33. MAE, Maroc, N.S. 405, Questions culturelles et religieuses, 1902–15. Dossier 1, "Écoles, missions scientifique, 1902–1907," Enclosing Chambre des Deputés, Projet de Résolution No. 1893, Lucien Hubert, "Institut marocain." Also ALC to Direction politique, Ministère des affaires étrangères, November 7, 1904, Le Chatelier Papers, Dossier A.

34. Ibid.

35. ALC to Saint-René-Taillandier, Paris, November 7, 1904, Le Chatelier Papers, Dossier A, Liasse III.

36. ALC Note "Au sujet de l'école d'application de la mission scientifique du Maroc," Enclosure No. 3, in ALC to Ministère des affaires étrangères, November 14, 1904, MAE, Maroc, N.S. 405. For the final parliamentary report, see Reglement, 1905, Mission scientifique du Maroc, Carton C-15, SHAT.

FOUR · WHEN PARADIGMS SHIFT

1. James Clifford, *The Predicament of Culture* (Cambridge, MA: Harvard University Press, 1988).

2. Edmund Burke III and David Prochaska, *Genealogies of Orientalism: History, Theory, Politics* (Lincoln: University of Nebraska Press, 2008), chap. 1.

3. See Pierre Bourdieu, *Sociology in Question,* trans. Richard Nice (Thousand Oaks, CA: Sage Publications, 1993); also Bourdieu, *Outline of a Theory of Practice,* trans. Richard Nice (Cambridge: Cambridge University, 1977).

4. On the Durkheim school, see Terry N. Clark, *Prophets and Patrons: The French University and the Emergence of the Social Sciences* (Cambridge, MA: Harvard University Press, 1973).

5. A. Maitrot de la Motte Capron, "Le Roghi," *Bulletin de la Société de géographie d'Alger,* 1929, 514–576. Also Jean du Taillis, *Le Maroc pittoresque* (Paris:

E. Flammarion, 1905), 65–70; Leonhard Karow, *Neun Jahre in marokkanischen Diensten* (Berlin: W. Weicher, 1909), 123.

6. Hubert Rapport.

7. Harry Alis was a strong proponent of African colonization and author of the following: *À la conquête du Tchad* (Paris: Librarie Hachette, 1891); *Promenade en Égypte* (Paris: Librarie Hachette, 1895); and the novels *Les pas de chance* (Brussels: Kistemaeckers, 1883) and *Hara-Kiri* (repr., Paris: Esprit des péninsules, 2000). His quarrel with Le Chatelier stemmed from a dispute over railroad investments in French Congo. On this, see Catherine Coquery-Vidovitch, "Les idées économiques de Brazza et les premières tentatives de compagnies de colonisation au Congo Français—1885–1898," *Cahiers d'études africaines* 5:17 (1965): 57–82; Raymond Messal, *La genèse de notre victoire au Maroc: Un précurseur, Alfred Le Chatelier (1855–1929)* (Paris: Dunod, 1931), 143–164.

8. Anouar Abdel-Malek, "The End of Orientalism," *Diogenes* 44 (1963): 103–140. From our present vantage point, Abdel-Malek's analysis seems overly optimistic.

9. Edward Said, *Orientalism* (New York: Pantheon, 1978).

10. See Edmund Burke III, "The First Crisis of Orientalism, 1890–1914," in *Connaissances du Maghreb: Sciences sociales et colonisation,* ed. Jean-Claude Vatin (Paris: Éditions du C.N.R.S., 1984), 213–226.

11. Which is not to say that in the post-9/11 world, the power of orientalist discourse has not returned full force. Nothing is forever.

12. On the critique of orientalism, see Burke and Prochaska, *Genealogies of Orientalism.*

13. For a more developed version of this argument, see the introduction to Burke and Prochaska, *Genealogies of Orientalism.*

14. Stanley Hoffman, *The Obstructed Path: French Social Thought in the Years of Desperation, 1930–1960* (New York: Transaction, 2001). While Hoffman refers to the post-1930 period, the pre-1914 Third Republic was at least as affected by social and political dysfunction.

15. Clifford Geertz, "In Search of North Africa," *New York Review of Books,* April 22, 1971.

16. Edmond Doutté, "Une mission d'études," *RC*, 1901, 171.

17. Eugène Aubin, *Le Maroc d'aujourd'hui* (Paris: A. Colin, 1904), 241 (quote), also 238–239.

18. Doutté, "Une mission d'études," 172.

19. Aubin, *Le Maroc d'aujourd'hui,* 245.

20. Edmund Burke III, *Prelude to Protectorate in Morocco: Precolonial Protest and Resistance, 1860–1912* (Chicago: University of Chicago Press, 1976), 68–75.

21. On French policy toward Morocco before 1904, see Edmond Doutté, "Les deux politiques," *Bulletin du Comité de l'Afrique française,* 1903, 306–311; and Robert de Caix, "La France et le Maroc," *Bulletin du Comité de l'Afrique française,* 1903, 298–306.

22. A clear exposition of Delcassé's policy of peaceful penetration can be found in Christopher Andrew, *Théophile Delcassé and the Making of the Entente Cordiale:*

A Reappraisal of French Foreign Policy, 1898–1905 (London: St. Martins, 1968). See also *Documents diplomatiques français,* Affaires du Maroc, I (1901–1905), 179–184.

23. Attempts were made to ease tensions in the region by the signing of diplomatic accords on the frontier in 1901 and 1902. But they failed to resolve the situation. A. Bernard, *Les confins algéro-marocains* (Paris: E. Larose, 1911) includes the complete texts of the accords.

24. The broad outlines of this policy seem first to have been suggested to Lyautey by Vaffier-Pollet, an employee of the Compagnie marocaine, in June of 1904. Cf. Louis Hubert Gonzalve Lyautey, *Vers le Maroc, lettres du sud-oranais, 1903–1906* (Paris: A. Colin, 1932), 66, 224–227.

25. Lyautey, *Vers le Maroc,* 224–227.

26. Exhaustively described by Pierre Guillen, "L'implantation de Schneider, les débuts de la Compagnie marocaine (1902–1906)," *Revue d'histoire diplomatique,* 1965, 113–168.

27. This history is related by Daniel Rivet, *Lyautey et l'institution du protectorat français au Maroc* (Paris: L'Harmattan, 1988), vol. 2. For the general background, see René Gallissot, *L'économie de l'Afrique du nord,* 3rd ed. (Paris: P.U.F., 1969).

28. "Discours de M. Etienne," *Bulletin du Comité de l'Afrique française,* 1904, 182.

29. Marquis René de Segonzac, *Au coeur de l'Atlas: Mission au Maroc, 1904–1905* (Paris: Émile Larose, 1910), 258.

30. Édouard Michaux-Bellaire, "L'organisme marocain," *Revue du monde musulman* 9 (1908): 1–33.

31. Edmond Ferry, "La réorganisation marocaine," *RC,* 1905, 519–528, esp. 526.

32. Lyautey, *Vers le Maroc,* 127.

33. Doutté, "Coup d'oeil sur le Maroc," *RC,* 1909, 135.

34. Doutté, "Le fanatisme musulman," *RC,* 1909, 164.

35. The influence of the *makhzan/siba* binary can be seen as well in Carleton Coon, *Caravan: The Story of the Middle East* (New York: Holt, 1958), 309–323, where it is used to explain the course of Middle Eastern history.

36. Henri Terrasse, *Histoire du Maroc des origines à l'établissement du protectorat français,* 2 vols. (Casablanca: Éditions Atlantides, 1950).

37. Terrasse, *Histoire du Maroc,* 2:357.

38. Ibid., 423.

39. Ibid., 357–358.

FIVE · TENSIONS OF EMPIRE

1. The summary that follows draws on Edmund Burke III, *Prelude to Protectorate in Morocco: Precolonial Protest and Resistance, 1860–1912* (Chicago: University of Chicago Press, 1976), chaps. 2–4.

2. Georges Salmon, "Une opinion marocaine sur la conquête de Touat (traduction)," *AM* 1:3 (1904): 416–424.

3. Burke, *Prelude,* chap. 3.

4. Ibid., 61–62.

5. Since the MSM did not begin operations until the fall of 1903 (and the first number of *AM* appeared in 1904), and the CAF missions started in 1900, the dates of their first phases do not quite coincide.

6. A. Le Chatelier to G. Salmon, Paris, October 26, 1903, MAE, Maroc, N.S. 405. In this lengthy letter Le Chatelier outlines in great detail exactly how he wishes Salmon to proceed in setting up the MSM and preparing the first issues of *AM* for publication.

7. On thick description, see Clifford Geertz, "Thick Description: Toward an Interpretive Theory of Culture," in *The Interpretation of Cultures* (New York: Basic Books, 1973), 3–30.

8. *AM* 1 :1–3 (1904).

9. Salmon to ALC, El Qsar [el-Kebir], October 15, 1904, Le Chatelier Papers, Bundle A, Folder III.

10. Charles-Robert Ageron, *Les algériens musulmans et la France, 1871–1919* (Paris: P.U.F., 1968), 1:67–102.

11. Chambre des Deputés, Session de 1904, No. 1893, Projet de Résolution ayant pour objet de créer un Institut marocain."

12. Georges Salmon, "Les chorfa idrisides de Fès d'après Ibn At-Tayyib al-Qadiry," *AM* 1:3 (1904): 425–453.

13. Evidence of this preoccupation can be found in Édouard Michaux-Bellaire, "Une tentative de restauration idrissite à Fez," *Revue du monde musulman* 5 (1908): 393–423.

14. On this, see Evariste Lévi-Provençal, *Les historiens des Chorfa: Essai sur la littérature historique et biographique au Maroc du XVIe au XXe siècle* (Paris: E. Larose, 1922), 371.

15. A. G. P. Martin, *Quatre siècles d'histoire marocaine: Au Sahara de 1504 à 1902, au Maroc de 1894 à 1912, d'après archives et documentations indigènes* (Paris: Alcan, 1923); and Martin, *Les oasis Sahariennes (Gourara—Touat—Tidikelt)* (Algiers: L'Imprimerie Algérienne, 1908). Also Frank E. Trout, *Morocco's Saharan Frontiers* (Geneva: Droz, 1969).

16. On the crisis of 1904–5, see Burke, *Prelude to Protectorate in Morocco*, 75–85.

17. Salmon to Le Chatelier, Tangier, November 20, 1904, Le Chatelier Papers, Dossier A.

18. Alfred Le Chatelier, "G. Salmon, Chef de Mission," *AM* 7 (1906): 463–473.

19. Ibid., 465–472.

20. *AF* (1906), 239.

21. Revoil to Minister of Foreign Affairs, May 31, 1906, MAE, Maroc, N.S. 405, Questions culturelles et religieux (1902–1915), Dossier I, Écoles, missions scientifiques (1902–7), not numbered.

22. Le Chatelier to George Louis, Paris, January 15, 1907, MAE, Maroc, Écoles et missions scientifiques, 1902–15, N.S. 405.

23. ALC to Revoil, Paris, April 1, 1906, MAE, Papiers d'Agents, Revoil MSS, in which it is also divulged that ALC proposed to provide complete sets of *AM* for distribution to the delegations at Algeciras.

24. See Herbert Feis, *Europe: The World's Banker, 1870–1915* (New York: W.W. Norton, 1965); William L. Langer, *European Alliances and Alignments, 1871–1890* (New York: Vintage, 1964); and David Landes, *Bankers and Pashas: International Finance and Economic Imperialism in Egypt* (London: Heinemann, 1958).

25. Burke, *Prelude to Protectorate in Morocco*, 85–93.

26. The Comité du Maroc was practically indistinguishable from a wholly owned subsidiary of the Comité de l'Afrique française, sharing the same offices, members, and funding sources.

27. Charles René-Leclerc, *Situation de la Délégation du Comité du Maroc à Tanger pendant 1906* (Algiers: Comité du Maroc), 79–81, 98.

28. Commandant Alfred-Henri Dyé (1874–1926) was a French explorer and hydrologist who participated in numerous French expeditions to Africa in the late nineteenth and early twentieth centuries. He was in Morocco continuously from 1904 to 1907 and is the author of *Les ports du Maroc: Leur commerce avec la France* (Paris: Imprimerie P. Brodard, 1909).

29. For a list of the CAF/CM-funded expeditions, see table 1.

30. Jonathan G. Katz, *Murder in Marrakech: Émile Mauchamps and the French Colonial Adventure* (Bloomington: Indiana University Press, 2006).

31. James Frazer, *The Golden Bough: A Study in Magic and Religion* (New York: Macmillan, 1947).

32. See chapter 3. His major work in this genre, *Magie et religion dans l'Afrique du Nord* (Paris: Geuthner, 1908) was published after the reports of his Morocco study missions.

33. George R. Trumbull, *An Empire of Facts: Colonial Power, Cultural Knowledge and Islam in Algeria, 1870–1914* (Cambridge: Cambridge University Press, 2009).

34. Edmond Doutté, *Merrakech* (Paris: Comité du Maroc, 1905).

35. Edmond Doutté, "Quatrième voyage d'études au Maroc: L'organisation domestique et sociale chez les H'h'a: Contribution à la sociologie marocaine," *RC*, 1905, 1–16.

36. See Paul Pascon, "Le rapport 'secret' d'Edmond Doutté," *Herodote* 11:3 (1978): 132–159, for the full text of Doutté's 1907 report, "Situation politique du Houz 1er Janvier 1907." See also Edmond Doutté, "A Rabat, chez Abdelaziz: Notes prises en 1907," *Bulletin de la Société de géographie et archéologie d'Oran* 33:1 (1910): 21–68.

37. Édouard Marie René Marquis de Segonzac, *Excursion au Sous avec quelques considérations préliminaires sur la question marocaine* (Paris: Challamel, 1901). The mission was undertaken in 1899 under the auspices of the Service géographique de l'Armée, in whose archives it slumbered for a year before it was published, thanks to the intervention of Auguste Mouliéras. Mouliéras, "La ville de Fez," *Bulletin de la Société de géographie d'Oran* 21 (April–June 1901): 1–31.

38. De Segonzac, *Voyages au Maroc, 1899–1901* (Paris: A. Colin, 1903).

39. De Segonzac, *Au Coeur de l'Atlas: Mission au Maroc, 1904–1905*. (Paris: Émile Larose, 1910). The full list of sponsors included the Société de géographie de Paris, Société de géographie de l'Afrique du Nord, Société normande de géographie,

Société de géographie commerciale, the Association française pour l'avancement des sciences, la Société géologique de France, the École d'Anthropologie de Paris, and the Société de secours aux blessés militaires.

40. Gentil led six missions in the period, while Brives conducted five. See Louis Gentil, *Dans le Bled es Siba: Explorations au Maroc* (Paris: Masson et cie, 1906) and *Le Maroc physique* (Paris: F. Alcan, 1912). Also Abel Brives, *Voyages au Maroc (1901–1907)* (Algiers: A. Jourdan, 1909).

41. Gentil, *Dans le Bled es Siba,* 524.

42. In 1920 Louis Gentil produced a "Carte géologique provisoire du Maroc" on the scale 1:1,500,000 for the protectorate. André Michard et al., eds. *Continental Evolution: The Geology of Morocco* (Berlin: Axel Springer Verlag, 2008), 385.

43. On the Zaer expedition, see Maurice Zimmerman, "Mission Louis Gentil dans le Maroc occidental," *Annales de géographie* 19:104 (1910) : 187–188.

44. Michard et al., *Continental Evolution.* Abel Brives mentioned the existence of phosphate beds in a 1908 publication and proposed that deposits were to be found in the Oum-er-Rbia valley, but only in 1917 did a French military engineer discover the phosphate deposits of Oued Zem (on which see Michard et al., *Continental Evolution,* 385).

45. Faouzi Houroro, *Sociologie politique coloniale au Maroc: Le cas de Michaux-Bellaire* (Casablanca: Afrique Orient, 1988).

46. R. Gerofi, "Michaux-Bellaire," *Tingu: Bulletin de la Société d'histoire et d'archéologie Tanger* 1 (1953): 79–85.

47. Procès-verbale du bureau de la mission scientifique, December 23, 1909, MAE, Maroc, Écoles et missions scientifiques, 1902–15, N.S. 405.

48. Le Chatelier Papers, Dossier A.

49. Révoil to Minister of Foreign Affairs, May 31, 1906, MAE, Maroc, N.S. 405.

50. Édouard Michaux-Bellaire, "La Mission scientifique du Maroc," *AM,* 1925, 1–22.

51. For example, Depont and Coppolani, Rinn, Lamartinière and Lacroix, and Bernard and Lacroix.

52. Alfred Le Chatelier, *Mémoire sur le Maroc: Situation actuelle de la France au Maroc, programme politique, questions économiques; Voyage au Maroc d'octobre 1889 à mars 1890* (Paris: Privately printed, 1890) ; Le Chatelier, *L'Islam dans l'Afrique Occidentale* (Paris: G. Steinheil, 1899).

53. On the institutionalization of the Durkheim school, see, among others, Terry N. Clark, *Prophets and Patrons: The French University and the Emergence of the Social Sciences* (Cambridge, MA: Harvard University Press, 1973).

54. Alex Padamasee, *Representations of Indian Muslims in British Colonial Discourse* (London: Palgrave Macmillan, 2005).

SIX · SOCIAL RESEARCH IN THE TECHNOCOLONY

1. Edmund Burke III, *Prelude to Protectorate in Morocco: Precolonial Protest and Resistance, 1860–1912* (Chicago: University of Chicago Press, 1976), chaps. 7 and 8.

See also Pierre Guillen, "L'implantation de Schneider, les débuts de la Compagnie marocaine (1902–1906)," *Revue d'histoire diplomatique,* 1965, 113–168.

2. [Edmond Doutté], "La réalisation du protectorat marocain (Note sur la future organisation politique du Maroc)," June 19, 1912, MAE, Maroc, Organisation administrative du protectorat, vol. 289, Dossier Général I (January—June 1912).

3. For the Cambon quotation, see Charles-Robert Ageron, *Les algériens musulmans et la France, 1871–1919* (Paris: P.U.F., 1968), 1:518–519. The phrase is from Cambon's description of Algerian society in 1890s as a "poussière d'hommes."

4. Émile Durkheim, *The Division of Labor in Society* (New York: Free Press, 1984).

5. Doutté, "La réalisation du protectorat marocain."

6. Ibid.

7. Daniel Rivet, *Lyautey et l'institution du protectorat français au Maroc, 1912–1925* (Paris: L'Harmattan, 1988), 2:161.

8. The authoritative survey of the development of its institutions is Rivet, *Lyautey.*

9. Hubert Lyautey, *Choix de lettres 1882–1919* (Paris: A. Colin, 1947), 25.

10. Clive Dewey, *Anglo-Indian Attitudes: The Mind of the Indian Civil Service* (London: Hambledon, 2003); and Abbot L. Lowell and H. Morse Stephens, *Colonial Civil Service: The Selection and Training of Colonial Officials in England, Holland, and France with an Account of the East India College at Haileybury (1806–1857)* (New York: Macmillan, 1900). Also Bernard S. Cohn, *Colonialism and Its Forms of Knowledge: The British in India* (Princeton, NJ: Princeton University Press, 1996).

11. Dewey, *Anglo-Indian Attitudes,* 3.

12. K.C. Arora, *The Steel Frame: Indian Civil Service since 1860* (New Delhi: Sanchar, 1996).

13. Kenneth Perkins, *Qaids, Captains and Colons: French Military Administration in the Colonial Maghrib, 1830–1934.* New York: Africana, 1981.

14. For an example, see John Gordon Lorimer, *Gazetteer of the Persian Gulf, 'Omān, and Central Arabia* (Calcutta: Superintendent Government Printing, 1915).

15. Will D. Swearingen, *Moroccan Mirages: Agrarian Dreams and Deceptions 1912–1986* (Princeton, NJ: Princeton University Press, 1987), chaps. 1–2.

16. Rivet, *Lyautey.*

17. Alfred Le Chatelier, "Propositions détaillés pour la constitution d'une service d'agents politiques du protectorat," 22 pages, January–February 1913, MAE, Maroc, Protectorat, Direction des affaires indigènes, Carton 227.

18. Ibid.

19. The original letter is referenced in Lyautey to Le Chatelier, May 15, 1912, Personal, MAE, Maroc, Protectorat, Direction des affaires indigènes, Carton 227.

20. Lyautey to Le Chatelier, May 15, 1912, Personal, MAE, Maroc, Protectorat, Direction des affaires indigènes, Carton 227.

21. Ibid.

22. Ibid.

23. Lyautey to minister of public instruction, Paris, January 31, 1913, No. 654 E.M.¹, MAE, Maroc, Écoles et missions scientifiques, 1902–15, N.S. 405. In the same letter Lyautey also discussed the future of the MSM, on which see below.

24. Lyautey to Stephen Pichon, Ministre des Affaires Étrangères, Paris, July 31, 1913, No. 656 E.M.², MAE, Maroc, Écoles et missions scientifiques, 1902–15, N.S. 405.

25. Ibid.

26. Ibid.

27. Lyautey to minister of public instruction, Paris, July 31, 1913, No. 971 B.P.², MAE, Maroc, Écoles et missions scientifiques, 1902–15, N.S. 405.

28. Pichon to Lyautey. Paris. August 27, 1913. No. 840, MAE, Maroc, Écoles et missions scientifiques, 1902–15, N.S. 405.

29. Lyautey to Pichon, Paris, September 25, 1913, No. 1123 B.P.², MAE, Maroc, Écoles et missions scientifiques, 1902–15, N.S. 405.

30. Ibid.

31. Robin Bidwell, *Morocco under Colonial Rule: French Administration of Tribal Areas, 1912–1956* (London: Frank Cass, 1973), 167.

32. Lyautey to Le Chatelier, May 15, 1912, Personal, MAE, Maroc, Protectorat, Direction des affaires indigenes, carton 227.

33. Mentioned in Lyautey to minister of public instruction, Paris, July 31, 1913, No. 971 B.P.², MAE, Maroc, Écoles et missions scientifiques, 1902–15, N.S. 405. I have not been able to find the original letter.

34. Lyautey to Alfred Le Chatelier, Rabat, January 31, 1913, No. 971 B.P.², MAE, Maroc, Écoles et missions scientifiques, 1902–15, N.S. 405.

35. Germain Ayache, *La guerre du Rif* (Paris: Harmattan, 1996). Also C. R. Pennell, *A Country with a Government and a Flag: The Rif War in Morocco, 1921–1926* (Boulder CO: Lynne Reiner, 1986).

36. Edmund Burke III, "Mouvements sociaux et mouvements de resistance au Maroc: La Grande Siba de la Chaouia, 1902–1906," *Hespéris-Tamuda* 17 (1976–77): 149–163; John Godfrey, "Overseas Trade and Rural Change in Nineteenth Century Morocco" (PhD diss., Johns Hopkins University, 1985); and André Adam, "Sur l'action du Galilée à Casablanca en août 1907," *Revue de l'Occident musulman et de la Méditerranée* 6:6 (1969): 9–22.

37. H. Lyautey, "Lettres de Rabat (1907)," *Revue des deux mondes,* 1921, 273–304.

38. Lyautey to minister of foreign affairs, Rabat, July 31, 1913, No. 656 E.M.¹, MAE, Maroc, Écoles et missions scientifiques, 1902–15, N.S. 405.

39. Mission scientifique du Maroc, *Documents et renseignements publié sous les auspices de la Résidence Générale: Casablanca et les Chaouia,* Villes et Tribus du Maroc (Paris: Ernest Leroux, 1913), 1:iii.

40. The exchange of correspondence between the two men can be found in Archives de la Légation de France à Tanger, Série A, Carton 227, Dossier on the Mission scientifique.

41. Dactylograph copy of Lyautey to Le Chatelier, December 11, 1913, No. 1551BP2, Archives de la Légation de France à Tanger, Série A, Carton 227, Dossier on the Mission scientifique.

42. Isabelle Grandgaud, *La ville impregnable: Une histoire sociale de Constantine au 18ième siècle* (Paris: Éditions de l'École pratique des hautes études en sciences sociales, 2002).

43. See Burke, "Mouvements sociaux," for such an attempt.

44. André Adam, *Casablanca: Essai sur la transformation de la société marocaine au contact de l'Occident,* 2nd ed. (Paris: Éditions du Centre national de la recherche scientifique, 1972). On sex workers, see Driss Maghraoui, "Gendering Colonial Urban Casablanca: The Case of the Quartier Reservé of Bousibir in Casablanca," in *Gendering Urban Space in the Middle East, South Asia and Africa,* ed. Kamran Asdar Ali and Martina Rieker (London: Palgrave, 2008), 17–44.

45. *Hespéris: Archives Berbères et Bulletin de l'Institut des hautes-études marocaines* (1921–59).

46. Évariste Lévi-Provençal, *Les historiens des Chorfa* (Paris: E. Larose, 1922); Émile Laoust, *Mots et choses berbères: Notes de linguistique et d'ethnographie; Dialectes du Maroc.* (Paris: A. Challamel, 1920).

47. Henry Comte de Castries et al., eds., *Les sources inédites de l'histoire du Maroc de 1530 à 1845* (Paris: E. Leroux, 1905).

SEVEN · BERBER POLICY

1. Today *thamazight* is the name given to the Berber language in Morocco.

2. Édouard Marie René, Marquis de Segonzac, *Au coeur de l'Atlas: Mission au Maroc, 1904–1905* (Paris: Émile Larose, 1910), 37, 43, 68, 105, and 270. The attentive reader will have noted that while Segonzac was ideologically opposed to the *makhzan* (and therefore disposed to have favorable views of Berbers), his views at the time about the relationship of the two were basically incoherent.

3. De Segonzac, *Au coeur de l'Atlas;* Eugène Aubin, *Le Maroc d'aujourd'hui* (Paris: A. Colin, 1904), 52.

4. Edmond Doutté, "Une mission d'études au Maroc: Rapport sommaire ensemble," " *RC,* 1901, 166.

5. Ibid., 167.

6. Doutté, "Troisième voyage d'études au Maroc: Rapport sommaire d'ensemble," *RC,* 1902, 158.

7. Augustin Bernard, *Les confins algéro-marocains* (Paris: E. Larose, 1911), 207.

8. Louis Hubert Gonzalves Lyautey, *Vers le Maroc, lettres du sud-oranais, 1903–1906* (Paris: A. Colin, 1937).

9. Paul Lemoine, "Mission dans le Maroc occidental," *RC,* 1905, 65–92.

10. Edmund Burke III, "Tribalism and Moroccan Resistance, 1890–1914: The Role of the Aith Ndhir," In *Tribe and State in Northwest Africa,* ed. George Joffe and Richard Pennell (London: M.E.N.A.S., 1991), 119–144.

11. Burke, "Tribalism and Moroccan Resistance."

12. Alfred Le Chatelier to Édouard Michaux-Bellaire, Paris, October 5, 1913, Papiers Le Chatelier, Dossier A, Folder III.

13. Général Paul Henrys to Lyautey, December 12, 1914, No. 183 FMR, Maroc/D.I.P. 51, Direction de l'instruction publique, Liasse 51.

14. Ibid.

15. Edmond Destaing, *Étude sur le dialecte berbère des Aït Seghrouchen (moyen atlas marocain)* (Paris: E. Leroux, 1920).

16. Lyautey to Gen. Division Nord (Meknes), January 9, 1915, No. 29 RDA, Maroc/D.I.P. 51, Direction de l'instruction publique, Liasse 51.

17. Lyautey to Alfred Le Chatelier, Rabat, March 15, 1915, No. 320 DR², MAE, Maroc, Protectorat, Direction des affaires indigènes, Carton 227.

18. General Franchet d'Esperey to Lyautey, Casablanca, April 10, 1913, No. 43 R.G., MAE, Maroc, Protectorat, Direction des affaires indigènes, Carton 227 .

19. François Doumergue, "Les *Archives Berbères,* Vol. 1," *Bulletin de la Société de géographie et d'archéologie de la province d'Oran* 35 (1915): 222–223.

20. Quoted in Daniel Rivet, *Lyautey et l'institution du protectorat français au Maroc, 1912–1925* (Paris: L'Harmattan, 1988), 1:186.

21. Robert Montagne, *Les Berbères et le makhzen dans le sud du Maroc: Essai sur la transformation politique des Berbères sédentaires (groupe chleuh)* (Paris: F. Alcan, 1930).

22. Rivet, *Lyautey,* 1:189.

23. The lack of knowledge is frankly set forth by Général Henrys in a report cited in Georges Surdon, *Institutions et coutumes des Berbères du Maghreb* (Tangier: Éditions internationales, 1938), 103: "Now, it must be admitted, what did we know at this time of the mores, customs and traditions specific to the Berbers of Morocco? Very little, if not nothing?"

24. On French operations in the Beni Mtir, see Mohammed Abès, "Monographie d'une tribu berbère: Les Aith Ndhir (Beni Mtir)," *Archives berbères* 2 (1917): 174–180; also Maurice Le Glay, "Notes contributives," Institut de France, Fonds Terrier, no. 5957. The circumstances of the Beni Mtir revolt are discussed in Burke, "Tribalism and Moroccan Resistance"; and Burke, "Mohand N'Hamoucha, Middle Atlas Berber," in *Struggle and Survival in the Modern Middle East,* ed. E. Burke (Berkeley: University of California Press, 1993), 100–113.

25. On the organization of the Cercle des Beni Mtir, see Pierre Lyautey, ed., *Lyautey l'Africain* (Paris: Plon, 1953), 1:220–225; and *Afrique française,* 1913, 118.

26. On Lyautey's sense of the importance of notables, cf. Lyautey, *Lyautey l'Africain,* 1:252–255. Also, for a striking instance, see Col. Henrys, Instructions politiques (June 6, 1914), No. 153z, SHAT, Série E-2. Maurice Le Glay's cynical observations on the Lyautey system provide a helpful contrast. Le Glay "Lyautey et le commandement indigène," *Afrique française,* 1936, 194–197. Other important characteristics of the Lyautey system included an emphasis on political over military action where possible, and the establishment of markets and medical dispensaries in newly pacified territory.

27. Adolphe Hanoteau and Aristide Letourneux, *La Kabylie et les coutumes kabyles,* 3 vols. (Paris: Imprimerie nationale, 1872–73). In addition, see A. Bernard, "La question berbère dans le Maroc central," (unpublished paper, 1914), in *Fonds*

Terrier No. 5957; and Maurice Le Glay, "Les populations berbères du Maroc et le droit coutumier des berbères du Maroc central," *Archives berbères* 3 (1917): 299.

28. Henrys, cited in Surdon, *Institutions et coutumes,* 106.

29. Ibid.

30. Henrys, Instructions politiques (June 6, 1914), No. 153z, SHAT, Série E-2. See also Bernard, "La question berbère."

31. Surdon, *Institutions et coutumes,* 107–8.

32. Introduction to Henrys report of July 7, 1914, cited in Surdon, *Institutions et coutumes,* 106. Bernard, "La question berbère."

33. Bruno, cited in Le Glay, "Les populations berbères," 299.

34. Le Glay, "Les populations berbères," 388–389.

35. Col. Henri Marie Martin Berriau, "L'Officier de Renseignements au Maroc," *RC,* 1918, 90. Berriau was a leading native affairs official in the protectorate.

36. Le Glay, "Les populations berbères," 396–397.

37. Bernard, "La question berbère."

38. Le Glay, "Les populations berbères," *Archives Berbères* 3 (1917): 397.

39. Bruno, cited in Le Glay, "Les populations berbères," 397.

40. Lyautey, cited in Surdon, *Institutions et coutumes,* 105.

41. The *dahir* of September 11, 1914, was specifically requested by Henrys on the recommendation of his native affairs staff regarding the question. The decree can be found in *Afrique française,* 1915, 81.

42. Surdon, *Institutions et coutumes,* 109, quoting Henry's letter of January 26, 1915.

43. Surdon, *Institutions et coutumes,* 105.

44. This concern was noted by Henrys in Instructions politiques (June 6, 1914), No. 153z, SHAT, Série E-2. On the fear of Arabization, see also Le Glay, "Les populations berbères," 403; and *Afrique française,* 1914, 31–37.

45. *Afrique française,* 1914, 36–37.

46. Le Glay, "Les populations berbères," 403.

47. Fanny Colonna, "Educating Conformity in French Colonial Algeria," in *Tensions of Empire,* ed. Frederick Cooper and Ann Laura Stoler (Berkeley: University of California Press, 1997), 346–372.

48. Robert Marquis de Caix Saint-Aymour, "L'oeuvre française au Maroc," *RC,* 1912, 248–250. Also Bernard, "La question berbère."

49. Fanny Colonna, *Instituteurs algériens: 1833–1939* (Paris: Les presses du Sciences Po, 1975).

50. Bernard, "La question berbère."

51. Capt. Feaugéas, "L'enseignement dans le Moyen Atlas" (May 19, 1948), MS no. 1336, Centre des hautes études sur l'Afrique et l'Asie moderne, Paris.

52. Bernard, "La question berbère." Feaugéas, "L'enseignement dans le Moyen Atlas."

53. Robert Montagne, *La vie sociale et la vie politique des berbères* (Paris: Éditions du Comité de l'Afrique française, 1931), 7; preface by the editors of *Afrique française.*

54. Montagne, *La vie sociale,* 18.

55. Charles-Robert Ageron, "La politique berbère du protectorat marocain," *Revue d'histoire moderne et contemporaine,* 1971, 50–90.

EIGHT · URBAN POLICY

1. For a bibliography of French urban studies of Morocco, 1894–1924, see André Adam, *Bibliographie critique de sociologie, d'ethnologie et de géographie humaine du Maroc* (Algiers: SNED, 1972). More generally, see *AM* and *AF* (in which most early urban studies first appeared).

2. Robert Montagne, *Naissance du prolétariat marocain* (Paris: Peyronnet, 1952); and André Adam, *Casablanca: Essai sur la transformation de la société marocaine au contact de l'Occident,* 2nd ed. (Paris: Éditions du Centre national de la recherche scientifique, 1972).

3. Auguste Mouliéras, *Fez* (Paris: Challamel, 1902), 80.

4. Auguste Mouliéras, "La ville de Fez," *Bulletin de la Société de géographie d'Oran* 21 (1901): 1–31.

5. Mouliéras, *Fez,* 158–159.

6. Ibid., chap. 32. It includes a detailed discussion of the role of the Alliance Israelite in Morocco; see pp. 231–247, 272–291.

7. Mouliéras, *Fez,* 114–120.

8. Ibid., 296–298. See especially his debate with the young *alim* Si Bou-Bekr, 391 ff.

9. Mouliéras, *Fez,* 350.

10. Émile Masqueray, *La formation des cités chez les populations sédentaires de l'Algérie: Kabyles du Djuradjura—Chaouias de l'Aures Beni Mzab* (Paris: E. Leroux, 1886).

11. Félix Weisgerber, "La ville de Fès," *Revue française de l'étranger* 24 (1899),: 591–596; and "Maroc, Voyage du Dr. Weisgerber," *Comptes-rendus des séances de la Société de géographie* (Paris, 1900), 259–264.

12. Gaetan Delphin, *Fas, son université et l'enseignement supérieur musulman* (Paris: E. Leroux, 1889); and Moulieras, *Fez* (.

13. Eugène Aubin [Collard-Descos], "Fez le dernier centre de la civilisation maure," *Revue de Paris,* February 15, 1904, 851–872; March 1, 1904, 173–196; March 15, 1904, 424–448. Later published as *Le Maroc d'aujourd'hui* (Paris: A. Colin, 1904); English trans., *Morocco Today.*

14. Henri Gaillard, *Une ville d'Islam: Fez; Esquisse historique et sociale* (Paris: J. André, 1905).

15. Charles René-Leclerc, "Le commerce et l'industrie à Fez," *RC,* supplement to *AF,* 1905, 229–253; 295–321; 337–350.

16. Georges Salmon, "Les chorfa idrissides de Fez," *AM* 1 (1904): 425–459.

17. Louis Massignon, "Les corps des métiers et la cité islamique," *Revue internationale de sociologie* 28 (1920): 473–489; and "Enquête sur les corporations musulmanes d'artisans et de commerçants au Maroc," *Revue du monde musulman* 58 (1924): 1–250.

18. Roger Le Tourneau, *Fès avant le protectorat: Étude économique et sociale d'une ville de l'Occident musulman* (Casablanca: L'Institut des hautes études marocaine, 1949).

19. Henri Gaillard (b. 1869) was a graduate of the École des langues orientales who began his Moroccan career in 1895 at Tangier, then served in Casablanca (1897–1900) and Fez (1900–1912). He became the first secretary-general of the protectorate, and finished his career as consul general in Cairo. Léon Eugène Aubin Collard-Descos (b. 1863) began his diplomatic career at Athens in 1885. He served at a variety of posts in the Middle East, China, Latin America, and Spain before being sent to Morocco in 1902.

20. See, Capt. Justinard, "E. Michaux-Bellaire," *AF,* 1930, 411–412; and R. Gerofi, "Michaux-Bellaire," *Tinga* 1 (1953): 79–85.

21. Antoine-Louis Martin (b. 1882), after graduating from the École des langues orientales, served as a member of the MSM from 1908 to 1910, and then held a number of diplomatic posts in Morocco. Léon-Marie-Jules-Simon Pérétié (b. 1879) had a diploma from the École des langues orientales. He served in Egypt from 1904 until 1909, when he came to Morocco, and was attached to the MSM. He later held diplomatic posts in the Middle East.

22. See the obituary by Alfred Le Chatelier, "G. Salmon, Chef de Mission," *AM* 7 (1906): 463–473. Also *AF,* 1906, 258.

23. Charles René-Leclerc held *brevet* in Arabic and Berber from the École des langues orientales. He began his Moroccan career as head of the Delegation Générale of the Comité du Maroc at Tangier in 1905, at which position he remained until 1912.

24. The following articles derived from Salmon's 1906 trip to Fez: Salmon, "Les chorfa idrissides de Fez"; Salmon, "Les chorfa filala et djilala de Fez," *AM* 3 (1905): 97–118; Salmon, "Le culte de Moulay Idris et la mosquée des chorfa à Fez," *AM* 3 (1905),:413–429; Édouard Michaux-Bellaire, "Description de la ville de Fez," *AM* 11 (1907): 1–115; Louis Martin, "Description de la ville de Fez, quartier du Keddan," *Revue du monde musulman* 9 (1909): 433–443 and 621–642; A. Pérétié, "Les médersas de Fez," *AM* 18 (1918): 257–372. For an account of the accomplishments of the Fez mission, see Le Chatelier, "G. Salmon, Chef de Mission."

25. Jonathan G. Katz, "The Most Parisian of Muslims: Kaddour ben Ghabrit (1873–1954)," paper presented at the Northwest World History Association annual conference, Vancouver, WA, October 16–17, 2004.

26. Aubin was the author of *La Perse d'aujourd'hui* (Paris, 1908); *Les Anglais aux Indes et en Égypte* (Paris, 1899); and *En Haiti* (Paris, 1910).

27. Fustel de Coulanges, *La cité antique* (Paris: Hachette, 1864); English trans., *The Ancient City.*

28. Aubin, *Le Maroc d'aujourd'hui,* 268–270, 312–355; Gaillard, *Une ville d'Islam: Fez,* 147–151, and 175–176.

29. Michaux-Bellaire to Colonel [Huot], Tangier, November 20, 1922, MAE, Maroc, Protectorat, Direction des affaires indigènes, vol. 228.

30. At the height of the first Moroccan crisis, the French foreign minister Delcassé assured his Tangier representative of his willingness to "buy" the acquies-

cence of key members of the Fez elite. See *Documents diplomatique français* 2, IV, No. 483.

31. The articles were also published separately as a book by the Comité de l'Afrique Française. See also G. Marchand, "La situation commerciale à Fez en 1906," *RC,* 1906, 421–422.

32. For Aubin's discussions, see *Le Maroc d'aujourd'hui,* chaps. 10–12. There is reason to believe that the pseudonym René Maudit, used by the author of "Le makhzan marocain," *RC,* 1903, 293–304, hides the pen of Gaillard. Cf. Gaillard's later article, "L'administration au Maroc: Le makhzen, étendue et limites de son pouvoir," *Bulletin de la Société de géographie d'Alger,* 1909, 433–470, which was used to brief French diplomats at the Algeciras conference.

33. The influence of Sir James Frazer's *The Golden Bough,* a particularly important work that operates on the assumption of the existence of historical survivals, has been explicitly acknowledged in the case of Edmond Doutté. The Fez ethnographers operated in an intellectual environment in which evolutionary views dominated, even if unacknowledged.

34. Le Tourneau, *Fès;* and Jean-Louis Miège, *Le Maroc et l'Europe, 1830–1894,* 4 vols. (Paris: P.U.F., 1961–63).

35. Évariste Lévi-Provençal, *Les historiens des Chorfa: Essai sur la littérature historique et biographique au Maroc du XVIe au XXe siècle*(Paris: E. Larose, 1922); and Abdullah Laroui, *Les origines du nationalisme marocain, 1830–1912* (Paris: Maspéro,1977).

36. On the organic fallacy, see, among others, Édouard Michaux-Bellaire, "L'organisme marocaine," *Revue du monde musulman* 9 (1909): 1–33.

37. Discussed in Burke, *Prelude,* 180–187.

38. On the role of the *ulama,* see Edmund Burke III, "The Political Role of the Moroccan Ulama, 1860–1912," in *Saints, Scholars, and Sufis,* ed. N. R. Keddie (Berkeley: University of California Press, 1972), 93–126. Also Muhammad Baqir al-Kattani, *Tarjamah al-Shaykh Muhammad al-Kattani al-Shahid* (Unpublished manuscript, 1962); and Laroui, *Les origines du nationalisme marocain.*

39. The only effort at a study is Michaux-Bellaire's remarkably biased effort, "Une tentative de réstoration idrissite à Fez," *Revue du monde musulman* 5 (1908): 393–423.

40. Édouard Michaux-Bellaire, "Fez et les tribus berbères en 1910," *Bulletin de l'enseignement publique du Maroc,* 1921, 3–10.

41. Michaux-Bellaire to Colonel [Huot], Tangier, November 20, 1922, MAE, Maroc, Protectorat, Direction des affaires indigènes, vol. 228.

42. Clifford Geertz, Hildred Geertz, and Lawrence Rosen, *Meaning and Order in Moroccan Society: Three Essays in Cultural Analysis* (Cambridge: Cambridge University Press, 1979).

43. The argument in this section is presented in greater detail in chapter 7.

44. See above, chapter 7.

45. At least as important was Mme Mellier, know to Fasis as "Madame Bureau." She spoke Arabic fluently and was a tireless advocate for mutual understanding in

the weeks that followed the siege. See MacLeod to foreign minister Grey, Fez, March 7, 1913, FO 174, No. 272, No. 1.

46. MacLeod to foreign minister Grey, Fez, March 7, 1913, FO 174, No. 272, No. 1.

47. Sultan Abd al-Aziz appointed the *majlis al-a'yan* at a critical point in the crisis in 1904. See Burke, *Prelude,* 81–82.

48. During the siege of Fez in 1911 there was a complete breakdown in relations between the *makhzan* and the population of Fez (who were inclined to take the side of the besiegers). With the traditional structures of governance not functioning, the heads of the quarters of Fez met to select a temporary leader, Maylay Idris al-Zarawti, as the *shaykh al-rabia* until the crisis was resolved. See Burke, *Prelude,* 161–162.

49. On the role of 'ar sacrifice, see Edouard Westermarck, *Ritual and Belief in Morocco,* 2 vols. (London: Macmillan, 1926).

50. For the legislation, see the *Bulletin Officiel du Protectorat* (1912).

51. The *majlis al-baladi* is discussed by Jean Vattier, "La municipalité de Fez," *RC* 12 (1924): 383.

52. For a discussion of the election results, see the correspondence of Fez consul James MacLeod. MacLeod to Kennard, Fez, September 12, 1912, FO 174, No. 272, No. 101.

53. Vattier, "La municipalité de Fez."

54. Daniel Rivet, *Lyautey et l'institution du protectorat français au Maroc, 1912–1925* (Paris: L'Harmattan, 1988), 2:157–159.

55. MacLeod to Grey, Fez, March 17, 1914, FO 413, No. 60.

56. Michaux-Bellaire to Colonel [Huot], Tangier, November 20, 1922, MAE, Maroc, Protectorat, Direction des affaires indigènes, vol. 228.

57. Michaux-Bellaire to Colonel [Huot], Tangier, November 12, 1922, MAE, Maroc, Protectorat, Direction des affaires indigènes, vol. 228.

58. Michaux-Bellaire to Colonel [Huot], Tangier, November 20, 1922, MAE, Maroc, Protectorat, Direction des affaires indigènes, vol. 228.

59. See Bourdieu, "Le champs scientifique," *Actes de recherche en sciences sociales* 2:2 (1976): 88–104; and Bourdieu, *Le sens pratique* (Paris: Minuit, 1980).

NINE • THE INVENTION OF MOROCCAN ISLAM

1. There was one major exception to the ethnographic inventory: the *tashilhyt*-speaking Berbers of the Middle Atlas, who as late as 1912 remained mostly unknown. See chapter 8.

2. Julia Clancy-Smith, "In the Eye of the Beholder: Sufi and Saint in North Africa and the Colonial Production of Knowledge, 1830–1900," *Africana Journal* 15 (1990): 220–257.

3. Jean Servier, *Le péril d'avenir: Le nationalisme musulman en Egypt, en Tunisie, en Algérie* (Constantine: E. Boet, 1913).

4. Jean-Louis Triaud, *La légende noire de la Sanusiyya: Une confrérie musulmane saharienne sous le regard français (1840–1930)* (Paris: Éditions de la Maison des sciences de l'homme, 1995).

5. Edmond Doutté, "Une mission d'études au Maroc," *RC*, 1901, 175.

6. Jamil M. Abun-Nasr, *The Tijaniyya: A Sufi Order in the Modern World* (Oxford: Oxford University Press, 1965), 58–82, for French attempts to ally with the Tijaniya in Algeria.

7. Abun-Nasr, *Tijaniyya*, 93–98. Also Jamil M. Abun-Nasr, "The Salafiyya Movement in Morocco: The Religious Basis of the Moroccan Nationalist Movement," *Middle Eastern Affairs*, no. 3, *St. Antony's Papers*, no. 16 (1963): 90–105.

8. David Robinson, *Paths of Accommodation: Muslim Societies and French Colonial Authorities in Senegal and Mauritania, 1880–1920*. Oxford: James Currey, 2001.

9. Abun-Nasr, "Salafiyya Movement," 96–99.

10. For example, see the lists of Sufi brotherhoods in the *Villes et Tribus du Maroc* series.

11. Georges Spillmann, *Esquisse d'histoire religieuse du Maroc: Confréries et zaouïas* (Paris: J. Peyronnet, 1951).

12. Charles-André Julien, *Le Maroc face aux imperialismes* (Paris: Éditions Jeune Afrique, 1978), chap. 8.

13. Edmond Doutté, *L'Islam algérien en l'an 1900*; Doutté, *Notes sur l'Islâm maghribin, les marabouts* (Paris: E. Leroux, 1900); and Doutté, *Magie et religion dans l'Afrique du Nord* (Paris: P. Geuthner, 1908).

14. Eugène Aubin, *Le Maroc d'aujourd'hui*, 8th ed. (1904; Paris: A. Colin, 1913), 332–334.

15. Georges Salmon, "Les chorfa idrissides de Fez d'après Ibn At-Tayyib al-Qadiry," *AM* 1:3 (1904): 425–459.

16. Doutté, "Une mission d'études au Maroc," 173.

17. Edouard Westermarck, *Ritual and Belief in Morocco* (London: Macmillan, 1926), 35–261; first published in Swedish as *The Moorish Concept of Holiness (Baraka)*, Ofversigt af Finska Vetenscaps—Societetens Forhandlingar 58 (1915–1916), sec. B, no. 1 (Helsinki, 1916).

18. Aubin, *Le Maroc d'aujourd'hui*; see also Henri Gaillard, *Une ville d'Islam: Fez; Esquisse historique et sociale* (Paris: J. André, 1905).

19. Nikki R. Keddie, ed. *Scholars, Saints, and Sufis: Muslim Religious Institutions since 1500* (Berkeley: University of California Press, 1972) marked the start of a trend.

20. Judith Schlanger, *Les métaphores de l'organisme* (Paris: Librairie Philosophique J. Vrin, 1971).

21. Édouard Michaux-Bellaire, "L'organisme marocaine," *Revue du monde musulman* 8 (1909): 1–43.

22. Alfred Bel, *La religion musulmane en Berbérie: Esquisse d'histoire et de sociologie religieuses* (Paris: P. Guethner, 1938).

23. Walter Harris, *The Morocco That Was* (London: Blackwood & Sons, 1921).

24. Nil Joseph Robin, *L'insurrection de la Grande Kabylie en 1871* (Paris: H. Charles-Lavauzelle, 1901); and Louis Rinn, *Histoire de l'insurrection de 1871 en Algérie* (Algiers: A. Jourdan, 1891).

25. At this precise instant, largely unnoticed by French experts, reformist Islam was already transforming the cultural and political context. See Ali Merad, *Le réformisme musulman en Algérie de 1925 à 1940* (Paris: Mouton, 1967). Also James McDougall, *History and the Culture of Nationalism in Algeria* (Cambridge: Cambridge University Press, 2006).

26. Edmond Doutté, "Les causes de la chute d'un sultan: Coup d'œil sur le Maroc et L'Islam marocain," *RC* 7–12 (1909): 129–136, 163–168, 185–189, 220–225, 246–250, 262–267.

27. Jacques Cagne, *Nation et nationalisme au Maroc: Aux racines de la nation marocaine* (Rabat: L'Institut Universitaire de la Recherche Scientifique, 1988). Also Abdullah Laroui, *Les origines du du nationalisme marocain, 1830–1912* (Paris: Maspéro, 1977).

28. Edmund Burke III, *Prelude to Protectorate in Morocco: Precolonial Protest and Resistance, 1860–1912* (Chicago: University of Chicago Press, 1976), 161, 205.

29. See Edmund Burke III, "Pan-Islam and Moroccan Resistance to French Colonial Penetration: 1900–1912," *Journal of African History* 13:1 (1972): 97–118.

30. There is an abundant literature on this subject. See Jean-Marie Mayeur, *La séparation de l'église et de l'état* (Paris: Le Seuil, 1998). Also see Jean Baubérot, *Laïcité 1905–2005: Entre passion et raison* (Paris: Le Seuil, 2004).

31. On the anti-Semitic crisis in Algeria, see Charles-Robert Ageron, *Les algériens musulmans et la France, 1871–1919* (Paris: P.U.F., 1968), 1:chaps. 21–22. See also Geneviève Dermenjian, *La crise anti-juive oranaise, 1895-1905: L'antisémitisme dans l'Algérie* (Paris: Harmattan, 1986); Joshua Schreier, *"Arabs of the Jewish Faith": The Civilizing Mission in Colonial Algeria* (New Brunswick, NJ: Rutgers University Press, 2010).

32. James Frazer, *The Golden Bough: A Study in Magic and Religion* (New York: Macmillan, 1947).

33. On him see Daniel Schroeter in the online *Encyclopedia of Jews in the Islamic World*. See also Daniel Schroeter and Joseph Chetrit, "Emancipation and Its Discontents: Jews in the Formative Period of Colonial Rule in Morocco," *Jewish Social Studies* (Fall 2006): 170–206.

TEN · FROM THE ETHNOGRAPHIC STATE
TO MOROCCAN ISLAM

1. Driss Alaoui Mdaghri, ed., *Une ambition marocaine: Des experts analysent la décennie 1999–2009* (Monaco: Koutoubia Editions Alphée, 2009).

2. Ernest Gellner, *Saints of the Atlas* (Chicago: University of Chicago Press, 1969).

3. Ernest Gellner, *Words and Things* (Boston: Beacon Press, 1960) is a polemical tour de force. For an overview of Gellner's life, see John A. Hall, *Ernest Gellner: An Intellectual Biography* (New York: Verso, 2012).

4. Ernest Gellner, *Muslim Society* (Cambridge: Cambridge University Press, 1983).

5. Ernest Gellner, "How to Live in Anarchy," in *Contemporary Thought and Politics* (London: Routledge, 1974), 87–94.

6. Clifford Geertz, *Islam Observed: Religious Development in Morocco and Indonesia* (New Haven, CT: Yale University Press, 1968).

7. Clifford Geertz, *After the Fact: Two Countries, Four Decades, One Anthropologist* (Cambridge, MA: Harvard University Press, 1995).

8. Clifford Geertz, *Religions of Java* (Glencoe, IL: Free Press, 1960). Geertz's other Indonesian work includes *Agricultural Involution: The Processes of Ecological Change in Indonesia* (Berkeley: University of California, 1963), *Pedlars and Princes* (Chicago: University of Chicago Press, 1963), and *The Social History of an Indonesian Village* (Cambridge, MA: M.I.T. Press, 1965).

9. Fred Inglis, *Clifford Geertz: Culture, Custom and Ethics* (New York: Polity Press, 2000).

10. Alfred Bel, *La religion musulmane en Berbérie; Esquisse d'histoire et de sociologie religieuses* (Paris: P. Guethner, 1938).

11. John Waterbury, *Commander of the Faithful: The Moroccan Political Elite—a Study of Segmented Politics* (London: Wiedenfeld & Nicolson, 1970).

12. David Montgomery Hart (1927–2001) was an American anthropologist who lived for many years in Morocco. A strong believer in the efficacy of British segmentary lineage theory for the study of Moroccan tribes, he had an encyclopedic knowledge of the anthropological literature on Morocco in English, French, and Spanish. Hart's major works include *The Aith Waryaghar of the Moroccan Rif: An Ethnography and History*, 2 vols. (Tucson: University of Arizona Press, 1976); *Dada 'Atta and His Forty Grandsons: The Socio-Political Organization of the Ait 'Atta of Southern Morocco* (Cambridge: MENAS Press, 1981); and *The Ait 'Atta of Southern Morocco: Daily Life & Recent History* (Cambridge: MENAS Press, 1984). A collection of Hart's essays, *Tribe and Society in Rural Morocco* (London: Frank Cass, 2000), gives a sense of his enthusiasm for Morocco, which proved contagious for the generation of American graduate students in Morocco in the 1960s and 1970s, among them Waterbury and myself.

13. Robert Rezette, *La partis politiques marocains* (Paris: Armand Colin, 1956); Douglas Ashford, *Political Change in Morocco* (Princeton, NJ: Princeton University Pres, 1961); and I. William Zartman, *Morocco: Problems of New Power* (New York: Atherton Press, 1964).

14. See, for example, Nathan Leites, *Du malaise politique en France* (Paris: Librairie Plon, 1958); Eng. trans., *On the Game of Politics in France* (Stanford, CA, Stanford University Press, 1959); and Philip M. Williams, *Politics in Post-war France: Parties and the Constitution in the Fourth Republic* (London: Longmans, 1955).

15. John Waterbury, *Le commandeur des croyants: La monarchie marocaine et son élite* (Paris: Presses universitaires de France, 1975).

16. Dale Eickelman, *Moroccan Islam: Tradition and Society in a Pilgrimmage Center* (Austin: University of Texas Press, 1976).

17. See Edmund Burke III and David Prochaska, "Orientalism: From Postcolonial Theory to World History," in *Genealogies of Orientalism: History, Theory, Politics,* ed. Edmund Burke III and David Prochaska (Lincoln: University of Nebraska Press, 2008), 2–73.

18. Eickelman, *Moroccan Islam,* 21–25.

19. Chris Bayly, *Empire and Information: Intelligence Gathering and Social Communication in Colonial India, 1780–1870* (Cambridge: Cambridge University Press, 1996).

20. Stuart H. Schaar, "Conflict and Change in Nineteenth-Century Morocco" (PhD diss., Princeton University, 1966).

21. Bernard S. Cohn, *Colonialism and Its Forms of Knowledge: The British in India* (Princeton, NJ: Princeton University Press, 1996), chap. 2.

22. Edward Said, *Orientalism* (New York: Pantheon, 1976).

23. Eric Stokes, *The Peasant Armed: The Indian Revolt of 1857* (Oxford: Oxford University Press, 1986).

24. Edmund Burke III, "Theorizing the Histories of Colonialism and Nationalism in the Arab Maghrib," *Arab Studies Quarterly* 20:2 (Spring 1998): 5–19.

25. Ranajit Guha, "The Prose of Counter-Insurgency," in *Selected Subaltern Studies,* ed. Ranajit Guha and Gayatri Chakravarty Spivak (Oxford: Oxford University Press, 1988), 45–86.

26. Douglas Porch, *The Conquest of Morocco* (New York: Alfred A. Knopf, 1983), 187.

27. Ibid.

28. William A. Hoisington Jr., *Lyautey and the Conquest of Morocco* (New York: St. Martin's Press, 1995), 205.

29. Martin Thomas, *Empires of Intelligence: Security Services and Colonial Disorder after 1914* (Berkeley: University of California Press, 2008).

30. Clifford D. Rosenberg, *Policing Paris: The Origins of Modern Immigration Control between the Wars* (Ithaca, NY: Cornell University Press, 2006).

31. Edmund Burke III, "Towards a Comparative History of the Modern Mediterranean, 1750–1919," *Journal of World History* 23:4 (December 2012).

32. Paul Rabinow, *French Modern: Norms and Forms of the Social Environment* (Cambridge, MA: M.I.T. Press, 1989).

33. Jocelyne Dakhlia, "Pouvoir du parasol et pouvoir nu: Un dépouillement islamique? Le cas de la royauté marocaine," *Bulletin du Centre de recherche du château de Versailles* 2 (2005), http://crcv.revues.org/233.

34. Dakhlia, "Pouvoir du parasol," 42, citing a 1920 poster "Le sultan du Maroc se rendant à la mosquée de Fez," by Maurice Romberg.

35. Dakhlia, "Pouvoir du parasol," 43.

A NOTE ON SOURCES

À LA RECHERCHE DU MAROC PERDU...

As one might expect from a book that is largely about the intertextual world of French ethnography and colonial policy, it all began with a library, in this case the Bibliothèque générale de Rabat. Newly arrived in Morocco in the summer of 1966, and possessed of the toolkit of a historian of modern Europe and the Arab world of my generation, I was pursuing a woolly-minded project of studying the early years of the French protectorate (1912–25). I was adept at political and institutional history and newly fascinated by social history (Lawrence Stone arrived at Princeton just as I headed off to the field), but innocent of anthropology (the Geertzes had yet to appear on the scene). Since most of my friends were studying nationalism, my project was in itself a bit out of sync with the times. By 1966 Morocco had been independent for a scant decade. Neither the Moroccan archives nor the French colonial archives were available to researchers. So I sat in the reading room of the Bibliothèque générale (that passed for the Moroccan national library at the time) and requested books in French on Moroccan colonial history (the ones in Arabic had, for the most part, yet to be written). Because the staff had learned their craft under the French, and because it was Morocco, the books appeared at a glacial pace. Indeed the Bibliothèque générale was the perfect union of French bureaucracy and Moroccan efficiency!

While I waited (I did a lot of that), I started to read the *usuels,* the crusty leather-bound books that lined the walls. I began with a set of volumes entitled *Archives marocaines,* since I was unable to have access to the real thing. I started with volume 1, number 1. By the time I was done many months later, I had read the all thirty-three volumes. As I did so, a world gradually opened before me. My dissertation topic was discarded along the way, and a new one begun. Reading *Archives marocaines* transformed my intellectual horizons and had an important influence on my early career. This book is in some ways the story of one man's continuing relationship with a historical source.

Because the research for this book was done over a long period of time, certain things have changed. The citations refer to the old system of classification in effect at the Service historique de l'armée de terre (Château de Vincennes) and the archives of the Ministère des affaires étrangères, Quai d'Orsay, in the 1970s and early 1980s. At times the documents cited no longer exist, as I have had occasion to verify, since they fell victim to periodic reduction policies under different administrations. In 1977 I was able to consult for one week the private papers of Alfred Le Chatelier, then in the possession of his nephew, Henri Le Chatelier, in Grenoble. Subsequently he self-published a compilation of some of the elements of this archive (on which, see below). I am enormously grateful to M. Le Chatelier for this privilege, but also chagrined as the Le Chatelier Papers appear subsequently to have gone missing. My citations of this archive reflect the nonprofessional classification system of these papers at the time I viewed them.

BIBLIOGRAPHY

ARCHIVAL SOURCES

Private Papers

Centre des hautes études sur l'Afrique et l'Asie moderne, Paris. [CHEAM]
    MS no. 1336. Capt. Feaugéas, "L'enseignement dans le Moyen Atlas" (May 19, 1948).
Institut de France, Paris.
    Bibliothèque de l'Institut de France, Paris. [BIF]
        Auguste Terrier MSS.
Ministère des affaires étrangères, Paris. [MAE]
    Papiers d'Agents. Revoil MSS.

Official Papers

France
Archives de la Légation de France à Tanger. [Nantes]
    MAE, Protectorat, Missions scientifique, Direction des affaires indigènes.
    Série A.
    MAE, Protectorat marocain, Direction des affaires indigènes. Vol. 228.
Archives nationales, Paris
    Archives nationales, Série F/17.
Archives d'Outre-Mer, Aix-en-Provence. [CAOM]
    Archives de l'Ancien Gouvernement Général de l'Algérie. Série 4H A.
        Affaires musulmanes et sahariennes.
Ministère de la guerre. Service historique de l'Armee. [SHAT]
    Série A²6, Serie C, Série E-2.
Ministère des affaires étrangères, Paris [MAE]
    Documents diplomatiques français, Affaires du Maroc (1901–12). 6 vols. Paris, 1905–12.

MAE, Maroc, Écoles et missions scientifiques, 1902–15, N.S. 405.
MAE, Maroc, Organisation administrative du protectorat. Vol. 289.
Maroc. Direction de l'instruction publique. Liasse 51.

Great Britain
Political Correspondence. Foreign Office, London. [FO]
    FO 174. Consular Correspondence. August 1912–December 1913.
    FO 413. Confidential Print Series. Affaires of Morocco, 1914–1915.

Memoirs and Correspondence

Lyautey, Louis Hubert Gonzalve. *Choix de lettres 1882–1919*. Paris: A. Colin, 1947.
———. "Lettres de Rabat (1907)." *Revue des deux mondes,* 1921, 273–304.
———. *Lettres de Tonkin et de Madagascar (1894–1899)*. Paris: A. Colin, 1921.
———. *Lettres du sud de Madagascar, 1900–1902*. Paris: A. Colin, 1935.
———. *Paroles d'action Madagascar, Sud-Oranais, Oran, Maroc (1900–1926)*. Paris: A. Colin, 1927.
———. *Vers le Maroc, lettres du Sud-Oranais, 1903–1906*. Paris: A. Colin, 1937.
Lyautey, Pierre, ed. *Lyautey l'Africain*. 4 vols. Paris: Plon, 1953.
Saint-Aulaire, Auguste de Beaupoil, comte de. *Confessions d'un vieux diplomate.* Paris: Flammarion, 1953.

SECONDARY SOURCES

Abdel-Malek, Anouar. "The End of Orientalism." *Diogenes* 44:44 (1963): 103–140.
Abrard, René. "Biographie de Paul Lemoine: Leçon inaugurale du Cours de géologie du Professeur René Abrard, Successeur de Paul Lemoine au muséum d'histoire naturelle." In *Paul Lemoine (1878–1940)*. www.annales.org/archives/x/lemoine4.html.
Abu-Lughod, Janet. *Rabat, Urban Apartheid in Morocco*. Princeton, NJ: Princeton University Press, 1981.
Abun-Nasr, Jamil M. "The Salafiyya Movement in Morocco: The Religious Basis of the Moroccan Nationalist Movement." *Middle Eastern Affairs,* no. 3, *St. Antony's Papers,* no. 16 (1963): 90–105.
———. *The Tijaniyya: A Sufi Order in the Modern World*. Oxford: Oxford University Press, 1965.
Adam, André. *Bibliographie critique de sociologie, d'ethnologie et de géographie humaine du Maroc*. Algiers: SNED, 1972.
———. *Casablanca: Essai sur la transformation de la société marocaine au contact de l'Occident*. 2nd ed. Paris: Éditions du Centre national de la recherche scientifique, 1972.
———. "Sur l'action du *Galilée* à Casablanca en août 1907." *Revue de l'Occident musulman et de la Méditerranée* 6:6 (1969): 9–22.

Adams, Julia, Elisabeth S. Clemens, and Ann Shola Orloff, eds. *Remaking Modernity: Politics, History and Sociology.* Durham, NC: Duke University Press, 2005.

Ageron, Charles-Robert. "La France a-t-elle eu une politique kabyle?" *Revue historique* 223 (1960): 311–352.

———. "La politique berbère du protectorat marocain." *Revue d'histoire moderne et contemporaine,* 1971, 50–90.

———. *Les algériens musulmans et la France, 1871–1919.* Paris: P.U.F., 1968.

Ahmida, Ali A., ed. *Beyond Colonialism and Nationalism in North Africa: History, Culture, and Politics.* London: St. Martin's Press, 2001.

Albergoni, Gianni, and François Pouillon. "Le fait berbère et sa lecture coloniale: L'extrême sud tunisien." In *Le mal de voir: Ethnologie et orientalisme; Politique et épistemologie, critique et autocritique,* edited by Henri Moniot, 349–396. Collection 10/18, Cahier Jussieu/2. Paris: Union Générale des Éditions, 1976.

Alis, Harry [Jules Hyppolite Percher]. *À la conquête du Tchad.* Paris: Librairie Hachette, 1891.

———. *Hara-Kiri.* Paris: Esprit des péninsules, 2000.

———. *Les pas de chance.* Brussels: Kistemaeckers, 1883.

———. *Promenade en Égypte.* Paris: Librarie Hachette, 1895.

al-Kattani, Muhammad Baqir. "Tarjamah al-Shaykh Muhammad al-Kattani al-Shahid." Unpublished manuscript, 1962.

al-Nasiri, Ahmad ibn Khalid. "Kitab al-Istiqsa li Akhbar Duwwal al-maghrib al-Aqsa." Translated by E. Fumey. *Archives marocaines* 10 (1907).

Anderson, Benedict. *Imagined Communities: Reflections on the Origin and Spread of Nationalism.* London: Verso, 1983.

Andrew, Christopher. *Théophile Delcassé and the Making of the Entente Cordiale: A Reappraisal of French Foreign Policy, 1898–1905.* London: St. Martins, 1968.

Andrew, Christopher, and A. S. Kanya-Forstner. "The French 'Colonial Party': Its Composition, Aims and Influences, 1885–1914." *Historical Journal* 14:1 (1971): 99–128.

Arora, K. C. *The Steel Frame: Indian Civil Service since 1860.* New Delhi: Sanchar, 1996.

Ashford, Douglas. *Political Change in Morocco.* Princeton, NJ: Princeton University Press, 1961.

Aubin, Eugène [Léon Eugène Aubin Coullard Descos]. *En Haiti: Planteurs d'autrefois; nègres d'aujourd'hui.* Paris: A. Colin, 1910.

———. "Fez le dernier centre de la civilisation maure." *Revue de Paris,* February 15, 1904, 851–872; March 1, 1904, 173–196; March 15, 1904, 424–448.

———. *La Perse d'aujourd'hui: Iran, Mesopotamie.* Paris: A. Colin, 1908.

———. *Le Maroc dans la tourmente, 1902–1903.* Preface by Jean-François Durand. Reprint. Casablanca: La croisée des chemins, 2009.

———. *Le Maroc d'aujourd'hui.* Paris: A. Colin, 1904.

———. *Les Anglais aux Indes et en Égypte.* Paris: A. Colin, 1899.

Aucapitaine, Henri. *Le pays et la société kabyle (Expédition de 1857).* Paris: A. Bertrand, 1857.

Ayache, Germain. *La guerre du Rif.* Paris: Harmattan, 1996.

Baratin, Marc, and Christian Jacob. *Le pouvoir des bibliothèques: La mémoire des livres en Occident.* Paris: Albin Michel, 1996.

Barthou, Louis. *Lyautey et le Maroc.* Paris: Éditions de Petit Parisien, 1931.

Baubérot, Jean. *Laïcité, 1905–2005: Entre passion et raison.* Paris: Le Seuil, 2004.

Bayly, C. A. *Empire and Information: Intelligence Gathering and Social Communication in Colonial India, 1780–1870.* Cambridge: Cambridge University Press, 1996.

———. "Knowing the Country." *Modern Asian Studies* 27:1 (1993): 3–43.

Bel, Alfred. *La religion musulmane en Berbérie: Esquisse d'histoire et de sociologie religieuses.* Paris: P. Guethner, 1938.

Benabdullah, Abdelaziz. *Les grands courants de la civilisation du Maghreb.* Tangier, 1957.

Bender, Donald Ray. "Early French Ethnography in Africa and the Development of Ethnology in France." PhD diss., Northwestern University, 1964.

Bernard, Augustin. *Les confins algéro-marocains.* Paris: E. Larose, 1911.

———. "Pour servir à l'étude du Nord-Ouest Africain." *Bulletin de la Société de géographie et d'archéologie de la province d'Oran* 17 (1897): 243–252.

———. "Une mission au Maroc: Rapport à M. le Gouverneur General de l'Algérie." *Renseignements coloniaux* 10 (1904).

Bernard, Augustin, and Nicolas Lacroix. *La pénétration saharienne.* Algiers: Imprimerie Algérienne, 1906.

———. *L'évolution de nomadisme en Algérie.* Paris: A. Challamel, 1906.

Berque, Jacques. *Al-Yousi: Problèmes de la culture marocaine au XVIIeme siècle.* The Hague: Mouton, 1958.

———. *Arabies.* Paris: Stock, 1980.

———. "Cent-vingt-cinq ans de sociologie maghrebine." *Annales, Economies, Sociétés, Civilisations* 11:3 (1956): 296–324.

———. *Le Maghreb entre les deux guerres.* Paris: Seuil, 1962.

———. *Mémoires des deux rives.* Paris: Seuil, 1989.

———. *Structures sociales du Haut-Atlas.* Paris: Presses Universitaires de France, 1955.

Berriau, Henri Marie Martin. "L'officier de renseignements au Maroc." *Renseignements coloniaux,* 1918.

Bidwell, Robin. *Morocco under Colonial Rule: French Administration of Tribal Areas, 1912–1956.* London: Frank Cass, 1973.

Bierman, Irene, ed. *Napoleon in Egypt.* Reading, UK: Ithaca Press, 2003.

Binger, Louis Gustave. *Le péril de l'Islam.* Paris: Comité de l'Afrique française, 1906.

Blachère, Régis. "Arabe litéral (1795)." In *Cent-Cinquantenaire de l'École nationale des langues orientales vivantes,* 47–55. Paris: Imprimerie nationale, 1948.

Bonnerot, Jules. *La Sorbonne.* Paris: P.U.F., 1935.

Boulifa, Ammar ben Saïd. *Textes berbères en dialecte de l'Atlas marocain.* Paris: A. Leroux, 1909.

Bourdieu, Pierre. Contributions to *Le mal de voir: Ethnologie et orientalisme; Politique et épistemologie, critique et autocritique,* edited by Henri Moniot. Paris: Union Générale d'Éditions, 1976.

————. *Esquisse d'une théorie de la pratique.* Paris: Droz, 1972.

————. "Le champ scientifique." *Actes de la recherche en sciences sociales* 2:2 (1976): 88–104.

————. *Le sens pratique.* Paris: Minuit, 1980.

————. *Outline of a Theory of Practice.* Translated by Richard Nice. Cambridge: Cambridge University Press, 1977.

————. "Quelques propriétés des champs." In *Questions de sociologie,* edited by Pierre Bourdieu, 113–120. Paris: Minuit, 1984.

————. *Sociology in Question.* Translated by Richard Nice. Thousand Oaks, CA: Sage Publications, 1993.

Bourguet, Marie-Noelle, Daniel Nordman, Vassilis Panayotopoulos, and Maroula Sinarellis, eds. *L'invention scientifique de la Mediterranée: Egypte, Morée, Algérie.* Paris: Écoles des hautes études en sciences sociales, 1998.

Bourquia, Rahma, and Susan Gilson Miller. *In the Shadow of the Sultan: Culture, Power and Politics in Morocco.* Cambridge, MA: Harvard University Press, 1999.

Boyer, Paul. "L'École nationale des langues orientales vivantes." In *La vie universitaire à Paris,* edited by Paul Boyer et al., 194–205. Paris: A. Colin, 1918.

Bramson, Leon. *The Political Context of Sociology.* Princeton, NJ: Princeton University Press, 1961.

Braudel, Fernand. "Personal Testimony." *Journal of Modern History* 44:4 (1972): 448–467.

Brignon, Jean, et al. *Histoire du Maroc.* Paris: Hatier, 1967.

Brives, Abel. *Voyages au Maroc (1901–1907).* Algiers: A. Jourdan, 1909.

Broc, Numa. "Les grandes missions scientifiques francaises au XIXe siècle (Morée, Algérie, Mexique) et leurs travaux géographiques." *Revue d'histoire des sciences* 34:3–4 (1981): 319–358.

Brower, Benjamin Claude. *A Desert Called Peace: The Violence of France's Empire in the Algerian Sahara, 1844–1902.* New York: Columbia University Press, 2009.

Brunschwig, Henri. *French Imperialism, 1870–1914: Myth and Realities.* New York: Praeger, 1966.

Burke, Edmund, III. "A Comparative View of French Native Policies in Morocco and Syria, 1912–1925." *Middle Eastern Studies* 9:2 (1973): 175–186.

————. "Extreme Ethnography: French Exploration and the Conquest of North Africa." 2009 Carson Lecture, Oregon State University, February 9, 2009.

————. "The First Crisis of Orientalism, 1890–1914." In *Connaissances du Maghreb: Sciences sociales et colonisation,* edited by Jean-Claude Vatin, 213–226. Paris: Éditions du C.N.R.S., 1984.

————. "France and the Classical Sociology of Islam, 1798–1962." *Journal of North African Studies* 18:1 (2007): 1–7.

————. "The Image of the Moroccan State in French Ethnological Literature: A New Look at the Origin of Lyautey's Berber Policy." In *Arabs and Berbers,* edited by Ernest Gellner and Charles Micaud, 175–199. London: Duckworth, 1972.

————. "The Institutionalization of the Social Sciences: Its Social and Political Significance." *International Social Science Journal* 102 (1984): 643–655.

————. "Islamic History as World History: Marshall Hodgson and *The Venture of Islam.*" *International Journal of Middle East Studies* 10:2 (1979): 241–264.

————. "La Hafidiya (Août 1907—Janvier 1908): Enjeux sociaux et luttes populaires." *Hespéris/Tamuda* 31 (1993): 101–115.

————. "Mouvements sociaux et mouvements de resistance au Maroc: La Grande Siba de la Chaouia, 1902–1906." *Hespéris-Tamuda* 17 (1976–77): 149–163.

————. "Orientalism Observed: France and the Sociology of Islam, 1798–1962." Unpublished manuscript.

————. "Pan-Islam and Moroccan Resistance to French Colonial Penetration: 1900–1912." *Journal of African History* 13:1 (1972): 97–118.

————. "The Political Role of the Moroccan Ulama, 1860–1912." In *Saints, Scholars, and Sufis: Muslim Religious Institutions since 1500*, edited by N. R. Keddie, 93–126. Berkeley: University of California Press, 1972.

————. *Prelude to Protectorate in Morocco: Precolonial Protest and Resistance, 1860–1912.* Chicago: University of Chicago Press, 1976.

————. "The Terror and Religion: Brittany and Algeria." In *Colonialism and the Modern World,* edited by Gregory Blue, Martin Bunton, and Ralph Croizier, 40–50. White Plains, NY: M. E. Sharpe, 2002.

————. "Theorizing the Histories of Colonialism and Nationalism in the Arab Maghrib." *Arab Studies Quarterly* 20:2 (Spring 1998): 5–19.

————. "Towards a Comparative History of the Modern Mediterranean, 1750–1919." *Journal of World History* 23:4 (December 2012).

————. "Tribalism and Moroccan Resistance, 1890–1914: The Role of the Aith Ndhir." In *Tribe and State in Northwest Africa,* edited by George Joffe and Richard Pennell, 119–144. London: M.E.N.A.S., 1991.

Burke, Edmund, III, and David Prochaska, "Orientalism: From Postcolonial Theory to World History." In *Genealogies of Orientalism: History, Theory, Politics,* edited by Edmund Burke III and David Prochaska, 2–73. Lincoln: University of Nebraska Press, 2008.

————. "Rethinking the Historical Genealogy of *Orientalism.*" *History and Anthropology* 18:2 (2007): 135–151.

Cagne, Jacques. "Les origins du mouvement jeune marocain." *Bulletin de la Société d'histoire du Maroc* 1 (1968): 8–17.

————. *Nation et nationalisme au Maroc: Aux racines de la nation marocaine.* Rabat: L'Institut Universitaire de la Recherche Scientifique, 1988.

Caix de Saint-Aymour, Robert, marquis de. "Au coeur de l'Atlas." *Bulletin du Comité de l'Afrique française,* 1910, 204.

————. "La France et le Maroc." *Afrique française,* 1903, 298–306.

————. "L'oeuvre française au Maroc." *Renseignements coloniaux,* 1912, 252.

————. "Notre politique au Maroc." *Bulletin du Comité de l'Afrique française,* 1903, 377.

Calhoun, C., E. LiPuma, and M. Postone, eds. *Bourdieu: Critical Perspectives.* Chicago: University of Chicago Press, 1993.

Cambon, Jules. *Le Gouvernement Général de l'Algérie.* Paris: E. Champion, 1918.

Cannadine, David. "The Context, Performance and Meaning of Ritual: 'The British Monarchy and the Invention of Tradition,' c. 1820–1977." In *The Invention of Tradition,* edited by Eric J. Hobsbawm and Terrence Ranger, chap. 4. Cambridge: Cambridge University Press, 1983.

———. *Ornamentalism: How the British Saw Their Empire.* Oxford: Oxford University Press, 2002.

Carette, Ernest. *Exploration scientifique de l'Algérie: Études sur la Kabylie proprement dite.* Vols. 4–5. Paris: Imprimerie nationale, 1848.

Castries, Henry, comte de, et al., eds. *Les sources inédites de l'histoire du Maroc de 1530 à 1845.* Paris: E. Leroux, 1905–.

Cent Cinquantenaire de l'École nationale des langues orientales vivantes. Paris: Imprimerie nationale de France, 1948.

Chailley-Bert, Joseph. *Dix années de politique coloniale.* Paris: A. Colin, 1902.

———. *Java et ses habitants.* Paris: A. Colin, 1900.

———. *L'Inde britannique: Société indigène, politique indigène, les idées directrices.* Paris: A. Colin, 1910.

Chalcraft, John, and Yaseen Noorani, eds. *Counterhegemony in the Colony and the Post Colony.* London: Palgrave Macmillan, 2007.

Chatterjee, Partha. *The Nation and Its Fragments: Colonial and Postcolonial Histories.* Princeton, NJ: Princeton University Press, 1993.

Cigar, Norman, ed. *Muhammad al-Quadiri's Nashr al Mathani: The Chronicles.* Translated by Norman Cigar. London: Oxford University Press, 1981.

Clancy-Smith, Julia. "In the Eye of the Beholder: Sufi and Saint in North Africa and the Colonial Production of Knowledge, 1830–1900." *Africana Journal* 15 (1990): 220–257.

Clark, Terry N. *Prophets and Patrons: The French University and the Emergence of the Social Sciences.* Cambridge, MA: Harvard University Press, 1973.

Clifford, James. *The Predicament of Culture: Twentieth-Century Ethnography, Literature, and Art.* Cambridge, MA: Harvard University Press, 1988.

Cohn, Bernard S. *Colonialism and Its Forms of Knowledge: The British in India.* Princeton, NJ: Princeton University Press, 1996.

———. "Representing Authority in British India," In *The Invention of Tradition,* edited by Eric J. Hobsbawm and Terrence Ranger, chap. 5. Cambridge: Cambridge University Press, 1983.

Cole, Juan. *Napoleon's Egypt: Invading the Middle East.* New York: Palgrave-Macmillan, 2007.

Colin, G. S. "Arabe vulgaire." In *Cent Cinquantenaire de l'École nationale des langues orientales vivantes,* 95–112. Paris: Imprimerie nationale de France, 1948.

Colonna, Fanny. "Educating Conformity in French Colonial Algeria." In *Tensions of Empire,* edited by Frederick Cooper and Ann Laura Stoler, 346–372. Berkeley: University of California Press, 1997.

———. *Instituteurs algériens: 1833–1939.* Paris: Les Presses du Sciences Po, 1975.

———. "Production scientifique et position dans le champ intellectuel et politique: Deux cas; Augustin Berque et Joseph Desparmet." In *Le mal de voir: Ethnologie et orientalisme; Politique et épistemologie, critique et autocritique,* edited by Henri Moniot, 397–415. Paris: Union Générale d'Éditions, 1976.

Colonna, Fanny, and Claude Haim Brahimi. "Du bon usage de la science colonial." In *Le mal de voir: Ethnologie et orientalisme: Politique et épistemologie, critique et autocritique,* edited by Henri Moniot, 397, 221–241. Paris: Union Générale d'Éditions, 1976.

Combs-Schilling, M. Elaine. *Sacred Performances: Islam, Sexuality, and Sacrifice.* New York: Columbia University Press, 1989.

Commission des sciences et des arts d'Égypte. *Description de l'Égypte, ou recueil des observations et des recherches qui ont été faites en Égypte pendant l'expédition de l'armée francaise, publié par les ordres de sa majesté Napoléon le Grand.* 23 vols. Paris: Imprimerie impériale, 1809–28.

Conklin, Alice. *A Mission to Civilize: The Republican Idea of Empire in France and West Africa, 1895–1930.* Stanford, CA: Stanford University Press, 1997.

Cooke, James. *New French Imperialism, 1880–1910: The Third Republic and Colonial Expansion.* Hamden, CT: Archon Books, 1973.

Coon, Carleton. *Caravan: The Story of the Middle East.* New York: Holt, 1958.

Cooper, Frederick. *Colonialism in Question: Theory, Knowledge, History.* Berkeley: University of California Press, 2005.

Cooper, Frederick, and Ann Laura Stoler, eds. *Tensions of Empire: Colonial Cultures in a Bourgeois World.* Berkeley: University of California Press, 1997.

Coquery-Vidovitch, Catherine. "Les idées économiques de Brazza et les premières tentatives des compagnies de colonisation au Congo Français—1885–1898." *Cahiers d'études africaines* 5:17 (1965): 57–82.

Cordier, Henri. *Un coin de Paris: L'École des langues orientales vivantes, 2, rue de Lille.* Paris: E. Leroux, 1913.

Coulanges, Fustel de. *La cité antique.* Paris: Hachette, 1864.

Cruickshank, Earl F. *Morocco at the Parting of the Ways.* Philadelphia: University of Pennsylvania Press, 1935.

Cunninghame Graham, Robert B. *Moghreb el Akca: A Journey in Morocco.* London: Duckworth, 1898.

Daadaoui, Mohammed. *Moroccan Monarchy and the Islamist Challenge: Maintaining Makhzan Power.* New York: Palgrave Macmillan, 2011.

Dakhlia, Jocelyne. "Pouvoir du parasol et pouvoir nu: Un dépouillement islamique? Le cas de la royauté marocaine." *Bulletin du Centre de recherche du château de Versailles* 2 (2005). http://crcv.revues.org/233.

Dalrymple, William. "Lessons from the British Raj." *Le monde diplomatique,* August 7, 2007.

Daughton, James. *An Empire Divided: Religion, Republicanism and the Making of French Colonialism, 1880–1914.* Oxford: Oxford University Press, 2006.

Daumas, Eugène. *Exposé de l'état actuel de la societé arabe, du gouvernement, de la legislation qui la régit.* Algiers: Imprimerie du gouvernement, 1844.

———. *Le Sahara algérien: Études géographiques, statistiques et historiques sur la region au sud des établissements français en Algérie.* Paris: Fortin, 1845.

————. *Moeurs et coutumes de l'Algérie: Tell, Kabylie, Sahara.* Paris: Hachette, 1853.

Davis, John H. R. *People of the Mediterranean: An Essay in Comparative Anthropology.* London: Routledge and Kegan Paul, 1976.

Decornoy, Jacques. *Péril jaune, peur blanche.* Paris: B. Grasset, 1970.

Dehérain, Henri. "Les établissements d'enseignements et de recherche de l'orientalisme à Paris." *Revue internationale de l'enseignement* 5 (July 15, 1939): 125–148 and (October 15, 1939): 222–238.

————. *Orientalistes et antiquaires: Silvestre de Sacy, ses contemporains et ses disciples.* Paris: Geuthner, 1938.

Delphin, Gaetan. *Fas, son université et l'enseignement supérieur musulman.* Paris: E. Leroux, 1889.

Depont, Octave, and Xavier Coppolani. *Les confréries religieuses musulmanes.* Algiers: Jourdan, 1897.

Dermenjian, Geneviève. *La crise anti-juive oranaise, 1895–1905: L'antisémitisme dans l'Algérie coloniale.* Paris: Harmattan, 1986.

Derrien, Lt.-Colonel. "Bibliographie." *Bulletin de la Société de géographie et archéologie de la province d'Oran* 21 (1901): 159–170.

d'Esme, Jean. *Ce Maroc que nous avons fait.* Paris: Hachette, 1955.

Destaing, Edmond. *Étude sur le dialecte berbère des Aït Seghrouchen (moyen atlas marocain).* Paris: E. Leroux, 1920.

Dewey, Clive. *Anglo-Indian Attitudes: The Mind of the Indian Civil Service.* London: Hambledon Press, 2003.

Digéon, Jean. *La crise allemande de la pensée française, 1870–1914.* Paris: P.U.F., 1959.

Direction des affaires indigènes. *Tanger et sa zone.* Vol. 7 of *Documents et renseignements publié sous les auspices de la Résidence Générale.* Paris: Leroux, 1918.

Dirks, Nicholas. *Castes of Mind: Colonialism and the Making of Modern India.* Princeton, NJ: Princeton University Press, 2001.

Dirks, Nicholas, Geoff Eley, and Sherry B. Ortner, eds. *Culture/Power/History: A Reader in Contemporary Social Theory.* Princeton, NJ: Princeton University Press, 1994.

"Discours de M. Etienne." *Bulletin du Comité de l'Afrique française,* 1904, 182.

Dosse, François. *New History in France: The Triumph of the Annales.* Translated by Peter V. Conroy Jr. Urbana: University of Illinois Press, 1987.

Douiri, Moumen. *À qui qppartient le Maroc?* Paris: Harmattan, 1992.

Doumergue, François. "Les *Archives berbères,* Vol. 1." *Bulletin de la Société de géographie et d'archéologie de la province d'Oran* 35 (1915): 222–223.

Doutté, Edmond. "À Rabat, chez Abdelaziz: Notes prises en 1907." *Bulletin de la Société de géographie et d'archéologie de la province d'Oran* 33:1 (1910): 21–68.

————. "Bulletin bibliographique de l'Islam maghrébin." *Bulletin de la Société de géographie et d'archéologie de la province d'Oran* 29 (1899): 37–123.

————. "Coup d'oeil sur le Maroc." *Renseignements coloniaux,* 1909, 135.

————. *Des moyens de développer l'influence française au Maroc: Rapport à M. le Gouverneur-Général de l'Algérie.* Paris: Imprimerie P. Levé, 1900.

————. *En tribu: Missions au Maroc.* Paris: Geuthner, 1914.

———. "La réalisation du protectorat marocain (Note sur la future organisation politique du Maroc)." June 19, 1912. MAE, Maroc. Vol. 289. Organisation administrative du protectorat. Dossier Général I (Janvier–Juin 1912).

———. "Le fanatisme musulman." *Renseignements coloniaux,* 1909, 164.

———. *Les Aissaoua à Tlemcen.* Chalons-sur-Marne: Martin, 1900.

———. "Les causes de la chute d'un sultan: Coup d'œil sur le Maroc et L'Islam marocain." *Renseignements coloniaux* 7–12 (1909): 129–136, 163–168, 185–189, 220–225, 246–250, 262–267.

———. "Les deux politiques." *Bulletin du Comité de l'Afrique française,* 1903, 306–311.

———. *L'Islam algérien en l'an 1900.* Algiers: Giralt, 1900.

———. *Magie et religion dans l'Afrique du Nord.* Paris: P. Geuthner, 1908.

———. *Merrakech.* Paris: Comité du Maroc, 1905.

———. *Notes sur l'Islam maghribin, les marabouts.* Paris: E. Leroux, 1900.

———. "Quatrième voyage d'études au Maroc: Rapport sommaire d'ensemble; L'organisation domestique et sociale chez les H'h'a; Contribution à la sociologie marocaine." *Renseignements coloniaux,* 1905, 1–16.

———. "Troisième voyage d'études au Maroc: Rapport sommaire d'ensemble." *Renseignements coloniaux,* 1902, 157–164.

———. "Une mission d'études au Maroc: Rapport sommaire ensemble." *Renseignements coloniaux,* 1901, 161–178.

Doutté, Edmond, and J. Gautier. *Enquête sur la dispersion de la langue berbère en Algérie, faite par l'ordre de M. le Gouverneur Général.* Algiers: A. Jourdan, 1913.

Durkheim, Émile. *The Division of Labor in Society.* New York: Free Press, 1984.

———. *Les formes élémentaire de la vie religieuse: Le système totémique en Australie.* Paris: F. Alcan, 1912.

du Taillis, Jean. *Le Maroc pittoresque.* Paris: E. Flammarion, 1905.

Duval, Jules, and Auguste Warnier. *Bureaux arabes et colons.* Paris: Challamel, 1869.

Duveyrier, Henri. *La confrérie musulmane de Sidi Mohammed ben Au es Senoussi.* Paris, 1884.

———. *Les Touaregs du nord: Exploration du Sahara.* Paris: Challamel, 1864.

Dyé, Alfred-Henri. "Les ports du Maroc: Leur commerce avec la France." *Bulletin de la Société de géographie commerciale,* 1908, 3–82.

———. *Les ports du Maroc: Leur commerce avec la France.* Paris: Imprimerie P. Brodard, 1909.

Eberhardt, Isabelle. *Œuvres complètes.* Paris: Grasset, 1988.

Eickelman, Dale. *Moroccan Islam: Tradition and Society in a Pilgrimage Center.* Austin: University of Texas Press, 1976.

El Adnani, Jilali. *Les origines d'une confrérie religieuse au Maghreb: La Tijaniyya, 1781–1881.* Rabat: Marsam, 2007.

El Gammal, Jean. "Lyautey et les droites: Reflexions sur un portrait politique." In *Regards sur Lyautey,* 97–118.

———, ed. *Regards sur Lyautey: Actes du colloque de Nancy, 17–18 septembre 2004.* Annales de l'Est, 6th ser., 54, no. spéc. Nancy: Association d'historiens de l'est, 2004.

Elliot, H.M. *Memoirs on the History, Folklore, and Distribution of the Races of the North-Western Provinces of India.* Revised by John Beames. London: Trubner, 1869.

Emerit, Marcel. *Les Saint-Simoniens en Algérie.* Algiers: Les Belles Lettres, 1941.

Erckmann, Jules. *Le Maroc moderne.* Paris: Challamel, 1885.

Étienne, Eugène. "L'Institut marocain." *Renseignements coloniaux,* 1904, 194–195.

———. "Notre Comité du Maroc." *Bulletin du Comité de l'Afrique française,* 1904, 3–4.

Febvre, Lucien. *Le problème de l'incroyance au XVIe siècle, la religion de Rabelais.* Paris: A. Michel, 1942.

Feis, Herbert. *Europe, the World's Banker, 1870–1915.* New York: W.W. Norton, 1965.

Ferry, Edmond. "La réorganisation marocaine." *Renseignements coloniaux,* 1905, 517–528.

Flaubert, Gustave. *Voyage en Égypte.* Paris: Grasset, 1991.

Flotte de Roquevaire, René de. *Cinq mois de triangulation au Maroc.* Algiers: A. Jourdan, 1909.

Forbes, Rosita. *El Raisuni, the Sultan of the Mountains.* London: Thornton Butterworth, 1924.

Foucauld, Charles de. *Reconnaissance au Maroc, 1883–1884: Journal de route.* Paris: Challamel, 1888. 2nd ed. Paris: Société d'éditions géographiques, 1939.

Foucault, Michel. *The Archeology of Knowledge and the Discourse on Language.* New York: Harper & Row, 1972.

———. *The Order of Things: An Archeology of the Human Sciences.* New York: Pantheon Books, 1970.

Fourier, Joseph. *Description de l'Égypte, ou recueil des observations et des recherches qui ont été faites en Egypte pendant l'expédition de l'armée française, publié par les ordres de sa majesté Napoléon le Grand.* 23 vols. Paris: Imprimerie impériale, 1809–28.

Frazer, James. *The Golden Bough: A Study in Magic and Religion.* 2nd ed. 3 vols. London: Macmillan, 1900.

G., Dr. J. "Edmond Doutté 1867–1926." *Académie des sciences colonials* 8: *Comptes-rendus des séances* (1926–27): 531–535.

Gaillard, Henri. "L'administration au Maroc: Le makhzen, étendue et limites de son pouvoir." *Bulletin de la Société de géographie d'Alger,* 1909, 438–470.

———. *Une ville d'Islam: Fez; Esquisse historique et sociale.* Paris: J. André, 1905.

Gallissot, René. *L'économie de l'Afrique du nord.* 3rd ed. Paris: P.U.F., 1969.

Gaudefroy-Desmombynes, Maurice. *Manuel d'arabe marocain.* Paris: E. Guilmoto, 1913.

Gautier, E.F. *Le passé de l'Afrique du nord: Les siècles obscurs.* Paris: Flammarion, 1937.

Geertz, Clifford. *After the Fact: Two Countries, Four Decades, One Anthropologist.* Cambridge, MA: Harvard University Press, 1995.

———. *Agricultural Involution: The Processes of Ecological Change in Indonesia.* Berkeley: University of California Press, 1963.

———. "In Search of North Africa." *New York Review of Books,* April 22, 1971.

———. *Islam Observed: Religious Development in Morocco and Indonesia.* New Haven, CT: Yale University Press, 1968.

———. *Pedlars and Princes.* Chicago: University of Chicago Press, 1963.

———. *Religions of Java.* Glencoe, IL: Free Press, 1960.

———. *The Social History of an Indonesian Village.* Cambridge, MA: MIT Press, 1965.

———. "Thick Description: Toward an Interpretive Theory of Culture." In *The Interpretation of Cultures,* 3–30. New York: Basic Books, 1973.

Geertz, Clifford, Hildred Geertz, and Lawrence Rosen. *Meaning and Order in Moroccan Society: Three Essays in Cultural Analysis.* Cambridge: Cambridge University Press, 1979.

Gellner, Ernest. "How to Live in Anarchy." In *Contemporary Thought and Politics,* 87–94. London: Routledge, 1974.

———. *Muslim Society.* Cambridge: Cambridge University Press, 1983.

———. *Nations and Nationalism.* Ithaca, NY: Cornell University Press, 1983.

———. "Review: The Struggle for Morocco's Past." *Middle East Journal* 15:1 (1961): 79–90.

———. *Saints of the Atlas.* Chicago: University of Chicago Press, 1969.

———. *Words and Things.* Boston: Beacon Press, 1960.

Gellner, Ernest, and Charles Micaud, eds. *Arabs and Berbers.* London: Duckworth; New York: D. C. Heath, 1973.

Gentil, Louis. *Dans le Bled es Siba: Explorations au Maroc.* Paris: Masson et cie, 1906.

———. *Le Maroc physique.* Paris: F. Alcan, 1912.

Gerofi, R. "Michaux-Bellaire." *Tingu: Bulletin de la Société d'histoire et d'archéologie Tanger* 1 (1953): 79–85.

Gide, André. *Si le grain ne meurt.* Paris: Gallimard, 1931.

Gillet, Maxime. *Principes de pacification du Maréchal Lyautey.* Paris: Economica, 2010.

Godfrey, John. "Overseas Trade and Rural Change in Nineteenth Century Morocco." PhD diss., Johns Hopkins University, 1985.

Gordon, D. C. *North Africa's French Legacy, 1954–1962.* Cambridge, MA: Harvard University Press, 1964.

———. *Self-Determination and History in the Third World.* Princeton, NJ: Princeton University Press, 1971.

Grangaud, Isabelle. *La ville impregnable: Une histoire sociale de Constantine au 18ième siècle.* Paris: Éditions de l'École pratique des hautes études en sciences sociales, 2002.

Guha, Ranajit. "The Prose of Counter-Insurgency." In *Selected Subaltern Studies,* edited by Ranajit Guha and Gayatri Chakravarty Spivak, 45–86. Oxford: Oxford University Press, 1988.

Guillen, Pierre. *Les emprunts marocains, 1902–1904.* Paris: Éditions Richelieu, 1971.

———. "L'implantation de Schneider, les débuts de la Compagnie marocaine (1902–1906)." *Revue d'histoire diplomatique,* 1965, 113–168.

Hall, John A. *Ernest Gellner: An Intellectual Biography*. New York: Verso, 2012.

Hamet, Ismael. "Obituary-René Basset." *Académie des sciences coloniales* 2 (1925): 257–259.

Hammoudi, Abdellah. *Master and Disciple: The Cultural Foundations of Moroccan Authoritarianism*. Chicago: University of Chicago Press, 1997.

Hannoum, Abdelmajid. "Colonialism and Knowledge in Algeria: The Archives of the Arab Bureau." *History and Anthropology*, 2001, 343–379.

Hanoteau, Adolphe, and Aristide Letourneux. *La Kabylie et les coutumes kabyles*. 3 vols. Paris: Imprimerie nationale, 1872–73.

Hanoteau, Maurice. "Quelques souvenirs sur les collaborateurs de *La Kabylie et les coutumes Kabyles*." *Revue africaine* 64 (1923): 134–149.

Harris, Walter B. *The Land of an African Sultan: Travels in Morocco, 1887–89*. London: Samson, Low, Marston and Rivington, 1889.

———. *The Morocco That Was*. London: Blackwood & Sons, 1921.

Hart, David Montgomery. *The Ait 'Atta of Southern Morocco: Daily Life and Recent History*. Cambridge: MENAS Press, 1984.

———. *The Aith Warayaghar of the Moroccan Rif: An Ethnography and History*. 2 vols. Tucson: University of Arizona Press, 1976.

———. *Dada 'Atta and His Forty Grandsons: The Socio-Political Organization of the Ait 'Atta of Southern Morocco*. Cambridge: MENAS Press, 1981.

———. *Tribe and Society in Rural Morocco*. London: Frank Cass, 2000.

Hobsbawm, Eric J. *Nations and Nationalism since 1780*. Cambridge: Cambridge University Press, 1990.

Hobsbawm, Eric J., and Terence Ranger, eds. *The Invention of Tradition*. Cambridge: Cambridge University Press, 1983.

Hoffman, Stanley. *The Obstructed Path: French Social Thought in the Years of Desperation, 1930–1960*. New York: Transaction, 2001.

Hoisington, William A., Jr. *Lyautey and the Conquest of Morocco*. New York: St. Martin's Press, 1995.

Houel, Christian. *Mes aventures marocaines*. Casablanca: Éditions Maroc-Demain, 1954.

Hourani, Albert. "Ottoman Reform and the Politics of Notables." In *Beginnings of Modernization in the Middle East*, edited by William R. Polk and Richard L. Chambers. Chicago: University of Chicago Press, 1968.

Houroro, Faouzi. *Sociologie politique coloniale au Maroc: Le cas de Michaux-Bellaire*. Casablanca: Afrique Orient, 1988.

Hubert, Lucien. "Institut marocain." Chambre des Deputés, Projet de Resolution No. 1893.

Hunter, William Wilson. *The Indian Musalmans: Are They Bound in Conscience to Rebel against the Queen?* London: Trubner, 1871.

Inglis, Fred. *Clifford Geertz: Culture, Custom and Ethics*. New York: Polity Press, 2000.

Jacques, Hubert. *Les journées sanglantes de Fez*. Paris: Librairie Chapelot, 1913.

Joffe, E. G. H. and C. R. Pennell. *Tribe and State: Essays in Honour of David Montgomery Hart*. Wisbech, UK: MENAS Press, 1991.

Johnson, Douglas. "Political Intelligence, Colonial Ethnography, and Analytical Anthropology in the Sudan." 309–335. In *Ordering Africa: Anthropology, European Imperialism, and the Politics of Knowledge*, edited by Helen Tilley, with Robert I. Gordon, 309–335. Manchester: Manchester University Press, 2007.

Jorgenson, Joseph G., and Eric R. Wolf. "Anthropology On the Warpath." *New York Review of Books*, November 19, 1970, 26–35.

Julien, Charles-André. *Le Maroc face aux imperialismes (1415–1956)*. Paris: Éditions Jeune-Afrique, 1978.

Justinard, Leopold Victor. "E. Michaux-Bellaire." *Bulletin du Comité de l'Afrique française*, 1930, 411–412.

———. *Les Aït ba Amran*. Villes et tribus du Maroc 8. Paris: Honoré Champion, 1930.

Karow, Leonhard. *Neun Jahre in marokkanischen Diensten*. Berlin: W. Weicher, 1909.

———. *Promenade en Égypte*. Paris: Librarie Hachette, 1895.

Katz, Jonathan G. "The Most Parisian of Muslims: Kaddour ben Ghabrit (1873–1954)." Paper presented at the Northwest World History Association annual conference, Vancouver, WA, October 16–17, 2004.

———. *Murder in Marrakech: Émile Mauchamps and the French Colonial Adventure*. Bloomington: Indiana University Press, 2006.

Keddie, Nikki R., ed. *Scholars, Saints, and Sufis: Muslim Religious Institutions since 1500*. Berkeley: University of California Press, 1972.

Kraemer, Martin. "Arabistik and Arabism: The Passions of Martin Hartmann." *Middle Eastern Studies* 25:3 (1989): 283–300.

La Blache, Pierre Vidal de. "La zone frontière de l'Algérie et du Maroc d'après de nouveaux documents." *Annales de géographie* 6:28 (1897): 357–363.

Lahbabi, Mohamed. *Le gouvernement marocain à l'aube de XXe siècle*. Rabat: Éditions techniques Nord-Africaines, 1957.

Lamartinière, H. M. P. de, and Nicolas Lacroix. *Documents pour servir à l'étude du nord-ouest africain*. 4 vols. Algiers: Gouvernement générale de l'Algérie, service des affaires indigènes, 1894–97.

Landes, David. *Bankers and Pashas: International Finance and Economic Imperialism in Egypt*. London: Heinemann, 1958.

Langer, William L. *European Alliances and Alignments, 1871–1890*. New York: Vintage, 1964.

Laoust, Émile. *Mots et choses berbères: Notes de linguistique et d'ethnographie; Dialectes du Maroc*. Paris: A. Challamel, 1920.

Laroui, Abdullah. *Les origines du nationalisme marocain, 1830–1912*. Paris: Maspéro, 1977.

Laurens, Henry. "Le Chatelier, Massignon, Montagne: Politique musulmane et orientalisme." In *Istanbul et les langues orientales*, edited by Frédéric Hitzel, Varia Turcica 31, 497–529. Paris: L'Harmattan, 1997.

Leared, Arthur. *Morocco and the Moors: Being an Account of Travels, with a General Description of the Country and Its People*. London: Sampson Low, 1876.

————. *A Visit to the Court of Morocco.* London, 1879.

Le Chatelier, Alfred. "Au Maroc: La politique nécessaire." *Revue bleue,* April 1908.

————. "G. Salmon, Chef de Mission." *Archives marocaines* 7 (1906): 463–473.

————. *Les confréries musulmans du Hedjaz.* Paris: Leroux, 1887.

————. *Les Médaganat.* Paris: Jourdan, 1888.

————. *L'Islam au XIXième siècle.* Paris: Leroux, 1888.

————. *L'Islam dans l'Afrique occidentale.* Paris: G. Steinheil, 1899.

————. *Mémoire sur le Maroc: Situation actuelle de la France au Maroc, programme politique, questions économiques; Voyage au Maroc d'octobre 1889 à mars 1890.* Paris: Privately printed, 1890.

————. "Nos erreurs au Maroc: Comment en sortir." *Revue bleue,* June 1908.

————. *Questions sahariennes: Touat-Chambaa-Touareg; Mission dans le sud algérien, juin-aout 1890.* Paris, 1890.

Leclerc, Gerard. *Anthropologie et colonialisme: Essai sur l'histoire de l'africanisme.* Paris: Fayard, 1972.

Le Glay, Maurice. "Les populations berbères du Maroc et le droit coutumier des berbères du Maroc central." *Archives berbères* 3 (1917).

————. "Lyautey et le commandement indigène." *Afrique française,* 1936, 194–197.

Leites, Nathan. *Du malaise politique en France.* Paris: Librairie Plon, 1958.

————. *On the Game of Politics in France.* Stanford, CA, Stanford University Press, 1959.

Lemaistre, Alexis. *L'Institut de France et nos grands établissements scientifiques.* Paris: Hachette, 1896.

Lemoine, Paul. "Mission dans le Maroc occidental." *Renseignements coloniaux,* 1905, 65–92.

Le Reverend, André. *Un Lyautey inconnu: Correspondance et journal inédits 1874–1934.* Paris: Perrin, 1980.

Leroy-Beaulieu, Paul. *De la colonisation chez les peuples modernes.* Paris: F. Alcan, 1908.

————. *L'Algérie et la Tunisie.* Paris: Guillaumin, 1897.

"Les chorfa dilala et djilala de Fez d'apres Ibn at-Tayyib al-Qadiry." *Archives marocaines* 3: 97–118.

"Les obsèques de Georges Salmon." *Dépêche de Tanger* 125 (1906).

Le Tourneau, Roger. *Fès avant le protectorat: Étude économique et sociale d'une ville de l'Occident musulman.* Casablanca: L'Institut des hautes études marocaine, 1949.

Lévi-Provençal, Évariste. *Les historiens des Chorfa: Essai sur la littérature historique et biographique au Maroc du XVIe au XXe siècle.* Paris: E. Larose, 1922.

L'exploration scientifique de l'Algérie pendant les années 1840, 1841, 1842, publié par l'ordre du gouvernement. 37 vols. Paris: Imprimerie impériale, 1844–67.

Liard, Louis. *L'enseignement supérieur en France, 1789–1893.* 2 vols. Paris: A. Colin, 1894.

"L'Institut marocain." *Renseignements coloniaux,* 1904, 194–195.

Lorcin, Patricia. *Imperial Identities: Stereotyping, Prejudice and Race in Colonial Algeria.* Society and Culture in the Modern Middle East. London: I. B. Tauris, 1995.

Lorimer, John Gordon. *Gazetteer of the Persian Gulf, 'Omān, and Central Arabia.* Calcutta: Superintendent Government Printing, 1915.

Lowell, Abbot L., and H. Morse Stephens, *Colonial Civil Service: The Selection and Training of Colonial Officials in England, Holland, and France with an Account of the East India College at Haileybury (1806–1857).* New York: Macmillan, 1900.

Lucas, Philippe, and Jean-Claude Vatin. *L'Algérie des anthropologies.* Paris: Maspéro, 1975.

Lukes, Steven. *Émile Durkheim: His Life and Work.* London: Penguin, 1975.

Lyall, Alfred. *Asiatic Studies, Religious and Social.* 2nd ed. London: J. Murray, 1884.

Maghraoui, Driss. "Gendering Colonial Urban Casablanca: The Case of the Quartier Reservé of Bousibir in Casablanca." In *Gendering Urban Space in the Middle East, South Asia and Africa,* edited by Kamran Asdar Ali and Martina Rieker, 17–44. London: Palgrave, 2008.

———. "Moroccan Colonial Troops: History, Memory and the Culture of French Colonialism." PhD diss., University of California, Santa Cruz, 2000.

Maghraoui, Driss, and Saloua Zerhouni. "Morocco." In *The Middle East,* edited by Ellen Lust-Okar, 576–602. Washington, DC: CQ Press, 2010.

Maitrot de la Motte Capron, A. "Le Roghi." *Bulletin de la Société de géographie d'Alger,* 1929, 514–576.

Marchand, G. "La situation commerciale à Fez en 1906." *Renseignements coloniaux,* 1906, 421–422.

"Maroc, Voyage du Dr. Weisgerber." *Comptes-rendus des séances de la Société de géographie,* 1900, 259–264.

Marseille, Jacques. *Empire coloniale et capitalisme française: Histoire d'un divorce.* Paris: Albin Michel, 1984.

Martin, A. G. P. *Les oasis Sahariennes (Gourara—Touat—Tidikelt).* Algiers: L'Imprimerie Algérienne, 1908.

———. *Quatre siècles d'histoire marocaine: Au Sahara de 1504 à 1902, au Maroc de 1894 à 1912, d'après archives et documentations indigènes.* Paris: F. Alcan, 1923.

Martin, Bradford G. *Muslim Brotherhoods in Nineteenth Century Africa.* Cambridge: Cambridge University Press, 1976.

Martin, Louis. "Description de la ville de Fez, quartier du Keddan." *Revue du monde musulman* 9 (1909): 433–443, 621–642.

Marty, Paul. "Les mourides d'Amadou Bamba." *Revue du monde musulman* 25 (1913): 3–164.

Masqueray, Émile. *La formation des cités chez les populations sédentaires de l'Algérie (Kabyles du Djuradjura, Chaouïas de l'Aurés, Béni Mzab).* Paris: Leroux, 1886.

Massé, Henri. "Les études arabes en Algérie (1830–1930)." *Revue africaine* 74 (1933): 208–258 and 458–505.

Massignon, Louis. "Enquête sur les corporations musulmanes d'artisans et de commerçants au Maroc." *Revue du monde musulman* 58 (1924): 1–250.

———. "Les corps des métiers et la cité islamique." *Revue internationale de sociologie* 28 (1920): 473–489.

Maudit, René. "Le makhzan marocain." *Renseignements coloniaux,* 1903, 293–304.

Mayeur, Jean-Marie. *La séparation de l'église et l'état*. Paris: Le Seuil, 1998.

McDougall, James. *History and the Culture of Nationalism in Algeria*. Cambridge: Cambridge University Press, 2006.

Mdaghri, Driss Alaoui, ed. *Une ambition marocaine: Des experts analysent la décennie 1999–2009*. Monaco: Koutoubia Editions Alphée, 2009.

Meakin, J. E. B. *The Land of the Moors*. London: Sonnenschein, 1901.

———. *Life in Morocco and Glimpses Beyond*. London: Chatto & Windus, 1905.

———. *The Moorish Empire: A Historical Epitome*. London: S. Sonnenschein, 1899.

———. *The Moors: A Comprehensive Description*. London: Sonnenschein, 1902.

Mélia, Jean. *L'épopée intellectuelle de l'Algérie: L'histoire de l'Université d'Alger*. Algiers: La Maison des Livres, 1950.

Merad, Ali. *Le réformisme musulman en Algérie de 1925 à 1940: Essai d'histoire religieuse et sociale*. Paris: Mouton, 1967.

Messal, Raymond. *La genèse de notre victoire au Maroc: Un précurseur, Alfred Le Chatelier (1855–1929)*. Paris: Dunod, 1931.

Metcalf, Thomas R. *An Imperial Vision: Indian Architecture and Britain's Raj*. Berkeley: University of California Press, 1989.

Michard, André, Omar Saddiqi, Ahmed Chalouan, and D. Frizon de Lamotte, eds. *Continental Evolution: The Geology of Morocco; Structure, Stratigraphy, and Tectonics of the Africa-Atlantic-Mediterranean Triple Junction*. Berlin: Axel Springer Verlag, 2008.

Michaux-Bellaire, Édouard. "Description de la ville de Fez." *Archives marocaines* 11 (1907): 1–115.

———. "El-Qçar El-Kebir: Une ville province au Maroc septentrional." *Archives marocaines* 2:2 (1904).

———. "Fez et les tribus berbères en 1910." *Bulletin de l'enseignement publique du Maroc*, 1921, 3–10.

———. "La maison de Ouezzan." *Revue du monde musulman*, 1908, 23–89.

———. "La Mission scientifique du Maroc." *Archives marocaines*, 1925, 1–22.

———. "L'organisme marocain." *Revue du monde musulman* 9 (1909): 1–43.

———. "Une tentative de restauration idrissite à Fez." *Revue du monde musulmane* 5 (1908): 393–423.

Miège, Jean-Louis. *Le Maroc et l'Europe, 1830–1894*. 4 vols. Paris: P.U.F., 1961–63.

Moniot, Henri, ed. *Le mal de voir: Ethnologie et orientalisme; Politique et épistemologie, critique et autocritique*. Paris: Union Générale d'Éditions, 1976.

Montagne, Robert. *La vie sociale et la vie politique des berbères*. Paris: Éditions du Comité de l'Afrique française, 1931.

———. *Les Berbères et le makhzen dans le sud du Maroc: Essai sur la transformation politique des Berbères sédentaires (groupe chleuh)*. Paris: F. Alcan, 1930.

———. *Naissance du prolétariat marocain, enquête collective exécutée de 1948 à 1950*. Paris: Peyronnet, 1952.

Mouliéras, Auguste. *Fez*. Paris: Challamel, 1902.

———. "La ville de Fez." *Bulletin de la Société de géographie et d'archéologie de la province d'Oran* 21 (1901): 1–31.

———. *Le Maroc inconnu: Étude géographique et sociologique.* Paris: A. Challamel, 1902.

Muchembled, Robert. *L'invention de la France moderne.* Paris: Armand Colin, 2002.

———. *Popular Culture and Elite Culture in France, 1400–1700.* Baton Rouge: Louisiana University Press, 1985.

Mudimbe-Boyi, Elizabeth. *Empire Lost: France and Its Other Worlds.* Lanham, MD: Lexington Books, 2009.

Murdock, George Peter, Clellan S. Ford, et al. *Outline of Cultural Materials.* 6th ed. New Haven, CT: Human Relations Area Files, 2006.

Neveu, François de. *Les Khouan: Ordres religieux chez les musulmans de l'Algérie.* Paris: A. Guyot, 1845.

Nora, Pierre. *Rethinking France: Les lieux de mémoire.* Vol. 1, *The State.* Chicago: University of Chicago Press, 2001.

Nordman, Daniel. "La Reconnaissance au Maroc." In *Profils du Maghreb: Frontières, figures et territoires (XVIIᵉ et XIXᵉ siècle),* 141–180. Publications de la Faculté des Lettres et des sciences humaines de Rabat. Casablanca: Imprimerie Najah el Jadida, 1996.

Nye, Robert A. *Masculinity and Male Codes of Honor in Modern France.* New York: Oxford University Press, 1993.

"Obituary." *Journal africaine* 12 (1908): 338–351.

Owen, Roger. "The Influence of Lord Cromer's Indian Experience on British Policy in Egypt, 1883–1907." In *St. Antony's Papers,* no. 17, edited by Albert Hourani, 109–139. London: Oxford University Press, 1965.

———. "Studying Islamic History." *Journal of Interdisciplinary History* 4:2 (1973): 287–298.

Padamsee, Alex. *Representations of Indian Muslims in British Colonial Discourse.* London: Palgrave Macmillan, 2005.

Pascon, Paul. "Le rapport 'secret' d'Edmond Doutté." *Hérodote* 11:3 (1978): 132–159.

Pein, Louis Auguste Théodore. *Lettres familières sur l'Algérie: Un petit royaume arabe.* Algiers: Jourdan, 1893.

Pelissier de Reynaud, Henri Jean François Edmond. *Exploration scientifique de l'Algérie pendant les années 1840, 1841, 1842, publié par l'ordre du gouvernement.* 39 vols. Paris: Imprimerie impériale, 1844–67.

Pennell, C. R. *A Country with a Government and a Flag: The Rif War in Morocco, 1921–1926.* Boulder, CO: Lynne Reiner, 1986.

———. *Morocco since. 1830: A History.* New York: NYU Press, 2001.

Pérétié, A. "Les médersas de Fez." *Archives marocaines* 18 (1918): 257–372.

Perkins, Kenneth. *Qaids, Captains and Colons: French Military Administration in the Colonial Maghrib, 1830–1934.* New York: Africana, 1981.

Persell, Stuart. *The French Colonial Lobby, 1889–1938.* Stanford, CA: Hoover Institution Press, 1983.

Pobéguin, E. *Sur la côte ouest du Maroc.* Paris: Comité du Maroc, 1908.

Porch, Douglas. *The Conquest of Morocco*. New York: Alfred A. Knopf, 1983.

Pouillon, François, ed. *Dictionnaire des orientalistes de langue française*. Paris: Éditions Karthala, 2008.

Rabinow, Paul. *French Modern: Norms and Forms of the Social Environment*. Cambridge, MA: M.I.T. Press, 1989.

———. "Representations Are Social Facts: Modernity and Postmodernity in Anthropology." In *Writing Cultures: The Poetics and Politics of Ethnography*, edited by James Clifford and George Marcus, 234–261. Berkeley: University of California Press, 1986.

"Rapport sur les travaux présentes au concours ouvert en 1900." *Bulletin de la Société de géographie de d'archéologie de la province d'Oran* 21 (1901): XXVIII–XXX.

Reig, Daniel. *Homo orientaliste: La langue arabe en France depuis le XIXᵉ siècle*. Paris: Maissonneuve & Larose, 1988.

Renaud, Pierre. "La correspondance de Lyautey et ses invariants, de l'Indochine à Madagascar (1894–1902)." In *Regards sur Lyautey: Actes du colloque de Nancy, 17–18 septembre 2004*, edited by Jean El Gammal, Annales de l'Est, 6th ser., 54, no. spéc., 23–40. Nancy: Association d'historiens de l'est, 2004.

René-Leclerc, Charles. "Le commerce et l'industrie à Fez." *Renseignements coloniaux,* 1905, 229–253, 295–321, 337–350.

———. *Situation de la Délégation générale du Comité du Maroc à Tanger pendant 1906*. Algiers: Comité du Maroc, 1907.

———. *Situation économique & commerciale du Maroc en 1907*. Algiers: Imprimerie Léon, 1909.

Rézette, Robert. *Les partis politiques marocains*. Paris: Armand Colin, 1956.

Richard, Charles. *Du gouvernement arabe et de l'institution qui doit l'exercer*. Algiers: Bastide, 1848.

———. *Étude sur l'insurrection du Dahra (1845–1846)*. Algiers: A. Besancènes, 1846.

Rinn, Louis. *Histoire de l'insurrection de 1871 en Algérie*. Algiers: A. Jourdan, 1891.

———. *Marabouts et Khouans: Étude sur l'Islam en Algérie*. Algiers: Jourdan, 1884.

Rivet, Daniel. *Le Maroc de Lyautey à Mohammed V: Le double visage du protectorat*. Paris: Éditions Denoel, 1999.

———. *Lyautey et l'institution du protectorat français au Maroc, 1912–1925*. 3 vols. Paris: L'Harmattan, 1988.

Robin, Nil Joseph. *L'insurrection de la Grande Kabylie en 1871*. Paris: H. Charles-Lavauzelle, 1901.

Robin, Nil Joseph, and Louis Rinn. *Histoire de l'insurrection de 1871 en Algérie*. Algiers: A. Jourdan, 1891.

Robinson, David. *The Holy War of Umar Tal*. Oxford: Oxford University Press, 1985.

———. *Muslim Societies in African History*. New York: Cambridge University Press, 2004.

———. *Paths of Accommodation: Muslim Societies and French Colonial Authorities in Senegal and Mauritania, 1880–1920*. Athens, OH: Ohio University Press; Oxford: James Currey, 2000.

Rodinson, Maxime. "Situation, acquis, et problèmes d'orientalisme islamisant." In *Le mal de voir: Ethnologie et orientalisme; Politique et épistemologie, critique et autocritique,* edited by Henri Moniot, 242–257. Paris: Union Générale d'Éditions, 1976.

———. "The Western Image and Western Studies of Islam." In *The Legacy of Islam,* edited by C. E. Bosworth and Joseph Schacht, 9–62. London: Oxford University Press, 1974.

Rollman, Wilfred. "The New Order in a Pre-Colonial Muslim Society: Military Reform in Morocco, 1844–1904." PhD diss., University of Michigan, 1983.

Rosenberg, Clifford D. *Policing Paris: The Origins of Modern Immigration Control between the Wars.* Ithaca, NY: Cornell University Press, 2006.

Roussillon, Alain. "Sociologie et identité en Egypte et au Maroc: Le travail de la colonisation." *Revue d'historie des sciences humaines* 2:7 (2002): 193–221.

Ruedy, John. *Modern Algeria: The Origins and Development of a Nation.* 2nd ed. Bloomington: Indiana University Press, 2005.

Sabatier, Camille. *Essai sur les berbères.* Algiers, 1882.

———. *Études sociologique sur les Kabyles.* Algiers, 1881.

Said, Edward. *Culture and Imperialism.* New York: Random House, 1993.

———. *Orientalism.* New York: Pantheon, 1978.

Salmon, Georges. *Études sur la topographie du Caire: La Kal'at al-Kabch et la Birkat al-Fil.* Cairo: Imprimerie de l'Institut francais d'archeologie orientale, 1902.

———. "Le culte de Moulay Idris et la mosquée des chorfa à Fez." *Archives marocaines* 3 (1905): 413–429.

———. "Le nom de Babîdj dans la géographie égyptienne." *Bulletin de l'Institut français d'archéologie orientale* 1 (1901): 235–239.

———. "Les chorfa idrissides de Fez d'après Ibn At-Tayyib al-Qadiry." *Archives marocaines* 1:3 (1904): 425–459.

———, trans. *L'introduction topographique à l'histoire de Bagdadh d'Abou Bakr Ahmad ibn Thabit al-Khatib al-Bagdadhi.* Paris: E. Bouillon, 1904.

———. "Notes d'épigraphie arabe." *Bulletin de l'Institut français d'archéologie orientale* 2 (1902): 109–112.

———. *Notes d'épigraphie arabe.* Cairo: Imprimerie de l'Institut français d'archéologie orientale, 1902.

———. "Notes sur la flore de Fayyoum d'après An-Naboulsi." *Bulletin de l'Institut français d'archéologie orientale* 1 (1901): 25–28.

———. "Rapport sur une mission à Damiette." *Bulletin de l'Institut français d'archéologie orientale* 2 (1902): 71–89.

———. "Répertoire géographique de la province du Fayyoûm d'après le Kitâb Târîkh al-Fayyoûm d'An-Nâboulsî." *Bulletin de l'Institut français d'archéologie orientale* 1 (1901): 29–77.

———, ed. *Silvestre de Sacy (1758–1838).* 2 vols. Cairo: L'Institut français d'archéologie orientale, 1905.

———. "Une opinion marocaine sur la conquête de Touat (traduction)." *Archives marocaines* 1:3 (1904): 416–424.

————, trans. *Un texte arabe inédit pour servir à l'histoire des chrétiens d'Egypte*. Cairo: Imprimerie éditions de l'Institut français d'archéologie orientale, 1906.

Satiya, Priya. *Spies in Arabic: The Great War and the Cultural Foundations of Britain's Covert Empire in the Middle East*. Oxford: Oxford University Press, 2008.

Schaar, Stuart H. "Conflict and Change in Nineteenth-Century Morocco." PhD diss., Princeton University, 1966.

Schlanger, Judith. *Les métaphores de l'organisme*. Paris: Librairie Philosophique J. Vrin, 1971.

Schreier, Joshua. *"Arabs of the Jewish Faith": The Civilizing Mission in Colonial Algeria*. New Brunswick, NJ: Rutgers University Press, 2010.

Schroeter, Daniel. "Orientalism and the Jews of the Mediterranean." *Journal of Mediterranean Studies* 4 (1994): 183–196.

Sebti, Abdelahad. "Colonial Experience and Territorial Practices," In *Revisiting the Colonial Past of Morocco,* edited by Driss Maghraoui, 38–56. London: Routledge, 2013.

Segonzac, Édouard Marie René, marquis de. *Au coeur de l'Atlas: Mission au Maroc, 1904–1905*. Paris: Émile Larose, 1910.

————. *Excursion au Sous avec quelques considerations préliminaires sur la question marocaine*. Paris: Challamel, 1901.

————. *Voyages au Maroc, 1899–1901*. Paris: A. Colin, 1903.

Servier, Andre. *Le péril d'avenir: Le nationalisme musulman en Egypt, en Tunisie, en Algérie*. Constantine: E. Boet, 1913.

Sibeud, Emmanuelle. "The Elusive Bureau of Colonial Ethnography in France, 1907–1925." In *Ordering Africa: Anthropology, European Imperialism, and the Politics of Knowledge,* edited by Helen Tilley, with Robert I. Gordon, 49–66. Manchester: Manchester University Press, 2007.

Silverstein, Paul. *Algeria in France: Transpolitics, Race and the Nation*. Bloomington: Indiana University Press, 2004.

Simon, Henri. "Les études berbères au Maroc et leurs applications en matière de politique et d'administration." *Afrique française,* 1915, 4–5.

Spillmann, Georges. *Districts et tribus de la Haute Vallée du Dra*. Villes et tribus du Maroc 9. Paris: Honoré Champion, 1931.

————. *Esquisse d'histoire religieuse du Maroc: Confréries et zaouïas*. Paris: J. Peyronnet, 1951.

Stoler, Ann Laura, et al., eds. *Imperial Formations*. Santa Fe, NM: School for Advanced Research Press; Oxford: James Currey, 2007.

Suolinna, Kirsti, Catherine af Hällström, and Tommy Lahtinen, eds. *Portraying Morocco: Edward Westermarck's Fieldwork and Photographs, 1898–1913*. Åbo: Åbo Akademis Förlag, 2000.

Surdon, Georges. *Institutions et coutumes des Berbères du Maghreb*. Tangier: Éditions internationales, 1938.

Swearingen, Will D. *Moroccan Mirages: Agrarian Dreams and Deceptions, 1912–1986*. Princeton, NJ: Princeton University Press, 1987.

Terrasse, Henri. *Histoire du Maroc des origines à l'établissement du protectorat français*. 2 vols. Casablanca: Éditions Atlantides, 1949.

Thibaudet, Albert. *La république des professeurs suivi de les princes lorrains*. Paris: B. Grasset, 1927. Reprint. Hachette littératures, 2006.

Thomas, Martin. *Empires of Intelligence: Security Services and Colonial Disorder after 1914*. Berkeley: University of California Press, 2008.

———. *The French Empire between the Wars: Imperialism, Politics and Society* Manchester: Manchester University Press, 2005.

———. *The French North African Crisis: Colonial Breakdown and Anglo-French Relations, 1945–62*. London: Macmillan, 2000.

Thompson, Richard A. *The Yellow Peril, 1890–1924*. New York: Arno Press, 1978.

Tilley, Helen, with Robert I. Gordon, eds. *Ordering Africa: Anthropology, European Imperialism, and the Politics of Knowledge*. Manchester: Manchester University Press, 2007.

Triaud, Jean-Louis. "Islam under French Colonial Rule." In *The History of Islam in Africa*, edited by Nehemia Levtzion and Randall Pouwell, 169–188. Athens: Ohio University Press, 2000.

———. *La légende noire de la Sanusiya: Une confrérie musulmane saharienne sous le regard français (1840–1930)*. 2 vols. Paris: Éditions de la Maison des sciences de l'homme, 1995.

Triaud, Jean-Louis, and David Robinson. *La Tijaniyya: Une confrérie musulmane à la conquête de l'Afrique*. Paris: Karthala, 2003.

Trout, Frank E. *Morocco's Saharan Frontiers*. Geneva: Droz, 1969.

Trumbull, George R. *An Empire of Facts: Colonial Power, Cultural Knowledge and Islam in Algeria, 1870–1914*. Cambridge: Cambridge University Press, 2009.

Turner, Bryan S. *Marx and the End of Orientalism*. London: Allen & Unwin, 1976.

Turner, Jonathan H., and Alexandra Maryanski. "Sociology's Lost Human Relations Area Files." *Sociological Perspectives* 31:1 (1988): 19–34.

"Une opinion marocaine sur la conquète du Touat." Translated by Georges Salmon. *Archives marocaines* 1:3 (1904): 416–424.

Urbain, Thomas Ismail. "Algérie: Du gouvernement des tribus, Chrétiens et musulmans, Français et Algériens." *Revue de l'Orient et de l'Algérie* 2 (1847): 241–259.

Valensi, Lucette. "Le Maghreb vu du centre: Sa place dans l'École sociologique française." In *Connaissances du Maghreb: Étude comparée des perceptions françaises et américaines*, edited by Jean-Claude Vatin, Aix-en-Provence: Éditions du C.N.R.S., 1976.

Vallerie, Pierre. *Conquérants & conquis au Maroc: Contribution à l'étude sociologique de la conquête des peuples*. Paris: Les éditions Domat-Montchrestien, 1934.

Vatin, Jean-Claude, ed. *Connaissances du Maghreb: Sciences sociales et colonization*. Paris: Éditions du C.N.R.S., 1984.

Vattier, Jean. "La municipalité de Fez." *Renseignements coloniaux* 12 (1924): 383.

Vavasseur-Desperriers, Jean. *République et liberté Charles Jonnart, une conscience républicaine (1857–1927)*. Paris: Presses universitaires du Septentrion, 1996.

Warnier, Auguste. *L'Algérie et les victimes de la guerre*. Algiers: Duclaux, 1871.

Warnier, Auguste, and Jules Duval. *Bureaux arabes et colons*. Paris: Challamel, 1869.

Waterbury, John. *The Commander of the Faithful: The Moroccan Political Elite—a Study in Segmented Politics*. London: Weidenfeld & Nicolson, 1970.

———. *Le commandeur des croyants: La monarchie marocaine et son élite*. Paris: Presses universitaires de France, 1975.

Weisgerber, Félix. *Au seuil du Maroc modern*. Rabat: La Porte, 1947.

———. "La ville de Fès." *Revue française de l'étranger* 24 (1899): 591–596.

———. "Maroc, Voyage du Dr. Weisgerber." *Comptes-rendus des séances de la Société de géographie,* 1900, 259–264.

Westermarck, Edouard. *The Belief in Spirits in Morocco*. Åbo: Åbo Akademi, 1920.

———. *Ritual and Belief in Morocco*. 2 vols. London: Macmillan, 1926.

———. *Wit and Wisdom in Morocco: A Study of Native Proverbs*. New York: Liveright, 1931.

Wilder, Gary. "Colonial Ethnology and Political Rationality in French West Africa." *Ordering Africa: Anthropology, European Imperialism, and the Politics of Knowledge,* edited by Helen Tilley, with Robert I. Gordon, 336–376. Manchester: Manchester University Press, 2007.

———. *The French Imperial Nation-State: Negritude and Colonial Humanism between the Two World Wars*. Chicago: University of Chicago Press, 2005.

Williams, Philip M. *Politics in Post-war France: Parties and the Constitution in the Fourth Republic*. London: Longmans, 1955.

Zartman, I. William. *Morocco: Problems of New Power*. New York: Atherton Press, 1964.

Zeldin, Theodore. *Émile Ollivier and the Liberal Empire of Napoleon III*. Oxford: Clarendon Press, 1963.

Zenagui, Abd El-Aziz. "Récit en dialecte tlemcénien." *Journal asiatique* 2:4 (1904): 45–116.

Zimmerman, Maurice. "Mission Louis Gentil dans le Maroc occidental." *Annales de géographie* 19:104 (1910): 187–189.

INDEX

council and, 16, 161–65, 175; *makhzan* and *siba*/tribes binary and, 158–59; *makhzan* officials and, 147, 152, 154–56, 158–60, 162, 164; Moroccan Islam in context of, 152; nationalism and, 157–58; native policy reform and, 160–65, 228n45; politics in France in context of, 156–58; racist stereotypes and, 148, 158–60; resistance in, 156, 160; sharifian-ism and, 152; siege and occupation in 1911 of, 78, 105, 107, 138, 156, 159–60, 162, 229n48; studies on, 122–23, 147–54, 157, 158, 164–65, 228n31; Treaty of Fez in 1912 and, 107; *turuq* or Sufi brother-hoods studies and, 152, 157, 173; ulama or religious scholars and, 147–49, 152, 156–57, 160, 164, 173, 175, 178–79, 198; *Villes et Tribus du Maroc* and, 122–23

fiches de tribu (file cards of each tribe), 44, 49–50, 86–87, 100, 118, 121–22, 193

Foucauld, Charles de, 24, 36–37, 97, 129, 209n61, 209n63

Foucault, Michel, 5, 10–11, 22, 66, 72

Foureau/Lamy expedition, 55–56, 213n10

France: anthropology or *anthropologie* studies in, 6, 39; Cambon-Lansdowne agreement in 1904 and, 84–85; colonial lobby in parliament and, 54, 56, 67, 79; colony and metropole interpenetration and, 8, 20; comparative native policy and, 42–43, 211n15; Dreyfus affair and, 13, 74, 180; Franco-Prussian War, 6, 32, 38; funding for native policy and, 58, 60, 64; higher education transformation in, 34, 38–39; intelligence gathering and, 194–95; Jews and anti-Semitism in, 13, 62, 74, 180, 214n22; military ethnogra-phy and, 43; native policy in context of protectorates and, 104; orientalism and, 23–26, 28, 39–41, 210n10, 211n11; poli-tics in, 74, 156–58, 216n14; positivism and, 6, 41–42, 64; public opinion in context of native policy of, 15, 42–43, 211n13, 211n15; racist stereotypes and, 22, 26; religion/church versus secular-ism/state in, 47, 53–54, 170–71, 179–81; science discipline in, 25; "scientific imperialism" and, 6, 11, 42; social sci-ences in, 6, 11; tribes policy and, 69, 70, 76, 80; world historical context and, 13–14, 108. *See also* Algeria and colonial ethnography; colonial forms of knowl-edge; protectorate of Morocco; Tunisia and Tunisian colonial archive

Franco-Prussian War, 6, 32, 38, 42

Frazer, James, *Golden Bough*, 48, 96, 173, 177, 179, 182, 228n33

French colonial archives, 7, 90–91, 209n60, 219n37. *See also Archives marocaines*

Gaillard, Henri (René Maudit pseud.?), 150–54, 161–62, 197, 227n19, 228n32

Gallieni, Joseph-Simon, 43, 104, 109, 193

Gaudefroy-Desmombynes, Maurice, 40, 211n11

Gautier, E. F., 24

Geertz, Clifford, and topics, 17, 21, 75, 187–89

Gellner, Ernest, 17, 187–90

Gentil, Louis, 97–98, 140, 220n40, 220n42

Germany, 6, 12–13, 32, 38, 42, 77, 85, 92, 185

governmental issues in Morocco, 16, 168. *See also* monarchy of Morocco; Moroc-can Islam

Gramsci, Antonio, 72

Great Britain: Cambon-Lansdowne agree-ment in 1904 and, 84–85; colonial forms of knowledge and, 35–36; cultural anthropology studies in, 17, 35–36, 39, 187–90; Egyptian native policy and, 162; intelligence gathering and, 194–95; segmentary lineage structures and, 27, 188. *See also* British India

Guha, Ranajit, 193

Hanoteau, Adolphe, 32, 139–40

Hart, David Montgomery, 189, 232n12

Henrys, Paul, 133–35, 138–40, 142, 224n23, 225n41, 225n44

Hoisington, William A., Jr., 194

Houdas, Octave, 40, 210n10

imperialism, in context of the other, 28. *See also* "scientific imperialism"

Indian Colonial Service (I.C.S.), 5, 110–11, 114–15

Middle Atlas *(continued)*
myth/Arab and Berber binary and,
138–41; Arabization and, 141; *Archives
berbères* and, 15; assimilation policy and,
141–42; bureaucratic confusion and,
132–33; customary law and, 139–42, 145;
Islamicization and, 141; *jama'at* or tribal
councils and, 139–41; Lyautey system
and, 138, 224n26; *makhzan* policy and,
137–41, 139; racist stereotypes and, 140;
resistance by, 128–29, 132–33, 138–39,
142; scientific research and, 132–44, 137,
224n23; sharia or Islamic law and, 141;
Villes et Tribus du Maroc and, 15. *See
also* Berber policy

military ethnography, 30–31, 34–35, 43, 49,
208n37

Mission scientifique du Maroc (MSM):
overview and purpose of, 9, 15, 60,
100–102, 218n6; Algeciras conference
and, 92–93, 218n23; Algerian model in
context of, 51; *Archives berbères* and, 15,
124–25, 135–36; authority of, 53, 58, 60,
64–65; Berber studies and, 129, 130,
133–35; CAF collaboration with, 70, 85;
Casablanca and Chaouia publication
and, 118–19, 120*table*, 121–23; collaborative writing system and, 70, 85, 100,
151–52; cultural research and, 123; Fez
studies, 150–51; *fiches de tribu* system
and, 86–87, 100, 118, 121–22; funding
and, 15, 58, 59–60, 64, 94, 117–18, 134;
institutionalization of native policy
and, 112–13; leadership of, 59, 214n18; as
leading academic knowledge center, 86,
91; *makhzan* policy and, 9; Moroccan
Islam and, 157; nationalism and, 157;
native policy and reform in context of,
9, 60–61, 90–91; politics and, 59–65,
67–71, 100, 102, 133; public opinion in
context of native policy and, 15; renam-
ing of, 118; reorganization of, 98–100,
112–18; scientific research and, 86–87,
117, 218n6; statistics in context of social
characteristics and, 123; technocratic
position of power and, 71, 112–14; thick
description in context of, 87, 102; *Villes
et Tribus du Maroc* and, 15, 116, 118–19,

120*table*, 121–24, 149. *See also Archives
marocaines;* politics, and Moroccan
colonial archive; Salmon, Georges, and
topics

monarchy of Morocco: alliances/connec-
tions under, 175, 198; *a'yan* or bourgeois/
notables and, 4; *baraka* or divine blessing and, 2, 190, 197; British India native
policy as influence on, 4; cultural
studies and, 190; Hasan I, 190; Hasan
II, 190, 200; as independent government, 17, 195, 198; magico-religious
practices and, 2, 174; modernization
and, 3–4, 199–200; Moroccan Islam in
context of, 2, 5, 174, 185–86, 195–200;
Muhammad V, 195–96, 198–200;
Muhammad VI, 185, 200; nationalism
and, 196–98; protectorate in context of,
1, 3–4, 195, 197; technocratic position of
power and, 1, 197–98

Montagne, Robert, 26–27, 137, 147

Moqrani rebellion, 32, 171, 178

Moroccan colonial archive: overview of,
7–9, 11, 21, 27, 38, 100–102, 181–83;
academicians' contributions to, 5, 49;
Algerian Kabyle myth/Arab and Berber
binary and, 37; Algerian model/influ-
ence and, 14, 27; Algero-Moroccan
frontier and, 44–45, 61–62, 69, 75, 77,
80, 89, 138; anthropology history and, 6;
anti-Islamic influence on, 7; archive
defined and, 5; assembly during 1900–
1914, 5; Berber policy in context of,
36–37; British studies and, 35–36;
colonial gospel binaries and, 102; confidential reports and, 36–37, 209n61;
cultural life in Morocco and, 4, 11;
customary law and, 110; description of,
7; discursive system and, 6–7, 79, 83,
101, 182; domestic politics, 7; early
sources from 1880–1900 and, 35–37,
209n61, 209n63; economic interests, 7;
Enlightenment tradition and, 5–6, 29;
ethnographic history and, 6–9; *Exploration scientifique du Maroc,* 28; government reports and, 49, 51; historicization
in context of, 5–11, 14, 83–84, 187;
Jewish population in context of, 36–37,

(MSM); Moroccan colonial archive;
Morocco question
Porch, Douglas, 194
post-9/11 world, 187, 216n11
power: knowledge relationship to, 9, 43, 72,
129, 132–36, 187, 192–93; technocratic
position of, 1, 4, 71, 111–14, 124, 197. *See
also* colonial forms of knowledge
Prochaska, David, 24
protectorate of Morocco: bureaucratic
confusion in early days of, 107–9, 115,
118, 132–33; establishment/inauguration
of, 1, 5, 38, 43, 191, 196; indirect rule and,
136–37, 195; intelligence gathering in
context of, 193; modernity in context of,
193–94; monarchy in context of, 1, 3–4,
111, 195, 197; Moroccan Islam in context
of, 191, 196–200; "scientific imperialism" in context of, 109, 169–70, 186,
194–95. *See also* institutionalization of
native policy and knowledge in
Morocco; Moroccan Islam; Morocco
question
public opinion, in context of native policy,
15, 42–43, 57, 78, 93–94, 211n13, 211n15

Regnault, Henri, 107, 115
Renan, Ernest, 23, 40, 58
René-Leclerc, Charles, 113, 150–51, 153–54,
227n23
Révoil, Paul, and topics: Algeciras confer-
ence and, 92–93, 218n23; chair at Col-
lège de France, 57; governor-general of
Algeria, 43–44, 54, 59; Moroccan
Institute, 64–65; Morocco question, 71;
MSM, 59, 64–65, 99, 214n18; native
policy and reform, 43–44, 54, 56
Richard, Charles, 26, 30
Rinn, Louis, 30, 43–44
Rivet, Daniel, 108–9, 137

Sabatier, Camille, 31, 33, 208n49
Saharan oases, 44, 84, 89, 172
Said, Edward W., and topics: colonial
critiques, 10; *Description de L'Égypte*,
24–25, 27–28; discursive systems and
orientalism, 10–11, 24–25, 66, 72; ethnography of the other, 24; historical

context critiques, 10–11, 28; Orient, the,
10, 24, 27–28, 66, 72; *Orientalism*, 10, 25,
27–28, 66, 72, 191; "ornamentalism," 3
Saint-Aulaire, Auguste de Beaupoil, comte
de, 104
Saint-Germain, André Gaston de, 43–47,
53, 63
Saint-René-Taillandier, Georges, 90
Saint-Simonians, 26, 29, 32
Salafiyya Islam, 50, 191
Salmon, Georges, and topics: *Archives
marocaines*, 60, 86–87, 89–90; biographical information, 59, 86, 91–92;
characteristics, 87, 214n17; collaborative
writing system, 100; document gathering expeditions, 89–91; École d'Alger
counteroffensive, 61–63, 214n22; Fez
studies, 151; funding for MSM position,
59; Islam in Morocco, 169; Jews and
anti-Semitism, 62, 214n22; MSM
leadership, 59, 71, 99, 102, 214n18;
scientific research in Morocco, 59–60,
62, 71, 174; writings, 59
Sanusiya brotherhood conspiracies, 35, 172
"scientific imperialism": Algerian colonial
ethnography and, 32, 35, 38; France and,
6, 11, 42; institutionalization of native
policy and, 101–2, 109, 114–15, 122–24,
193–95, 197; Moroccan colonial archive
and, 6, 11; protectorate of Morocco and,
109, 169–70, 186, 194–95; social engineering in context of, 101–2, 193, 197
Segonzac, Édouard Marie René, marquis de,
79, 95*table*, 96–97, 129, 219n37, 223n2
Servier, André, 172
sharia (Islamic law), 27, 32, 35, 38, 110, 141
sharifianism, 16, 89, 152, 170, 174, 176, 182,
190–91
Silvestre de Sacy, Antoine Isaac, 23, 39, 59
Simon, Henri, 125, 134, 140
Slousch, Nahum, 183
social engineering, 101–2, 193, 197. *See also*
"scientific imperialism"
social history: cultural/historical survivals
and, 16, 96–97, 155, 173–74, 177–79,
181–82, 228n33; cultural research in
context of, 27, 86–88, 91, 117, 123; folklore studies and, 41, 48, 50–51, 150, 173;

urban centers and studies: Algerian colonial ethnography and, 26, 47, 149; Casablanca and, 27, 118–19, 120*table*, 121–23; Moroccan colonial archive and, 4, 26, 122–23, 149; Moroccan Islam in context of, 175, 183; *Villes et Tribus du Maroc* and, 149. *See also* Fez

Villes et Tribus du Maroc, 15, 116, 118–19, 120*table*, 121–24, 149
Von Paasen, Pierre, 168

Warnier, August, 31
Waterbury, John, 189–90, 232n12
West African colonial ethnography, 14, 27, 30, 34–35, 54, 172
Westermarck, Edward, 175
world history, and Islamic studies, 12–14, 108, 177–79, 187, 192–93, 216n11. *See also* social history

Youssef, Moulay, 1, 197